Motivation, Language Identity and the L2 Self

SECOND LANGUAGE ACQUISITION
Series Editor: Professor David Singleton, *Trinity College, Dublin, Ireland*

This series brings together titles dealing with a variety of aspects of language acquisition and processing in situations where a language or languages other than the native language is involved. Second language is thus interpreted in its broadest possible sense. The volumes included in the series all offer in their different ways, on the one hand, exposition and discussion of empirical findings and, on the other, some degree of theoretical reflection. In this latter connection, no particular theoretical stance is privileged in the series; nor is any relevant perspective – sociolinguistic, psycholinguistic, neurolinguistic, etc. – deemed out of place. The intended readership of the series includes final-year undergraduates working on second language acquisition projects, postgraduate students involved in second language acquisition research, and researchers and teachers in general whose interests include a second language acquisition component.

Full details of all the books in this series and of all our other publications can be found on http://www.multilingual-matters.com, or by writing to Multilingual Matters, St Nicholas House, 31-34 High Street, Bristol BS1 2AW, UK.

SECOND LANGUAGE ACQUISITION
Series Editor: David Singleton, *Trinity College, Dublin, Ireland*

Motivation, Language Identity and the L2 Self

Edited by
Zoltán Dörnyei and Ema Ushioda

MULTILINGUAL MATTERS
Bristol • Buffalo • Toronto

Library of Congress Cataloging in Publication Data
A catalog record for this book is available from the Library of Congress.
Motivation, Language Identity and the L2 Self
Edited by Zoltán Dörnyei and Ema Ushioda.
Second Language Acquisition
Includes bibliographical references and index.
1. Second language acquisition. 2. Motivation in education.
3. Identity (Psychology) 4. Self.
I. Dörnyei, Zoltán. II. Ushioda, Ema.
P118.2.M676 2009
418.0071–dc22 2008035198

British Library Cataloguing in Publication Data
A catalogue entry for this book is available from the British Library.

ISBN-13: 978-1-84769-128-6 (hbk)
ISBN-13: 978-1-84769-127-9 (pbk)

Multilingual Matters
UK: St Nicholas House, 31-34 High Street, Bristol BS1 2AW, UK.
USA: UTP, 2250 Military Road, Tonawanda, NY 14150, USA.
Canada: UTP, 5201 Dufferin Street, North York, Ontario M3H 5T8, Canada.

The policy of Multilingual Matters/Channel View Publications is to use papers that are natural, renewable and recyclable products, made from wood grown in sustainable forests. In the manufacturing process of our books, and to further support our policy, preference is given to printers that have FSC and PEFC Chain of Custody certification. The FSC and/or PEFC logos will appear on those books where full certification has been granted to the printer concerned.

Typeset by Datapage International Ltd.

Contents

Contributors

Abdullah Al-Shehri is a trainer and English language curriculum developer in the Department of English Training Centre for SWCC (Saline Water Conversion Corporation), Saudi Arabia. He has published a number of articles related to issues on culture, religion, politics, change management and self-development. He is the author of several books, including *Truth Exposed* (Cooperative Office, 2003), *This is for You* (Cooperative Office, 2002), *The Important Lessons* (Cooperative Office, 2002).

Richard Clément is Professor of Psychology and Director of the Official Languages and Bilingualism Institute at the University of Ottawa. His current research interests include issues related to bilingualism, second language acquisition, identity change and adjustment in the acculturative process. In 2001 he was awarded the Otto Klineberg Intercultural and International Relations Prize by the Society for the Psychological Study of Social Issues, and in 2002 he received the Robert C. Gardner Award from the International Association of Language and Social Psychology. He is a fellow of both the Canadian and the American Psychological Association.

Kata Csizér is an Assistant Professor at the Department of English Applied Linguistics, School of English and American Studies, Eötvös Loránd University, Budapest. She holds a PhD in Language Pedagogy and her main field of research interest focuses on the socio-psychological aspects of second language learning and teaching as well as second and foreign language motivation. She has published over 30 academic papers on L2 motivation and related issues and a book titled *Motivation, Language Attitudes and Globalisation* (Multilingual Matters, 2006, co-authored by Zoltán Dörnyei and Nóra Németh).

Alex Ding is a university teacher at the Centre for English Language Education, University of Nottingham. He is involved in technology enhanced language teaching and learning as well as in carrying out research into teacher autonomy and new technology. He is also currently engaged in PhD research at the University of Nottingham.

Zoltán Dörnyei is Professor of Psycholinguistics in the School of English Studies, University of Nottingham. He has published over 60 academic papers on various aspects of second language acquisition and language teaching methodology, and is the author of several books, including *Teaching and Researching Motivation* (Longman, 2001), *The Psychology of the Language Learner* (Lawrence Erlbaum, 2005), *Motivation, Language Attitudes and Globalisation* (Multilingual Matters, 2006, co-authored by Kata Csizér and Nóra Németh) and *Research Methods in Applied Linguistics* (Oxford University Press, 2007).

Elizabeth Gatbonton is Associate Professor of Applied Linguistics at Concordia University in Montréal. She is involved in two strands of research: (1) investigating the role of ethnic group identity factors in the development of L2 fluency in general and L2 pronunciation accuracy in particular, and (2) examining pedagogical and methodological issues in the development of L2 fluency and idiomaticity.

Tae-Young Kim is Assistant Professor in the Department of English Education at Chung-Ang University, South Korea. He recently completed his PhD in Second Language Education at the Ontario Institute for Studies in Education, University of Toronto. He teaches courses and conducts research on ESL/EFL learning and teaching, motivation, sociocultural theory, L2 learner factors, SLA theories, and qualitative research methodology.

Judit Kormos is a Senior Lecturer at the Department of Linguistics and English Language, Lancaster University. She formerly worked at Eötvös Lorand University, Budapest. Together with Kata Csizér, she has conducted several research projects on the motivation of Hungarian language learners. She has published a number of papers on the psychological aspects of second language acquisition and is the author of the book *Speech Production and Second Language Acquisition* (Lawrence Erlbaum, 2006).

Maggie Kubanyiova is a Lecturer in Educational Linguistics at the School of Education, University of Birmingham. Her research interests lie in broad areas of instructed second language acquisition (particularly the social psychological processes in instructed settings), language teacher development and classroom-based research. She has published empirical and methodological papers in all these areas. Her recent longitudinal mixed methods research project concerned language teacher development and led to the advancement of a novel theoretical model of Language Teacher Conceptual Change (LTCC).

Martin Lamb is a Senior Lecturer in TESOL in the School of Education, University of Leeds, where he teaches undergraduate and postgraduate courses on various aspects of language acquisition and teaching. His research interests are in learner motivation and autonomy, the social contexts of English language education, and language assessment.

Zachary Lyons is a Research Fellow with the Trinity Immigration Initiative English Language Support Programme, Trinity College, Dublin, and a former lecturer in French and post-primary mathematics teacher. Research interests include teacher/learner motivation and identity in *gaelscoileanna* (Irish-medium primary and secondary schools) and pressurised learning environments.

Peter D. MacIntyre is a Professor of Psychology in the School of Science and Technology at Cape Breton University in Sydney, Nova Scotia. He has published over 50 papers on topics including anxiety, motivation, personality, stereotypes, attitudes, public speaking, and willingness to communicate. In addition to awards for teaching and service to students, his research has been recognized with awards from the Modern Language Association, the International Association for Language and Social Psychology, and the Canadian Psychological Association.

Sean Mackinnon is a Masters candidate in social psychology at Wilfrid Laurier University, Waterloo, Ontario. His pre-graduate school research focused primarily on second language acquisition, public speaking anxiety and attributional biases. His postgraduate work has shifted towards implicit attitudes, particularly the impact of implicit self esteem on both defensive behaviour and seating preference. His publication record includes work published in the *Journal of Fluency Disorders* (2007) and a chapter in the book *Cultural Identity and Language Anxiety* (Guangxi Normal University Press, in press).

Michael Magid is a research student in the School of English Studies, University of Nottingham. His research interests include psycholinguistics, sociolinguistics, bilingualism, second language motivation, teaching methodology, second language acquisition and materials development. His main research outputs have been his Masters thesis entitled 'The Attitudes of Chinese People towards Fluent Chinese Speakers of English' (Concordia University, Canada, 2004) and the paper 'Learners' Ethnic Group Affiliation and L2 Pronunciation Accuracy: A Sociolinguistic Investigation' (*TESOL Quarterly* 39 (3), 2005, co-authored by Elizabeth Gatbonton and Pavel Trofimovich). Michael has experience teaching English in Canada, England, China, and Japan.

Kimberly A. Noels is a Professor in the Social and Cultural Psychology area of the Department of Psychology at the University of Alberta. Her research concerns the social psychology of language and communication, with a focus on intercultural communication. Her publications include articles on motivation for language learning, the role of communication in the process of cross-cultural adaptation, and the relation between language and ethnic identity. Her research has received awards from The Modern Language Association, the International Communication Association, the International Association of Language and Social Psychology, and the Society for the Psychological Study of Social Issues.

Mostafa Papi is an official teacher of English at the Iranian Ministry of Education. He is also a graduate student majoring in Teaching English as a Foreign Language at the Iranian University of Science and Technology. His main research interests are the psycholinguistic aspects of second language learning, especially second language motivation.

Stephen Ryan is an Associate Professor in the Department of Foreign Languages at Seitoku University, Japan. He has been involved in language education for over 20 years, spending more than 15 years teaching and researching in Japan. He recently completed his PhD at the University of Nottingham, where his research is based around exploring the ideal L2 selves of Japanese learners of English.

Norman Segalowitz is Professor of Psychology at Concordia University in Montréal and Associate Director of the Centre for the Study of Learning and Performance. His research focuses on the cognitive processes underlying adult second language acquisition and use. In particular, his work addresses the roles automatic and attention-based cognitive mechanisms may play in second language oral and reading fluency and the implications these roles may have for language instruction.

Tatsuya Taguchi is a PhD student in the School of English Studies, University of Nottingham. He obtained his Masters degree from the University of Melbourne and has worked in the field of foreign language teaching at the primary and secondary levels as well as at several universities in Japan. His research interests include second language acquisition (motivation and learning strategies) and quantitative research methodology. He has published in the area of learning strategies in Australia.

Pavel Trofimovich is an Associate Professor of Applied Linguistics at the TESL Centre/Department of Education at Concordia University in Montréal. His research and teaching focus on cognitive aspects of second language processing, second language phonology, sociolinguistic aspects of second language acquisition, and computer-assisted language learning.

Ema Ushioda is an Associate Professor in ELT and Applied Linguistics at the Centre for Applied Linguistics, University of Warwick, where she teaches MA courses and coordinates the Doctorate in Education. Her research interests include language motivation, autonomy, sociocultural theory and teacher development. Her publications include *Learner Autonomy 5: The Role of Motivation* (Authentik, 1996), *Towards Greater Learner Autonomy in the Foreign Language Classroom* (Authentik, 2002, co-authored by David Little and Jennifer Ridley), and *Learner Autonomy in the Foreign Language Classroom: Teacher, Learner, Curriculum and Assessment* (Authentik, 2003, co-edited by David Little and Jennifer Ridley.

Cynthia White is Professor of Applied Linguistics in the School of Language Studies, Massey University, New Zealand. She has research interests in online and distance language learning, learner autonomy, teacher cognition and language and settlement issues among immigrants and refugees. In 2004 she received the TESOL Virginia French Allen Award for Scholarship and Service. Her books include *Language Learning in Distance Education* (Cambridge University Press, 2003), and *Distance Education and Languages: Evolution and Change* (Multilingual Matters, 2005, co-edited by Borje Holmberg and Monica Shelly). In 2006 she edited a special issue of *Language Teaching Research* on web-based and online language teaching.

Tomoko Yashima is a Professor of Applied Linguistics and Intercultural Communication at Kansai University. Her research interests include intercultural contact, acculturation, language identity, as well as attitudes, motivation and affect in L2 communication. Her studies have been published in international journals such as *Psychological Reports, The Modern Language Journal, Language Learning, and Language Testing*. She is the author of several books published in Japanese including *Motivation and Affect in Foreign Language Communication* (Kansai University Press, 2004), and has published a translation of Zoltán Dörnyei's *Questionnaires in L2 Research* (Shohakusha, 2006, co-translated by Osamu Takeuchi).

Chapter 1

Motivation, Language Identities and the L2 Self: A Theoretical Overview

EMA USHIODA and ZOLTÁN DÖRNYEI

Introduction: Why a New Book on L2 Motivation Now?

As Pit Corder famously put it some 40 years ago, '*given motivation*, it is inevitable that a human being will learn a second language if he is exposed to the language data' [italics original] (Corder, 1967: 164). Since then, of course, we have witnessed a vast amount of theoretical discussion and research examining the complex nature of language learning motivation and its role in the process of SLA. At the same time, during the latter decades of the 20th century and the first decade of this century, we have also witnessed the phenomena of globalisation, the fall of communism and European reconfiguration, widespread political and economic migration, increased mobility with the rise of budget airlines, ever-developing media technologies and electronic discourse communities – all contributing in one way or another to the inexorable spread of 'global English', the growth of World English varieties, and repercussions for the loss or maintenance of various national, local or heritage languages. In short, over the past decades the world traversed by the L2 learner has changed dramatically – it is now increasingly characterised by linguistic and sociocultural diversity and fluidity, where language use, ethnicity, identity and hybridity have become complex topical issues and the subject of significant attention in sociolinguistic research. Yet, surprisingly perhaps, it is only within the last few years that those of us working in the L2 motivation field have really begun to examine what this changing global reality might mean for how we theorise the motivation to learn another language, and how we theorise the motivation to learn Global English as target language for people aspiring to acquire global identity in particular. Put simply, L2 motivation is currently in the process of being radically reconceptualised and re-theorised in the context of contemporary notions of self and identity. This volume brings together the first comprehensive anthology of key conceptual and empirical papers that mark this important paradigmatic shift.

Re-theorising L2 Motivation in Relation to Self and Identity

Without the critical detachment of historical analysis, it is not easy to pinpoint the root causes of this paradigmatic shift in thinking. Instead, the aim of this introductory chapter is to sketch some of the contributing factors and developments which have brought questions of self and identity to the core of L2 motivation theorising.

Within the L2 motivation field, the theoretical concept that has garnered most attention to date is, of course, integrative orientation, defined by Gardner and Lambert (1972: 132) as 'reflecting a sincere and personal interest in the people and culture represented by the other group'. As Gardner and Lambert explain (Gardner & Lambert, 1972: 12), the integrative concept derived from a parallel they drew with processes of social identification underpinning first language acquisition, whereby the infant attempts to imitate the verbalisations of its care-givers for the reinforcing feedback which this imitation provides. They reason that a process similar to social identification 'extended to a whole ethnolinguistic community' may sustain the long-term motivation needed to master a second language. In short, notions of social identification and ethnolinguistic identity have always been implicit in the integrative concept. Moreover, such notions have been very much explicit in related social psychological research on second language communication and intergroup behaviour, and was used to explain motivation for developing and adopting particular linguistic codes and speech patterns among minority ethnic groups (Giles & Byrne, 1982). However, the basic premise underlying the integrative concept, namely that the L2 learner 'must be willing to identify with members of another ethnolinguistic group and take on very subtle aspects of their behaviour' (Gardner & Lambert, 1972: 135), has provoked considerable debate. Through the 1980s, there was much discussion about strong (social identification and integration) versus weak (sense of affiliation and interest) versions of the integrative concept. McDonough (1981: 152), for example, speculated that the strong form would be unrealistic for many language learners, while Clément and Kruidenier (1983) put the strong form to the empirical test and found little evidence that a truly integrative orientation of this kind was common among language learners.

In recent years, the debate about the integrative concept has intensified and taken on a new turn, prompted by the burgeoning discussions within applied linguistics and at large about the global spread of English. A basic question we have begun to ask is whether we can apply the concept of integrative orientation when there is no specific target reference group of speakers. Does it make sense to talk about integrative attitudes when ownership of English does not necessarily rest with a specific community of speakers, whether native speakers of British or American English varieties or speakers of World English varieties? Moreover, does the notion of integrative motivation for learning English have any real meaning, given the increasing curricular reframing of English as a universal basic skill to be taught from primary level alongside literacy and numeracy, and given the predicted decline in numbers of English (as a foreign language) learners by the end this decade (Graddol, 2006)?

Among L2 motivation researchers, questions of this kind about the special status of English as target language have prompted the rethinking of the integrative concept. For example, Yashima (2002; see also this volume) expands the notion of integrativeness to refer to a generalised international outlook or 'international posture' which she defines with reference to Japanese learners of English as 'interest in foreign or international affairs, willingness to go overseas to stay or work, readiness to interact with intercultural partners, and [...] openness or a non-ethnocentric attitude toward different cultures' (Yashima, 2002: 57). The concept of international posture thus considerably broadens the external reference group from a specific geographic and ethnolinguistic community to a non-specific global community of English language users. As Ushioda (2006: 150) points out, however, precisely because it is a global community, is it meaningful to conceptualise it as an 'external' reference group, or as part of one's internal representation of oneself as a *de facto* member of that global community? It is this theoretical shift of focus to the internal domain of self and identity that marks the most radical rethinking of the integrative concept.

An ambitious research project that has pushed forward this rethinking was a large-scale longitudinal survey of Hungarian students' attitudes to learning foreign languages spanning the period from 1993 to 2004 (Dörnyei & Csizér, 2002; Dörnyei *et al.*, 2006). Commenting on the salience and multifaceted composition of an integrative motivation factor in their data, Dörnyei and Csizér (2002: 453) speculated that the process of identification theorised to underpin integrativeness might be better explained as an internal process of identification within the person's self-concept, rather than identification with an external reference group. Dörnyei (2005) developed this speculation further by drawing on the psychological theory of 'possible selves'. According to this theory, possible selves represent individuals' ideas of 'what they might become, what they would like to become, and what they are afraid of becoming', and so 'provide a conceptual link between the self-concept and motivation' (Markus & Nurius, 1987: 157). Dörnyei (2005; see also this volume) builds on this theory of possible selves to develop a new conceptualisation of L2 motivation, the 'L2 Motivational Self System'. Its central concept is the *ideal self*, which refers to the representation of the

attributes that someone would ideally like to possess (i.e. a representation of personal hopes, aspirations or wishes). A complementary
self-guide is the *ought-to self*, referring to the attributes that one believes
one ought to possess (i.e. a representation of someone else's sense of
duty, obligations or responsibilities). A basic hypothesis is that if
proficiency in the target language is part and parcel of one's *ideal* or
ought-to self, this will serve as a powerful motivator to learn the language
because of our psychological desire to reduce the discrepancy between
our current and possible future selves.

While Dörnyei has drawn on developments in self research in
psychology to reframe L2 motivation, other scholars have looked to
contemporary discussions of identity in the globalising and postmodern
world (e.g. Giddens, 1991) to rethink the nature of L2 motivation and
integrative orientation. For example, Lamb (2004; see also this volume)
draws on self-report data from junior high school students in Indonesia
and speculates that their motivation to learn English may partly be
shaped by the pursuit of a bicultural identity – that is, a global or world
citizen identity on the one hand, and a sense of local or national identity
as an Indonesian on the other. Such students may thus aspire to 'a vision
of an English-speaking globally-involved but nationally responsible
future self' (Lamb, 2004: 16). Lamb further speculates that changes in
motivation to learn English may partly be explained with reference to
changing perceptions and the reconstruction of identities, especially
during the formative years of adolescence.

In relation to L2 motivation and identity, the push for new thinking
has also come from much stronger voices of dissent among those
working in the area of language and identity in sociolinguistics. Several
scholars have openly criticised traditional social psychological notions of
identity inherent in much L2 motivation research to date. For example,
Norton (2000: 4) argues that SLA theorists have not developed a
comprehensive theory of identity that integrates the language learner
and the language learning context. She uses the term identity to reference
how a person understands his or her relationship to the world, how that
relationship is constructed across time and space, and how the person
understands possibilities for the future. She also develops the motivational concept of 'investment' to capture the 'socially and historically
constructed relationship of learners to the target language, and their
often ambivalent desire to learn and practice it' (Norton, 2000: 10). When
learners invest in a language, they do so with the understanding that they
will acquire a wider range of symbolic and material resources, which will
enhance their cultural capital, their identity and their desires for the
future. Thus an investment in the target language is also an investment
in the learner's own identity. However, Norton questions the assumption that language learners can be unproblematically characterised as

motivated or unmotivated, with clear-cut target identities, since motivation and identity are socially constructed, often in inequitable relations of power, changing over time and space, and possibly coexisting in contradictory ways in the individual.

This poststructuralist perspective on identity (and motivation) as being multiple, complex and a site of struggle is similarly developed by Pavlenko (2002) in her critique of social psychological approaches to L2 motivation. Pavlenko also draws attention to what she calls 'the monolingual and monocultural bias' in these approaches which implies a view of the world in terms of 'homogeneous and monolingual cultures, or in-groups and out-groups, and of individuals who move from one group to another' (Pavlenko, 2002: 279). As she argues, such a view does not reflect the complexity of the modern globalised multilingual world where more than half the inhabitants are not only bilingual or multilingual but also members of multiple ethnic, social and cultural communities. Very recently, a similar argument has been put forward by Coetzee-Van Rooy (2006) in her incisive critique of the concept of integrativeness in relation to learners and speakers of World English. In particular, she exposes what she calls its 'simplex' view of identity which presupposes that learning a second language somehow results in loss of the first language and the establishment of a new 'simple' identity as monolingual speaker of the target language. As she argues, such a simplex view seriously misrepresents the complex sociolinguistic realities of language learning, language use and cultural identity in postcolonial World English contexts, where multidimensional identities and pluralism (rather than integration) are the norm. She concludes her paper with a strong statement urging critical re-examination of the integrative concept which she regards as untenable in such World English contexts.

In summary, from both within the L2 motivation field and beyond it, there have been a number of parallel developments pushing for change in how we theorise L2 motivation, and pushing for contemporary notions of self and identity to be brought to the core of this re-theorising. Such a paradigmatic shift in L2 motivation theory not only serves to advance our thinking and understanding about issues of language learning motivation in the modern globalised multilingual world. It also brings L2 motivation theory firmly in line with current and highly topical analyses of language and identity in multilingual contexts, and serves to illuminate fundamental underlying processes of motivation in these analyses. In short, there is now very real potential for much greater synergy between L2 motivation theory and mainstream SLA and sociolinguistics than in the past, where we motivation researchers have traditionally rather ploughed our own furrow. It is hoped that this current collection of papers will help set the agenda for such synergy.

A Brief Overview of This Book

This anthology brings together a diverse range of conceptual and empirical perspectives on motivation, identity and the L2 self. Following this introductory chapter, the anthology begins with Dörnyei's most up-to-date and detailed theoretical elaboration of the L2 Motivational Self System (Chapter 2), which provides key background for the remaining chapters. Three chapters by Taguchi, Magid and Papi (Chapter 4), Csizér and Kormos (Chapter 5) and Ryan (Chapter 6) report on extensive empirical investigations of the L2 Motivational Self System, focusing on learners of English from a range of countries (Japan, China, Iran, Hungary) and levels of education (secondary school, university and adult education). Three chapters develop particular theoretical or empirical perspectives relating to Dörnyei's model: MacIntyre, Mackinnon and Clément (Chapter 10) discuss the development of a measurement scale to assess possible selves; Al-Shehri (Chapter 8) explores the role of imaginative capacity and visual learning style in fashioning *ideal* selves; Segalowitz, Gatbonton and Trofimovich (Chapter 9) consider how aspects of ethnolinguistic affiliation and identity are psychologically realised through the L2 Motivational Self System, affecting selective engagement in L2 use which, in turn, impacts on cognitive-perceptual processing and ultimately L2 proficiency.

Two chapters offer critical or alternative perspectives: MacIntyre, Mackinnon and Clément (Chapter 3) express caution about re-theorising L2 motivation from a self perspective and urge us not to throw out the baby with the bathwater, suggesting instead that possible selves and integrative motivation be viewed as complementary rather than competing frameworks; Ushioda (Chapter 11) problematises ontological assumptions in linear models of motivation in general and presents an alternative relational view of motivation and identity emergent through interaction.

Two chapters develop connections between Dörnyei's self approach and other major theoretical frameworks: Kim (Chapter 14) draws on sociocultural *activity theory* to examine the interface between the *ideal* and *ought-to* self, while Noels (Chapter 15) critically explores *self-determination* and *autonomy* theory and finds connections with the motivational self system. Three chapters integrate discussion of possible selves with related theoretical constructs: Yashima (Chapter 7) relates *ideal* self to the notion of *international posture* in the Japanese EFL context; Lamb (Chapter 12) integrates concepts of *ideal* and *ought to* selves with concepts of *identity* and *Bourdieuan habitus* in his qualitative analysis of Indonesian learners of English, as does Lyons (Chapter 13) in his analysis of the unique language learning setting of the French Foreign Legion.

Finally, two chapters extend the self approach to the analysis of language teacher motivation and teacher development: Kubanyiova (Chapter 16) applies the self approach to examine conceptual change (and lack of change) among EFL teachers in Slovakia during in-service training, while White and Ding (Chapter 17) use the *ideal* and *ought-to* self perspectives to illuminate understanding of how teachers engage with the new practice of e-language teaching.

The anthology concludes with a discussion of future research directions. First we raise several specific issues concerning the 'self' approach to L2 motivation and then we examine briefly how the two main theoretical strands underlying the material in this book – the motivational relevance of future self guides and a situated, dynamic view of motivation – might potentially be integrated by adopting a dynamic systems perspective.

References

Clément, R. and Kruidenier, B. (1983) Orientations in second language acquisition: I. The effects of ethnicity, milieu, and target language on their emergence. *Language Learning* 33, 273–291.

Coetzee-Van Rooy, S. (2006) Integrativeness: Untenable for world Englishes learners? *World Englishes* 25 (3/4), 437–450.

Corder, S.P. (1967) The significance of learners' errors. *International Review of Applied Linguistics* 5 (2/3), 161–169.

Dörnyei, Z. (2005) *The Psychology of the Language Learner. Individual Differences in Second Language Acquisition*. Mahwah, NJ: Lawrence Erlbaum.

Dörnyei, Z. and Csizér, K. (2002) Some dynamics of language attitudes and motivation: Results of a longitudinal nationwide survey. *Applied Linguistics* 23 (4), 421–462.

Dörnyei, Z., Csizér, K. and Németh, N. (2006) *Motivation, Language Attitudes and Globalisation: A Hungarian Perspective*. Clevedon: Multilingual Matters.

Gardner, R.C. and Lambert, W.E. (1972) *Attitudes and Motivation in Second-Language Learning*. Rowley, MA: Newbury House.

Giddens, A. (1991) *Modernity and Self-Identity: Self and Society in the Late Modern Age*. Cambridge: Polity Press.

Giles, H. and Byrne, J.L. (1982) An intergroup approach to second language acquisition. *Journal of Multilingual and Multicultural Development* 3, 17–40.

Graddol, D. (2006) *English Next: Why Global English May Mean the End of 'English as a Foreign Language'*. London: British Council.

Lamb, M. (2004) Integrative motivation in a globalizing world. *System* 32, 3–19.

Markus, H. and Nurius, P. (1987) Possible selves: The interface between motivation and the self-concept. In K. Yardley and T. Honess (eds) *Self and Identity: Psychosocial Perspectives* (pp. 157–172). Chichester: John Wiley and Sons.

McDonough, S. (1981) *Psychology in Foreign Language Teaching*. London: George Allen and Unwin.

Norton, B. (2000) *Identity and Language Learning: Gender, Ethnicity and Educational Change*. Harlow: Longman.

Pavlenko, A. (2002) Poststructuralist approaches to the study of social factors in second language learning and use. In V. Cook (ed.) *Portraits of the L2 User* (pp. 277–302). Clevedon: Multilingual Matters.

Ushioda, E. (2006) Language motivation in a reconfigured Europe: Access, identity and autonomy. *Journal of Multilingual and Multicultural Development* 27 (2), 148–161.

Yashima, T. (2002) Willingness to communicate in a second language: The Japanese context. *Modern Language Journal* 86 (1), 54–66.

Chapter 2
The L2 Motivational Self System

ZOLTÁN DÖRNYEI

> *The space of what might be is a uniquely human domain*
> *that is still to be fully mapped. Some is roughly charted,*
> *but much more remains to be surveyed.*
> Markus, 2006

In 2005, I outlined the basis of a new approach to conceptualising second language (L2) learning motivation within a 'self' framework (Dörnyei, 2005), calling the new theory the 'L2 Motivational Self System'. The purpose of this chapter is to provide a detailed theoretical description of this construct and to show its foundations and the ways by which I believe it broadens the scope of L2 motivation research. As part of an extended validity argument, I will refer to several empirical studies that tested some tenets of the theory, and I will also discuss how the model is compatible with other influential conceptualisations of motivation by Gardner (2001), Noels (2003) and Ushioda (2001). Finally, I will argue that the new theory has considerable practical implications as it opens up a novel avenue for motivating language learners.

The L2 Motivational Self System represents a major reformation of previous motivational thinking by its explicit utilisation of psychological theories of the self, yet its roots are firmly set in previous research in the L2 field. Indeed, L2 motivation researchers have always believed that a foreign language is more than a mere communication code that can be learnt similarly to other academic subjects, and have therefore typically adopted paradigms that linked the L2 to the individual's personal 'core,' forming an important part of one's identity. Thus, proposing a system that explicitly focuses on aspects of the individual's self is compatible with the whole-person perspective of past theorising.

The actual model has grown out of the combined effect of two significant theoretical developments, one taking place in the L2 field, the other in mainstream psychology. Looking at our own field first, we can conclude that for several decades L2 motivation research had been centred around the highly influential concept of *integrativeness/integrative motivation*, which was first introduced by Gardner and Lambert (1959). However, during the past 20 years there has been growing concern with the theoretical content of this concept, partly because it did not offer any obvious links with the new cognitive motivational concepts that had

9

been emerging in motivational psychology (such as goal theories or self-determination theory) and partly because the label 'integrative' was rather limiting and, quite frankly, did not make too much sense in many language learning environments. The second theoretical development that contributed to the genesis of the L2 Motivational Self System took place in psychological research on the self, leading to a convergence of self theory and motivation theory in mainstream psychology. I will start by describing this movement and the resulting conception of 'possible selves' and 'future self-guides', followed by discussing how these have informed L2 motivation research.

The Contribution of Psychology: Possible Selves and Future Self-Guides

MacIntyre *et al.* (this volume, Chapter 3) are right when they point out that the notion of 'self' is one of the most frequently – and most diversely – used concepts in psychology. A cursory scan of the PSYCHINFO database they conducted revealed more than 75,000 articles with 'self' in their titles and a very long list of self-related concepts used in the literature (e.g. self-esteem, self-concept, self-determination, etc.). Similarly, Higgins (1996: 1062) also concluded that 'Psychologists are fascinated with the "self". It headlines more psychological variables than any other concept.'

While there is indeed a confusing plethora of self-related issues, from a motivational point of view one area of self-research stands out with its relevance: the study of *possible selves* and *future self-guides*. The emergence of this subfield has been a direct consequence of the success of personality trait psychology in defining the major and stable dimensions of personality (e.g. the Big Five model; see Dörnyei, 2005). These advances, according to Cantor (1990), have paved the way for paying more attention to questions about how individual differences in personality are translated into behavioural characteristics, examining the '"doing" sides of personality' (Cantor, 1990: 735). Thus, over the past two decades self theorists have become increasingly interested in the active, dynamic nature of the self-system, gradually replacing the traditionally static concept of self-representations with a self-system that mediates and controls ongoing behaviour (Markus & Ruvolo, 1989; for a recent review, see Leary, 2007). This move resulted in the introduction of a number of self-specific mechanisms that link the self with action (e.g. self-regulation), and thus an intriguing interface has been formed between personality psychology and motivational psychology.

Markus and Ruvolo (1989: 214) explain that although the interwoven nature of the self-system and motivated behaviour is seldom made explicit, 'yet the belief that the two *must be linked* can be inferred from the writing of a variety of personality and motivation theorists' (emphasis mine). One of the most powerful mechanisms intended to make this link explicit and describe how the self regulates behaviour by setting goals and expectations was proposed by Markus and Nurius (1986) in their theory that centred around the concept of 'possible selves'. Due to its versatile character, the possible selves approach also lends itself to various educational applications and, as we will see later, has indeed been successfully applied to a variety of educational contexts.

Possible selves

A person's self-concept has traditionally been seen as the summary of the individual's self-knowledge related to how the person views him/ herself at present. Carver *et al.* (1994) emphasise that *possible selves –* representing the individuals' ideas of what they *might* become, what they *would like* to become, and what they are *afraid of* becoming (Markus & Nurius, 1986) – denote a unique self-dimension in that they refer to future rather than current self states. Furthermore, while the self-concept is usually assumed to concern information derived from the individual's past experiences, Markus and Nurius's notion of possible selves concerns how people conceptualise their as-yet unrealised potential, and as such, it also draws on hopes, wishes and fantasies. In this sense, possible selves act as 'future self-guides', reflecting a dynamic, forward-pointing conception that can explain how someone is moved from the present toward the future. At the heart of this movement is the complex interplay of current and imaginative self-identities and its impact on purposive behaviour (Yowell, 2002). Looking back on two decades of research on possible selves, Markus (2006) summarised this as follows:

> Our excitement with the notion of possible selves had multiple sources. Focusing on possible selves gave us license to speculate about the remarkable power of imagination in human life. We also had room to think about the importance of the self-structure as a dynamic interpretive matrix for thought, feeling, and action, and to begin to theorize about the role of sociocultural contexts in behaviour. Finally, the concept wove together our mutual interests in social psychology, social work, and clinical psychology. (Markus, 2006: xi)

We should note that the third point Markus (2006) mentions in the above quote, the inclusion of clinical psychology, is related to the fantasy element of possible selves. As Segal (2006) explains, Markus and Nurius's (1986) conceptualisation meant that social psychology was taking on the subtleties of psychodynamic processes that are so prominent in psycho-analytic theory. His summary is enlightening:

> For their contribution to our understanding of the self, Markus and Nurius essentially married a social-cognitive instrument with a

projective. Future possible selves are fantasy tempered by expectation (or expectations leavened by fantasy) and so, conceptually,
eliciting them invokes two central actions of mental life: The social
cognitive act of future planning with the equally human act of
generating fantasy. (Segal, 2006: 82)

In their seminal paper, Markus and Nurius (1986: 954) distinguished
between three main types of possible selves: (1) 'ideal selves that we
would very much like to become', (2) 'selves that we could become', and
(3) 'selves we are afraid of becoming'. The ideal or hoped-for selves
might include 'the successful self, the creative self, the rich self, the thin
self, or the loved and admired self', whereas the feared selves could be
'the alone self, the depressed self, the incompetent self, the alcoholic self,
the unemployed self, or the bag lady self'. While these two extremes are
easy to grasp and illustrate, what exactly are the selves of the third type,
the 'selves that we could become'? In one sense, this description can be
seen as merely a synonym of the generic term 'possible self' (because
'possible' is what 'we can become'), which was surely not the authors'
intention. So, it is more likely that these selves refer to 'expected' or
'likely' selves (Carver *et al.*, 1994), that is, to the default option. Thus, the
three main types of possible selves proposed by Markus and Nurius refer
to the best case, the worst case and the default scenarios.

There are two important points to note about these self types. First, we
should not forget that they all come under the label of *possible* selves, that
is, even the ideal, hoped-for self is not completely detached from reality
(i.e. it cannot be an utterly implausible fantasy). The second point is that
Markus and Nurius (1986) clearly meant this list to provide a broad
outline of the scope of possible selves rather than a specific taxonomy,
because later in their article they mention hoped-for selves and ideal
selves as two separate entries within a list (Markus & Nurius, 1986: 957).
Interestingly, they also mention 'ought selves' in their paper (which we
are going to look at in more detail later), defining it as 'an image of self
held by another' (Markus & Nurius, 1986: 958). Thus, Markus and
Nurius believed in multiple future-oriented possible selves and outlined
in their paper the scope of these selves with a number of illustrations but
without providing a finite taxonomy.

A final point that needs to be emphasised about Markus and Nurius's
(1986) proposal is central to the conception of possible selves yet it tends
to be curiously ignored or overlooked in most work on the subject. It
concerns the fact that possible selves involve tangible *images* and *senses*;
as Markus and Nurius emphasise, possible selves are represented in the
same imaginary and semantic way as the here-and-now self, that is, they
are a *reality* for the individual: people can 'see', 'hear' and 'smell' a
possible self (although I am not that sure about the benefits of the latter).

Markus and Ruvolo (1989) argue that it is a major advantage to frame future goals in this way because this representation seems to capture some elements of what people actually experience when they are engaged in goal-directed behaviour. As the authors state, by focusing on possible selves we are 'phenomenologically very close to the actual thoughts and feelings that individuals experience as they are in the process of motivated behaviour and instrumental action' (Markus & Ruvolo, 1989: 217). This is a crucial point that I will come back to later.

Future self-guides: Ideal and ought selves

Possible selves are often referred to as 'future self-guides', but strictly speaking, not every type of possible self has this guiding function. As mentioned earlier, the expected, 'could-become' self refers to the default situation and therefore it does not so much guide as predict the likely future scenario. In contrast, the ideal self has a definite guiding function in setting to-be-reached standards and, in a negative way, the feared self also regulates behaviour by guiding the individual *away* from something. It does not need much justification that from the point of view of acting as academic self-guides the learner's ideal self is particularly important, which is an area that has been the subject of a great deal of research by Tory Higgins and his associates (e.g. Higgins, 1987, 1998; Higgins *et al.*, 1985; Higgins *et al.*, 1994). It is important to know that Higgins's work on selves precedes that of Markus and Nurius (1986), with the latter authors acknowledging Higgins's contribution (by citing, for example, not only Higgins *et al.*, 1985, but also an unpublished manuscript by him from 1983).

The two key components of Higgins's (1987; Higgins *et al.*, 1985) self theory are the *ideal self* and the *ought self*. As we have seen above, Markus and Nurius (1986) also mention these concepts, but Higgins used them as precisely defined technical terms in his more general theory of motivation and self-regulation. The *ideal self* refers to the representation of the attributes that one would ideally like to possess (i.e. representation of hopes, aspirations, or wishes), while the *ought self* refers to the representation of attributes that one believes one ought to possess (i.e. representation of someone else's sense of duties, obligations or moral responsibilities) and which therefore may bear little resemblance to one's own desires or wishes. In his 1987 paper Higgins points out that both the ideal and the ought selves can derive from either the individual's own or someone else's views, which means that the ideal self might represent attributes that another person would like the individual to possess in an ideal case. However, because it is not clear how this meaning would be different from an ought self, it has typically not been included in subsequent uses of the term, and the ideal sense has been usually interpreted in the literature as the individual's own vision for him/herself, while the ought self as someone else's vision for the individual.

An important difference between Higgins's and Markus and Nurius's conceptualisations of the future-oriented self dimensions is that while the latter authors talk about multiple possible selves, including, for example, more than one ideal self, Higgins talks about a single ideal and a single ought self for each individual, viewing these as composite self-guides that sum up all the relevant attributes. However, he also accepts (e.g. Higgins, 1987, 1996) that there are several other types of self-representations beyond the ideal or ought self concepts.

Boyatzis and Akrivou (2006) highlight a potential source of confusion in the distinction between the ideal and the ought selves concerning the level of internalisation of the ought self. They argue that because various reference groups (to which every individual belongs) affect the individual by anticipatory socialisation or value induction, it is not always straightforward to decide at times of social pressure whether an ideal-like self state represents one's genuine dreams or whether it has been compromised by the desire for role conformity. Indeed, group norms, as their name suggests, impose a normative function on group members and because humans are social beings, most of us adhere to some extent to these norms (see Dörnyei, 2007). This means that there is a pressure to internalise our ought selves to some extent, resulting in various degrees of integration.

The graded internalisation of external motives has been well described in Deci and Ryan's (1985) self-determination theory, which offers an internalisation continuum of extrinsic regulation, identifying four stages of the process: (1) *external regulation*, which refers to the least self-determined form of extrinsic motivation, coming entirely from external sources such as rewards or threats (e.g. teacher's praise or parental confrontation); (2) *introjected regulation*, which involves externally imposed rules that the individual accepts as norms he/she should follow in order not to feel guilty (e.g. some laws of a country); (3) *identified regulation*, which occurs when people engage in an activity because they highly value and identify with the behaviour, and see its usefulness (e.g. learning a language which is necessary to pursue one's hobbies or interests); and (4) *integrated regulation*, which is the most developmentally advanced form of extrinsic motivation, involving choiceful behaviour that is fully assimilated with the individual's other values, needs and identity (e.g. learning English because proficiency in this language is part of an educated cosmopolitan culture one has adopted). At first sight, (1) and (2) appear to be linked to the ought self and (3) and (4) to the ideal self, but where exactly is the boundary? We will come back to this question below when we look at the development of the two self dimensions.

Finally, the ought self raises one more issue. In Higgins's (1987; Higgins *et al.*, 1985) original conceptualisation it referred to a positive reference point (i.e. the person whom I believe I ought to be), but Higgins (1996) suggests that this meaning may be extended to include a negative reference point (i.e. the person I don't want to be), similar to Markus and Nurius's (1986) feared self. This is an important point that I will recall when we look at the motivational capacity of the future self-guides below.

Future self-guides versus future goals

Human action is caused by purpose, and this purpose has often been operationalised in terms of *goals* both in professional and everyday discourse. Thus, goals refer to desired future end-states and this definition is rather close to the definition of future-oriented self-guides. So, are the ideal/ought dimensions merely a subset of goals? The answer is a definite no, and being aware of the difference is a prerequisite to understanding the essence of possible selves. In psychology there is a multitude of cognitive constructs that serve as future-oriented motives, ranging from self-actualisation needs to the different types of goals and orientations in various goal theories. The proponents of each construct present intellectually convincing arguments, which makes it difficult to choose from the wide variety of available constructs. The main attraction of possible self theory for me has been that it goes beyond logical, intellectual arguments when justifying the validity of the various future-oriented self types. As mentioned earlier, possible selves involve images and senses, approximating what people actually experience when they are engaged in motivated or goal-directed behaviour. This is why Markus keeps emphasising that possible selves involve self-relevant imagery (e.g. Markus, 2006; Markus & Nurius, 1986; Ruvolo & Markus, 1992). Thus, possible selves can be seen, according to Markus and Ruvolo (1989: 217), as the result of the various motivational factors (e.g. expectancies, attributions, value beliefs) 'that is psychologically experienced and that is a durable aspect of consciousness'.

Reading the possible selves literature I have found it remarkable how most authors seem to ignore this crucial distinction between goals and future self-guides in spite of the prominent emphasis on it in Markus's writings. Pizzolato (2006), for example, is quite right when she states that 'Unlike goal theory, possible selves are explicitly related to a long-term developmental goal involving goal setting, volition (via adherence to associated schemas), and goal achievement, but are larger than any one or combination of these constructs' (p. 58), but she could have gone one step further to state that it is the experiential element that makes possible selves 'larger' than any combinations of goal-related constructs. Similarly, Miller and Brickman (2004: 14) state that possible selves are examples of long-term, future goals and define these as 'self-relevant, self-defining goals that provide incentive for action', regulating behaviour 'through self-identification with the goals or the integration of the goals into the system of self-determined goals'. Yet, they seem to overlook the key element, namely that possible selves are 'self states' that people experience as reality.

The role of imagination and imagery

Having argued for a prominent place of imagery in possible selves theory, let us examine the notion of imagery/imagination and its motivational impact more closely. Imagination has been known to be related to motivation since the ancient Greeks. Aristotle, for example, defined imagination as 'sensation without matter' and claimed that 'There's no desiring without imagination' (Modell, 2003: 108). As McMahon (1973) explains, Aristotle defined the image in the soul as the prime motivating force in human action; he believed that when an image of something to be pursued or avoided was present in imagination, the soul was moved in the same manner as if the objects of desire were materially present.

Interestingly, contemporary definitions of mental imagery are very similar to that of Aristotle. Kosslyn *et al.* (2002), for example, define it as 'the ability to represent perceptual states in the absence of the appropriate sensory input' and they also confirm the assumption that humans respond to mental images similarly to visual ones. They report on neuroimaging studies that indicate that visual mental imagery and visual perception activate about two thirds of the same brain areas (for a recent summary of relevant research, see Kosslyn *et al.*, 2006). These results provide a neuropsychological basis for Markus and Ruvolo's (1989) claim that 'imaging one's own actions through the construction of elaborated possible selves achieving the desired goal may thus directly facilitate the translation of goals into intentions and instrumental actions' (p. 213) and a similar idea has been expressed by Wenger (1998) when he described the concept of 'imagination':

> My use of the concept of imagination refers to a process of expanding our self by transcending our time and space and creating new images of the world and ourselves. Imagination in this sense is looking at an apple seed and seeing a tree. It is playing scales on a piano, and envisioning a concert hall. (Wenger, 1998: 176)

The motivating power of mental imagery has been well documented in the field of sport psychology as well. Inspired by Paivio's (1985) influential model of cognitive functions of imagery in human performance, hundreds of studies have examined the relationship between mental imagery and sport performance, and as Gregg and Hall (2006) summarise, it has been generally concluded that imagery is an effective performance enhancement technique (see also Cumming & Ste-Marie, 2001, for a similar conclusion). As a result, virtually every successful athlete in the world applies some sort of imagery enhancement technique during training.

Thus, Markus and Nurius's (1986) possible selves concept has opened up a channel to harness the powerful motivational function of imagination (see Taylor *et al.*, 1998), which explains why Markus (2006) emphasised this aspect first in her retrospective summary cited earlier. In the same overview, she added the following:

> We were impressed by the fact that people spend an enormous amount of time envisioning their futures. We now know that this imaginative work has powerful consequences. Possible selves can work to energize actions and to buffer the current self from everyday dragons and many less overt indignities as well. ... In the U.S., it is both a birthright and a moral imperative to tailor one's personal version of the American Dream. The notion that one should 'dream on,' 'keep the dream alive,' and that 'if you dream it, you can become it' is a critical element in the world's cultural imagination about the U.S. ... People across a wide array of contexts are capable and willing to generate possible selves. (Markus, 2006: xii)

In summary, let me reiterate that the inclusion of imagery is a central element of possible selves theory. As Segal (2006) emphasises, it is the integration of fantasy with the self-concept construct that marks Markus and Nurius's (1986) work as truly innovative. This is certainly the aspect that grasped my own attention when I first encountered this work, and this is, I believe, what makes the concept of future self-guides such as the ideal and the ought selves suitable to be the lynchpins of a broad theory of L2 motivation. In their analysis of the ideal self, Boyatzis and Akrivou (2006) share Markus's (2006) conclusion that the dream or image of a desired future is the core content of the ideal self. And, as the following quote shows, they also believe that imagination has played a key role in the whole history of the human race:

> Throughout history of mankind, humans are driven by their imagination and their ability to see images of the desired future. Leaders, poets, writers, composers, artists, dreamers, athletes have been able to be inspired, stay inspired and inspire others through such images. These images, once shared, have the power to become a force, and in that sense an inspiration for social development and growth, for intentional change at many levels of social organization, not just for the individual. (Boyatzis & Akrivou, 2006: 633)

The motivational function of future self-guides: Self-discrepancy theory

We saw in the previous section that the imagery component of future self-guides is a powerful motivational tool. Let us examine how this tool fits into a broader theory of the motivational function of the ideal and ought selves. In this respect the most coherent framework has been offered by Higgins's (1987, 1996) *self-discrepancy theory*, which postulates that people are motivated to reach a condition where their self-concept matches their personally relevant self-guides. In other words, motivation in this sense involves the desire to reduce the discrepancy between one's actual self and the projected behavioural standards of the ideal/ought selves. Thus, future self-guides provide incentive, direction and impetus for action, and sufficient discrepancy between these and the actual self initiates distinctive self-regulatory strategies with the aim to reduce the discrepancy – future self-guides represent points of comparison to be reconciled through behaviour (Hoyle & Sherrill, 2006).

An important point to note is that although the ideal and ought selves are similar to each other in that they are both related to the attainment of a desired end-state, Higgins (1998) emphasises that the predilections associated with the two different types of future selves are motivationally distinct from each other: ideal self-guides have a *promotion* focus, concerned with hopes, aspirations, advancements, growth and accomplishments; whereas ought self-guides have a *prevention* focus, regulating the absence or presence of negative outcomes associated with failing to live up to various responsibilities and obligations. As Higgins adds, this distinction is in line with the age-old motivational principle that people approach pleasure and avoid pain.

Conditions for the motivating capacity of the ideal and ought selves

Although the above description of possible selves theory has pointed to the conclusion that future self-guides motivate action by triggering the execution of self-regulatory mechanisms, several studies have found that this does not always happen automatically (e.g. Oyserman *et al.*, 2006; Yowell, 2002). Past research suggests that there are certain conditions that can enhance or hinder the motivational impact of the ideal and ought selves, the most important of which are the following ones: (1) availability of an elaborate and vivid future self image, (2) perceived plausibility, (3) harmony between the ideal and ought selves, (4) necessary activation/priming, (5) accompanying procedural strategies, and (6) the offsetting impact of a feared self.

Availability of an elaborate and vivid future self image

The primary and obvious prerequisite for the motivational capacity of future self-guides is that they *need to exist*. It has been observed that people differ in how easily they can generate a successful possible self (Ruvolo & Markus, 1992) and, therefore not everyone is expected to possess a developed ideal or ought self guide (Higgins, 1987, 1996). This can explain the absence of sufficient motivation in many people. Furthermore, even if the self image does exist, it may not have a sufficient degree of elaborateness and vividness to be effective. It has been found that the more elaborate the possible self in terms of imaginative, visual and other content elements, the more motivational power it is expected to have. People display significant individual differences in the vividness of their mental imagery (Richardson, 1994), and a possible self with insufficient specificity and detail may not be able to stir up the necessary motivational response.

Perceived plausibility

Ruvolo and Markus (1992: 96) argue that it is the individual's 'specific representations of what is possible for the self that embody and give rise to generalised feelings of efficacy, competence, control, or optimism, and that provide the means by which these global constructs have their powerful impact on behaviour'. In other words, possible selves are only effective insomuch as the individual does indeed perceive them as *possible*, that is, realistic within the person's individual circumstances. The significance of the subjective appraisal of future self-guides has been echoed by others as well; for example, Segal (2006: 91) points out that 'It is well established that the degree to which participants expect their feared or wished for possible selves to come true affects their self-esteem, current mood, and optimism', and MacIntyre *et al.* (this volume, Chapter 10: 197) also conclude that 'it is also important to find out how *likely* participants consider a possible self to be; a highly unlikely possible self probably will have little relation to motivation'.

Norman and Aron (2003) make an important point when they emphasise the relevance of the individual's perceived control in the context of possible selves. 'Perceived behavioural control' was introduced as a key component in Ajzen's (1988) theory of planned behaviour, referring to the perceived ease or difficulty of performing the behaviour (e.g. perceptions of required resources and potential impediments or obstacles). With regard to possible selves, Norman and Aron argue that perceived control is the degree to which individuals believe their behaviours can influence the attainment, or avoidance, of a possible self. 'If individuals believe they have control over attaining or avoiding a possible self, they will be more inclined to take the necessary steps to do so' (p. 501). Interestingly, Carver *et al.* (1994) see the main difference between pessimists and optimists exactly in their ability to translate hoped-for possible selves into realistic expectations. As they conclude, because pessimists' hopes 'fail to evolve into expected selves, these hopes may thus be less likely to engage the motivational control systems that cause their realization in behaviour' (p. 139).

Harmony between the ideal and ought selves

We have seen earlier that the ought self is closely related to peer group norms and other normative pressures (e.g. ethnic community expectations). Thus, learners' (and especially adolescents') ought self may contain certain peer-induced views about academic attainment (e.g. low-achieving expectations that are often called the 'norm of mediocrity') that are in conflict with the individual's ideal self. Put in another way, there can be a clash between a learner's personal and social identity. Oyserman *et al.* (2006) found that among school children negative group images are often highly accessible, making social group membership feel like it conflicts with academic self-guides, and in such cases teenagers tend to regulate their behaviours to fit in with their peers (Pizzolato, 2006). Thus, an important condition for effective desired possible selves is that they should feel congruent with important social identities, that is, that the ideal and the ought selves should be in harmony.

Necessary activation/priming

Even if the learner does have a well-developed and plausible ideal/ought self image, this may not always be active in the working memory. Hoyle and Sherrill (2006) argue that possible selves become relevant for behaviour only when they are recruited into the working self-concept and for this to happen they need to be activated. This priming of the self image can be triggered by various reminders and self-relevant events, and they can also be deliberately invoked by the individual in response to an event or situation. Ruvolo and Markus (1992), for example, maintain that simulating a desired end-state can activate the future self-guide and they provide empirical evidence that imagery manipulations (in their case, asking participants to imagine themselves as successful or unsuccessful before a task) increased the accessibility of possible selves, as evidenced by the subjects' performance. I come back to the question of the enhancement of self-representations at the end of this chapter when discussing the practical implications of the theory.

Accompanying procedural strategies

Let us consider a learner who is energised by an attractive future ideal self-guide. In order to translate the aroused motivational potential into action, he/she needs to have a roadmap of tasks and strategies to follow in order to approximate the ideal self. For example, it is obviously not enough for an Olympic athlete merely to imagine herself walking into the Olympic stadium or stepping onto the podium if she has no coach or training plan. For this reason, along with many others, Oyserman *et al.* (2006) argue that future self-guides are only effective if they are accompanied by a set of specific predeveloped and plausible action plans, which are cued automatically by the image. Thus, effective future self-guides need to come as part of a 'package', consisting of an imagery component and a repertoire of appropriate plans, scripts and self-regulatory strategies. This idea of a rich, closely networked package of information about how to achieve their hoped-for possible selves is expressed very clearly by Cross and Markus (1994):

> A possible self may serve as a node in an associative network of experiences, strategies, and self-knowledge. In this way, the possible self may link effective steps and strategies...with beliefs about one's ability and competence in the domain. (Cross & Markus, 1994: 434)

A study by Pizzolato (2006) of American minority students provided clear empirical confirmation that without procedural schemas for achieving their educational aspirations the participants could not make specific plans, which jeopardised the achievement of their ideal selves. Miller and Brickman (2004) also emphasise that because future self-guides specify distant goals, people have to create proximal guides themselves, setting concrete courses of action that lead to distal attainments, which is of course a central tenet in goal-setting theory (Locke & Latham, 1990). As Miller and Brickman (2004) argue, it is this system of specific proximal subgoals, or goal-focused strategies, that distinguishes reality-based future goals from empty dreams and fantasies. In their view, the absence of an appropriate system of meaningful paths to pursue the desired selves can be caused by two factors: a lack of sufficient knowledge or experience (e.g. no relevant role models or knowledgeable significant others) and ineffective cognitive skills for planning and problem-solving. On the other hand, if the possible self is accompanied by the necessary procedural knowledge, it will turn from a hoped-for into an expected self (Yowell, 2002).

Offset by feared self

The last condition to be mentioned with regard to the motivational capacity of possible selves concerns an interesting proposal made by Oyserman and Markus (1990). They argued that a desired possible self will have maximal motivational effectiveness when it is offset or balanced by a counteracting feared possible self in the same domain. Indeed, focusing on what would happen if the original intention failed has often been seen in motivational psychology as a powerful source of energy to keep us going (see Dörnyei, 2001a) – in academia, for example, it is often not the imagined success of a paper that makes us get down to writing it but rather the fear of missing the deadline. Thus, according to Oyserman and Markus (1990), for best effect the negative consequences of not achieving a desired end-state need to be elaborated and be cognitively available to individuals.

In an educational intervention study, Oyserman *et al.* (2006) demonstrated that positive self-guides and their negative counterparts are not simply inverse factors but have distinct impacts on the students' self-regulatory behaviour: learners with academically focused desired future selves spent more time doing homework and were less disruptive and more engaged in classroom activities, whereas feared possible selves resulted in fewer school absences. This suggests that the most effective condition for future self-guides is a balanced combination of pairs of countervailing selves; in Higgins's paradigm this would suggest a balanced combination of the ideal and the ought selves, which is related to the question of the harmony between the selves mentioned above. Hoyle and Sherrill (2006) argue similarly, stating that the motivation conferred by balanced possible selves is additive, involving both approach and avoid tendencies, and is therefore greater than the motivation conferred by the hoped-for or feared self alone.

The Contribution of L2 Motivation Research: Growing Dissatisfaction with the Integrative Motive

Having described the theoretical advances in psychology that acted as one of the two main sources of inspiration for proposing the L2 Motivational Self System, let us now turn to the second source, which is rooted in developments within L2 motivation research. It concerns a growing dissatisfaction with the concept of integrativeness/integrative motivation, which, as I stated in the introduction of this chapter, has been at the centre of L2 motivation research for almost five decades (for reviews, see Dörnyei, 2001b; Gardner, 2001; MacIntyre, 2002; MacIntyre *et al.*, this volume, Chapter 3).

Integrativeness refers to the desire to learn an L2 of a valued community so that one can communicate with members of the community and sometimes even become like them. Gardner (2001) characterised the concept as follows:

> Integrativeness reflects a genuine interest in learning the second language in order to come closer to the other language community. At one level, this implies an openness to, and respect for other cultural groups and ways of life. In the extreme, this might involve complete identification with the community (and possibly even

withdrawal from one's original group), but more commonly it might well involve integration within both communities. (Gardner, 2001: 5)

Integrative motivation is a more complex, multi-componential construct, consisting of three main constituents: 'integrativeness', 'attitudes towards the learning situation' and 'motivation' (see Figure 2.1). The latter is seen as the driving force of motivated behaviour, subsuming effort, desire and affect (Gardner, 2001); that is, it is concerns a central motivational engine that needs to be ignited by some specific learning goal such as an integrative orientation.

As I pointed out in my 2005 review (Dörnyei, 2005), a closer look at the L2 motivation literature reveals a certain amount of ambivalence about integrativeness/integrative motivation, amounting sometimes to a kind of 'love–hate' relationship amongst researchers outside Gardner's Canadian circle. The concept is certainly an enigma. It has been without any doubt the most researched and most talked about notion in L2 motivation studies and yet it has no obvious equivalent in any other theories in mainstream motivational and educational psychology. In addition, the label 'integrative' is ambiguous because it is not quite clear what the target of the integration is, and in many language learning environments it simply does not make much sense. In a multicultural

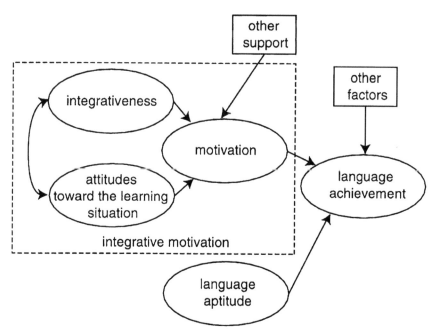

Figure 2.1 The integrative motive within Gardner's 'Socio-Educational Model of Second Language Acquisition' (Gardner, 2001: 4)

setting such as Montreal, where Gardner first developed his theory, we can talk about potential 'integration', but in learning situations where a foreign language is taught as a school subject without any direct contact with its speakers (e.g. teaching English or French in Hungary, China, Japan or other typical 'foreign language learning' contexts) the 'integrative' metaphor does not have any obvious meaning. Partly for these reasons and partly because the actual empirical findings did not always fit Gardner's original interpretation of the notion, several scholars in the past have questioned the validity and relevance of integrativeness (e.g. Coetzee-Van Rooy, 2006; Dörnyei *et al.*, 2006; Irie, 2003; Lamb, 2004; Ushioda, 2006; Warden & Lin, 2000; Yashima, 2000; for a review, see Dörnyei, 2005). Interestingly, this even happened amongst Canadian scholars close to Gardner, as the following quotation shows:

> Although it was originally suggested that the desire for contact and identification with members of the L2 group [i.e. integrative orientation] would be critical for L2 acquisition, it would now appear that it is not fundamental to the motivational process, but has relevance only in specific sociocultural contexts. Rather, four other orientations may be seen to sustain motivation. (Noels *et al.*, 2000: 60)

The four orientations – or learning goals – the researchers were advocating are *travel, friendship, knowledge,* and *instrumental orientation,* which echoes the findings of Clément and Kruidenier's (1983) seminal paper in the early 1980s that was the first 'insider challenge' to the integrative construct proposed by Gardner.

The problematic nature of integrativeness has been amplified by the worldwide globalisation process and the growing dominance of Global/World English as an international language (Dörnyei *et al.*, 2006). In the new globalised world order, as Arnett (2002) argues, the pressure for most people is to develop a *bicultural identity,* in which part of their identity is rooted in their local culture while another part is associated with a global identity that links them to the international mainstream. The language of this global identity is English, and from this perspective it is not at all clear who EFL (English as a foreign language) learners believe the 'owner' of their L2 is. This lack of a specific target L2 community, in turn, undermines Gardner's theoretical concept of integrativeness: in Gardner's (2001) definition cited above, for example, what exactly would be – to quote Gardner (2001) – 'the other language community' that the learner would want to 'get closer to'?

As a result of these and other concerns – particularly the under-theorised nature of the concept of integrativeness from a cognitive psychological point of view (see Ushioda, 2007) – integrative motivation has played a rapidly diminishing role in L2 motivation research during the past decade, to the extent that currently few active motivation researchers include the concept in their research paradigms. In a recent article specifically devoted to this issue with regard to the learning of World English, Coetzee-Van Rooy (2006) came to the following summary:

> In conclusion, I want to return to the question posed in the title of this paper: is the notion of integrativeness untenable for world Englishes speakers? Findings from a review of theoretical criticism as well as empirical projects suggest that the answer is: Yes, the notion of integrativeness is untenable for second-language learners in world Englishes contexts. Researchers who use the construct should at least interrogate its use within the context in which the second language is learnt and the extent of multidimensionality of the learner's identity. (Coetzee-Van Rooy, 2006: 447)

The Formation of the 'L2 Motivational Self System'

In accordance with the above considerations, at the beginning of the new millennium I was ready to move beyond integrativeness, and possible selves theory seemed to offer the most promising way forward. Consequently, in an article describing the results of a large-scale investigation in Hungary (Dörnyei & Csizér, 2002), we called for a general rethinking of the concept of integrativeness:

> ...the term may not so much be related to any actual, or metaphorical, *integration* into an L2 community as to some more basic *identification process* within the individual's *self-concept*. Although further research is needed to justify any alternative interpretation, we believe that rather than viewing 'integrativeness' as a classic and therefore 'untouchable' concept, scholars need to seek potential new conceptualizations and interpretations that extend or elaborate on the meaning of the term without contra-dicting the large body of relevant empirical data accumulated during the past four decades. (Dörnyei & Csizér, 2002: 456)

As already mentioned briefly, the main personal attraction of possible selves theory for me lay in its imagery component. Language learning is a sustained and often tedious process with lots of temporary ups and downs, and I felt that the secret of successful learners was their possession of a superordinate vision that kept them on track. Indeed, language learning can be compared in many ways to the training of professional athletes, and the literature is very clear about the fact that a successful sports career is often motivated by imagery and vision. The point when this line of thinking went beyond mere speculation was during the re-analysis of our Hungarian motivation data using structural equation modelling (Csizér & Dörnyei, 2005), when I realised that the results supported the possible reinterpretation of integrativeness as the 'Ideal L2 Self'. Let us look at these results in more detail.

Empirical findings pointing to the need to reinterpret integrativeness

Over the past 15 years I have been heading a research team in Hungary with the objective of carrying out a longitudinal survey amongst teenage language learners by administering an attitude/ motivation questionnaire at regular intervals so that we can gauge the changes in the population's international orientation. So far three successive waves of data collections have been completed (in 1993, 1999 and 2004) involving over 13,000 learners (for a detailed summary, see Dörnyei *et al.*, 2006). The survey questionnaire targeted attitudes towards five target languages: English, German, French, Italian and Russian. It was originally developed in collaboration with one of Robert Gardner's closest associates, Richard Clément, and therefore integrativeness had a prominent place in it, but we also measured several other attitudinal/motivational dimensions, such as *Instrumentality* (i.e. the pragmatic utility of learning the L2); *Direct contact with L2 speakers* (i.e. attitudes towards actually meeting L2 speakers and travelling to their country); *Cultural interest* (i.e. the appreciation of cultural products associated with the particular L2 and conveyed by the media; e.g. films, TV programs, magazines and pop music); *Vitality of L2 community* (i.e. the perceived importance and wealth of the L2 communities in question); *Milieu* (i.e. the general perception of the importance of foreign languages in the learners' school context and in friends' and parents' views); and finally *Linguistic self-confidence* (i.e. a confident, anxiety-free belief that the mastery of an L2 is well within the learner's means).

We submitted the data from all three waves of the survey to structural equation modelling, treating each language and each year separately (so we computed separate models for, say, German in 1993 and French in 2004) and found that the structure underlying the examined variables was remarkably stable across time and languages: The multiple models we obtained produced the same overall result with only minor varia- tions. Figure 2.2 presents the schematic representation of the final construct, which had excellent goodness of fit indices for all the versions (for details, see Dörnyei *et al.*, 2006).

The most important aspect of the model in Figure 2.2 is, from our perspective, that *Integrativeness* was found to play a key role in L2 motivation, mediating the effects of all the other attitudinal/motivational variables on the two criterion measures *Language choice* and *Intended effort to study the L2*. The immediate antecedents of *Integrativeness* were *Attitudes toward L2 speakers/community* and *Instrumentality*, which indicated that the

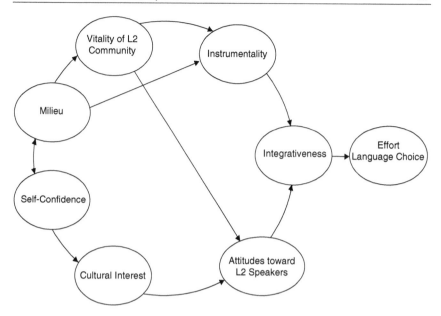

Figure 2.2 Schematic representation of the structural equation model in Dörnyei *et al.*'s (2006) study

central component in the motivation paradigm was defined by two very different variables, faceless pragmatic incentives and personal attitudes toward members of the L2 community. The question was how we could explain these consistent but theoretically far-from-straightforward findings. After some consideration I came to the conclusion that the possible selves approach described earlier offered a good account of the data. Looking at 'integrativeness' from the self perspective, the concept can be conceived of as the L2-specific facet of one's ideal self: if our ideal self is associated with the mastery of an L2, that is, if the person that we would like to become is proficient in the L2, we can be described in Gardner's (1985) terminology as having an integrative disposition. Thus, the central theme of the emerging new theory was the equation of the motivational dimension that has traditionally been interpreted as 'integrativeness/ integrative motivation' with the *Ideal L2 Self*.

Does the self account explain the two antecedents of integrativeness in Figure 2.2, 'attitudes toward members of the L2 community' and 'instrumentality'? I believe it does, and does it very well:

(1) *Attitudes toward members of the L2 community:* There is no doubt that L2 speakers are the closest parallels to the idealised L2-speaking self. This suggests that our attitudes towards members of the L2 community must be related to our ideal language self image. I would

suggest that the more positive our disposition toward these L2 speakers, the more attractive our idealised L2 self; or, to turn this equation around, it is difficult to imagine that we can have a vivid and attractive ideal L2 self if the L2 is spoken by a community that we despise. Therefore, the self interpretation of integrativeness is fully compatible with the direct correlation of the concept with 'attitudes toward members of the L2 community'. We find confirmation for this link in the psychological literature. Herbst *et al.*'s own research and the studies they cite confirm that 'people are attracted to others who emulate the person they want to be rather than the person they actually are' (Herbst *et al.*, 2003: 1206), and, more specifically, 'similarity to the ideal self drives the similarity–attraction association' (p. 1207). Therefore, the correlation in Figure 2.2 not only makes sense but actually validates the reinterpretation of integrativeness as the ideal L2 self.

(2) *Instrumentality:* In our idealised image of ourselves we naturally want to be professionally successful and therefore instrumental motives that are related to career enhancement are logically linked to the ideal L2 self. We should note here, however, that from a self perspective the term 'instrumentality' can be divided into two distinct types. Recall that Higgins (1987, 1998) highlighted a contrasting *approach/avoid* tendency in our future self-guides: ideal self-guides have a *promotion* focus, concerned with hopes, aspirations, advancements, growth and accomplishments (i.e. approaching a desired end-state); whereas ought-to self-guides have a *prevention* focus, regulating the absence or presence of negative outcomes, concerned with safety, responsibilities and obligations (i.e. avoidance of a feared end-state). Looking at it from this perspective, traditionally conceived 'instrumentality/instrumental motivation' mixes up these two aspects: when our idealised image is associated with being professionally successful, instrumental motives with a promotion focus – for example, to learn English for the sake of professional/career advancement – are related to the ideal self; in contrast, instrumental motives with a prevention focus – for example, to study in order not to fail an exam or not to disappoint one's parents – are part of the ought self. Interestingly, a study by Kyriacou and Benmansour (1997) proposed a data-based five-factor construct that seems to reflect this duality well as it comprises a component labelled 'long-term instrumental motivation,' focusing on acquiring the L2 to enhance one's future professional career, and also a 'short-term instrumental motivation' factor, focusing on getting good grades.

The L2 Motivational Self System

So far this chapter has described how both empirical findings and theoretical considerations led me to a reconceptualisation of L2 motivation as part of the learner's self system. The good fit between the new theoretical approach and the Hungarian data convinced me that future self-guides – more specifically, the ideal and the ought selves – are central components of this system. However, I also felt that we needed to add a third major constituent, which is associated with the direct impact of the students' learning environment. After all, one of the main achievements of the new wave of motivational studies in the 1990s was to recognise the motivational impact of the main components of the classroom learning situation, such as the teacher, the curriculum and the learner group (for reviews, see Dörnyei, 1994a, 2001b; Ushioda, 2003). For some language learners the initial motivation to learn a language does not come from internally or externally generated self images but rather from successful engagement with the actual language learning process (e.g. because they discover that they are good at it). Thus, in 2005 I proposed that the 'L2 Motivational Self System' was made up of the following three components:

(1) *Ideal L2 Self*, which is the L2-specific facet of one's 'ideal self': if the person we would like to become speaks an L2, the *'ideal L2 self'* is a powerful motivator to learn the L2 because of the desire to reduce the discrepancy between our actual and ideal selves. Traditional integrative and internalised instrumental motives would typically belong to this component.

(2) *Ought-to L2 Self*, which concerns the attributes that one believes one *ought to* possess to meet expectations and to *avoid* possible negative outcomes. This dimension corresponds to Higgins's ought self and thus to the more extrinsic (i.e. less internalised) types of instrumental motives.

(3) *L2 Learning Experience*, which concerns situated, 'executive' motives related to the immediate learning environment and experience (e.g. the impact of the teacher, the curriculum, the peer group, the experience of success). This component is conceptualised at a different level from the two self-guides and future research will hopefully elaborate on the self aspects of this bottom-up process.

Parallels with other conceptualisations of L2 motivation

Although future self-guides may seem rather different in nature from integrativeness, the two theories are not at all incompatible. They both grew out of a social psychological approach to understanding the foundations of action, and both paradigms are centred around identity and identification. With the self system this aspect is obvious, but a closer look at integrativeness also reveals that its core aspect is some sort of a psychological and emotional identification with the L2 community (Gardner, 2001). Indeed, we find several similarities with the L2 Motivational Self System in Gardner's theory. For example, a model put forward by Tremblay and Gardner (1995) as an extension of Gardner's traditional construct includes a broad composite 'Language attitudes' factor at its base, which bears a close resemblance to the proposed concept of Ideal L2 Self in that it subsumes integrative orientation, instrumental orientation, and L2-speaker-related attitudes.

More importantly, Gardner's (2001) socio-educational model described in Figure 2.1 is also compatible with the proposed motivational self system if we consider (1) that the 'motivation' subcomponent in Gardner's construct is, in effect, a measure of motivated behaviour, as indicated by the items that measure it in Gardner's (1985) Attitude/Motivation Test Battery (see Dörnyei, 1994b); and (2) that Gardner (2001) attached a possible instrumental motivational link to the Motivation subcomponent in his construct (as the key element of the 'other support' box in Figure 2.1). After these changes, Gardner's motivation construct suggests, in effect, that motivated behaviour is determined by three major motivational dimensions, Integrativeness, Instrumentality, and Attitudes toward the learning situation, which corresponds closely with the proposed L2 Motivational Self System.

Looking at parallels with more recent influential conceptualisations, the proposed self perspective also corresponds with the motivation constructs suggested by Noels (2003) and Ushioda (2001). Noels conceived L2 motivation as being made up of three interrelated orientations: (1) intrinsic reasons inherent in the language learning process, (2) extrinsic reasons for language learning, and (3) integrative reasons. These three components are a close match to the L2 Learning Experience, the Ought-to L2 Self and the Ideal L2 Self, respectively.

Using qualitative rather than quantitative methods, Ushioda identified a more complex motivation construct which, however, is conceptually related both to the one offered by Noels and the L2 Motivation Self System. Her findings pointed to eight motivational dimensions, which in turn can be grouped into three broad clusters: (1) *actual learning process* (subsuming 'Language-related enjoyment/liking', 'Positive learning history' and 'Personal satisfaction'); (2) *external pressures/incentives*; and (3) *integrative disposition* (subsuming 'Personal goals'; 'Desired levels of L2 competence', which consists of language-intrinsic goals; 'Academic interest', which had the greatest contribution from interest in French literature; and 'Feelings about French-speaking countries or people'). Here again the parallels with the L2 Motivational Self System are obvious.

Thus, we can conclude that a number of different L2 motivation theories appear to converge in a common tripartite construct, which is fully compatible with the L2 Motivational Self System. This provides theoretical validation for the new model. Let us examine now whether empirical data also confirm the proposed assumptions.

Empirical validation of the L2 Motivational Self System

Over the last three years several quantitative studies have been conducted to specifically test and validate the L2 Motivational Self System, and the most important of these are included in this volume (Al-Shehri; Csizér & Kormos; Ryan; Taguchi *et al.*). These investigations took place in five different countries (China, Hungary, Iran, Japan and Saudi Arabia) and involved over 6000 participants in four different sample types: secondary pupils, English-major and non-English-major university students and adult learners. Without wanting to reiterate the findings reported in the specific papers, let me draw five general conclusions:

(1) All these studies found solid confirmation for the proposed self system.
(2) The studies which specifically tested the relationship between Integrativeness and the Ideal L2 Self produced an average correlation of .54 between the two variables across the various subsamples, leaving no doubt that the two concepts are closely related.
(3) The Ideal L2 Self was consistently found to correlate highly with the criterion measure (Intended effort), explaining 42% of the variance, which is an exceptionally high figure in motivation studies. In the studies where it was measured, Integrativeness also did a good job at explaining variance in the criterion measure, but the amount of variance it accounted for was considerably less, only 32%.
(4) When instrumentality was divided into two types in accordance with Higgins's (1987, 1998) promotion/prevention distinction, all the studies found – in line with the theory – higher correlations of the *Ideal L2 Self* with *Instrumentality-promotion* than with *Instrumentality-prevention*, while *Ought-to L2 Self* displayed the reverse pattern. Furthermore, the promotion and the prevention aspects were largely independent from each other, with even the highest correlations between the two types of instrumental factors explaining less than 12% of shared variance. Thus, these figures prove that traditionally conceived 'instrumental motivation' can indeed be divided into two distinct types, one relating to the Ideal L2 Self, the other to the Ought-to L2 Self.
(5) Structural equation models including the full L2 Motivational Self System displayed fine goodness of fit with the data.

Besides these studies that were specifically conducted for validation purposes, several other empirical investigations reported in this anthology considered some aspect of the validity of the L2 Motivational Self System. We will summarise these in the final chapter in more detail, but as a preliminary it is fair to say that the proposed model came out of these studies in a favourable light. Thus, we can conclude that there exists robust theoretical and empirical confirmation of the soundness of the proposed self-based approach.

Practical Implications of the Self-based Approach to Motivation

One benefit of reinterpreting L2 motivation within the L2 Motivational Self System is that it offers new avenues for motivating language learners. The novel area of motivational strategies concerns the promotion of the first component of the system, the Ideal L2 Self, through generating a language learning vision and through imagery enhancement. Because the source of the second component of the system, the Ought-to L2 Self, is external to the learner (as it concerns the duties and obligations imposed by friends, parents and other authoritative figures), this future self-guide does not lend itself to obvious motivational practices. The third component of the system, the L2 Learning Experience, is associated with a wide range of techniques that can promote motivation, but because these have been described well in past discussions of traditional motivational strategies, I will not focus on them here (for a review, see Dörnyei, 2001a). The new set of motivational techniques associated with the Ideal L2 Self complements these known strategies.

In the first part of this Chapter I summarised the conditions that are necessary for future self-guides to exert their motivational power. Accordingly, the Ideal L2 Self is an effective motivator if (1) the learner has a desired future self-image, (2) which is elaborate and vivid, (3) which is perceived as plausible and is in harmony – or at least does not clash – with the expectations of the learner's family, peers and other elements of the social environment, (4) which is regularly activated in the learner's working self-concept, (5) which is accompanied by relevant and effective procedural strategies that act as a roadmap towards the goal, and finally (6) which also contains elaborate information about the negative consequences of not achieving the desired end-state. Of this list, points (1–4) are specific to the self approach, whereas the final two points involve more general motivational and instructional strategies that have been, in one way or another, part of the traditional conception of motivational teaching practice: point (4) concerns the generation of a realistic and situated action plan while point (5) involves the general idea that we can be both pulled and pushed towards the same goal and the most effective way is to coordinate these forces. Let us look at the strategic implications of these six points.

Construction of the Ideal L2 Self: Creating the vision

We saw earlier that the (obvious) prerequisite for the motivational capacity of future self-guides is that they *need to exist*. It was also mentioned that people differ in how easily they can generate a successful possible self, which means that a major source of any absence of L2 motivation is likely to be the lack of a developed ideal self in general or an Ideal L2 Self component of it in particular. Therefore, the first step in a motivational intervention following the self approach is to help learners to construct their Ideal L2 Self, that is, to *create their vision*.

Strictly speaking, the term 'constructing' the Ideal L2 Self is not really accurate because it is highly unlikely that any motivational intervention will lead a student to generate an ideal self out of nothing – the realistic process is more likely to involve awareness raising and guided selection from the multiple aspirations, dreams, desires, etc. that the students have already entertained in the past. Dunkel *et al.* (2006) explain that during the formation of their identities, adolescents produce a wide variety of possible selves as potential identity alternatives to explore and 'try on' without full commitment. The origins of these tentative possible selves go back to views held by others, most notably to the ideals that parents hold for themselves and for their children (Zentner & Renaud, 2007). Alternatively, they can also stem from the students' peer groups, which act as powerful reference groups exerting social pressure (Boyatzis & Akrivou, 2006), and a third common route is related to the impact of role models that the students have seen in films, on TV or in real life.

Thus, igniting the vision involves, in effect, increasing the students' mindfulness about the significance of ideal selves, guiding them through a number of possible selves that they have entertained in their minds in the past, and presenting powerful role models. Oyserman *et al.* (2002) also emphasise the importance of helping students to synthesise the potential hypothetical images with what they know about themselves, their own traits and abilities, as well as their past successes and failures in order to capitalise on existing strengths and avoid weaknesses. In a successful intervention programme with American low-income, minority teenagers, for example, Oyserman *et al.* (2006) asked students to introduce each other in terms of the skills or ability they possessed, and in the second session participants picked photographs that fitted their adult 'visions'. A different approach was taken in Sheldon and Lyubomirsky's (2006) 'Best Possible Selves' writing project, in which students were directed to outline their 'ideal future life' in as much detail as they could.

In another programme developed by Hock *et al.* (2006) for demotivated elementary to post-secondary students in the US, the first phase included a series of activities designed to help students identify areas in which they have interest and skills and feel good about themselves. This was followed by a semi-structured interview with a teacher or counsellor, either individually or as part of a group, in which the students were asked to identify words or phrases that described them in targeted areas (as a learner, a person, a worker, and in a strength area), and to define their hopes, expectations and fears for the future in each area. The interviews were recorded and students were also encouraged to write down the answers to each question. As a follow-up, in the third phase of the programme they were asked to draw a 'Possible Selves Tree' with branches and other elements (e.g. lightning, termites) representing both their desired and feared possible selves. Interestingly, they were instructed to use the exact words they recorded in the interview to add branches and roots to the tree and the dangers around it.

So far no research has been directed at specifically developing an ideal language self. However, it seems to me that in an era when international holidays are becoming increasingly accessible and cross-cultural communication is a standard part of our existence in the 'global village', it is possible to devise creative ideal-self-generating activities drawing on past adventures, on the exotic nature of encounters with a foreign culture, and on role models of successful L2 learning achievers.

Imagery enhancement: Strengthening the vision

I argued earlier that even if a desired self image exists, it may not have a sufficient degree of elaborateness and vividness in some learners to be effective. The good news is that methods of imagery enhancement have been explored in several areas of psychological, educational and sport research in the past, and the techniques of creative or guided imagery can be utilised to promote ideal L2 self images and thus to *strengthen the students' vision*. (For reviews and resources, see for example, Berkovits, 2005; Fezler, 1989; Gould *et al.*, 2002; Hall *et al.*, 2006; Horowitz, 1983; Leuner *et al.*, 1983; Singer, 2006; Taylor *et al.*, 1998). The impact of imagery training is evident from an Olympic champion springboard diver's account:

> It took me a long time to control my images and perfect my imagery, maybe a year, doing it every day. At first I couldn't see myself, I always saw everyone else, or I would see my dives wrong all the time. I would get an image of hurting myself, or tripping on the board, or I would 'see' something done really bad. As I continued to

work at it, I got to the point where I could feel myself doing a perfect dive and hear the crowd yelling at the Olympics. But it took me a long time. (Gould *et al.*, 2002: 70)

As Gould *et al.* (2002) describe, imagery training for athletes is designed to enhance the vividness and controllability of an athlete's imagery. These can involve a variety of exercises, starting from very simple ones (e.g. imagining one's bedroom and gradually adding details) to complex ones that include controlling and manipulating the content of elaborate image sequences. However, the authors stress that, regardless of which area an athlete is working on, 'imagery is a skill like any other, requiring consistent effort to attain a high level of proficiency' (Gould *et al.*, 2002: 70). In psychotherapy, too, there is a number of different approaches, from the 'positive imagery approach' (which involves the use of highly pleasurable, relaxing images to counteract anxiety), to behaviourists' systematic desensitisation or to guided imagery in the treatment of conditions as diverse as anorexia or childhood phobias (see Leuner *et al.*, 1983; Singer, 2006).

Guided imagery is also utilised in medical practice. According to Roffe *et al.* (2005), it has been identified as one of the 10 most frequently recommended complementary cancer therapies on the internet, and Fezler (1989) reports on using imagery successfully even on skin disorders such as acne. Finally, imagery has definite educational potential. Taylor *et al.* (1998), for example, present evidence that mental simulation was beneficial for university students preparing for an exam, and Berkovits (2005) argues passionately that imagery is the ideal way to work with children:

> When a child uses imagery to find solutions to problems in her current life or from the past, she obtains a sense of autonomy and confidence in her ability to resolve situations she may have felt controlled her. These situations run the gamut of the child's experience, pertaining to her relationship with herself, her peers, her parents, siblings, teachers, authority figures, and learning situations in school, to name a few. Using imagination to find solutions to these situations has the added advantage of improving the child's verbal ability, because the images are clear and precise, and they lend themselves to clarity and precision of expression. (Berkovits, 2005: xvii)

Thus, there is a considerable body of literature on the conscious use of imagery to good effect in varied disciplines. What would be needed in applied linguistics now is a systematic review of the techniques utilised with a view of their potential applicability to promoting L2 motivation and the vision to master a foreign language. An intriguing recent publication by Arnold *et al.* (2007) has taken the important first step towards introducing mental imagery in the L2 classroom, and although the details of an effective 'language vision programme' are still to be worked out, let there be no doubt about it: 'Our capacity for imagery and fantasy can indeed give us a kind of control over possible futures!' (Singer, 2006: 128).

Making the Ideal L2 Self plausible: Substantiating the vision

We saw earlier that possible selves are only effective insomuch as the individual perceives them as possible, that is, realistic within the person's particular circumstances. It is a central tenet in expectancy-value theories of motivation that the greater the perceived likelihood of goal-attainment, the higher the degree of the individual's positive motivation. Indeed, it is obvious that if people are convinced that they cannot succeed no matter how hard they try, they are unlikely to invest effort in the particular task (see Dörnyei, 2001b). This principle also applies to ideal self-images: in order for them to energise sustained behaviour, they must be anchored in a sense of realistic expectations. In other words, they need to be *substantiated*, resulting in the curious mixed aura of imagination and reality that effective images share. As Pizzolato (2006: 59) puts it, 'The relation between what students want to become and what students actually become may be mediated by what students feel they are able to become (i.e. expected possible selves).'

In the self-oriented training programme by Oyserman *et al.* (2006: 191) mentioned above, the reality component was added to the desired self image by asking students to draw role models and negative forces, implying the metamessage that 'everyone faces obstacles and difficulties; this does not make the PSs [possible selves] less part of the "true" self'. Then, in the following session students drew timelines into the future, including forks in the road and obstacles, thus reinforcing this message. In the 'Possible Selves Tree' programme described briefly earlier, Hock *et al.* (2006) also included a reality check component called 'Reflecting', which encouraged students to evaluate the condition of their Possible Selves Tree and to realise the need for the conscious nurturing of the tree. The authors argued that once students had examined their possible selves, they were more inclined to believe that they could do well in school and in life:

> In effect, they begin to view learning as a pathway to their hopes and expectations and as a way to prevent feared possible selves from materializing. Thus, learning becomes more relevant, and students increase their willingness to put forth effort and commit to learning. (Hock *et al.*, 2006: 214)

Activating the Ideal L2 Self: Keeping the vision alive

Very little is said in the literature about activating the ideal self, but this is an area where language teachers have, perhaps unknowingly, a great deal of experience. Classroom activities such as warmers and icebreakers as well as various communicative tasks (see for example, Dörnyei & Murphey, 2003) can all be turned into effective ways of *keeping the vision alive*, and inviting role models to class, playing films and music, and engaging in cultural activities such as French cheese parties or 'Cook Your Wicked Western Burger' evenings can all serve as potent ideal self reminders. Indeed, good teachers in any subject matter seem to have the instinctive talent to provide an engaging framework that keeps the enthusiasts going and the less-than-enthusiasts thinking.

Developing an action plan: Operationalising the vision

It was argued earlier, and virtually all the researchers in the area of possible/ideal selves point out in one way or another, that future self-guides are only effective if they are accompanied by a set of concrete action plans. Therefore, the ideal self needs to come as part of a 'package' consisting of an imagery component and a repertoire of appropriate plans, scripts and self-regulatory strategies. This is clearly an area where L2 motivation research and language teaching methodology overlap. An effective action plan will contain a goal-setting component, which is a motivational issue, but it will also include individualised study plans and instructional avenues, which are methodological in nature. For an Olympic athlete the coach and the training plan are just as much a part of the complete vision as the image of stepping onto the top of the podium. Thus, in many ways, several of the components underpinning the ideal self package are not strictly speaking self-specific and have in fact been addressed in detail in the past. The important lesson from our point of view is that these methodological aspects must not be overlooked because even the most galvanising vision might fall flat without any concrete pathways into which to channel the individual's energy. For this reason, in Hock *et al.*'s (2006: 214) training programme the final component involves a thorough check-up phase, in which 'task completion is reviewed, goals and action plans are modified, goal attainment is celebrated, new goals are added, and hopes, expectations, and fears are continually examined'.

Considering failure: Counterbalancing the vision

Oyserman and Markus (1990) proposed that for maximum effectiveness, the desired self should be offset by the feared self. That is, future self-guides are most potent if they utilise the cumulative impact of both approach and avoid tendencies – we do something because we want to do it but also because not doing it would lead to undesired results. Indeed, the perceived consequences of action abandonment have been known to have great energising potential (Dörnyei, 2001b), but a common human tendency is to focus on the positive goals and turn to considering the dire alternatives only when everything else fails. Oyserman and Markus's proposal intends to change this practice by making awareness of the two sides of the coin more balanced; it can be seen, therefore, as a call for the regular activation of the dreaded self. In language teaching terms this would involve regular reminders of the limitations of not knowing languages as well as recurrently priming the learners' Ought-to L2 Self by highlighting the duties and obligations the learners have committed themselves to.

Conclusion

This chapter discussed a major theoretical shift in L2 motivation research, describing how a new paradigm has emerged from both theoretical considerations and research results, and then presenting the main components of the newly proposed 'L2 Motivational Self System'. I would not like to draw detailed conclusions here because this will be done in the final chapter of this volume, which also outlines future research directions. Let me only make here three concluding points:

(1) Reframing L2 motivation in a 'possible/ideal-self' perspective does not invalidate the results accumulated in the field of L2 motivation research in the past. On the contrary: I believe that these results will come to life and receive a new meaningfulness within the self framework.

(2) Zentner and Renaud (2007) claim that stable ideal-self representations do not emerge before adolescence, and neither can younger children consider multiple perspectives on the self, most notably the ought self projected by significant others. Therefore, the self approach may not be appropriate for pre-secondary students.

(3) In everyday parlance 'vision' and 'visionary' are highly loaded words, having life-changing connotations. For me this transformational potential is a real attraction of the ideal self, and therefore it has been reassuring to read Oyserman *et al.*'s (2006) summary:

> Our results demonstrate the real-world power of a social psychological conceptualization of the self as a motivational resource...we developed a process model that, when operationalized, produced lasting change on PSs [possible selves], self-regulation, academic outcomes, and depression. (Oyserman *et al.*, 2006: 201)

So, the self approach allows us to think BIG, and this is exactly what Markus (2006) did in the conclusion of her retrospective overview:

> The realm of what I might be has come under empirical and theoretical scrutiny and has yielded more than we might have imagined some twenty years ago. ... I hope the volume succeeds in convincing other researchers not to be faint-hearted about the imaginative capacities of the human mind and our abilities to invent ourselves and our worlds. As humans our great evolutionary advantage is our capacity for self-making and world making. ... In fact, our futures may rest with our shared willingness to experiment with possible selves and possible worlds, and to redesign ourselves and our worlds so that there is room for all of us. (Markus, 2006: xiv)

References

Ajzen, I. (1988) *Attitudes, Personality and Behavior.* Chicago: Dorsey Press.

Arnett, J.J. (2002) The psychology of globalization. *American Psychologist* 57 (10), 774–783.

Arnold, J., Puchta, H. and Rinvolucri, M. (2007) *Imagine That! Mental Imagery in the EFL Classroom.* Cambridge: Cambridge University Press.

Berkovits, S. (2005) *Guided Imagery: Successful Techniques to Improve School Performance and Self-Esteem.* Duluth, MN: Whole Person Associates.

Boyatzis, R.E. and Akrivou, K. (2006) The ideal self as the driver of intentional change. *Journal of Management Development* 25 (7), 624–642.

Cantor, N. (1990) From thought to behavior: 'Having' and 'doing' in the study of personality and cognition. *American Psychologist* 45 (6), 735–750.

Carver, C.C., Reynolds, S.L. and Scheier, M.F. (1994) The possible selves of optimists and pessimists. *Journal of Research in Personality* 28, 133–141.

Clément, R. and Kruidenier, B. (1983) Orientations in second language acquisition: 1. The effects of ethnicity, milieu and target language on their emergence. *Language Learning* 33, 273–291.

Coetzee-Van Rooy, S. (2006) Integrativeness: Untenable for world Englishes learners? *World Englishes* 25 (3/4), 437–450.

Cross, S.E. and Markus, H.R. (1994) Self-schemas, possible selves, and competent performance. *Journal of Educational Psychology* 86 (3), 423–438.

Csizér, K. and Dörnyei, Z. (2005) The internal structure of language learning motivation: Results of structural equation modelling. *Modern Language Journal* 89 (1), 19–36.

Cumming, J.L. and Ste-Marie, D.M. (2001) The cognitive and motivational effects of imagery training: A matter of perspective. *The Sport Psychologist* 15, 276–288.

Deci, E.L. and Ryan, R.M. (1985) *Intrinsic Motivation and Self-Determination in Human Behaviour.* New York: Plenum.

Dörnyei, Z. (1994a) Motivation and motivating in the foreign language classroom. *Modern Language Journal* 78, 273–284.

Dörnyei, Z. (1994b) Understanding second language motivation: On with the challenge! *Modern Language Journal* 79, 505–518.

Dörnyei, Z. (2001a) *Motivational Strategies in the Language Classroom.* Cambridge: Cambridge University Press.

Dörnyei, Z. (2001b) *Teaching and Researching Motivation*. Harlow: Longman.

Dörnyei, Z. (2005) *The Psychology of the Language Learner: Individual Differences in Second Language Acquisition*. Mahwah, NJ: Lawrence Erlbaum.

Dörnyei, Z. (2007) Creating a motivating classroom environment. In J. Cummins and C. Davison (eds) *International Handbook of English Language Teaching* (Vol. 2) (pp. 719–731). New York: Springer.

Dörnyei, Z. and Csizér, K. (2002) Some dynamics of language attitudes and motivation: Results of a longitudinal nationwide survey. *Applied Linguistics* 23, 421–462.

Dörnyei, Z., Csizér, K. and Németh, N. (2006) *Motivation, Language Attitudes and Globalisation: A Hungarian Perspective*. Clevedon: Multilingual Matters.

Dörnyei, Z. and Murphey, T. (2003) *Group Dynamics in the Language Classroom*. Cambridge: Cambridge University Press.

Dunkel, C., Kelts, D. and Coon, B. (2006) Possible selves as mechanisms of change in therapy. In C. Dunkel and J. Kerpelman (eds) *Possible Selves: Theory, Research and Applications* (pp. 187–204). New York: Nova Science.

Fezler, W. (1989) *Creative Imagery: How to Visualize in All Five Senses*. New York: Simon & Schuster.

Gardner, R.C. (1985) *Social Psychology and Second Language Learning: The Role of Attitudes and Motivation*. London: Edward Arnold.

Gardner, R.C. (2001) Integrative motivation and second language acquisition. In Z. Dörnyei and R. Schmidt (eds) *Motivation and Second Language Acquisition* (pp. 1–20). Honolulu, HI: University of Hawaii Press.

Gardner, R.C. and Lambert, W.E. (1959) Motivational variables in second language acquisition. *Canadian Journal of Psychology* 13, 266–272.

Gould, D., Damarjian, N. and Greenleaf, C. (2002) Imagery training for peak performance. In J.L. Van Raalte and B.W. Brewer (eds) *Exploring Sport and Exercise Psychology* (2nd edn, pp. 49–74). Washington, DC: American Psychological Association.

Gregg, M. and Hall, C. (2006) Measurement of motivational imagery abilities in sport. *Journal of Sports Sciences* 24 (9), 961–971.

Hall, E., Hall, C., Stradling, P. and Young, D. (2006) *Guided Imagery: Creative Interventions in Counselling and Psychotherapy*. London: Sage.

Herbst, K.C., Gaertner, L. and Insko, C.A. (2003) My head says yes but my heart says no: Cognitive and affective attraction as a function of similarity to the ideal self. *Journal of Personality and Social Psychology* 84 (6), 1206–1219.

Higgins, E.T. (1987) Self-discrepancy: A theory relating self and affect. *Psychological Review* 94, 319–340.

Higgins, E.T. (1996) The 'self-digest': Self-knowledge serving self-regulatory functions. *Journal of Personality and Social Psychology* 71 (6), 1062–1083.

Higgins, E.T. (1998) Promotion and prevention: Regulatory focus as a motivational principle. *Advances in Experimental Social Psychology* 30, 1–46.

Higgins, E.T., Klein, R. and Strauman, T. (1985) Self-concept discrepancy theory: A psychological model for distinguishing among different aspects of depression and anxiety. *Social Cognition* 3 (1), 51–76.

Higgins, E.T., Roney, C.J.R., Crowe, E. and Hymes, C. (1994) Ideal versus ought predilections for approach and avoidance: Distinct self-regulatory systems. *Journal of Personality and Social Psychology* 66 (2), 276–286.

Hock, M.F., Deshler, D.D. and Schumaker, J.B. (2006) Enhancing student motivation through the pursuit of possible selves. In C. Dunkel and J. Kerpelman (eds) *Possible Selves: Theory, Research and Application* (pp. 205–221). New York: Nova Science.

Horowitz, M.J. (1983) *Image Formation and Psychotherapy.* Northvale, NJ: Jason Aronson.

Hoyle, R.H. and Sherrill, M.R. (2006) Future orientation in the self-system: Possible selves, self-regulation, and behavior. *Journal of Personality* 74 (6), 1673–1696.

Irie, K. (2003) What do we know about the language learning motivation of university students in Japan? Some patterns in survey studies. *JALT Journal* 25 (1), 86–100.

Kosslyn, S.M., Cacioppo, J.T., Davidson, R.J., Hugdahl, K., Lovallo, W.R., Spiegel, D. and Rose, R. (2002) Bridging psychology and biology: The analysis of individuals in groups. *American Psychologist* 57 (5), 341–351.

Kosslyn, S.M., Thompson, W.L. and Ganis, G. (2006) *The Case for Mental Imagery.* New York: Oxford University Press.

Kyriacou, C. and Benmansour, N. (1997) Motivation and learning preferences of high school students learning English as a foreign language in Morocco. *Mediterranean Journal of Educational Studies* 2 (1), 79–86.

Lamb, M. (2004) Integrative motivation in a globalizing world. *System* 32, 3–19.

Leary, M.R. (2007) Motivational and emotional aspects of the self. *Annual Review of Psychology* 58, 317–344.

Leuner, H., Horn, G. and Klessmann, E. (1983) *Guided Affective Imagery with Children and Adolescents.* New York: Plenum.

Locke, E.A. and Latham, G.P. (1990) *A Theory of Goal Setting and Task Performance.* Englewood Cliffs, NJ: Prentice Hall.

MacIntyre, P.D. (2002) Motivation, anxiety and emotion in second language acquisition. In P. Robinson (ed.) *Individual Differences in Second Language Acquisition* (pp. 45–68). Amsterdam: John Benjamins.

Markus, H.R. and Nurius, P. (1986) Possible selves. *American Psychologist* 41, 954–969.

Markus, H.R. and Ruvolo, A. (1989) Possible selves: Personalized representations of goals. In L.A. Pervin (ed.) *Goal Concepts in Personality and Social Psychology* (pp. 211–241). Hillsdale, NJ: Lawrence Erlbaum.

Markus, H.R. (2006) Foreword. In C. Dunkel and J. Kerpelman (eds) *Possible Selves: Theory, Research and Applications* (pp. xi–xiv). New York: Nova Science.

McMahon, C.E. (1973) Images as motives and motivators: A historical perspective. *American Journal of Psychology* 86 (3), 465–490.

Miller, R.B. and Brickman, S.J. (2004) A model of future-oriented motivation and self-regulation. *Educational Psychology Review* 16 (1), 9–33.

Modell, A.H. (2003) *Imagination and the Meaningful Brain.* Cambridge, MA: MIT Press.

Noels, K.A. (2003) Learning Spanish as a second language: Learners' orientations and perceptions of their teachers' communication style. In Z. Dörnyei (ed.) *Attitudes, Orientations, and Motivations in Language Learning* (pp. 97–136). Oxford: Blackwell.

Noels, K.A., Pelletier, L.G., Clément, R. and Vallerand, R.J. (2000) Why are you learning a second language? Motivational orientations and self-determination theory. *Language Learning* 50, 57–85.

Norman, C.C. and Aron, A. (2003) Aspects of possible self that predict motivation to achieve or avoid it. *Journal of Experimental Social Psychology* 39, 500–507.

Oyserman, D., Bybee, D. and Terry, K. (2006) Possible selves and academic outcomes: How and when possible selves impel action. *Journal of Personality and Social Psychology* 91 (1), 188–204.

Oyserman, D. and Markus, H.R. (1990) Possible selves and delinquency. *Journal of Personality and Social Psychology* 59, 112–125.

Oyserman, D., Terry, K. and Bybee, D. (2002) A possible selves intervention to enhance school involvement. *Journal of Adolescence* 25, 313–326.

Paivio, A. (1985) Cognitive and motivational functions on imagery in human performance. *Canadian Journal of Applied Sport Sciences* 10, 22S–28S.

Pizzolato, J.E. (2006) Achieving college student possible selves: Navigating the space between commitment and achievement of long-term identity goals. *Cultural Diversity and Ethnic Minority Psychology* 12 (1), 57–69.

Richardson, A. (1994) *Individual Differences in Imaging: Their Measurement, Origins, and Consequences*. Amityville, NY: Baywood.

Roffe, L., Schmidt, K. and Ernst, E. (2005) A systematic review of guided imagery as an adjuvant cancer therapy. *Psycho-Oncology* 14, 607–617.

Ruvolo, A.P. and Markus, H.R. (1992) Possible selves and performance: The power of self-relevant imagery. *Social Cognition* 10 (1), 95–124.

Segal, H.G. (2006) Possible selves, fantasy distortion, and the anticipated life history: Exploring the role of imagination in social cognition. In C. Dunkel and J. Kerpelman (eds) *Possible Selves: Theory, Research and Applications* (pp. 79–96). New York: Nova Science.

Sheldon, K.M. and Lyubomirsky, S. (2006) How to increase and sustain positive emotion: The effects of expressing gratitude and visualizing best possible selves. *Journal of Positive Psychology* 1 (2), 73–82.

Singer, J.L. (2006) *Imagery in Psychotherapy*. Washington, DC: American Psychological Association.

Taylor, S.E., Pham, L.B., Rivkin, I.D. and Armor, D.A. (1998) Harnessing the imagination: Mental simulation, self-regulation, and coping. *American Psychologist* 53 (4), 429–439.

Tremblay, P. and Gardner, R.C. (1995) Expanding the motivation construct in language learning. *Modern Language Journal* 79, 505–518.

Ushioda, E. (2001) Language learning at university: Exploring the role of motivational thinking. In Z. Dörnyei and R. Schmidt (eds) *Motivation and Second Language Acquisition* (pp. 91–124). Honolulu, HI: University of Hawaii Press.

Ushioda, E. (2003) Motivation as a socially mediated process. In D. Little, J. Ridley and E. Ushioda (eds) *Learner Autonomy in the Foreign Language Classroom: Teacher, Learner, Curriculum and Assessment* (pp. 90–102). Dublin: Authentik.

Ushioda, E. (2006) Language motivation in a reconfigured Europe: Access, identity, autonomy. *Journal of Multilingual and Multicultural Development* 27 (2), 148–161.

Ushioda, E. (2007) Motivation, autonomy and sociocultural theory. In P. Benson (ed.) *Learner Autonomy 8: Teacher and Learner Perspectives* (pp. 5–24). Dublin: Authentik.

Warden, C. and Lin, H.J. (2000) Existence of integrative motivation in Asian EFL setting. *Foreign Language Annals* 33, 535–547.

Wenger, E. (1998) *Communities of Practice: Learning, Meaning, and Identity*. Cambridge: Cambridge University Press.

Yashima, T. (2000) Orientations and motivations in foreign language learning: A study of Japanese college students. *JACET Bulletin* 31, 121–133.

Yowell, C.M. (2002) Dreams of the future: The pursuit of education and career possible selves among ninth grade Latino youth. *Applied Developmental Science* 6 (2), 62–72.

Zentner, M. and Renaud, O. (2007) Origins of adolescents' ideal self: An intergenerational perspective. *Journal of Personality and Social Psychology* 92 (3), 557–574.

Chapter 3

The Baby, the Bathwater, and the Future of Language Learning Motivation Research

PETER D. MACINTYRE, SEAN P. MACKINNON and
RICHARD CLÉMENT

> *'(Don't) throw the baby out with the bath water' [is] an easily understandable*
> *metaphor: the only too human inclination towards extreme reactions.*
> *All of us, whether we like it or not, are from time to time guilty*
> *of the universally practiced act of throwing the baby out*
> *with the bath water...*
> Mieder, 1995

The entry of possible selves into the SLA literature, and in particular the field of language learning motivation, is most welcome and has the potential to open new avenues of study, providing new insights into the language learning process. However, there is much that has been gained already, over the past 50 years or so, from the study of integrative motivation in the context of the Socio-Educational (SE) Model. This chapter outlines the position that the possible selves and integrative motivation perspectives are not mutually exclusive, and are instead complementary concepts that map much of the same phenomenological territory. Indeed, it will be argued that the two frameworks present complementary aspects.

The Socio-Educational (SE) Model

The relevance of social psychology in the study of second language learning was demonstrated by Gardner and Lambert's (1959) seminal work in Montreal, Canada. Their study of high school students showed that motivation for language learning, defined as a combination of goal-directed effort and desire, predicted second language achievement at a level similar to the predictive value of language aptitude. Gardner and Lambert's (1959) research was one of the first demonstrations of social psychology's importance to language learning, as well as one of the first uses of a methodology that could be used to study the psychology of motivation and intergroup processes. The seemingly simple idea that intergroup attitudes and motives *matter* in language learning, in addition to aptitude and the linguistic features of language, evolved into the SE model of second language learning (Gardner, 1985; Gardner & Lambert, 1972). Broader still is the international interest in the social psychological study of second languages (Agnihotri *et al.*, 1998; Taylor & Usborne, 2007). Gardner and Lambert's (1959) study opened the field of second language learning to a distinctly social psychological perspective, with a focus on attitudes, affect, intergroup relationships and motives.

The SE model features a set of 11 interrelated concepts (Gardner, 2001) that combine to form three major factors influencing language learning: integrativeness, attitudes toward the learning situation and motivation. Integrativeness is defined by attitudes reflecting a genuine desire to meet, communicate with, take on characteristics of, and possibly identify with another group (Gardner & Lambert, 1972). Attitudes toward the learning situation assesses how much language students enjoy their teacher and course. Motivation is the engine that drives the system, and is defined by having a desire to learn the language, enjoyment of the task, and putting forward effort toward learning (Gardner, 1985). At the heart of the model, integrativeness and attitudes toward the learning situation combine to support motivation. In turn, motivation supports the behaviours necessary to learn a language. The relationship with members of another language group is the central theme of integrative motivation, that is, the underlying motive is to create 'real bonds of communication with another people' (Gardner, 2001). Extensive research by Gardner and his associates under the rubric of the SE model (reviewed by Masgoret & Gardner, 2003) has confirmed that this principle is sound. The importance of communicating with the target language group in SLA has been repeatedly confirmed as well in studies that adopt different theoretical orientations (Alalou, 2001; Allard & Landry, 1994; Clément, 1986; Clément & Gardner, 2001; Giles & Byrne, 1982; Noels, 2001; Spada, 1986; Ushioda, 2001; Yashima, 2002).

MacIntyre (2004) argued that the SE model can be considered unique, even ahead of its time in significant ways, especially as compared to motivation theories in the field of psychology. Through various phases of development, the SE model retained the core idea that the constellation of affective, cognitive and social factors defining the integrative motive for second language learning was predictive of success (Gardner & Lambert, 1972; Gardner, 1985; Gardner & MacIntyre, 1992; Gardner *et al.*, 1997). The SE model conceptualises a uniquely human motive, one whose complex interactions of cognitive and affective processes could not be captured by a single conceptual frame in psychology. Even from the perspective of social psychology, the SE model represents a departure from standard conceptual and methodological techniques that focus on laboratory-oriented, experimental concepts.

In addition to the theoretical uniqueness of the SE model, the statistical techniques used to test it have been state of the art. The language learning processes studied (e.g. individual differences in motivation, anxiety, achievement, and contact) lend themselves to correlational procedures that describe the tendencies for those variables to rise and fall in regular patterns. Correlation, regression, and factor analysis underpin structural equation modelling procedures which are widely applied in research today, but were highly unusual when Gardner and associates introduced them to the study of motivation (Dörnyei, 2005).

Although the SE model influenced international conceptualisations of motivation for second language learning for decades, particularly among pedagogues, the model has its detractors. It has been suggested that the SE model, and particularly the notion of integrativeness, dominated to the extent that no other approaches to the issue were seriously considered for a long period of time (Crookes & Schmidt, 1991; Dörnyei, 1994). Moreover, because motivational processes were hypothesised to be based on intergroup processes that generally took place outside the language classroom, it was unspecified how teachers could foster language learning motivation in their students and thereby facilitate language learning. Picking up this gauntlet, Clément et al. (1994) conducted a study of L2 attitudes and motivation in post communist Hungary, among students of English who had had very little direct contact with native English speakers. Surprisingly, and detracting from Crookes and Schmidt's allegation, it was found that attitudes and motivations of the type proposed under the integrative motive were related to classroom dynamics (cohesion and cooperation) as perceived by both the students and the teachers. The argument has been made that an expanded, less socio-politically oriented, more education-relevant framework would re-open the motivation research agenda (Crookes & Schmidt, 1991), thereby increasing the applied value of theorising and research for teachers, programme developers, and other language professionals. It would seem, however, that such a framework ought to include elements of the integrative motive.

More generally, the call for an expanded study of motivation in second language learning appears to be returning the field to a pre-paradigmatic state. The various approaches being developed span neurological investigations of brain-based motives (Schumann et al., 2004) to rich qualitative descriptions of learners' interpretations of experience (Norton, 2001; Ushioda, 2003). The avenue under consideration in the present chapter, exploring possible selves as a source of language learning motivation, has the potential to organise many of the current approaches; there is much new conceptual ground to be explored using possible selves as a theoretical framework. However, if the social psychological and political dimensions of language are drained away as the bathwater, we must be careful not to lose the conceptual baby, which is the relevance of those individual differences in the motivations to communicate with people who speak the target language. These motives affect the learning process, whether we frame them in terms of the SE model, other models of motivation, or in terms of possible selves.

Possible Selves

Over years, the conceptualisation of the self has come a long way. As Markus and Wurf (1987: 301) note: 'What began as an apparently singular, static lump-like entity has become a multidimensional, multi-faceted dynamic structure that is systematically implicated in all aspects of social information processing'. There is an understanding that the self is constantly changing and evolving as goals, attitudes and potentials for the future change (Greenwald & Pratkanis, 1984). Moreover, research has shown that a person may have many different selves – including academic, physical and social selves – which may not necessarily be closely related to one another (Marsh & Craven, 1997).

The possible selves literature became firmly established in mainstream psychology with Markus and Nurius's (1986) original work. They described possible selves as a form of future-oriented self-knowledge that can be divided into three distinct parts: the expected self, the hoped-for self and the feared self, each with varying impacts on motivation and self-regulation. The expected self is a future self that a person feels he or she can realistically achieve, and it may be positive or negative in valence. The hoped-for self represents a highly desired possible future, which is often not fully grounded in reality. A feared self is what a person is afraid of becoming in the future, despite wanting to avoid that future. It is important to note that these differentiated possible selves can, and typically do occur concurrently. For example, a French immersion student might hope to become bilingual, expect to develop fluency in French, and fear getting lost during a trip to Québec because he is unable to speak French, all of which provide reasons for language study. In this example, all three aspects of the self motivate and support learning; they are all pushing or pulling in the same direction.

Possible selves are important because they function as incentives of future behaviour and provide an interpretive context for the current view of the self (Markus & Nurius, 1986). Possible selves are motivating because they are future-oriented; they provide an end-state for potential behaviour, as well as providing potential incentives to perform or avoid certain behaviours (Oyserman & Markus, 1990). Individuals are motivated to act in order to reaffirm their sense of identity with their present sense of self, or as a potential goal in the case of possible selves. So, under this conceptualisation, motivation is the conscious striving to approach or avoid possible selves in order to achieve one's inner-most potential (Carver & Sakina, 1994; Leondari *et al.*, 1998; Markus & Nurius, 1986;

Markus & Ruvolo, 1989; Oyserman & Markus, 1990). Possible selves also provide an individualised, interpretive context for current behaviour. Consider the different interpretations of achieving a grade of B-minus in a language class by a student with a clear bilingual possible self compared to a student who does not see the language as part of his or her future self.

One year before Markus and Nurius's (1986) study, Higgins *et al.* (1985) presented a similar conceptual scheme called Self-Discrepancy Theory. Though there are some important differences between the conceptualisations of the self, both Higgins's approach and that of Markus and Nurius espouse a similar central thesis: future, as-yet-unrealised selves have the potential to be powerful motivational influences on behaviour. Higgins suggests that there are two types of idealised future selves that influence behaviour. The *ideal self* is what people hope or wish they could become. The *ought-to self* is what a person feels obliged or duty-bound to become. Moreover, Higgins makes the distinction between selves that are based on self-perceptions (i.e. 'I should be fluent in French') versus the perceptions of others (i.e. 'My mother thinks I should be fluent in French'). In general, ideal selves have a promotion focus, where the concern is on growth, achievement, and goal-reaching. Conversely, ought-to selves have a prevention focus, and are concerned with regulation of behaviour in order to stay responsible and safe (Higgins, 1998).

Self-Discrepancy Theory (Higgins, 1987) postulates that these selves are motivating because discrepancies between one's current sense of self and these future selves causes discomfort, which in turn motivates a person to increase congruence between the two selves in order to reduce that feeling of discomfort. Higgins acknowledges, however, that this process is not always conscious: 'one's self-discrepancies can be used to assign meaning to events without one's being aware of either the discrepancies or their impact on processing' (Higgins, 1987: 324). For example, a woman might experience tension if she envisions working at a bilingual job over the summer (an ideal self) but cannot currently speak the language fluently (current self), so to reduce that feeling of discomfort, she decides to enrol in an advanced language course. The emotions experienced are critical to understanding the motivational properties of possible selves.

Emotions are fundamentally important motivators (Brehm & Brummett, 1998; Lazarus, 1991; Izard, 1977). Without a strong tie to the learner's emotional system, possible selves exist as cold cognition, and therefore lack motivational potency. When emotion is a prominent feature of a possible self, including a strong sense of fear, hope, or even obligation, a clear path exists by which to influence motivation and action (see Higgins, 1987). At the end of this chapter we present an 'Interview with Linda' that demonstrates the powerful motivational potential of possible selves as well as the emotional investment they create. Linda describes her experience learning conversational phrases in Russian. Her story shows that a clear image of a future possible self can sustain motivation for language learning. The emotional tone of the story centres on expected feelings of pride and accomplishment; we suggest that without this emotional component, the motivational implications of the possible self vision would be all but absent.

Linda's story also demonstrates a second key process; as her learning progressed the imagined conversations grew more interpersonally satisfying. Even in this brief passage, the motivational potential of possible self imagery becomes clear. Linda describes imagined conversations with the Russian speaking mother of a colleague for whom she was learning conversational phrases. She says, '*As I had more phrases to say, my imagined conversations with her grew longer and her approval greater. My motivation to learn became more intense. In fact, I studied harder*'. This clearly shows a developmental process by which present learning alters the vision of the future self and with it language learning motivation. This sort of narrative corresponds with the experience of many language learners, and is one of the main reasons for the introduction of possible selves in the SLA literature.

Based on the above literature review, it becomes clear that possible selves have links to motivated behaviour generally, and to motivation for language learning in particular. The relevance of possible selves to language learning motivation has been discussed in detail by Dörnyei (2005) in relation to his L2 Motivational Self System (see also Dörnyei, this volume).

Dörnyei's Reconceptualisation of the Integrative Motive

In his book *The Psychology of the Language Learner*, Dörnyei (2005) proposes a new, broad construct of L2 learning called the *L2 Motivational Self System*. This construct is composed of three dimensions: the ideal L2 self, the ought-to self, and the L2 learning experience. The ideal L2 self houses the vision of oneself in the future. Ushioda's (2001) study of Irish learners of French describes their visions of travelling to France and speaking the French language with people they hope to meet. Norton's (2001) work describes the imagined community that the learner anticipates joining. This visioning of a future time in which one will be able to use the language *in situ* can sustain motivation during difficult times. Ushioda (2001) notes that even students who were not experiencing success still felt motivated by what Dörnyei (2005) would later call the ideal L2 self. The ought-to self is focused on duties and obligations imposed by external authorities, drawing upon various types of extrinsic (Noels, 2001) and instrumental (Gardner & MacIntyre, 1991) motives that have been discussed in the SLA literature. The ought-to self also might be linked to the imperatives of maintaining the linguistic dimension of ethnic identity, as when a heritage language is under threat, forming a potentially potent conceptual integration. The third dimension, L2 learning experience, is related to the motivation inspired by prior experience interacting with the present learning environment. The tendency for prior success to promote future success is a basic tenet of motivation theory generally (Reeve, 2005), and is explicitly captured by this dimension of the L2 Motivational Self System (see Ushioda, 2001).

Dörnyei (2005) described possible selves in the construction of his notion of the ideal L2 self, and in the process brought into play a vast body of research on the self. As we argue below, the vastness of the literature is a double edged sword. Whereas there is a great deal of prior research on the self, there also are conceptual complications.

Dörnyei (2005) presents his concept of the L2 Motivational Self System as a reframing of Gardner's (2001) concept of the integrative motive. Much of Dörnyei's (2005) initial empirical support for this reconceptualisation comes from a large ($N = 8593$) study of Hungarian language learners conducted by Csizér and Dörnyei (2005). Using structural equation modelling (SEM), they found that integrativeness subsumes all other factors in Gardner's model, even instrumentality. Based on these results, Csizér and Dörnyei suggest that integrativeness represents a broader construct than Gardner's (2001) definition would suggest[1]. Dörnyei (2005; Dörnyei & Csizér, 2002; Csizér & Dörnyei, 2005) goes on to propose that integrativeness can be interpreted as an idealised view of the L2 self, as presented in the L2 Motivational Self System.

We can draw out three principal reasons – of many – that Dörnyei suggests this reconceptualisation is necessary (see Csizér & Dörnyei, 2005: 28–30; Dörnyei, 2005: 65–119):

(1) As English spreads throughout the globe, it has become less and less associated with any particular culture, and as a result, a possible selves framework – uncoupled from any particular culture – could have more explanatory power for language learners;

(2) a self perspective can look at different motivational vectors, such as the convergence of both motivating and demotivating factors;

(3) the terminology in Gardner's model is unnecessarily confusing and sometimes vague, leading to conceptual difficulties in the literature (see also Dörnyei, 1994).

There is potentially much to be learned by taking this reconceptualisation seriously. However, we must be cautious not to adopt new theoretical and methodological problems in our haste to respond to the criticism of Gardner's SE model by throwing the baby out with the bathwater. Thus, in the sections that follow we will discuss the potential advantages and cautions involved in reconceptualising integrativeness using a possible selves framework.

Future Conceptual Development

Currently, the research into the L2 Motivational Self System is still in its infancy, and there are many questions to be explored. If we are to use possible selves as a framework to understand L2 motivation, research is needed to clearly define what is appropriately conceptualised as a possible L2 self. Moreover, it will be necessary to study the relationships between the L2 self and L1 self, as has been done with research into identity. If we contemplate the nature of the L2 possible self, it seems likely that it would involve: images of interactions with speakers of the target language, skilful action using the target language, feelings of accomplishment of communicative goals, travelling to experience the target language in its cultural context, fears of being embarrassed in the L2, worries about self-presentation when speaking to members of the language community, and so on. That is, we are going to be talking about the target language community, expressed in terms related to changes in the self rather than attitudes or interests, but mapping much of the same experiential territory.

Dörnyei (2005: 107) notes that Gardner's integrative motive 'corresponds closely' with the proposed L2 self system. We agree. The story of Linda learning Russian (see end of this chapter) could be accounted for by a Possible Selves approach, as we have attempted, or by using the SE model. In an SE model account, positive attitudes toward learning the language coupled with effort and enjoyment sustain the specific behaviours undertaken to learn the target language. The overlap between Possible Selves and the SE model can be noted clearly when one avoids the often-made mistake of building integrativeness into a straw man that simply means assimilation into the target language group.

The potential strength of the L2 self formulation lies in its ability to map out new conceptual linkages by taking the self as the starting point. New types of research questions can be generated. For example, in Linda's story, motivation derived from imagined conversations is foregrounded. The specificity of these future conversations is remarkable, but how common is the experience? How many different imagined persons do learners create and can object relations theory (e.g. Kohut, 1977), and its conceptual offspring attachment theory (e.g. Ainsworth, 1989), be applied to language learning?

Whereas it is difficult to predict the future development of possible selves in the area of language learning motivation, contributions to the present volume show that the topic will be taken seriously in future research (see chapters in this volume by, for example, Csizér & Kormos; Ryan; Taguchi *et al.*). Studies that examine the role of possible selves will be successful to the extent that they build on the existing literature, using new questions as a starting point. Gardner (2005) warns that simply translating integrative motivation into a possible selves framework might prove problematic, suggesting that equating his concept of integrativeness with Csizér and Dörnyei's (2005) ideal L2 self 'might confuse things considerably; it certainly will make communication about integrativeness difficult' (Gardner 2005: 8). As the field moves forward, it is worthwhile to consider that which is gained and lost by using a possible selves approach. In the space remaining, we will outline three benefits and six cautions that we identify with respect to possible selves. These arguments might serve as a starting point for discussion of the concept. They are not intended to be exhaustive.

Benefits of the Possible Selves Approach

Benefit 1: An educator-friendly approach

One of the earliest criticisms of Gardner's SE model suggests that a more educator-friendly approach to L2 learning is crucial (Crookes & Schmidt, 1991; Dörnyei, 1994). Using a possible selves framework does that; in fact, much of the research conducted on possible selves has focused on increasing motivation in numerous educational areas (Leondari *et al.*, 1998; Oyserman & Markus, 1990; Oyserman *et al.*, 2002, 2004, 2006; Yowell, 2002). Though research on possible selves in second language learning is just beginning, the existing body of research on possible selves combined with the theoretical model proposed by Dörnyei (2005) suggests that the approach has utility. In comparison with the SE model, possible selves shift the focus from desirable attributes of the target language group, which are largely fixed, to the changing personal attributes of the learner. The process by which individual language learners change their view of self would be an interesting theoretical avenue to explore, and techniques for changing possible selves could be of practical use to educators, addressing the concerns of some researchers (Crookes & Schmidt, 1991; but see Clément *et al.*, 1994).

Benefit 2: Addressing language contexts outside Canada

The first of Dörnyei's (2005) arguments described earlier in this paper suggests that taking a possible selves perspective is beneficial when addressing language contexts outside of Canada's unique sociocultural milieu. One of the prominent criticisms of Gardner's model is that much of the research has been conducted in Canada, and might not generalise to language learning situations in other cultures (Dörnyei, 2005: 94). In the case of a rapidly spreading World English, there is no clear, discrete cultural-linguistic identity that unifies L2 speakers in the potential learner's mind. In this case, using possible selves escapes the complications of defining a specific linguistic group model by focusing on the hopes, aspirations and fears of the L2 learner instead of their integration into an existing L2 community (*cf.* Norton's, 2001, concept of imagined communities). It might not be the personal or collective attributes of a local group of L2 speakers that drive possible selves but rather the actions that an L2 speaker can take and the goals they can accomplish as they acquire a new language.

Benefit 3: Multiple motivations

Dörnyei's (2005) second point discussed above suggests that language learning motivation, with respect to possible selves, must expand the focus on language to include the other kinds of motives a learner will experience. Motivation is multiply determined, with any single action involving a variety of competing motivational forces (MacIntyre *et al.*, in press; Reeve, 2005). For example, an adolescent learner might simultaneously experience both a desire to learn French and support from parents/teachers AND a fear of ridicule from peers as a 'geek', 'nerd', or 'teacher's pet'. To add further complications to this example, adolescent language learners are typically experiencing numerous developmental milestones such as developing a sense of personal competence and autonomy, negotiating new identities, and nourishing close friendships, all of which may or may not impact on a student's motivation to learn at any given moment (Manning, 1988). As Dörnyei (2005: 87) notes, 'hardly any research has been done to examine how people deal with multiple actions and goals, how they prioritize between them, and how the hierarchies of superordinate and subordinate goals are structured'.

Language learning is integrated with all of the other activities in which a learner occupies his or her time, and we can enhance our understanding of the learner by asking about the relative importance of various motives, language-related and otherwise. This is an area that can and should be explored, and seems easily approached from a possible selves perspective. The self, like motivation, is multifaceted and constantly changing (Greenwald & Pratkanis, 1984; Markus & Wurf, 1987) and the open-ended format typically utilised in possible selves research (for an example, see Oyserman, 2004) allows researchers to examine a wide variety of motivational and identity-based qualities. Such an approach may best be seen as a complement to, rather than a replacement for, the more domain specific analysis provided by the integrative motive. Nevertheless, research into the various competing motives experience by a language learner, expressed as various possible selves that guide action, would be a significant advance for SLA research.

Cautions for Future Research

The possible selves framework represents an important avenue for studying language learning motivation. Using a possible selves framework is not without important limitations. There are several areas in which caution is warranted. These cautions arise primarily from the complexity of studying the self, rather than specifically from Dörnyei's (2005) L2 Motivational Self System.

Caution 1: Measurement of possible selves

The measurement of possible selves is going to be a serious issue in the future. One of the strengths of the SE model is its link to a high quality measurement tool, the Attitude and Motivation Test Battery (AMTB, Gardner, 1985; Gardner & MacIntyre, 1991). The use of a possible selves approach brings diverse and inconsistent measurement methods. Typically, the research on possible selves takes a distinct qualitative bent, often asking participants to spontaneously generate possible selves in open-ended surveys (Carver & Sakina, 1994; Leondari *et al.*, 1998; Norman & Aron, 2003). As with much qualitative research, both the data collection and analysis methods vary greatly from one study to the next. Though Oyserman and colleagues have developed a well-established, replicable coding scheme in their research programme (Oyserman & Markus, 1990; Oyserman *et al.*, 2002, 2006) this has been inconsistently used in the possible selves literature. In contrast, the majority of research on the SE model uses consistent, quantitative methods of measurement which have been utilised in dozens of studies (see Masgoret & Gardner, 2003). To the extent that measurement is inconsistent from one study to the next, there is a concern that reconceptualising integrative motivation using a possible selves framework might actually make research into second language motivation more difficult to interpret. Elsewhere in this volume (MacIntyre *et al.*, Chapter 10) we offer a new scale designed to assess possible selves.

A source of concern related to measurement and interpretation of possible selves is the questionable veracity and impartiality in representations of the self. A variety of errors, biases, and defence mechanisms (Cramer, 2006) have the powerful effect of protecting the self from negativity:

> People have a need to view themselves positively. This is easily the most common and consensually endorsed assumption in research on the self. (Heine *et al.*, 1999: 766)

It is possible that a switch from established methodologies and instruments that measure language-related attitudes (such as the AMTB) to methodologies that measure possible future selves might exacerbate the influence of self-serving biases on data provided by research participants. Alternatively, the need to view one's self positively may still provide a basis for motivation even if biases are operating to make the self-view unrealistic or unattainable.

Caution 2: The naming problem

In addition to potential problems with measurement, tapping into the literature on the self might turn out to be a double edged sword. Dörnyei (1994) identified a problem with the multiple uses of the term 'integrative' within the SE model (integrative orientation, integrativeness, and integrative motivation) eventually proposing his L2 Motivational Self System (Dörnyei, 2005) as a way of overcoming both the terminology problem and potential theoretical inconsistencies in Gardner's (2005) model. Unfortunately, the terminology problem faced by Gardner's model might not be improved by adopting the terminology of possible selves; the multitude of overlapping concepts in the literature on the self is more confusing than integrativeness ever could be. With such an enormous base of literature at the researcher's disposal, tying together a coherent theoretical explanation for the role of the self in language learning may prove daunting and even frustrating at times. There are so many self-related concepts (a cursory scan of the PSYCHINFO database reveals more than 75,000 articles with 'self' in their title and a very long list of 'self' related concepts used in the literature[2]) that differentiating one from another can be a formidable task. The variations in approach to possible selves shown in Higgins's and Markus's work should be kept in mind as the concept of possible selves is studied in the language learning domain. These two approaches have interesting conceptual differences, but one risks losing sight of the big picture of language learning if one becomes too engrossed in the nuances of conceptualising the details of the self-system.

Caution 3: Cultural variation in the concept of self

Another potential complication is the impact of culture on a person's self-concept. It is especially important in the SLA literature that we be conscious of the differing cross-cultural meanings of self. Dörnyei (2005) argues that the ubiquitous nature of World English severs the ties to specific cultural groups (especially British and American as exemplars of speakers of English) making possible selves more portable across cultures. As we consider the implications of this idea, we must acknowledge the various culture-bound definitions of self that may impact on the motivational properties of possible selves.

In Markus and Kitayama's (1991) article, they suggest that Eastern and Western cultures construe the self in very different ways: Western cultures are more likely to view the self as independent, distinct and separate from others while Eastern cultures view the self as interdependent, deeply intertwined with others. Unemori *et al.* (2004) found that English–American participants tend to report intrapersonal (e.g. anxious, happy, etc.) themes in their possible selves while Japanese participants tend to focus more on professional and/or academic accomplishment. Numerous other studies also reveal differences in self-conception between Eastern and Western cultures; East-Asians report lower self-esteem than North Americans (Heine *et al.*, 1999), are more likely to portray their behaviour as constrained by context (Kanagawa *et al.*, 2001; Triandis *et al.*, 1990) and are less likely to engage in attributional biases such as the fundamental attribution error (Jaspars & Hewstone, 1982).

Li *et al.* (2006) caution that the pen-and-paper nature of many cross-cultural studies on self construal can depend heavily on language:

> Because words or sentences that are equivalent in meaning and form in two or more languages are sometimes very difficult or impossible to find ... participants in different language or cultural groups may interpret the questionnaires differently. (Li *et al.*, 2006: 592)

Bilingual speakers (Chinese–English) have been shown to endorse more Chinese values when responding in Chinese than when speaking in English (Bond, 1983). Ross *et al.* (2002) suggest that Eastern and Western identities are stored in separate knowledge structures in bicultural individuals, and those differing ethnic identities may be activated by speaking in the corresponding language. The self appears to be a highly variable concept, not only cross culturally but also intra-individually, as research with bicultural individuals shows. It is clear then that future research in the areas of SLA must take into account the varied effects of culture on the construction of the self when using possible selves as a framework for interpreting L2 motivation.

Caution 4: Possible selves as goals

Possible selves capture a set of interrelated goals for language learning by envisioning the future. This implicates two processes, goal setting and time judgments, both of which carry their own cautions for researchers new to the area. A major problem with goal-setting and motivation is that humans often fail to translate goals into appropriate behaviour. Merely setting a goal does not necessarily affect performance. Kuhl (1994) has identified numerous individual factors which can mediate the translation from motivation to actual performance in his theory of Action Control. The theory describes individual differences in the ability to initiate and maintain behaviour (action orientation) and in the tendency to become preoccupied and hesitant to the point of non-action (state orientation), which can explain seemingly paradoxical behaviour such as why a person might choose to ruminate on an unpleasant past event rather than engaging in a pleasant or otherwise productive activity.

Moreover, goals that exert influence on motivation tend to show certain qualities. Only specific, moderately difficult goals are likely to provide strong motivational support (Locke *et al.*, 1981) and even then, the support appears to be limited to tasks that are routine or boring. Oyserman and colleagues have shown that possible selves – which can be loosely interpreted as future-oriented self goals – do not necessarily provide motivation or influence performance. They argue that possible selves must involve both specific plans for self-regulation and a counter-vailing feared self in the same domain to truly motivate behaviour (Oyserman & Markus, 1990; Oyserman *et al.*, 2004). Though plans for goal achievement may be included in a possible self, future research would do well to look at how clear the implementation intentions are (e.g. a willingness to communicate when the opportunity arises, see MacIntyre, 2007) and whether or not the plans allow for recovery of motivational processes when language learning is delayed or the learner experiences a setback.

Caution 5: Possible selves change over time

In addressing the debate over the proper theoretical approach to take regarding L2 motivation, Dörnyei (2003) commented:

> I have now come to believe that many of the controversies and disagreements in L2 motivation research go back to an insufficient temporal awareness ... that different or even contradictory theories do not exclude one another, but may simply be related to different phases of the motivated behavioral process. (Dörnyei, 2003: 18)

The phenomenological quality of the possible selves seems likely to change significantly as milestone dates approach. Linda's story shows a strengthening of self-related imagery as language learning progressed. It might also be possible for elements of the possible self vision to become unrealistic or impossible as time goes by (Pizzolato, 2007). For this reason, possible selves might work better as long term goals than as short term ones. For example, the final exams at the end of a four-year degree programme may be seen as more of an obstacle or a nuisance than an opportunity for performance feedback. Research corroborates this notion. Smith (2004) found that academic motivation can sharply decrease, and self-handicapping strategies and fear of demonstrating a lack of ability to others (i.e. 'looking stupid' in front of peers) increase, as students approach completion of high school.

The quality of motivation can vary greatly depending on the time-frame of the goal and the level of interest in the task. Generally speaking, short term (or 'proximal') goals increase motivation for uninteresting tasks (Bandura & Schunk, 1981), while long-term (or 'distal') goals tend to increase motivation and performance for interesting tasks. Short-term goals provide more chance for feedback and competence building (Latham & Seijts, 1999). Bolstering self-confidence has a positive effect on academic motivation and performance. However, on the one hand, for tasks that people find interesting, a multitude of short-term goals are seen as more intrusive than fewer, more distal goals (Reeve, 2005: 211). On the other hand, for long-term goals to increase motivation, a person must be relatively free to both set and pursue those goals in their own particular fashion (Manderlink & Harackiewicz, 1984).

Caution 6: Possible selves and identity

The desire to integrate numerous explanatory concepts defining the individual in interaction with her or his context is not new in social psychology. 'Identity', and particularly 'social identity' have attracted considerable attention as explanatory constructs of interpersonal and intergroup relations (e.g. Hogg, 2003; Turner & Reynolds, 2001). Fundamental to the identification process is the problem of categorisation – that is, how one construes oneself and 'others' in a given context. This process, resulting in one's identity, has been shown to have emotional, cognitive, affective and behavioural correlates and to vary in salience as a function of specific aspects of the situation (see Ashmore et al., 2004); characteristics also attributed to the self. Furthermore, social identity theory has been used to explain a plethora of language-related phenomena, including all forms of intergroup communication (e.g. Noels et al., 2003) and, specifically, L2 learning motivation (Giles & Byrne, 1982).

The process of categorisation through which we identify self and non-self features is also basic to the integrative motive and the production of subtractive and additive forms of bilingualism (Lambert, 1978). Furthermore, following the work by Higgins (1987) and Markus and Nurius (1986) as well as that of cross-cultural psychologists (e.g. Weinreich, 1996), the contrasts between actual, desired and reflected (that which is assigned to you by others) identities has been shown to be related to experiencing discrimination and second language confidence (Clément et al., 2001).

Progress made within the identity framework linking L2 language and communication to both theoretical and applied issues, can be brought to bear on the L2 self system as a motivational paradigm. That is, the theoretical strength of discussing the self does not lie in reiterating processes of identity formation and change. However, given that social identity is that aspect of the self-concept derived from group membership, there may be other aspects of identity that are not represented through the social identity paradigm. More importantly, social identity theory does not provide a description of how identities become meshed to ensure temporal and spatial continuity of the self (Abrams, 1996; Learey & Tangney, 2003). Given their relevance to intergroup interaction, a L2 motivational self paradigm must account for identity processes. In particular, a specific contribution of the L2 self system could be to provide a functional structure accounting for the integration of identity processes.

Conclusion

The notion of possible selves is an interesting approach and deserves serious study in SLA. The expansive literature on integrative motivation can be a solid basis on which to build the literature on the L2 Motivational Self System, knowing that some key questions already have been answered. As a conceptual scheme, the L2 Motivational Self System (Dörnyei, 2005; see also this volume) including the concept of possible selves, holds a great deal of promise. The strength of the concept of possible selves lies in its focus on the learner as applicable to education research contexts, its focus on who individuals plan to use language with apart from a specific cultural group, and its ability to integrate multiple, sometimes conflicting motives. SLA researchers should be aware of, and as far as possible avoid several potential pitfalls, such as the measurement of possible selves, the proliferation of self-related concepts (the naming problem), cultural variations in the concept of self, conditions that affect the relevance of goals as motives, changes in the selves over time and the junction with identity. It will be necessary to be cautious as we move forward to ensure that we advance our understanding rather than merely rephrasing it. If we avoid the temptation to throw out the baby with the bathwater, the future of language learning motivation research looks very interesting indeed.

Notes

1. A comment is necessary on the false dichotomy of integrative and instrumental motives (see Rueda & Chen, 2005). The notion that integrative and instrumental reasons for language learning are opposing forces simply is not consistent with Gardner's position (Gardner & Tremblay, 1994). Indeed, there is no theoretical reason to suggest that the two are mutually exclusive. The data show a strong tendency for integrative and instrumental orientations to be positively correlated, and this occurs in samples with various degrees of contact (Clément & Kruidenier, 1983; Gardner & MacIntyre, 1993; Gardner *et al.*, 1997; MacIntyre *et al.*, 2001). There simply is no good reason to believe that a person who sees the value of the target language as a means of communication and social interaction would not also see the value of the

language in instrumental terms, and the empirical results support that idea, whether from scholars critical of the SE model or from Gardner's own data.

2. The list of self-related concepts retrieved from the PSYCHINFO database on July 4, 2007 includes the following 50 items: self-actualization, self-esteem, self-efficacy, self-consciousness, self-concept, self-identity, self-extension, self-image, ought-to self, self perception, real self, ideal self, academic self, physical self, social self, emotional self, hoped-for self, expected self, feared self, looking-glass self, self-worth, self-acceptance, self-regard, self-evaluation, self-respect, self-regulation, self as subject ('I'), self as object ('me'), material me, social me, spiritual me, good-me, bad-me, not-me, self-affirmation theory, self-determination theory, self-monitoring theory, self-verification theory, self-completion theory, dialogical self, interpersonal self, individual self, collective self, selfhood, selfness, self-awareness, self-respect, self-confidence, and self-perception theory.

References

Abrams, D. (1996) Social identity, self as structure and self as process. In W.P. Robinson (ed.) *Social Groups and Identities* (pp. 65–94). Oxford: Butterworth-Heinemann.

Agnihotri, R.K., Khanna, A.L. and Sachdev, I. (eds) (1998) *Social Psychological Perspectives on Second Language Learning*. New Delhi: Sage.

Ainsworth, M.D.S. (1989) Attachments beyond infancy. *American Psychologist* 44, 109–716.

Alalou, A. (2001) Reevaluating curricular objectives using students' perceived needs: The case of three language programs. *Foreign Language Annals* 34, 453–469.

Allard, R. and Landry, R. (1994) Subjective ethnolinguistic vitality: A comparison of two measures. *International Journal of the Sociology of Language* 108, 117–144.

Ashmore, R.D., Deaux, K. and McLaughlin-Volpe, T. (2004) An organizing framework for collective identity: Articulation and significance of multi-dimensionality. *Psychological Bulletin* 130, 80–114.

Bandura, A. and Schunk, D.H. (1981) Cultivating competence, self-efficacy, and intrinsic interest through proximal self-motivation. *Journal of Personality and Social Psychology* 41, 586–598.

Bond, M.H. (1983) How language variation affects inter-cultural differentiation of values by Hong Kong bilinguals. *Journal of Language and Social Psychology* 2, 57–66.

Brehm, J.W. and Brummett, B.H. (1998) The emotional control of behavior. In M. Kofta, G. Weary and G. Sedek (eds) *Personal Control in Action* (pp. 133–153). New York: Plenum Press.

Carver, C.S. and Sakina, R.L. (1994) The possible selves of optimists and pessimists. *Journal of Research in Personality* 28, 133–141.

Clément, R. (1986) Second language proficiency and acculturation: An investigation of the effects of language status and individual characteristics. *Journal of Language and Social Psychology* 5, 271–290.

Clément, R., Dörnyei, Z. and Noels, K.A. (1994) Motivation and the foreign language classroom: A study of Hungarians learning English. *Language Learning* 44, 417–448.

Clément, R. and Gardner, R.C. (2001) Second language mastery. In H. Giles and P. Robinson (eds) *The New Handbook of Language and Social Psychology* (pp. 489–504). London: Wiley.

Clément, R. and Kruidenier, B.G. (1983) Orientations in second language acquisition: The effects of ethnicity, milieu and target language on their emergence. *Language Learning* 33, 273–291.

Clément, R., Noels, K.A. and Deneault, B. (2001) Interethnic contact, identity and psychological adjustment: The mediating and moderating roles of communication. *Journal of Social Issues* 57, 557–577.

Cramer, P. (2006) *Protecting the Self: Defense Mechanisms in Action.* New York: Guilford Press.

Crookes, G. and Schmidt, R.W. (1991) Motivation: Reopening the research agenda. *Language Learning* 41, 469–512.

Csizér, K. and Dörnyei, Z. (2005) The internal structure of language learning motivation: Results of structural equation modelling. *Modern Language Journal* 89 (1), 19–36.

Dörnyei, Z. (1994) Understanding second language motivation: On with the challenge! *Modern Language Journal* 78, 515–523.

Dörnyei, Z. (2003) Attitudes, orientations, and motivations in language learning: Advances in theory, research, and applications. In Z. Dörnyei (ed.) *Attitudes, Orientations, and Motivations in Language Learning* (pp. 3–32). Oxford: Blackwell.

Dörnyei, Z. (2005) *The Psychology of the Language Learner: Individual Differences in Second Language Acquisition.* London: Lawrence Erlbaum Associates.

Dörnyei, Z. and Csizér, K. (2002) Some dynamics of language attitudes and motivation: Results of a longitudinal nationwide survey. *Applied Linguistics* 23 (4), 421–462.

Gardner, R.C. (1985) *Social Psychology and Second Language Learning: The Role of Attitudes and Motivation.* London: Edward Arnold.

Gardner, R.C. (2001) Integrative Motivation: Past, Present and Future. Temple University Japan, Distinguished Lecturer Series, Tokyo, February 17, 2001; Osaka, February 24, 2001. Retrieved from http://publish.uwo.ca/~gardner/GardnerPublicLecture1.pdf. Accessed 30 July 2008.

Gardner, R.C. (2005) Integrative motivation and second language acquisition. Canadian Association of Applied Linguistics Joint Plenary Talk, London, Ontario, May 30, 2005. Retrieved from http://publish.uwo.ca/~gardner/caaltalk5final.pdf. Accessed 30 July 2008.

Gardner, R.C. and Lambert, W.E. (1959) Motivational variables in second language acquisition. *Canadian Journal of Psychology* 13, 266–272.

Gardner, R.C. and Lambert, W.E. (1972) *Attitudes and Motivation in Second Language Learning.* Rowley, MA: Newbury House.

Gardner, R.C. and MacIntyre, P.D. (1991) An instrumental motivation in language study: Who says it isn't effective? *Studies in Second Language Acquisition* 13, 57–72.

Gardner, R.C. and MacIntyre, P.D. (1992) A student's contribution to second language learning: Part I, cognitive factors. *Language Teaching* 25, 211–220.

Gardner, R.C. and MacIntyre, P.D. (1993) On the measurement of affective variables in second language learning. *Language Learning* 43, 157–194.

Gardner, R.C. and Tremblay, P.F. (1994) On motivation, research agendas and theoretical frameworks. *The Modern Language Journal* 78, 359–368.

Gardner, R.C., Tremblay, P.F. and Masgoret, A.M. (1997) Towards a full model of second language learning: An empirical investigation. *The Modern Language Journal* 81, 344–362.

Giles, H. and Byrne, J.L. (1982) An intergroup approach to second language acquisition. *Journal of Multilingual and Multicultural Development* 1, 17–40.

Greenwald, A.G. and Pratkanis, A.R. (1984) The self. In R.S. Wyer and T.R. Srull (eds) *Handbook of Social Cognition* (Vol. 3) (pp. 129–178). Hillsdale, NJ: Erlbaum.

Heine, S.J., Lehman, D.R., Markus, H.R. and Kitayama, S. (1999) Is there a universal need for positive self-regard? *Psychological Review* 106, 766–794.

Higgins, E.T., Klein, R. and Strauman T. (1985). Self-concept discrepancy theory: A psychological model for distinguishing among different aspects of depression and anxiety. *Social Cognition* 3, 51–76.

Higgins, E.T. (1987) Self-discrepancy: A theory relating self and affect. *Psychological Review* 94 (3), 319–340.

Higgins, E.T. (1998) Promotion and prevention: Regulatory focus as a motivational principle. In M.P. Zanna (ed.) *Advances in Experimental Social Psychology* (Vol. 30) (pp. 1–46). New York: Academic Press.

Hogg, M.A. (2003) Social identity. In M.R. Leary and J.P. Tangney (eds) *Handbook of Self and Identity* (pp. 462–479). New York: The Guilford Press.

Izard, C.E. (1977) *Human Emotions.* New York: Plenum.

Jaspars, J. and Hewstone, M. (1982) Cross-cultural interaction, social attribution and inter-group relations. In S. Bochner (ed.) *Cultures in Contact: Studies in Cross-Cultural Interaction* (pp. 75–81). Oxford: Pergamon.

Kanagawa, C., Cross, S.E. and Markus, H.R. (2001) 'Who am I?' The cultural psychology of the conceptual self. *Personality and Social Psychology Bulletin* 27, 90–103.

Kohut, H. (1977) *The Restoration of the Self.* Madison, CT: International Universities Press.

Kuhl, J. (1994) A theory of action and state orientations. In J. Kuhl and J. Beckmann (eds) *Volition and Personality* (pp. 9–46). Gottingen: Hogrefe & Huber Publishers.

Lambert, W.E. (1978) Cognitive and socio-cultural consequences of bilingualism. *Canadian Modern Language Review* 34, 537–547.

Latham, G.P. and Seijts, G.H. (1999) The effects of proximal and distal goals on performance on a moderately complex task. *Journal of Organizational Behavior* 20 (4), 421–429.

Lazarus, R.S. (1991) *Emotion and Adaptation.* London: Oxford University Press.

Leary, M.R. and Tangney, J.P. (eds) (2003) *Handbook of Self and Identity.* New York: The Guilford Press.

Leondari, A., Syngollitou, E. and Kiosseoglou, G. (1998) Academic achievement, motivation and future selves. *Educational Studies* 24 (2), 153–164.

Li, H.Z., Zhang, Z., Bhatt, G. and Yum, Y.O. (2006) Rethinking culture and self-construal: China as a middle land. *The Journal of Social Psychology* 146 (5), 591–610.

Locke, E.A., Shaw, K.N., Saari, L.M. and Latham, G.P. (1981) Goal setting and task performance: 1969–1980. *Psychological Bulletin* 90 (1), 125–152.

MacIntyre, P.D. (2004) Volition and personality: Bringing motivational tendencies to life. Paper presented at the 9th International Congress of Language and Social Psychology, State College PA, July, 2004.

MacIntyre, P.D. (2007) Willingness to communicate in the second language: Understanding the decision to speak as a volitional process. *Modern Language Journal* 91, 564–576.

MacIntyre, P.D., Mackinnon, S.P. and Clément, R. (in press) Embracing affective ambivalence: A research agenda for understanding the interdependent processes of language anxiety and motivation. In P. Cheng and J.X. Yan (eds) *Cultural Identity and Language Anxiety*. Guilin: Guangxi Normal University Press.

MacIntyre, P.D., MacMaster, K. and Baker, S. (2001) The convergence of multiple models of motivation for second language learning: Gardner, Pintrich, Kuhl and McCroskey. In Z. Dörnyei and R. Schmidt (eds) *Motivation and Second Language Acquisition* (pp. 461–492). Honolulu, HI: University of Hawaii Press.

Manderlink, G. and Harackiewicz, J.M. (1984) Proximal versus distal goal setting and intrinsic motivation. *Journal of Personality and Social Psychology* 47 (4), 918–928.

Manning, L. (1988) Erikson's psychosocial theories help explain early adolescence. *NASSP Bulletin* 72, 95–100.

Markus, H. and Kitayama, S. (1991) Culture and the self: Implications for cognition, emotion, and motivation. *Psychological Review* 98 (2), 224–253.

Markus, H. and Nurius, P. (1986) Possible selves. *American Psychologist* 41 (9), 954–969.

Markus, H. and Ruvolo, A. (1989) Possible selves: Personalized representations of goals. In L.A. Pervin (ed.) *Goal Concepts in Personality and Social Psychology* (pp. 211–241). Hillsdale, NJ: Erlbaum.

Markus, H. and Wurf, E. (1987) The dynamic self-concept: A social psychological perspective. *Annual Review of Psychology* 38, 299–337.

Marsh, H.W. and Craven, R. (1997) Academic self-concept: Beyond the dustbowl. In G. Phye (ed.) *Handbook of Classroom Assessment: Learning, Achievement, and Adjustment* (pp. 131–198). Orlando, FL: Academic.

Masgoret, A.M. and Gardner, R.C. (2003) Attitudes, motivation and second language learning: A meta-analysis of studies conducted by Gardner and associates. In Z. Dörnyei (ed.) *Attitudes, Orientations, and Motivations in Language Learning* (pp. 167–210). Oxford: Blackwell.

Mieder, W. (1995) '(Don't) throw the baby out with the bathwater': The Americanization of a German proverb and proverbial expression. *Deproverbio* 1. Retrieved from http://www.deproverbio.com/DPjournal//DP,1,1,95// BABY.html#. Accessed 30 July 2008.

Noels, K.A. (2001) New orientations in language learning motivation: Towards a model of intrinsic, extrinsic and integrative orientations. In Z. Dörnyei and R. Schmidt (eds) *Motivation and Second Language Acquisition* (pp. 43–68). Honolulu, HI: University of Hawaii Press.

Noels, K.A., Giles, H. and Le Poire, B. (2003) Language and communication processes. In M.A. Hogg and J. Cooper (eds) *The Sage Handbook of Social Psychology* (pp. 232–257). London: Sage.

Norman, C.C. and Aron, A. (2003) Aspects of possible self that predict motivation to achieve or avoid it. *Journal of Experimental Social Psychology* 39, 500–507.

Norton, B. (2001) Non-participation, imagined communities, and the language classroom. In M. Breen (ed.) *Learner Contributions to Language Learning: New Directions in Research* (pp 159–171). Harlow: Pearson Education.

Oyserman, D. (2004) Possible Selves Citations, Measure, and Coding Instructions. http://www.sitemaker.umich.edu/culture.self/files/possible_selves_measure.doc. Accessed June 1 2007.

Oyserman, D., Bybee, D. and Terry, K. (2006) Possible selves and academic outcomes: How and when possible selves impel action. *Journal of Personality and Social Psychology* 91 (1), 188–204.

Oyserman, D., Bybee, D., Terry, K. and Hart-Johnson, T. (2004) Possible selves as roadmaps. *Journal of Research in Personality* 38, 130–149.

Oyserman, D. and Markus, H.R. (1990) Possible selves and delinquency. *Journal of Personality and Social Psychology* 59 (1), 112–125.

Oyserman, D., Terry, K. and Bybee, D. (2002) A possible selves intervention to enhance school involvement. *Journal of Adolescence* 25, 313–326.

Pizzolato, J.E. (2007) Impossible selves: Investigating students' persistence decisions when their career-possible selves border on impossible. *Journal of Career Development* 33 (3), 201–223.

Reeve, J. (2005) *Understanding Motivation and Emotion* (4th edn). Hoboken, NJ: Wiley.

Ross, M. Xun, W.Q.E. and Wilson, A.E. (2002) Language and the bicultural self. *Personality and Social Psychology Bulletin* 28, 1040–1050.

Rueda, R. and Chen, C. (2005) Assessing motivational factors in foreign language learning: Cultural variation in key constructs. *Educational Assessment* 10, 209–229.

Schumann, J., Crowell, S., Jones., N., Lee, N., Scuchert, S. and Wood, A. (2004) *The Neurobiology of Learning: Perspectives from Second Language Acquisition*. Mahwah, NJ: Erlbaum.

Smith, L. (2004) Changes in student motivation over the final year of high school. *Journal of Educational Enquiry* 5 (2), 64–85.

Spada, N. (1986) The interaction between types of content and type of instruction: Some effects on the L2 proficiency of adult learners. *Studies in Second Language Acquisition* 8, 181–199.

Taylor, D.M. and Usborne, E. (2007) Is the social psychology of language a genuine field of study? *Journal of Language and Social Psychology* 26, 204–211.

Triandis, H.C., McCusker, C. and Hui, C.H. (1990) Multimethod probes of individualism and collectivism. *Journal of Personality and Social Psychology* 59, 1006–1020.

Turner, J.C. and Reynolds, K.J. (2001) The social identity perspective in intergroup relations: Theories, themes and controversies. In R. Brown and S. Gaertner (eds) *Blackwell Handbook of Social Psychology: Intergroup Processes* (pp. 133–152). Oxford: Blackwell.

Unemori, P., Omoregie, H. and Marksu, H.R. (2004) Self-portraits: Possible selves in European American, Chilean, Japanese and Japanese-American cultural contexts. *Self and Identity* 3, 321–338.

Ushioda, E. (2001) Language learning at university: Exploring the role of motivational thinking. In Z. Dörnyei and R. Schmidt (eds) *Motivation and Second Language Acquisition* (pp. 93–125). Honolulu, HI: University of Hawaii Press.

Ushioda, E. (2003) Motivation as a socially mediated process. In D. Little, J. Ridley and E. Ushioda (eds) *Learner Autonomy in the Foreign Language Classroom: Teacher, Learner, Curriculum and Assessment* (pp. 90–102). Dublin: Authentik.

Weinreich, P. (1996) Ethnic stereotyping and identification in a multicultural context: Acculturation, self-esteem and identity diffusion in Hong Kong Chinese university students. *Psychology and Developing Societies* 8, 107–169.

Yashima, T. (2002) Willingness to communicate in a second language: The Japanese EFL context. *Modern Language Journal* 86, 54–66.

Yowell, C.M. (2002) Dreams of the future: The pursuit of education and career possible selves among ninth grade Latino youth. *Applied Developmental Science* 6 (2), 62–72.

Interview with Linda

Linda* is an experienced language learner. Her native language is one of five major regional languages in the Philippines and her second language is English. She speaks fluently in Pilipino and is functional in French and Spanish. She has lived in North America for 35 years and has a faculty position in a large university. English is her main language of communication both at home and at work. Dmitri, a close friend and colleague of Linda's, was due to host his mother on a visit from Russia. Linda became intrigued by the idea of conversing with Dmitri's mother during her visit and began to learn Russian. Linda has provided the following reflections on her learning experience and the motivational role played by possible selves.

PM:	When you first thought about learning Russian, what sort of language use did you envision, what did you see yourself doing? Did you find this vision motivating?
L:	*My friend told me a lot about his mother and I sort of envisioned a very interesting person who would be worth getting to know very well. So when Dmitri told me that his mother was coming, I actually really got excited. I remember one day thinking: Wouldn't it be nice to be able to converse with her in Russian? My husband could speak Russian and I felt I could ask him to teach me a few useful phrases. I could also learn from Dmitri, of course. I have already started to ask him how to say a few useful phrases in Russian (How are you? I like cookies, etc.).*
PM:	As the time of the visit drew close (within weeks or days of the visit), did this vision of yourself speaking Russian change? Did your motivation for learning Russian change?
L:	*My vision of myself talking to my friend's mom, with both Dmitri and my husband watching, was always there. As I had more phrases to say, my imagined conversations with her grew longer and her approval greater. My motivation to learn became more intense. In fact, I studied harder and I asked my husband to teach me more phrases and how to write them down so I would remember. I practiced them over and over again, saying the phrases in my imagined conversation with her.*
	I formulated a plan to learn English so that when Dmitri's mom came I would be able to talk to her. I already had visions of myself talking to her, asking her numerous questions about herself and about Dmitri because part of my motivation to learn Russian at that time was to be able to ask questions about how he grew up and what it was like raising children in her part of the world.

	I have had a lot of occasions in the past to try to converse with people who spoke very little English and found this to be a very enriching experience. One person I remember most was a woman from Brazil, wife of a Brazilian visiting professor who came to dinner at my house. She did not speak English and I did not speak Portuguese. I knew a bit of Spanish so I tried out a few Spanish phrases, learning from her the equivalent Portuguese phrases. At the end of the evening we had exchanged quite a bit of information about ourselves and our family. The other was a Serbo-Croatian mother of my daughter's violin teacher whom he brought one day to visit. I spoke to her in combination of a few useful phrases in Serbian that I had learned earlier from her son and wife and phrases in English and we also had a successful exchange of information.
	As I learned to say a few phrases in Russian, I had one of these women in my mind. More often it was the Serbo-Croatian lady because, for some reason, I imagined Dmitri's mom to be like her. When I thought of her, especially at the beginning, I had a picture of her arriving at the airport and my husband and I picking her up. I would be greeting her and saying phrases rehearsed for that purpose. (How are you? How was the trip? Are you tired?). Later I imagined her sitting in our house and I asking her questions (Do you work? Where do you work? How is your husband? Does he speak English?)
	Always in my mind I would be facing her so that I could see her reaction and I would be using a phrase, usually one I had rehearsed a lot. I would be gesturing a lot to get my meaning across. I would be watching her face intently, wondering if I had said the phrase well enough so that she could recognize it. I imagined that if I succeeded she would be laughing, pleased that I was trying to use her language. I imagined her giving me a response that I could barely understand but I would ask more questions and with gestures and miming I would be able to figure out what to say and so on. And, of course, part of the scenario would be Dmitri pleased and proud of my efforts to speak the language, and my husband also beaming with pride that I am delivering the phrases he had helped me learn.
	The funny thing is that when she actually appeared at the airport and I could finally say all the appropriate phrases I had rehearsed for welcoming her, I opened my mouth to say something and the first words were frozen in mid air!
	Nevertheless, things went well. As I expected, she was very receptive to my efforts to learn. She spoke slowly for my benefit and taught me many new phrases. In the weeks she was here we spent many hours talking, and my Russian, broken at first, found mending as we began to know more about each other.

*The names have been changed

Chapter 4

The L2 Motivational Self System among Japanese, Chinese and Iranian Learners of English: A Comparative Study

TATSUYA TAGUCHI, MICHAEL MAGID and MOSTAFA PAPI

Introduction

Since the 1990s, L2 motivation researchers have been struggling to find a new professional identity that goes beyond the classic traditions set by Canadian social psychologist Robert Gardner and his associates. Several theories have been proposed in the Canadian context (e.g. Noels *et al.*, 2000) as well as in contexts outside of Canada (e.g. Ushioda, 2001; Yashima, 2000) (see Dörnyei, 2001, 2005, for comprehensive reviews). These theories either complemented Gardner's theoretical framework or looked at second language (L2) motivation through the lens of a different research paradigm. The most recent approach, initiated by Zoltán Dörnyei, has been the proposal of a new L2 motivation construct, the L2 Motivational Self System. This system offers a synthesis of two recent conceptualisations of motivation by Noels (2003) and Ushioda (2001), as well as research in personality psychology on possible selves, identity, self-regulatory processes, and self-discrepancy theory. The proposed new framework is described in detail in Chapter 2 and in Dörnyei's (2005) seminal work on the psychology of the language learner. One of the main objectives in our comparative motivational study of learners of English in Japan, China and Iran has been to validate Dörnyei's L2 Motivational Self System in three important Asian contexts.

The Hungarian Study

Dörnyei (2005) explained that the stimulus for his L2 Motivational Self System was his research with Kata Csizér in which they conducted a repeated stratified national survey of the motivation of 13,391 middle school students in Hungary toward studying five target languages (English, German, French, Italian and Russian). The Hungarian study was the largest L2 motivation study ever and its findings have been published in a book (Dörnyei *et al.*, 2006) and numerous articles (e.g. Csizér & Dörnyei, 2005a, 2005b; Dörnyei & Csizér, 2002).

Structural equation modelling (SEM) of the various language data in the different phases of the survey revealed a consistent relationship between the key variables of integrativeness, instrumentality, attitudes toward L2 speakers/community, and two criterion measures – language choice preference and the learners' intended learning effort. One of the main findings was that integrativeness was the most important component of the L2 motivation construct in the sense that, as demonstrated by Dörnyei and Csizér (2002: 453), it 'explained almost as much of the variance of the criterion measures as all the motivation components together'. Although the power of integrativeness was supported by Gardner's (1985) work, it did not make sense that it would have such an impact in a foreign language context like Hungary in which there was practically no English speaking community which English learners could join. The potency of integrativeness in a country without a salient L2 group certainly remains an enigma and we did wonder whether the results from the Hungarian study could have been country-specific. By replicating the Hungarian study in other countries where there is an absence of a substantial L2 group, our purpose is to explore the role of integrativeness in contexts that are vastly different from the Hungarian one. Our first objective then is to partially replicate the Hungarian study in three key Asian countries: Japan, China and Iran.

Another key finding in the Hungarian study was that integrativeness was determined by two antecedent variables: instrumentality and attitudes toward L2 speakers/community. These three variables mediated the contribution of all the other components to the criterion measures. It is reasonable that integrativeness is determined by both attitudes toward L2 speakers and pragmatic incentives if it is an aspect of our ideal self to be personally agreeable and professionally successful. Indeed, in proposing his L2 Motivational Self System, Dörnyei (2005) suggested that integrativeness can be interpreted as being an L2-specific facet of an L2 learner's ideal self. Thus, the ideal L2 self is a central component of the construct of L2 motivation within the L2 Motivational Self System, which consists of three dimensions: the ideal L2 self, the ought-to L2 self, and the L2 learning experience. However, so far, there has not been any empirical evidence for the validity of equating the ideal L2 self with integrativeness, so our second objective is to determine whether or not a relationship exists between these two variables.

According to Dörnyei's (2005) L2 Motivational Self System, there are two types of instrumentality based on Higgins's (1998) distinction: promotional and preventional. The first is related to the ideal L2 self as it regulates positive outcomes, that is, goals and hopes of becoming professionally and personally successful in the L2. The second type is related to the ought-to L2 self as it controls negative outcomes associated with the duties and obligations individuals perceive they have toward others. In spite of this theoretical distinction, in the Hungarian study instrumentality had not been divided into the two categories. Since the ought-to L2 self was assumed to play a particularly significant role in Asian learning environments because of the important influence from family in Asian cultures (e.g. Lockwood *et al.*, 2005; Markus & Kitayama, 1998), we decided to examine both types of instrumentality separately in our study. Therefore, our third objective is to test whether or not there are indeed two distinct types of instrumentality and if so, how they are related to each other as well as to the ideal and ought-to L2 selves.

Finally, our investigation also offers an overall validity study of Dörnyei's tripartite model of the L2 Motivational Self System in an Asian context. By using SEM, our objective is to determine the causal relationships among the attitudinal and motivational factors making up the construct. In particular, we want to examine the relationships between the ideal L2 self, attitudes toward learning English, and the criterion measures. As was mentioned above, Dörnyei (2005) had proposed that the L2 learning experience, which refers to situation-specific motives connected to the immediate learning environment and experience, is one of the three main dimensions of motivation within the L2 Motivational Self System. However, with its focus being on generalised motives, the learning experience dimension was not assessed in the Hungarian study. Therefore, the tripartite construct as a whole had never been empirically tested. We believe that if learners have a strong ideal L2 self, this will be reflected in their positive attitudes toward language learning and they will exhibit greater efforts toward that end as well. By including questions about the participants' attitudes toward learning English, our specific goal is to examine the third dimension of the L2 Motivational Self System and produce empirical evidence of its crucial role in the overall construct.

The Three Asian Contexts of our Research

As was mentioned before, one objective of our study was to examine the findings from the Hungarian study in strikingly different contexts to verify if the results were country-specific or if they could be generalised to other countries. If it can be shown that the L2 Motivational Self System applies to diverse cultural contexts, this will demonstrate the potency and generalisability of the system. For this reason, we decided to compare three countries in Asia that differ considerably in terms of their population, history, economy and religions. The first two countries, Japan and China, have been the subject of a fair amount of motivation research in the past. There is an established tradition of conducting research on English learners in Japan and with the emergence of China onto the global arena as a superpower, we are witnessing a substantial increase in research on English learning in China as well. With regard to

Iran, an opportunity arose for us to conduct an investigation there and we thought it would be enlightening to include a completely different Asian country from Japan and China which nevertheless has a similar foreign language learning context. Space limitations do not allow us to give detailed descriptions of each country or extensive reviews of available research findings. Instead, we will highlight a few general differences pertaining to the cultures, educational systems and the status of English, and present some key motivational studies from each country.

Japan and China

There are, obviously, vast differences between Japan and China although they also share some cultural and linguistic similarities. The majority of people in both countries are not religious and the writing system based on characters is similar in some respects. At the same time, China is a rapidly developing centralised (Communist) system which has been undergoing significant changes in recent years, whereas Japan is one of the most technologically advanced welfare democracies in the world. It was only in the 1990s that China's involvement in world trade became truly substantial; in the past decade, China has opened its doors to the world and the world has come streaming in. When China joined the World Trade Organisation on November 11, 2001, it was a major breakthrough in China's economy. These changes have substantially increased the importance of English in China. In recent years, there has also been a greater emphasis on the importance of English in Japan due to rapid globalisation.

With regard to their educational contexts, Japan and China do share some common features, especially in terms of the extremely exam-oriented nature of the educational system, and in both countries, English is one of the featured subjects in the university entrance exams. In spite of this prominence of English, the two countries differ in the level of importance accorded to English by the general population. Although recently, Japanese industries have started to require potential candidates to possess practical English abilities and many students are keen on raising their English proficiency test scores, it is not always the case that English proficiency is as strongly related to successful job-hunting in Japan as it is in China. Therefore, English is less valued by many learners of English in Japan than in China, where knowing English has become a must for anyone who wants to compete in the global marketplace. A knowledge of English is a requirement in most international companies in China as well as in many Chinese ones.

We were curious to see the ways in which the motivation to learn English in Japan and China would be similar and different since there have not been a great deal of comparative studies between both countries in the past. Miyahara *et al.* (1997) carried out a large-scale study with university students who were learning English in China and Japan in order to compare their motivation as well as other aspects related to learning. The researchers identified a factor in both countries representing an interest in travelling and making friends with people from L2 communities and they labelled this Personal Communication. It is intriguing to note that the researchers also found a factor associated with the desire to become integrated into the L2 communities in the Chinese sample which they labelled Integrative Motivation. Miyahara *et al.* suggested that this factor may explain why Chinese students had a higher average in English proficiency than their Japanese counterparts.

Matsukawa and Tachibana (1996) carried out a survey of Japanese and Chinese junior high school students to measure their motivation and attitudes toward studying English. The main finding was that the Chinese students showed more interest toward studying English than the Japanese students did. Furthermore, the Chinese students' interest was maintained regardless of the grade they were in, whereas Japanese students tended to lose interest as they progressed in grade level. Matsukawa and Tachibana interpreted the findings by suggesting that the motivation of the Japanese students was multifaceted since it was both instrumental and integrative because it consisted of interest in the learning process, high achievement, and English culture. In contrast, the motivation of the Chinese students was solely instrumental because the Chinese participants only cared about the utility of English in their future job and in gaining a high salary.

Yashima (2000) conducted a study with Japanese university students who were majoring in informatics in Japan. The objectives of the study were to discover the reasons why those students wanted to learn English, identify their motivational orientations, and determine which factors were the best predictors of motivation and proficiency. The main finding was that the participants perceived instrumental and intercultural friendship orientations as being the most important. Yashima (2000: 131) stated that Japanese students 'feel vaguely it will become a necessity to use English in the "internationalised" society, but they do not have a clear idea of how they are going to use it'. They did not believe that identification with the target group was important, which supports the findings from Miyahara *et al.*'s (1997) study. In addition, working in the international community was considered the least important by the students.

Iran

Iran shares certain similarities with Japan and China, but in some key aspects it is quite different. For instance, Iran is officially a religious country and the official language of the country, Farsi, is an Indo-European language. Iran contains fewer native speakers of English than Japan or China since political obstacles have inhibited the economic, professional and even academic relations between Iran and English-speaking countries. At the same time, like in Japan and China, the urban youth in Iran are quite westernised and interested in English.

Iranian people usually learn English these days in order to enter prestigious universities and thereby proceed to the highest levels of education and strata in their society. They are also attracted by the opportunity of studying and living abroad, having access to the huge amount of new information resources, and becoming familiar with the cultural products of western countries.

Research on English language attitudes and motivation in the context of Iran has been following the Gardnerian tradition and has typically focused on the relationship between learners' motivational orientations on the one hand and their success in language learning on the other. The literature review below outlines some of the main motivational studies in Iran.

Dastgheib (1996) investigated the relationship between the attitudes and motivation of university undergraduate students of different medical majors and their language proficiency. The main finding involved the discovery of a significant positive correlation between the students' attitudes toward learning English and their desire to learn English. These two variables were positively correlated with motivational intensity and integrativeness. Also, there was a significant positive correlation between instrumental and integrative orientations.

Sadighi and Maghsudi (2000) carried out a study with undergraduates majoring in Teaching English as a Foreign Language in order to compare the language proficiency of instrumentally oriented students with that of integratively oriented students. In addition, personal, social and educational factors were addressed in terms of their relationship with English language learning motivation. The findings of the study demonstrated that the integratively oriented students did significantly better than the students who were instrumentally oriented on the TOEFL test of English language proficiency. It was also found that the participants' educational, personal, and social reasons for learning English were positively correlated with their general motivation to learn English. While all three correlation scores were significant, the first two factors, that is, the educational and the personal factors showed higher correlations ($r = 0.78$ and 0.75, respectively) with the students' motivation than the social factor did ($r = 0.67$).

In a recent study, Matin (2007) investigated the motivational characteristics of university students in Tehran. The results of the study showed that the participants did not differ in terms of their general orientation to learn English. In fact, they were almost equally motivated by instrumental and integrative reasons. The knowledge promotion and employment factors were the highest and lowest ranked factors, respectively on the instrumental scale while interest in the English language ranked the highest and interest in English culture ranked the lowest on the integrative scale.

Method

Participants

The total number of the participants in the current survey was nearly 5000 (see Table 4.1 for a breakdown of the sample according to country, gender and employment status). The Japanese students ranged in age from 18 to 43 with a mean age of 19.1; the Chinese students ranged from 11 to 53 with a mean age of 21.1; and the Iranian students ranged from 12 to 44 with a mean age of 17.4. The participants' exposure to native English teachers, their overseas experiences and their self-assessed English levels were diverse (see Table 4.2).

In the present study, we used the total samples from all three countries for most analyses even though they contained certain sub-samples. However, for the SEM comparisons, we focused only on the university students in each sample.

Instruments

The current study employed three versions of a questionnaire, adapted for use in Japan, China and Iran. Each version is comprised of two major parts: the first part consists of items measuring the learners' attitudes and motivation concerning English learning, and the second

Table 4.1 The sample investigated in the survey

Country	Total	Gender		Employment status			
					University student		
		Male	Female	Middle school student	English major	Non-English major	Working professional
Japan	1586	678	898	–	1534		–
					319	1180	
China	1328	458	869	214	940		173
					182	758	
Iran	2029	892	1137	1309	719		–
					394	325	

Note: Some questionnaires had missing data

Table 4.2 The participants' native teacher, overseas experiences, and self-reported English proficiency

	Native teacher	Overseas experience	Self-reported English proficiency level				
			Beginner	Post-beginner	Lower intermediate	Intermediate	Upper-intermediate and over
Japan	1481 (93.4%)	165 (10.4%)	231 (14.6%)	436 (27.5%)	582 (36.7%)	279 (17.6%)	32 (2%)
China	1098 (82.7%)	100 (7.5%)	25 (1.9%)	111 (8.4%)	437 (32.9%)	612 (46.1%)	88 (6.6%)
Iran	199 (2.5%)	50 (2.5%)	381 (18.8%)	450 (22.2%)	347 (17.1%)	495 (24.4%)	241 (11.9%)

part consists of questions about the learners' background information (e.g. gender, age, native English teacher experience, overseas experience, and self-rated English proficiency levels).

The first of the three questionnaires was developed for Japan, and its design followed the procedures suggested in Dörnyei (2003) (see Taguchi, in progress, for more detail). Because the current study is to validate Dörnyei's L2 motivation theory by replicating the Hungarian studies in the framework of his L2 Motivational Self System, the main components were chosen from Dörnyei *et al.*'s (2006) Hungarian studies (i.e. integrativeness, cultural interest, attitudes to L2 community, and criterion measures) and the L2 Motivational Self System (ideal L2 self, ought-to L2 self, and attitudes to learning English). In addition, other components which are considered important to learner motivation were also included in the questionnaire (e.g. fear of assimilation and ethnocentrism). Most of the items for the components were based on established questionnaires (Clément & Baker, 2001; Dörnyei, 2001; Gardner, 1985; Mayumi, in progress; Noels *et al.*, 2000; Ryan, this volume) and some of them were newly designed. In the second stage, the Chinese version was developed based on the Japanese version but also drawing on other sources (e.g. Neuliep & McCroskey, 1997; Yashima *et al.*, 2004). Finally, the Iranian version followed the same procedures as the Chinese version. All these versions were fine-tuned through extensive piloting in each of the three countries.

The final versions (see Appendix A) adopted statement-type and question-type items; the former were measured by six-point Likert scales while the latter by six-point rating scales with 'not at all' anchoring the left end and 'very much' anchoring the right end. The total number of questionnaire items was 67 in the Japanese and Chinese versions and 76 in the Iranian version.

The following 10 factors were used in the study (for the specific items and the Cronbach Alpha internal consistency reliability coefficients, see Table 4.3):

(1) *Criterion measures* assessing the learners' intended efforts toward learning English.
(2) *Ideal L2 self,* which, according to Dörnyei (2005: 106), refers to the 'L2-specific facet of one's ideal self'.
(3) *Ought-to L2 self,* which measures 'the attributes that one believes one *ought* to possess (i.e. various duties, obligations, or responsibilities) in order to avoid possible negative outcomes' (Dörnyei, 2005: 106).
(4) *Family influence* examining active and passive parental roles.
(5) *Instrumentality-promotion* measuring the regulation of personal goals to become successful such as attaining high proficiency in English in order to make more money or find a better job.

Table 4.3 Composites of attitudinal/motivational variables with Cronbach Alpha coefficients in Japan, China and Iran

Factor name	Japan		China		Iran	
	Item no.	*α*	*Item no.*	*α*	*Item no.*	*α*
Criterion measures	5, 17, 28, 41	0.83	3, 13, 23, 31, 37, 45	0.75	8, 16, 24, 32, 40, 50	0.79
Ideal L2 self	8, 20, 33, 58, 66	0.89	6, 14, 29, 38, 46	0.83	9, 17, 25, 33, 41, 51	0.79
Ought-to L2 self	13, 25, 38, 62	0.76	5, 12, 19, 27, 36, 42, 49	0.78	1, 10, 18, 26, 34, 43	0.75
Family influence	2, 14, 29, 40	0.83	2, 11, 21, 30, 40	0.70	2, 11, 19, 27, 35, 44	0.69
Instrumentality – promotion	6, 18, 31, 55, 64	0.82	4, 10, 16, 22, 28, 35, 41, 48	0.78	3, 12, 20, 28, 37, 45	0.67
Instrumentality – prevention	10, 23, 36, 60, 67	0.73	7, 18, 25, 33, 43	0.84	4, 13, 29, 36, 42, 48, 53	0.81
Attitudes to learning English	12, 24, 37, 61	0.90	50, 55, 60, 65	0.81	54, 59, 63, 67, 71, 75	0.82
Cultural interest	43, 46, 49, 52	0.77	53, 58, 63	0.67	57, 61, 65, 74	0.76
Attitudes to L2 community	44, 47, 50, 53	0.86	54, 59, 64, 67	0.76	58, 62, 66, 70	0.76
Integrativeness	45, 48, 51	0.64	52, 57, 62	0.63	56, 69, 73	0.56

(6) *Instrumentality-prevention* measuring the regulation of duties and obligations such as studying English in order to pass an examination[1].

(7) *Attitudes to learning English* measuring situation-specific motives related to the immediate learning environment and experience.

(8) *Attitudes to L2 community* investigating the learner's attitudes toward the community of the target language.

(9) *Cultural interest* measuring the learner's interest in the cultural products of the L2 culture, such as TV, magazines, music and movies.

(10) *Integrativeness*, which is assessed with items from Dörnyei *et al.*'s (2006) Integrativeness factor, which entails having a positive attitude toward the second language, its culture and the native speakers of that language.

Procedure

The data was collected in all three countries in 2006 and 2007. In order to make our results robust, we attempted to collect as large a sample as we could in each context. The main procedure in all three contexts was similar. We used all of the possible contacts we could activate to find willing participants within the same broad categories: middle school students, university students majoring in English, non-English majors, and adult learners of English.

Data analysis

All the data obtained were analysed with SPSS version 15.0. For the second and third research objectives, correlation techniques were used to describe the strength and direction of the linear relationship between two variables. In assessing relationships between variables, Dörnyei (2007: 223) indicates that correlations of 0.3 to 0.5 can be meaningful and that, when two variables show correlations of 0.6 and above, they measure more or less the same thing.

For the fourth research objective, the datasets from the three versions were submitted to 'Analysis of Moment Structures' (AMOS) version 7.0 (Arbuckle, 2006), one of the popular programs for SEM analysis. Before proceeding to SEM analysis, some approach has to be taken to handle missing cases because AMOS does not tolerate missing data and needs a complete dataset. In our dataset, as missing values were scattered throughout the cases and variables, instead of using *listwise deletion*, we employed the expectation-maximisation algorithm which is a widely used approach among SEM users (Allison, 2003; Hair *et al.*, 2006; Kline, 2005).

The general SEM model can be decomposed into two submodels: a measurement model and a structural model (Byrne, 2001). The main role of the measurement model is to specify the relationships between the latent variables and the actual questionnaire items that assess them and to test the fit and validity of these proposed links. The main purpose of the structural model is to define relations among the unobserved latent variables and to specify the manner by which particular latent variables directly or indirectly influence changes in other latent variables in the model. In this study, the estimation of parameters was based on the maximum likelihood method.

The adequacy of the specified measurement and structural models are usually evaluated on the basis of various criteria: parameters such as values of factor loadings and residuals, the overall model fit indices, and theoretical consideration of the constructs under investigation. In particular, the overall model fit measures are useful to decide on the adequacy of the final model. AMOS provides many types of goodness-of-fit indices.

Byrne (2001) and Hair *et al.* (2006) offer general guidelines of which indices to report. One of the most important indices is χ^2. However, concerns have been raised about using the χ^2 statistic for large samples because it has an inherent bias against sample sizes that are larger than 200 (Schumacker & Lomax, 2004: 100). Therefore, we need to look at other fit indices. These are the goodness-of-fit index (GFI), the comparative fit index (CFI), and the root mean square error of approximation (RMSEA). Regarding GFI and CFI, generally > 0.90 on the 0–1.0 scale is considered as indicative of good fit. However, some researchers (e.g. Hu & Bentler, 1999) recommend a cut-off value close to 0.95. With regard to RMSEA, a value of 0.05 or less means that the model's fit to the data is considered good (Browne & Cudeck, 1993). As these fit criteria are general guidelines, Hair *et al.* (2006) claim to adjust the index cut-off values based on model characteristics, such as the complexity of the model and sample size. Therefore, given our model's complexity and the large sample size, the cut-off values may be less strict.

Results and Discussion

Correlational analyses

Table 4.4 shows the correlation coefficients between the *ideal L2 self* and *integrativeness* in Japan, China and Iran. The *ideal L2 self* was positively correlated with *integrativeness* in all three groups. The average correlation coefficient for each group was over 0.50. There were further significant correlations between the two variables across all the sub-groups. These results demonstrate that the two variables are tapping into the same construct domain and can therefore be equated.

Table 4.5 displays the correlation of the *ideal L2 self* and *integrativeness* with the *criterion measures*. Results from all the groups show that except

Table 4.4 The relationship between the ideal L2 self and integrativeness

	Total	*Middle school students*	*University students (English majors)*	*University students (non-English majors)*	*Adult learners*
Japan (1534)	0.59	–	0.48	0.59	–
China (1328)	0.51	0.66	0.46	0.46	0.53
Iran (2029)	0.53	0.55	0.35	0.43	–

Note: All the correlations are significant at the $p < 0.01$ level

Table 4.5 The relationship between the ideal L2 self, integrativeness and the criterion measures

		Total	Middle school students	University students (English majors)	University students (non-English majors)	Adult learners
Japan (1534)	Ideal L2 self	0.68	–	0.59	0.68	–
	Integrativeness	0.64	–	0.51	0.64	–
China (1328)	Ideal L2 self	0.55	0.69	0.51	0.52	0.51
	Integrativeness	0.52	0.63	0.53	0.47	0.44
Iran (2029)	Ideal L2 self	0.61	0.63	0.45	0.60	–
	Integrativeness	0.58	0.59	0.41	0.55	–

Note: All the correlations are significant at the $p < 0.01$ level

for one sub-group (English majors in China), all the sub-groups show higher correlations between the *ideal L2 self* and the *criterion measures* than between *integrativeness* and the *criterion measures*. The average variance in the *criterion measures* explained by *integrativeness* is 29% while the average variance explained by the *ideal L2 self* is 34%, which is 17% higher. These findings justify the replacement of *integrativeness* with the *ideal L2 self*.

We measured the promotion and prevention aspects of instrumentality separately in order to test whether Higgins's (1998) distinction between promotion and prevention would apply to our data. Table 4.6 presents the correlations of the *ideal* and *ought-to L2 selves* with *instrumentality-promotion* and *instrumentality-prevention*. In this analysis, the *ought-to L2 self* was combined with *family influence*, since the ought-to L2 self contains not only aspects related to friends and colleagues, but also to family.

As the table indicates, in all three groups *instrumentality-promotion* correlates more highly with the *ideal L2 self* than *instrumentality-prevention* does. In contrast, *instrumentality-prevention* correlates more highly with the *ought-to L2 self* than *instrumentality-promotion* does. In addition, the two aspects of instrumentality show low intercorrelations, which means that these aspects are distinctly separate: even the highest one explains less than 10% of the variance. However, the substantial correlations between the promotional aspect of instrumentality with the *ought-to L2 self* in the Chinese and Iranian samples was unexpected. We will look at this issue in more detail first in the Chinese data, where the promotional aspect correlated with the *ideal* and *ought-to L2 selves* equally, and then in

Table 4.6 The relationship between instrumentality (promotion) and instrumentality (prevention)

	Ideal L2 self			Ought-to L2 self			Instrumentality (promotion)		
	Japan	China	Iran	Japan	China	Iran	Japan	China	Iran
Ought-to L2 self	0.14**	0.07*	0.26**	–	–	–	–	–	–
Instrumentality (promotion)	0.60**	0.46**	0.63**	0.27**	0.46**	0.44**	–	–	–
Instrumentality (prevention)	–0.05	–0.13**	0.00	0.45**	0.68**	0.62**	0.31**	0.26**	0.29**

$*p < 0.05$ (2-tailed); $**p < 0.01$ (2-tailed)

the Iranian data where there was also a substantial correlation between *instrumentality-promotion* and the *ought-to L2 self*.

Instrumentality promotion and the ought-to L2 self in China

If we examine the specific items that make up the *instrumentality-promotion* variable in the Chinese questionnaire and consider the Chinese culture, we can understand the results. The two items that were used for the model were items 10 (*Studying English is important to me because English proficiency is necessary for promotion in the future*) and 16 (*Studying English can be important to me because I think I'll need it for further studies*). The majority of Chinese people living in mainland China aspire to gain promotion at work in order to secure a higher salary that would be used to support family members. This reason is associated with their ought-to L2 self. Ever since the one child policy was enforced in 1978, young people have had a heavy burden placed on their shoulders to support their ageing parents. People retire at a relatively early age in China, usually with extremely low pensions, so their children have the responsibility and obligation to take care of them as they become the sole breadwinners of the family.

Along the same lines, we can explain why studying English in order to pursue further studies is related to one's ought-to L2 self. Many young Chinese people are pressured by their family to continue their studies so that they can obtain a high status, high paying job. In this way, Chinese people often feel a great obligation to their parents to study, even though they may not be intrinsically motivated to do so themselves. They view themselves not only in individualistic terms like many Westerners do, but also as a direct extension of their family. Therefore, as their status in society increases, so does the position of their family. Many believe that since their parents raised them, they have a duty to support them in their old age and carry out their wishes. This is why in China, parents will often choose a major for their children. Most young people will obey their parents even if they are not interested in the major or career that their parents have chosen for them. These days, young people may voice their opinion more openly than in the past, but most are still controlled by their parents since their parents support them financially during their studies. In China, it is almost impossible for university students to support themselves by finding a part-time job like in Western countries because employers prefer to hire university graduates.

Instrumentality promotion and the ought-to L2 self in Iran

By considering the specific items that make up the *instrumentality-promotion* variable in the Iranian questionnaire and reflecting on the Iranian culture, we can understand why there was a relatively high correlation between *instrumentality-promotion* and the *ought-to L2 self* in Iran. The two items that were used for *instrumentality-promotion* in the model were items 12 (*Studying English is important to me because English proficiency is necessary for promotion in the future*) and 37 (*I study English in order to keep updated and informed of recent news of the world*). In Iran, studying English is necessary in order to find a good job because it is a required component of a university education, and having a higher degree greatly increases one's chances of finding a secure job with a stable income. Studying English for a promotion is related to one's ought-to L2 self in the same way that it is in China. Since average salaries in Iran are usually not very high, young people should try their best to support their entire family on their income. In fact, it is one of the main responsibilities that they have toward their family as well as getting married. In Iran, usually the selection of a future spouse is highly influenced and sometimes even determined by the parents who will consider the socio-economic status and educational level of the potential spouse. With regard to item 12, a promotion at work will elevate one's socio-economic status which will bring honour to one's entire family, thereby positively reinforcing one's ought-to L2 self. With regard to item 37, in Iranian society, those who are knowledgeable about the outside world will build an excellent reputation, which will garner prestige for their family, and is thus related to their ought-to L2 self. Also, since the majority of the world's resources pertaining to science and technology are published in English, it is necessary to know English in order to advance in many careers in Iran.

The high correlation between *instrumentality-promotion* and the *ought-to L2 self* in the Iranian sample reflects the current social and economic situation in Iran. As a result of all of the political turmoil, revolutions, and wars in Iran, especially during the last 30 years, many Iranian parents today believe that they did not have a fulfilling youth and have not been able to achieve their dreams. Therefore, they place almost all of their hope onto their children. They believe that if their children will be successful, that will be a sign of their own success as well. Like in China, though to a lesser extent, parents in Iran also influence their children in their choice of a major and a career.

Since English language teaching in the academic and formal educational system in Iran lacks the capability to equip learners with the required level of English to pass the university entrance exam, students usually resort to language institutes and private teachers to achieve their goal. Although these private classes are expensive, especially relative to the insufficient income of the majority of the people in Iran, many families accept all the costs based on the expectation that their children will be successful. In exchange for their financial sacrifice, parents expect their children to bring them honour and prestige by being successful.

Summary of the main findings

As we have seen, our results indicate that the concept of *integrativeness* can be re-interpreted in a broader frame of reference – the *ideal L2 self* – and our findings indicate that the *ideal L2 self* achieved a better explanatory power toward learners' intended efforts than *integrativeness* did.

In the case of instrumentality, we found that the concept can be divided into two distinct types from a self perspective, one closely associated with the ideal L2 self and the other with the ought-to L2 self. Depending on the context, even the same phenomenon or event can be perceived differently in this respect. For example, studying English for going overseas is promotional for those who desire to study overseas, but it can be preventional for those who will be commanded to work overseas by a company. Thus, the interpretation is a function of the extent of internalisation of the extrinsic motives that make up instrumentality (Csizér & Dörnyei, 2005a).

Structural equation modelling analyses

Our main purpose for employing structural equation modelling was to examine the causal relationships among the attitudinal/motivational factors including the components of the L2 Motivational Self System. Before making any attempt to evaluate the structural models of our datasets, it is necessary to first test the validity of the measurement models. For this purpose, we set out to test three measurement models. The first model consists of four latent variables (*ideal L2 self, instrumentality-promotion, attitudes to L2 community,* and *cultural interest*). There was a problem of discriminant validity on *attitudes to L2 community* and *cultural interest*. As cultural interest in the L2 can be considered to be a part of attitudes to the L2 community, the factors were combined with the label *attitudes to L2 culture and community*. The second measurement model comprises factors relating to the ought-to L2 self. Given the strong influence of the family on student motivation described above, we separated the unified ought-to L2 self from the original *ought-to L2 self* and *family influence* factors[2]. Finally, the third measurement model is made up of two latent variables (*attitudes to learning English* and *criterion measures*). The goodness-of-fit measures indicated that after some modifications the measurement models fit the data well for all the Japanese, Chinese, and Iranian samples.

The second step in SEM is to develop a full structural model by integrating the measurement models; in constructing our structural model we followed Dörnyei *et al.*'s (2006) Hungarian model and Dörnyei's (2005) L2 Motivational Self System. The models with standardised path coefficients for the three samples are shown in Figures 4.1, 4.2 and 4.3.

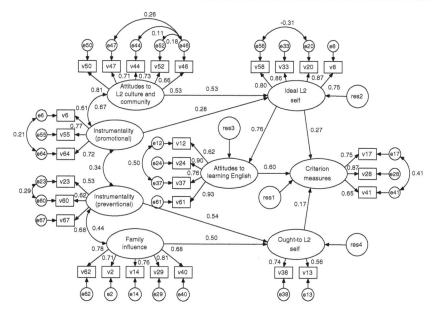

Figure 4.1 The final model with standardised estimates for the Japanese university students
Note: N = 1534. All path coefficients are significant at *p* < 0.001. $\chi^2(358) =$ 1777.47, *p* < 0.001; GFI = 0.92; CFI = 0.94; RMSEA = 0.05.

The three figures show that all the paths were significant at the *p* < 0.001 level except for one path in the Iranian model (*instrumentality-promotion↔instrumentality-prevention*). Because of the large sample size, the chi-square tests are significant, $\chi^2(358) = 1777.47$, *p* < 0.001 in the Japanese group, $\chi^2(284) = 1002.85$, *p* < 0.001 in the Chinese group, and $\chi^2(284) = 748.93$, *p* < 0.001 in the Iranian group. However, other goodness-of-fit indices indicate that our models are appropriate to describe the three samples. The GFI, CFI and RMSEA values were 0.93, 0.94 and 0.05, respectively, for the Japanese model, 0.93, 0.92 and 0.05 for the Chinese model, and 0.93, 0.93 and 0.05 for the Iranian model. The results of the goodness-of-fit measures and the standardised estimates of the various relationships in all three figures indicate that the proposed final models are stable across the various samples. Therefore, we can conclude that the models provide an adequate representation of our Japanese, Chinese, and Iranian datasets.

A closer look at the coefficients of the models

While the overall relationship patterns in the models in Figures 4.1, 4.2 and 4.3 are stable, the standardised estimate values (which can be

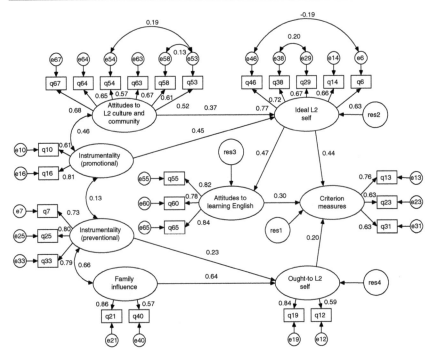

Figure 4.2 The final model with standardised estimates for the Chinese university students
Note: $N = 940$. All path coefficients are significant at $p < 0.001$. $\chi^2(284) = 1002.85$, $p < 0.001$; GFI $= 0.93$; CFI $= 0.92$; RMSEA $= 0.05$.

thought of as correlation coefficients) describing the strength of the specific relationships among the various variables did not remain constant across the cultures (see Figure 4.4). Although there are several cross-cultural differences between the coefficients across the models, two particular clusters stand out in this respect, both involving the *ideal L2 self*: the interrelationship of (1) *ideal L2 self, attitudes to L2 culture and community,* and *instrumentality-promotion,* and (2) *ideal L2 self, attitudes to learning English* and the *criterion measures.*

Ideal L2 self, attitudes to L2 culture and instrumentality

One remarkable cross-cultural difference concerns the influence of *attitudes to L2 culture and community* and *instrumentality-promotion* on the *ideal L2 self.* In the Japanese model the impact from *attitudes to L2 culture and community* on the *ideal L2 self* is nearly twice as large as from *instrumentality-promotion,* whereas in the Chinese and the Iranian data the contribution of the two aspects is roughly equal.

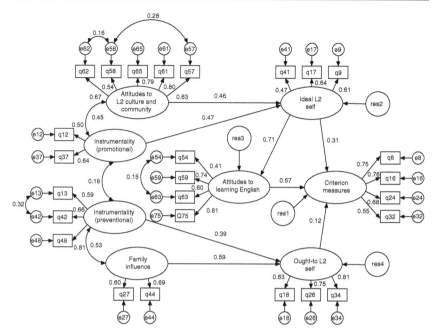

Figure 4.3 The final model with standardised estimates for the Iranian university students

Note: $N = 719$. All path coefficients except for one between two types of instrumentality are significant at $p < 0.001$. $\chi^2(284) = 748.93$, $p < 0.001$; GFI = 0.93; CFI = 0.93; RMSEA = 0.05.

The relatively balanced influence of *attitudes to L2 culture and community* and *instrumentality-promotion* on the *ideal L2 self* in the Chinese and Iranian participants, suggests that the ideal L2 self they tend to develop is fully fledged and rounded in terms of being both personally agreeable and professionally successful. Perhaps they are similar to the most motivated group of Hungarian learners which Csizér and Dörnyei (2005b) identified through cluster analysis. In their survey, these authors identified four groups of language learners. Group 1 consisted of students who scored lower than average on all of the motivational scales (and subsequently also on the criterion measures) and were therefore labelled the *least motivated students*. Group 2 students had a more positive attitude toward the L2 community and culture like the Japanese in our study, but they did not seem to realise how English would be relevant in their professional life. Group 3 scored high on instrumentality and were motivated by their ought-to L2 self without sufficient support by attitudes toward the L2 community and culture. Group 4 participants scored higher than average in every motivational area and were labelled

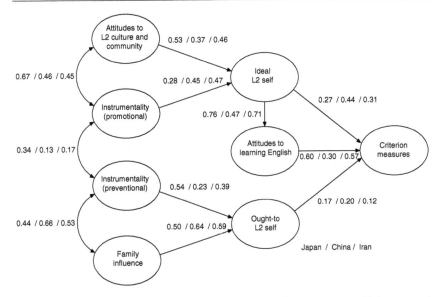

Figure 4.4 Comparison of coefficients among the Japanese, Chinese and Iranian models

the *most motivated students*. They also performed the highest on the criterion measures which assessed the learners' effort and language choice. The Chinese and Iranian students from our study had a much higher average on the *criterion measures* than the Japanese students did (4.38 and 4.69 in contrast to 3.68) and they also had a more salient *ideal L2 self* (4.78 and 4.74 in contrast to 3.62). This type of balanced ideal L2 self was associated with a mastery of the second language in the Hungarian study, and therefore, in a follow-up investigation we intend to conduct a cluster analysis of our dataset to examine whether we find the same learner pattern.

Thus, Japanese learners behave differently from Chinese and Iranian ones in the sense that there is an imbalance in the effect of the two components on the *ideal L2 self*. Certainly, the Japanese think that they need to study English to obtain a job, but their idealised English self is not strongly linked with a professionally successful self. This could be because good English ability represented with high scores on English proficiency tests is just one of the favourable conditions for finding a job. As Kobayashi (2007: 64) claims, the supposedly beneficial effects of English skills are implicitly restricted to 'those prospective and current professional employees who are already in good standing regardless of their English levels'. Therefore, the professionally successful English self is accorded less importance than the personally agreeable English self by the Japanese participants. Interestingly, while the promotional aspect is not that relevant, instrumentality maintains its impact because, as shown in Figure 4.4, the preventional aspect in Japan has the strongest impact on the *ought-to L2 self* among the three countries. This is a good illustration of why it is worth distinguishing the two instrumentality aspects. We find a similar overall volume of instrumentality but this sum hides a major qualitative difference.

Ideal L2 self, attitudes to learning English and the criterion measures

Another salient cross-cultural difference can be found in the *ideal L2 self → criterion measures* relationships. In the three models, the *ideal L2 self* predicts the *criterion measures* both directly and indirectly through *attitudes to learning English*. In Japan and Iran, the indirect route is considerably stronger than the direct one, whereas in China both routes are quite balanced. Thus, it seems that in China, *attitudes to learning English* play a less important role than in Japan and Iran in influencing the amount of effort learners expend on learning English. The items related to *attitudes to learning English* in the Chinese questionnaire are concerned with a high interest in learning English, looking forward to English classes, and enjoying the process of learning English. We would argue that while many Chinese students enjoy learning English, enjoyment does not play a decisive role in their overall motivation: even if learning English is a painstaking task, Chinese students will typically be able to control their negative attitudes for the sake of achieving their ultimate goal, a high level of proficiency in English or at the very least a passing mark in their English exams. Owing to the enormous pressure Chinese students are under to achieve their future desired selves, the classroom experience is far less important for them than for the Japanese and Iranian university students. Broadly speaking, they simply cannot afford the luxury of caring for the niceties of the classroom experience.

In summary, the models we constructed fit our data well and describe English language learners in Asia with culturally and educationally different backgrounds. It was expected that there would be some variations in the models due to the cross-cultural differences in the three Asian countries we have described above, but this diversity is limited and does not affect the overall validity of the L2 Motivational Self System.

Conclusion

We can draw four main conclusions based on our findings. Firstly, the Hungarian line of research which has provided so much theorising on L2 motivation research in the past two decades is not country-specific since we found a similar pattern in three countries that differ greatly from Hungary and from each other. This confirms Dörnyei's assumption that Hungary can be seen as a prototype of a general foreign language learning context; therefore, the Hungarian findings have external validity. Secondly, our findings support the underlying tenet of the L2 Motivational Self System that integrativeness can be relabelled as the ideal L2 self. In fact, we found that the new concept possesses increased explanatory power in foreign language contexts. Thirdly, from a self perspective, our results confirm that instrumentality can be classified into two distinct constructs, associated with promotion versus prevention tendencies, depending on the extent of internalisation of external incentives. Finally, the structural equation modelling analysis presented in this article not only confirmed the validity of the entire tripartite L2 Motivational Self System, but also helped us to understand certain cross-cultural differences in different educational contexts.

Although our surveys have not been based on stratified random sampling, given the depth and breadth of the populations that were sampled from three major countries it is difficult to imagine that the strong tendencies uncovered would be untrue. Also, we were pleased to see that other chapters in this anthology (e.g. Ryan; Csizér & Kormos) fully converge on this issue with our findings.

Notes

1. The original *instrumentality-prevention* in the Iranian version contained eight items with the 0.78 alpha coefficient. However, because item 21 reduced the reliability of the scale, the item was deleted from the table and further analysis.
2. Two items (25 and 62) in the *ought-to L2 self* in the Japanese version are related to family dimensions, so these items were moved to *family influence*.

References

Allison, P.D. (2003) Missing data techniques for structural equation modelling. *Journal of Abnormal Psychology* 112 (4), 545–557.

Arbuckle, J.L. (2006) *AMOS* (Version 7.0). Chicago, IL: SPSS.

Browne, M.W. and Cudeck, R. (1993) Alternate ways of assessing model fit. In K.A. Bollen and J.S. Long (eds) *Testing Structural Equation Models* (pp. 136–162). Newbury Park, CA: Sage.

Byrne, B.M. (2001) *Structural Equation Modelling with AMOS: Basic Concepts, Applications, and Programming*. Mahwah, NJ: Lawrence Erlbaum Associates.

Clément, R. and Baker, S.C. (2001) *Measuring Social Aspects of L2 Acquisition and Use: Social Characteristics and Administration* (Technical Report). Ottawa: School of Psychology, University of Ottawa.

Csizér, K. and Dörnyei, Z. (2005a) Language learners' motivational profiles and their motivated learning behaviour. *Language Learning* 55 (4), 613–659.

Csizér, K. and Dörnyei, Z. (2005b) The internal structure of language learning motivation and its relationship with language choice and learning effort. *Modern Language Journal* 89 (1), 19–36.

Dastgheib, A. (1996) The role of attitudes and motivation in second/foreign language learning. PhD thesis, Islamic Azad University of Tehran.

Dörnyei, Z. (2001) *Teaching and Researching Motivation.* Harlow: Longman.

Dörnyei, Z. (2003) *Questionnaires in Second Language Research: Construction, Administration, and Processing.* Mahwah, NJ: Lawrence Erlbaum Associates.

Dörnyei, Z. (2005) *The Psychology of the Language Learner: Individual Differences in Second Language Acquisition.* Mahwah, NJ: Lawrence Erlbaum Associates.

Dörnyei, Z. (2007) *Research Methods in Applied Linguistics: Quantitative, Qualitative and Mixed Methodologies.* Oxford: Oxford University Press.

Dörnyei, Z. and Csizér, K. (2002) Some dynamics of language attitudes and motivation: Results of a longitudinal nationwide survey. *Applied Linguistics* 23 (4), 421–462.

Dörnyei, Z., Csizér, K. and Németh, N. (2006) *Motivation, Language Attitudes, and Globalisation: A Hungarian Perspective.* Clevedon: Multilingual Matters.

Gardner, R.C. (1985) *Social Psychology and Second Language Learning: The Role of Attitudes and Motivation.* London: Edward Arnold.

Hair, J.F., Black, W.C., Babin, B.J., Anderson, R.E. and Tatham, R.L. (2006) *Multivariate Data Analysis* (6th edn). Upper Saddle River, NJ: Prentice Hall.

Higgins, E.T. (1998) Promotion and prevention: Regulatory focus as a motivational principle. *Advances in Experimental Social Psychology* 30, 1–46.

Hu, L.T. and Bentler, P.M. (1999) Cutoff criteria for fit indexes in covariance structure analysis: Conventional criteria versus new alternatives. *Structural Equation Modelling: A Multidisciplinary Journal* 6 (1), 1–55.

Kline, R.B. (2005) *Principles and Practice of Structural Equation Modelling* (2nd edn). New York, NY: The Guilford Press.

Kobayashi, Y. (2007) Japanese working women and English study abroad. *World Englishes* 26 (1), 62–71.

Lockwood, P., Marshall, T.C. and Sadler, P. (2005) Promoting success or preventing failure: Cultural differences in motivation by positive and negative role models. *Personality and Social Psychology Bulletin* 31 (3), 379–392.

Markus, H.R. and Kitayama, S. (1998) The cultural psychology of personality. *Journal of Cross-Cultural Psychology* 29 (1), 63–87.

Matin, M. (2007) The relationship between attitudes and orientation toward English learning and preferences in the use of language learning strategies MA thesis, Iran University of Science and Technology.

Matsukawa, R. and Tachibana, Y. (1996) Junior high school students' motivation towards English learning: A cross-national comparison between Japan and China. *ARELE: Annual Review of English Language Education in Japan* 7, 49–58.

Mayumi, K. (in progress) Temporal changes in language learner motivation in Japan. PhD thesis, University of Nottingham.

Miyahara, F., Namoto, M., Yamanaka, S., Murakami, R., Kinoshita, M. and Yamamoto, H. (1997) *Konomamade Yoika Daigaku Eigokyoiku* [Current status of university English education: Comparison of university students' ability in English and learning behaviour in China, Korea, and Japan]. Tokyo: Shohakusya.

Neuliep, J.W. and McCroskey, J.C. (1997) The development of a U.S. and generalised ethnocentrism scale. *Communication Research Reports* 14 (4), 385–398.

Noels, K.A. (2003) Learning Spanish as a second language: Learners' orientations and perceptions of their teachers' communication style. In Z. Dörnyei (ed.) *Attitudes, Orientations, and Motivations in Language Learning* (pp. 97–136). Oxford: Blackwell.

Noels, K.A., Pelletier, L.G., Clément, R. and Vallerand, R.J. (2000) Why are you learning a second language? Motivational orientations and self-determination theory. *Language Learning* 50 (1), 57–85.

Sadighi, F. and Maghsudi, N. (2000) The relationship between motivation and English proficiency among Iranian EFL learners. *Indian Journal of Applied Linguistics* 26 (1), 39–52.

Schumacker, R.E. and Lomax, R.G. (2004) *A Beginner's Guide to Structural Equation Modelling* (2nd edn). Mahwah, NJ: Lawrence Erlbaum Associates.

Taguchi, T. (in progress) The L2 motivational self system amongst Japanese university learners of English. PhD thesis, University of Nottingham.

Ushioda, E. (2001) Language learning at university: Exploring the role of motivational thinking. In Z. Dörnyei and R. Schmidt (eds) *Motivation and Second Language Acquisition* (pp. 99–125). Honolulu, HI: University of Hawaii Press.

Yashima, T. (2000) Orientations and motivations in foreign language learning: A study of Japanese college students. *JACET Bulletin* 31, 121–133.

Yashima, T., Zenuk-Nishide, L. and Shimizu, K. (2004) The influence of attitudes and affect on willingness to communicate and second language communication. *Language Learning* 54 (1), 119–152.

Appendix A

Scales for statement-type items:
1 (Strongly disagree), **2** (Disagree), **3** (Slightly disagree), **4** (Slightly agree), **5** (Agree), and **6** (Strongly agree)

Scales for question-type items:
1 (not at all), **2** (not so much), **3** (so-so), **4** (a little), **5** (quite a lot), and **6** (very much)

Note:
For each item, the following tables provide the sequence number of the item in the instrument (in bold), as well as the item's mean and the standard deviation (the latter in brackets).

Criterion measures

Item	*Japanese*	*Chinese*	*Iranian*
If an English course was offered at university or somewhere else in the future, I would like to take it.	**5**—4.26 (1.44)		
If an English course was offered in the future, I would like to take it.		**45**—4.49 (1.11)	**32**—4.76 (1.34)
I am working hard at learning English.	**17**—3.69 (1.24)		

	Japanese	Chinese	Iranian
I am prepared to expend a lot of effort in learning English.	28—3.54 (1.23)	23—4.75 (1.2)	16—5.04 (1.18)
I think that I am doing my best to learn English.	41—3.29 (1.24)	3—4.61 (1.07	
I would like to spend lots of time studying English.		13—4.40 (1.11)	8—4.62 (1.33)
I would like to concentrate on studying English more than any other topic.		31—4.11 (1.24)	24—4.08 (1.46)
Compared to my classmates, I think I study English relatively hard.		37—3.78 (1.17)	
If my teacher would give the class an optional assignment, I would certainly volunteer to do it.			40—4.45 (1.53)
I would like to study English even if I were not required.			50—4.33 (1.63)

Ideal L2 self

Item	Japanese	Chinese	Iranian
I can imagine myself living abroad and having a discussion in English.	8—2.90 (1.41)	6—4.80 (1.08)	
I can imagine myself living abroad and using English effectively for communicating with the locals.			51—4.34 (1.52)
I can imagine a situation where I am speaking English with foreigners.	20—3.70 (1.45)		
I can imagine myself speaking English with international friends or colleagues.		38—4.71 (1.04)	17—4.46 (1.53)
I imagine myself as someone who is able to speak English.	33—3.76 (1.52)	14—4.90 (0.98)	
I can imagine myself speaking English as if I were a native speaker of English.		29—4.70 (1.17)	9—4.81 (1.34)
Whenever I think of my future career, I imagine myself using English.	58—3.33 (1.62)	46—4.77 (1.06)	25—4.36 (1.48)
The things I want to do in the future require me to use English.	66—4.55 (1.43)		

| I can imagine myself studying in a university where all my courses are taught in English. | | | 33—4.49 (1.52) |
| I can imagine myself writing English e-mails fluently. | | | 41—4.29 (1.48) |

Ought-to L2 self

Item	Japanese	Chinese	Iranian
I study English because close friends of mine think it is important.	13—2.51 (1.27)	5—2.69 (1.30)	1—4.12 (1.71)
I have to study English, because, if I do not study it, I think my parents will be disappointed with me.	25—2.22 (1.25)		
Learning English is necessary because people surrounding me expect me to do so.	38—2.59 (1.38)	19—2.78 (1.34)	34—3.25 (1.61)
My parents believe that I must study English to be an educated person.	62—2.50 (1.42)		
I consider learning English important because the people I respect think that I should do it.		12—3.19 (1.31)	18—3.57 (1.60)
Studying English is important to me in order to gain the approval of my peers/teachers/family/boss.		27—3.14 (1.38)	26—3.65 (1.62)
It will have a negative impact on my life if I don't learn English.		36—3.54 (1.32)	
Studying English is important to me because an educated person is supposed to be able to speak English.		42—3.68 (1.34)	
Studying English is important to me because other people will respect me more if I have a knowledge of English.		49—3.49 (1.26)	43—3.33 (1.59)
If I fail to learn English, I'll be letting other people down.			10—2.42 (1.49)

Family influence

Item	Japanese	Chinese	Iranian
My parents encourage me to study English.	2—3.41 (1.57)		

My parents encourage me to take every opportunity to use my English (e.g. speaking and reading).	14—2.55 (1.37)		
My parents encourage me to study English in my free time.	29—2.35 (1.41)		
My parents encourage me to attend extra English classes after class (e.g. at English conversation schools).	40—2.00 (1.26)		
My parents encourage me to practise my English as much as possible.			35—4.35 (1.47)
My parents/family believe that I must study English to be an educated person.		2—4.24 (1.27)	2—4.03 (1.61)
Studying English is important to me in order to bring honours to my family.		11—3.10 (1.33)	11—4.03 (1.63)
I must study English to avoid being punished by my parents/relatives.		21—2.73 (1.28)	
Being successful in English is important to me so that I can please my parents/relatives.		30—3.97 (1.28)	19—3.43 (1.64)
My family put a lot of pressure on me to study English.		40—3.02 (1.36)	27—2.33 (1.55)
I have to study English, because, if I don't do it, my parents will be disappointed with me.			44—2.11 (1.43)

Instrumentality (promotion)

Item	Japanese	Chinese	Iranian
Studying English can be important to me because I think it will some day be useful in getting a good job.	6—5.08 (1.06)	4—5.02 (0.99)	
Studying English is important because with a high level of English proficiency I will be able to make a lot of money.		22—4.39 (1.10)	
Studying English can be important to me because I think it will some day be useful in getting a good job and/or making money.			3—4.85 (1.30)

Studying English is important to me because English proficiency is necessary for promotion in the future.	18—4.64 (1.21)	10—5.00 (1.05)	12—4.88 (1.24)
Studying English is important to me because I would like to spend a longer period living abroad (e.g. studying and working).	31—4.20 (1.56)		
Studying English is important to me because I am planning to study abroad.			45—3.89 (1.71)
Studying English can be important for me because I think I'll need it for further studies on my major.	55—4.48 (1.35)		
Studying English can be important to me because I think I'll need it for further studies.		16—5.14 (0.97)	20—5.11 (1.14)
Studying English is important to me because with English I can work globally.	64—4.74 (1.19)		
The things I want to do in the future require me to use English.		28—4.93 (1.06)	
Studying English is important to me because it offers a new challenge in my life.		35—4.41 (1.07)	
Studying English is important to me in order to achieve a special goal (e.g. to get a degree or scholarship).		41—4.14 (1.28)	28—4.34 (1.51)
Studying English is important to me in order to attain a higher social respect.		48—3.85 (1.25)	
I study English in order to keep updated and informed of recent news of the world.			37—4.77 (1.35)

Instrumentality (prevention)

Item	Japanese	Chinese	Iranian
I have to learn English because without passing the English course I cannot graduate.	10—4.04 (1.52)		
I have to learn English because without passing the English course I cannot get my degree.			13—3.77 (1.76)

	Japanese	Chinese	Iranian
I have to learn English because I don't want to fail the English course.		33—3.21 (1.39)	42—4.20 (1.75)
I have to study English because I don't want to get bad marks in it at university.	23—3.86 (1.35)		
I have to study English because I don't want to get bad marks in it.		7—3.36 (1.53)	4—3.98 (1.84)
I have to study English; otherwise, I think I cannot be successful in my future career.	36—3.43 (1.47)		21—4.05 (1.53)
Studying English is necessary for me because I don't want to get a poor score or a fail mark in English proficiency tests.	60—3.94 (1.41)	25—3.46 (1.39)	
Studying English is necessary for me because I don't want to get a poor score or a fail mark in English proficiency tests (TOEFL, IELTS,…).			36—4.36 (1.51)
Studying English is important to me because, if I don't have knowledge of English, I'll be considered a weak student.	67—2.91 (1.42)	18—2.75 (1.32)	29—3.24 (1.73)
Studying English is important to me, because I would feel ashamed if I got bad grades in English.		43—3.02 (1.35)	48—4.08 (1.65)
Studying English is important to me because I don't like to be considered a poorly educated person.			53—4.59 (1.45)

Attitudes to learning English

Item	Japanese	Chinese	Iranian
I like the atmosphere of my English classes.	12—4.06 (1.31)		
Do you like the atmosphere of your English classes?		50—3.92 (1.28)	54—4.08 (1.56)
I find learning English really interesting.	24—4.32 (1.34)		
Do you find learning English really interesting?		55—4.22 (1.29)	59—4.81 (1.35)
I always look forward to English classes.	37—3.65 (1.37)		

Do you always look forward to English classes?		60—3.83 (1.34)	67—4.62 (1.47)
I really enjoy learning English.	61—4.12 (1.39)		
Do you really enjoy learning English?		65—4.34 (1.30)	75—4.68 (1.45)
Would you like to have more English lessons at school?			71—4.22 (1.60)
Do you think time passes faster while studying English?			63—3.70 (1.64)

Cultural interest

Item	Japanese	Chinese	Iranian
Do you like the music of English-speaking countries (e.g. pop music)?	43—4.69 (1.33)	53—4.81 (1.17)	57—3.85 (1.81)
Do you like English films?	46—5.05 (1.16)	58—5.17 (1.03)	61—3.94 (1.84)
Do you like English magazines, newspapers, or books?	49—3.73 (1.41)		74—3.96 (1.68)
Do you like TV programmes made in English-speaking countries?	52—4.07 (1.43)	63—4.73 (1.17)	65—3.85 (1.70)

Attitudes to L2 community

Item	Japanese	Chinese	Iranian
Do you like to travel to English-speaking countries?	44—4.63 (1.36)	64—5.28 (1.00)	66—4.76 (1.50)
Do you like the people who live in English-speaking countries?	47—4.52 (1.21)	54—4.35 (1.12)	58—3.64 (1.55)
Do you like meeting people from English-speaking countries?	50—4.86 (1.27)	59—4.58 (1.12)	62—4.20 (1.66)
Would you like to know more about people from English-speaking countries?	53—4.68 (1.31)	67—4.89 (1.08)	70—4.44 (1.49)

Integrativeness

Item	Japanese	Chinese	Iranian
How important do you think learning English is in order to learn more about the culture and art of its speakers?	**45**—4.84 (1.07)	**57**—5.15 (1.06)	**69**—4.70 (1.28)
How much would you like to become similar to the people who speak English?	**48**—4.06 (1.38)	**52**—5.11 (1.12)	**56**—4.39 (1.62)
How much do you like English?	**51**—4.42 (1.35)	**62**—4.51 (1.19)	**73**—4.82 (1.37)

Chapter 5

Learning Experiences, Selves and Motivated Learning Behaviour: A Comparative Analysis of Structural Models for Hungarian Secondary and University Learners of English

KATA CSIZÉR and JUDIT KORMOS

Introduction

There is a Hungarian proverb, which says 'you are as many men as many languages you speak'. This proverb is usually interpreted in two different ways: the more languages you speak, the more opportunities open up for you in your life, or when using another language, you become a different person. The proverb's first meaning is especially important for Hungarians since there are only around 15 million L1 speakers of Hungarian in the world. The second meaning of the proverb expresses that language and identity are hardly separable and when learning another language, one's self also undergoes a change. Guiora and Acton argue for the existence of a different self in the foreign language, termed 'language ego', which is based on the psychological experience shared by many language learners that 'one feels like a different person when speaking a second language and often indeed acts very differently as well' (Guiora & Acton, 1979: 199). Whereas the role of self-concept has been thoroughly researched in studies of foreign language learning anxiety (e.g. Young, 1992), it is only recently that the self-concept has become a subject of investigation and theorising in the L2 motivation literature (Dörnyei, 2005).

L2 learners' self-concept was implicitly incorporated in Gardner's construct of integrative motivation, which implies varied psychological and emotional identification either with the target language community (Gardner, 2001), or if no salient L2 community is present in the immediate learning environment, identification with values associated with the L2 community and/or the language or identification with the language itself (Dörnyei, 1990). By the 21st century, however, English has become an international language serving as a lingua franca in a globalised world (e.g. Crystal, 2003; Widdowson, 1994). Therefore the

English language has become separated from its native speakers and their cultures (Skutnabb-Kangas, 2000). Integrativeness in the sense as defined by Gardner involves the language learners' identification with native speakers of the L2, but in today's world it seems to be more appropriate to talk about 'World English identity' (Dörnyei, 2005) or 'international posture' (Yashima, 2002), which includes 'interest in foreign or international affairs, willingness to go overseas to study or work, readiness to interact with intercultural partners ... and a non-ethnocentric attitude toward different cultures' (Yashima, 2002: 57; see also Yashima, this volume). The lack of identification with native speakers of English as a significant motivating factor has been demonstrated in a number of studies in a variety of settings (e.g. Lamb, 2004; Warden & Lin, 2000; Yashima, 2000). It has also been shown that in the case of English, it is very difficult to distinguish instrumentality, that is, the utilitarian benefits associated with the knowledge of the language, from integrativeness (Kimura *et al.*, 2001; Lamb, 2004). As Lamb (2004: 15) argues, 'meeting with westerners, using pop-songs, studying and travelling abroad, pursuing a desirable career – all these aspirations are associated with each other'.

In an attempt to answer these challenges, Dörnyei (2005) proposed the model of the L2 Motivational Self System, which consists of three main components: ideal L2 self, ought-to L2 self and the L2 learning experience (see also Dörnyei, this volume). In this model integrativeness is included in the construct of the ideal L2 self, which is one's ideal self-image expressing the wish to become a competent L2 speaker. The ought-to L2 self contains 'attributes that one believes one ought to possess (i.e. various duties, obligations, or responsibilities) in order to avoid possible negative outcomes' (Dörnyei, 2005: 106). L2 learning experience covers 'situation specific motives related to the immediate learning environment and experience' (Dörnyei, 2005: 106). The model of the Motivational Self System is based on Higgins's self-discrepancy theory (1987), in which it is argued that motivation is the result of someone's wish to reduce the discrepancy between one's ideal self, that is, one's image of what one would like to become, and one's actual self, that is, one's actual self-state. Motivation also comes about from the intention to lessen the gap between one's actual self and one's ought-to self, that is, one's perception of what significant others would like one to become.

The aim of the study presented in this paper was to investigate the role of the ideal L2 self and ought-to L2 self as well as L2 learning experience in two important language learner populations who study English in a single context, Budapest, the capital city of Hungary, and thereby provide empirical support for the theory of the L2 Motivational Self System. For this purpose, we applied multiple-group structural equation modelling and set up a model describing the interplay of students' learning experiences, self-concept and motivated behaviour. Using the same measurement scales and within the framework of the same model, we compared how the motivational and attitudinal dispositions of secondary school pupils and university students differed.

Our hypothetical model is presented in Figure 5.1. The criterion measure employed in our study was *motivated learning behaviour,* one of the most important antecedents of learning achievement (Dörnyei, 2005), which was defined as effort expended to achieve a goal, desire to learn the language, and importance attached to the task of learning the language. In accordance with Dörnyei's (2005) model, three antecedent variables were linked to the criterion measure: the *ideal L2 self,* the *ought-to L2 self* and *L2 learning experience.* As the ought-to L2 self dimension supposedly contains extrinsic motivational forces, we hypothesised that it would be affected by *parental encouragement,* that is, parents' views on the importance and necessity of language learning, *knowledge orientation,* which covers the instrumental value of English with the help of which students can gain more knowledge about the world, and *international posture,* that is, students' views of the role of English as a lingua franca. As for the *ideal L2 self,* we proposed that *L2 learning experience, international posture* and the *ought-to L2 self* will have an influence on students' wish to become competent speakers of English. We postulated that positive experiences concerning L2 learning will help the formation of students' images of themselves as competent language users, and

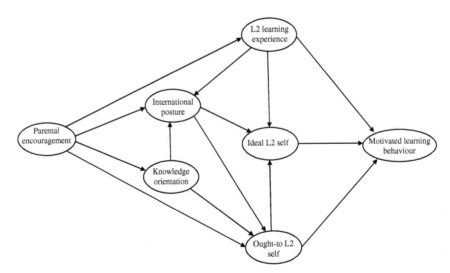

Figure 5.1 Schematic representation of the initially tested model for both samples

other extrinsic motivational variables such as the international position of English and the respondents' ought-to L2 selves will also contribute to the process of developing salient L2 selves. In a previous study using the same data set, we found that in the regression equation with ideal L2 self as the criterion variable, *L2 learning experience* and *international posture* were the best predictor variables (Kormos & Csizér, 2008). Previous studies carried out in Hungary showed that milieu plays an important role in forming and sustaining students' L2 learning motivation (see for example Dörnyei *et al.*, 2006; Kormos & Csizér, 2005), therefore we hypothesised that parental encouragement would contribute to the participants' L2 learning experience, knowledge orientation and their ought-to L2 selves.

Method

Participants

In our research we investigated language learners from Budapest, the capital of Hungary. Budapest is the largest city in the country, where one fifth of the total Hungarian population resides. In many respects, Budapest is similar to major metropolitan cities in Europe, with the exception that in Hungary most of the population is mono-lingual: according to the 2000 census, 92.3% of the population claimed to be ethnic Hungarian and the proportion with Hungarian as their mother tongue was even higher, 98.2% (Demographic Yearbook, 2004). In our research we used criterion-sampling. As for secondary school students, we included three schools that fell into the range of institutions with an average quality of teaching and average student population based on the rank order of schools in terms of the number of students admitted to university (National Institute for Public Education, 2004). Two of the schools were state schools, and in order to represent learners from the private sector of education, we also selected a church-owned school. The three schools were from different geographical locations of the city in order to represent students from various social backgrounds. All the students in the second and third year studying English were asked to fill in the questionnaires. Altogether 202 learners, 80 male and 122 female, responded to our questions in the secondary school sample. The average age of students was 16.5 years. English is not a compulsory language in Hungarian secondary schools, but it is the most frequently studied language (Halász & Lannert, 2007). When enrolling in secondary school, students can choose which foreign language they would like to study. The level of students' proficiency in the investigated sample was between pre-intermediate and intermediate.

In selecting the university students, we paid attention to representing the various fields of study one can pursue in Budapest and to including

Table 5.1 Summary of participants

	N	*Male*	*Female*
Sample 1			
Secondary school students	202	80	122
Sample 2			
College students	124	29	95
University students	106	44	62
Total	432	153	279

learners both from colleges and universities (see Table 5.1). 124 college students and 106 university students responded to our questions. The students' average age was 21.5 years, and 157 of them were female and 73 male. Studying foreign languages is voluntary at universities, and students are required to pay for foreign language instruction. Most students in the sample were preparing for one of the accredited intermediate level proficiency exams.

Instruments

Each of the latent variables in the model was measured by several five-point scale Likert-type questionnaire items. The questions were adapted from two sources: a previous motivation questionnaire used by Dörnyei and Csizér in a variety of Hungarian research projects (for an overview see Dörnyei *et al.*, 2006) and from a newly developed questionnaire by Ryan (2005). The questionnaire consisted of 65 Likert-scale items and a ten item section containing multiple choice and short answer questions that provided background information about the participants. Below we give a brief summary of the definitions of the latent motivational concepts that the questionnaire intended to measure with sample items.

- *Parental encouragement*: The extent to which parents encourage their children to study English. Example: My parents really encourage me to study English.
- *L2 learning experience*: The extent to which students like learning English. Example: I really enjoy learning English.
- *Knowledge orientation*: Students' views on how learning English will help them gain information about the world around them. Example: Studying English will help me to become more knowledgeable.

- *International posture:* Students' attitudes to English as an international language. Example: Studying English will help me to understand people from all over the world.
- *Ideal L2 self:* Students' views of themselves as successful L2 speakers. Example: I like to think of myself as someone who will be able to speak English.
- *Ought-to L2 self:* Students' perceptions of how important learning English is in the opinion of significant others. Example: If I fail to learn English, I will be letting other people down.
- *Motivated learning behaviour:* Students' efforts and persistence in learning English. Example: I am willing to work hard at learning English.

Procedures

Gálik (2006) translated the questionnaire and piloted it by asking two secondary school students to think aloud while filling it in. Potentially problematic items were reworded, and the instrument was administered to 111 secondary school students (Gálik, 2006). Following the factor and reliability analysis of this pilot run, we omitted or reworded unreliable items. The final version of the questionnaire was either mailed or personally delivered to the secondary schools, universities and colleges, where a person who agreed to take charge of the administration of the questionnaires distributed them among teachers and collected the filled in questionnaires. (A copy of the final version of the questionnaire is available in Appendix A.)

Multiple-group structural equation modelling (SEM) was applied to evaluate the relations between the various latent variables investigated in the study, using the software AMOS 4.0. First, *measurement models* were drawn up in accordance with the earlier factor analytical results reported in Csizér and Dörnyei (2005), Dörnyei *et al.* (2006) and Kormos and Csizér (2008) on similar datasets. Following this, the various latent variables were combined into a *full structural model* on the basis of theoretical considerations as well as the correlational and regression analyses conducted in the previous phases of the research (see above). The two models for secondary school students and university students were compared by a multi-group procedure, that is, the two models were fitted simultaneously in order to assess possible differences in the structural models. To assess the overall model fit, we used indices most often advised in the SEM literature (Byrne, 2001) and besides the chi-square statistics and the CMIN/df (chi-square divided by the degrees of freedom), we report additional indices: Comparative Fit Index (CFI) (Fan *et al.*, 1999; Hu & Bentler, 1999), the Bentler-Bonett normed fit index (NFI), the Tucker-Lewis coefficient (TLI), the root mean square error of approximation (RMSEA) (Browne & Cudeck, 1993; Fan *et al.*, 1999; Hu & Bentler, 1999) and the Parsimony-adjusted Comparative Fit Index (PCFI).

Results

The final models

As a first step, the initial model was submitted to evaluation using maximum likelihood estimation simultaneously for both the secondary school and university samples (Byrne, 2001). It was found that although the hypothetical model provided acceptable joint model-data fit indices for the two samples (e.g. CFI = 0.985 and chi square/df = 1.879), there were two relations that turned out to be non-significant for both samples (international posture → ought-to L2 self and knowledge orientation → ought-to L2 self), and thus these paths were removed from the initial models. In addition, there were three paths that proved to be significant only for one of our samples (ought-to L2 self → motivated learning behaviour for the university student sample, and parental encouragement → international posture and ought-to L2 self → ideal L2 self for the secondary school sample). In sum, the final model contains 11 significant relationships for secondary school students and ten for the university student sample. Figure 5.2a and b present the schematic representation of the final model with the standardised estimates for each sample studied, and Table 5.2 presents various joint goodness of fit measures.

As can be seen in Table 5.2, the chi square/df ratio is under the usually recommended value of 2 (Byrne, 1989). Nevertheless, as we pointed out earlier, it is advisable to rely on more than one fit index, therefore, we also examined alternative fit indices. These all indicate a very good fit for the joint models, and thus we can conclude that the models in Figure 5.2a and b provide an adequate representation of our data. As a next step, we compared the paths in the structural model in order to find out whether there are any significant differences between the structural models for the two investigated samples. Apart from the three paths that are not present in both models (*parental encouragement →international posture, ought-to L2 self →ideal L2 self,* and *ought-to L2 self →motivated learning behaviour*), there is one path for which the critical ratio for differences showed significant difference. The relation between *ideal L2 self→ motivated learning behaviour* is significantly stronger for university students (C.R. = 2.164) than for secondary students.

Discussion

Overall the results of the structural equation modelling of our questionnaire data provide support for Dörnyei's (2005) theory of the Motivational Self System in a Hungarian context. The model reveals that

(a)

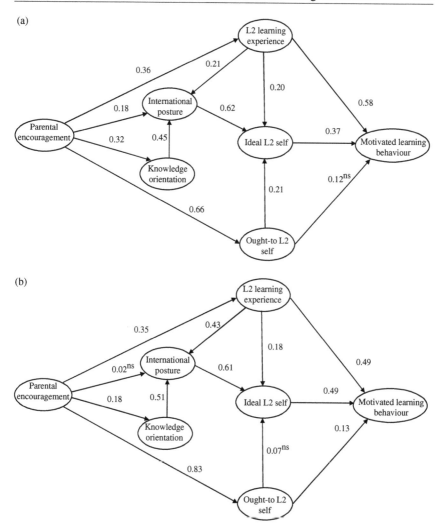

(b)

Figure 5.2 (a) The final model for secondary school students with standardised estimates. (b) The final model for university students with standardised estimates

the latent dimensions measuring ideal L2 self and L2 learning experience contribute significantly to motivated learning behaviour in both of the investigated populations. The ought-to L2 self, however, seems to play a limited role in predicting the effort Hungarian students invest in language learning, as in the university student sample its relation to motivated behaviour is very weak, and in the case of the secondary school students, the correlation between ought-to L2 self and motivated

Table 5.2 Joint selected fit measures for the final models

Chi square/df ratio	1.876
CFI	0.985
NFI	0.968
NNFI	0.980
RMSEA	0.045
PCFI	0.845

behaviour is not significant. In the model the three components of Dörnyei's model – the ideal L2 self, ought-to L2 self and L2 learning experience – are either not related at all to each other or show only weak correlations. This indicates that these three constructs are clearly different and independent motivational variables.

Our model reveals that the ideal L2 self seems to play a more substantial role in determining motivated behaviour than the ought-to L2 self. This finding is not surprising in the light of studies on the psychology of education, which have shown that intrinsic interest and a strong self-concept, as embodied by the construct of the ideal L2 self, are more powerful predictors of how much effort students are willing to invest in learning than extrinsic motivational forces (Deci & Ryan, 1985, 2002). A strong self-concept, which expresses students' self-perceptions and their confidence about succeeding in the learning task, has not only been assumed to be a predictor variable but even a prerequisite for achieving a particular learning goal (for a review see Zimmerman, 1989; Zimmerman & Schunk, 2007). The highly important role of the ideal L2 self in influencing motivated behaviour also indicates that this new construct might rightfully take over the place of integrativeness in the field of L2 motivation research (for comparative data on integrativeness and the ideal L2 self, see Taguchi *et al.*, this volume; Ryan, this volume).

In our initial model we hypothesised that both the ideal L2 self and the ought-to L2 self would be influenced by students' attitudes to the international status of the English language. Our results, however, suggest that international posture is only related to students' idealised images of themselves, and it does not correlate with students' ought-to L2 self. Our study thus supports previous investigations that have shown in an Asian setting (e.g. Lamb, 2004; Warden & Lin, 2000; Yashima, 2000, 2002) and in Hungary (Kormos & Csizér, 2008) that students' attitude to the role of English in our globalised world is not only a highly important driving force in L2 learning, but also contributes to students' future image of themselves as successful language learners. It seems therefore that in the Hungarian setting the students' views about the global significance of English do not act as an extrinsic motivating factor, but are internalised motives that are very strongly related to the students' L2 self-concept. The finding that knowledge orientation contributes positively to attitudes related to international English shows that for Hungarian learners, English serves as an important tool for gaining knowledge about the world around them via the information channels provided by globalised mass media such as the Internet.

Regarding the ought-to L2 self, the model supports our initial hypothesis that parental influence would positively contribute to the formation of this type of self-concept for both age groups. Our model indicates that even for young adults the relationship between parental encouragement and ought-to L2 self is very strong. This shows that in the investigated setting, the ought-to L2 self is entirely socially constructed, that is, students' views of what attributes they should possess to meet the expectations of their environment are formed by the attitudes of their immediate learning environment. Higgins's (1987) self-discrepancy theory also indicates that one's ought-to self is primarily shaped by significant others, and in the case of teenagers and young adults, the environmental influences concerning language learning in a Hungarian setting primarily originate from the students' parents. From interviews we conducted with Hungarian language learners aged 13 and 14 (Kormos & Csizér, 2007), it became apparent that language learners receive a great amount of encouragement and if possible, also actual help from their families. Our interviewees reported that parents, regardless of whether they speak foreign languages or not, consider it highly important that their children successfully acquire English. As the model reveals, parental encouragement has a number of direct and indirect effects, and many of the values attached to English language competence are internalised by the students in their ideal L2 self. The model shows that parental encouragement also contributes to the students' non-internalised L2 self-concept, but the ought to L2 self is not an important component of the model of language learning motivation in the investigated Hungarian sample. In the Hungarian setting, where the language of the country is spoken by very few people in Europe and where the national economy is highly dependent on foreign investments and multi-national enterprises, learners from a very young age are aware of the fact that their career prospects are dependent on L2 competence. Children are also surrounded by the products of globalised mass media in English as early as when they start using computers. These factors are responsible for the finding that by the age of 16 students internalise the values attached to the importance of speaking English, and external incentives embodied by the ought-to L2 self play a limited role in how much effort students invest in language learning.

The third important component of the model is L2 learning experience, which expresses students' attitude to learning English. Previous research in the field of L2 learning motivation also indicates that classroom factors including the teacher exert an important influence on what learning experiences students have and how much effort they are willing to invest in language learning (Nikolov, 1999). Our results also show that although it seems imperative that students have an intrinsic interest in learning an L2 and have a strong L2 self-concept, the role of the language learning situation is also essential. Positive attitudes to the learning context and the teacher as well as motivating activities, tasks, and teaching materials seem to influence both the learners' self-concept as well as how enthusiastically they study an L2. Thus, our findings highlight the importance of Dörnyei's (2001) argument that it is largely the teachers' responsibility to motivate students.

If we examine the significant differences between the models of the two groups of students, we find that the ideal L2 self has a stronger effect on motivated learning behaviour in the case of university students than for secondary school students. If we consider the students' self-concept in general, we can see that students' self-image goes through considerable changes in the period of adolescence (Carlson, 1965), and therefore their ideal L2 self is also under transformation at this age. University students, however, are in a period of their lives when they have a fairly stable self-image, but it is still flexible (Carlson, 1965); therefore the L2 self can easily form part of their self-image. In line with this, Kormos and Csizér (2008) found that university students had the strongest L2 self-concept out of the three populations (secondary school children, university students and adult learners) they investigated. The formation of the ideal L2 self can also be influenced by several factors not included in this study. For example, significant differences in students' future image of themselves as competent speakers of English might also be due to the fact that secondary school students experience a limited amount of contact with speakers of English, and thus do not yet perceive the high importance of being able to use English in the future. The finding that for secondary school students the role of the ideal L2 self is smaller than that of language learning experience, whereas for university students these two factors are of equal importance, might also be explained with reference to the results of previous Hungarian studies. These studies indicate that language learning experiences are slightly more important for younger learners (see Kormos & Csizér, 2008). We should not forget that for secondary school students, English is just another subject at school. Therefore L2 learning experiences gained in the classroom have a great effect on how much effort students are willing to invest in language learning. For university students, attitudes to language learning might be somewhat less important, as their relatively stronger and more developed L2 concept might potentially compensate even for the negative experiences of the learning situation.

The important role of L2 learning experiences in affecting attitudes to English as an international language in the case of university students might be related to the fact that most participating university students were taking part in ESP (English for Special Purposes) courses. It seems that the extent to which ESP courses provided students with positive learning experiences, that is, were among others relevant to their future needs and succeeded in demonstrating the importance of English as a lingua franca in their future profession might have a considerable impact on their international posture.

Conclusion

The research we reported in this Chapter investigated the effects of the ideal and ought-to L2 selves on Hungarian foreign language learners' motivated learning behaviour by means of structural equation modelling. The two groups we compared represented secondary school students and non-language major university students in a primarily monolingual context, where language learning is usually confined to classroom settings. Our models indicated that both in the case of secondary school and university students, motivated learning behaviour was partly determined by the ideal L2 self, that is, the extent to which students could imagine themselves as competent language users in the future. The other important determinant of language learning effort in our samples was the dimension of language learning experiences, the effect of which was found to be stronger than that of the ideal L2 self in the case of secondary school students, while for university students the ideal L2 self and language learning experiences played an equally important role. This finding suggests that motivational forces originating from the language classroom have great influence on how much effort students are willing to invest in language learning, and highlights the importance of motivational teaching practice (Dörnyei, 2001). The role of the ought-to L2 self seemed to be marginal, as its contribution to shaping students' learning behaviour was weak and reached the level of significance only for the university student population. The main determinants of the students' self-concept were international posture, knowledge orientation, language learning experiences and parental encouragement. Students' ought-to L2 self was found to be socially constructed as parental encouragement was the only factor with a significant contribution towards this type of self. The students' idealised images of themselves were influenced by language learning attitudes and students' attitudes towards English as an international language. Our research underlines the importance of self-concept in affecting motivated behaviour and shows that self-regulated learning is hardly possible unless students have a positive image of themselves as users of another language.

Our results reveal that how students see themselves as future language users might change with age, and therefore the impact of future self images on motivated learning might also vary. In line with Dörnyei and Ottó's (1998) process model of motivation, we have to bear in mind that both the ideal and ought-to L2 self might also be subject to changes in students' language learning history.

Our model is highly context-specific as its structure is largely influenced by the fact that only two age groups from one particular setting participated in our study. The main limitation of our research is that our participants were only from one region of the country, the capital city, which is thought to be much more cosmopolitan than other settlements of Hungary. Therefore, it is expected that certain scales such as English as an international language might play a different role if other parts of the country were surveyed. Finally, we have to note that future research should also be targeted at investigating the role of language learning experience and other possible determinants of the ideal and ought-to L2 self.

Acknowledgements

The research presented in this article was completed as part of the T047111 project of the Hungarian Academy of Sciences Research Funds (OTKA). We thank Stephen Ryan for making the questionnaire available to us. We are grateful to Éva Barta, Klára Bereczky, Judit Borbély, Mariann Dolgos, Myrtil Fóris, Szilvia Hegyi, Dénes Neumayer, Ildikó Káldosné Szendrői, Júlia Láng, Mónika Sápi, Judit Sárvári, Mónika Victor, Katalin Zöldi as well as to Babilon and Tudomány Language Schools for helping us administer the questionnaires.

References

Browne, M.W. and Cudeck, R. (1993) Alternative ways of assessing model fit. In K.A. Bollen and J.S. Long (eds) *Testing Structural Models* (pp. 136–162). Newbury Park, CA: Sage.
Byrne, B.M. (1989) *A Primer of LISREL: Basic Applications and Programming for Confirmatory Factor Analytic Model.* New York: Springer-Verlag.
Byrne, B.M. (2001) *Structural Equation Modeling with AMOS: Basic Concepts, Applications, and Programming.* Mahwah, NJ: Lawrence Erlbaum.
Carlson, R. (1965) Stability and change in the adolescent's self-image. *Child Development* 36, 659–666.
Crystal, D. (2003) *English as a Global Language* (2nd edn). Cambridge: Cambridge University Press.

Csizér, K. and Dörnyei, Z. (2005) The internal structure of language learning motivation and its relationship with language choice and learning effort. *Modern Language Journal* 89 (1), 19–36.

Deci, E.L. and Ryan, R.M. (1985) *Intrinsic Motivation and Self-Determination in Human Behaviour.* New York: Plenum.

Deci, E.L. and Ryan, R.M. (eds) (2002) *Handbook of Self-Determination.* Rochester, NY: University of Rochester Press.

Demographics Yearbook (2004) Budapest: Central Statistical Office.

Dörnyei, Z. (1990) Conceptualizing motivation in foreign-language learning. *Language Learning* 40, 45–78.

Dörnyei, Z. (2001) *Motivational Strategies.* Cambridge: Cambridge University Press.

Dörnyei, Z. (2005) *The Psychology of the Language Learner: Individual Differences in Second Language Acquisition.* Mahwah, NJ: Lawrence Erlbaum.

Dörnyei, Z. and Ottó, I. (1998) Motivation in action: A process model of L2 motivation. *Working Papers in Applied Linguistics* (Thames Valley University, London) 47, 173–210.

Dörnyei, Z., Csizér, K. and Németh, N. (2006) *Motivation, Language Attitudes and Globalisation: A Hungarian Perspective.* Clevedon: Multilingual Matters.

Fan, X., Thomson, B. and Wang L. (1999) Effects of sample size, estimation methods, model specification on structural modelling fit indexes. *Structural Equation Modelling: A Multidisciplinary Journal* 6, 56–83.

Gálik, N. (2006) An investigation into the relationship of motivational and attitudinal dispositions and the L2 Motivational Self-System. Unpublished M.A. thesis. Budapest: Eötvös University.

Gardner, R.C. (2001) Integrative motivation and second language acquisition. In Z. Dörnyei and R. Schmidt (eds) *Motivation and Second Language Acquisition* (pp. 1–19). Honolulu, HI: University of Hawaii Press.

Guiora, A. and Acton, W. (1979) Personality and language: A restatement. *Language Learning* 29, 193–204.

Halász, G. and Lannert, J. (2007) Report on the Hungarian state education, 2006. Budapest: OKI.

Higgins, E.T. (1987) Self-discrepancy: A theory of relating self and affect. *Psychological Review* 94, 319–340.

Hu L-T. and Bentler, P.M. (1999) Cutoff criteria for indexes in covariance structure analysis: Conventional criteria versus new alternatives. *Structural Equation Modelling: A Multidisciplinary Journal* 6, 1–55.

Kimura, Y., Nakata, Y. and Okumura, T. (2001) Language learning motivation of EFL learners in Japan: A cross-sectional analysis of various learning milieus. *JALT Journal* 23 (1), 47–68.

Kormos, J. and Csizér, K. (2005) A szülők szerepe az idegen nyelvi motivációban. [The role of parents in foreign language motivation]. *Magyar Pedagógia* 105 (1), 29–40.

Kormos, J. and Csizér, K. (2008) Age-related differences in the motivation of learning English as a foreign language: Attitudes, selves and motivated learning behaviour. *Language Learning* 58 (2), 327–355.

Lamb, M. (2004) Integrative motivation in a globalizing world. *System* 32, 3–19.

National Institute for Public Education, Hungary (2004) The list of secondary schools. Online at http://www.oki.hu/oldal.php?tipus = cikk&kod = kozepiskolai-Neuwirth-Kozepiskolak. Accessed 30 July 2008.

Nikolov, M. (1999) 'Why do you learn English?' 'Because the teacher is short.' A study of Hungarian children's foreign language motivation. *Language Teaching Research* 3, 33–56.

Ryan, S. (2005) *Motivational Factors Questionnaire*. Nottingham: School of English Studies, University of Nottingham.

Skutnabb-Kangas, T. (2000) *Linguistic Genocide in Education – or Worldwide Diversity and Human Rights?* Mahwah: NJ: Lawrence Erlbaum.

Warden, C.A. and Lin, H.J. (2000) Existence of integrative motivation in Asian EFL setting. *Foreign Language Annals* 33, 535–547.

Widdowson, H.G. (1994) The ownership of English. *TESOL Quarterly* 28, 377–389.

Yashima, T. (2000) Orientations and motivations in foreign language learning: A study of Japanese college students. *JACET Bulletin* 31, 121–134.

Yashima, T. (2002) Willingness to communicate in a second language: The Japanese EFL context. *Modern Language Journal* 86, 54–66.

Young, D.J. (1992) Language anxiety from the foreign language specialist's perspective: Interviews with Krashen, Omaggio Hadley, Terrell, and Rardin. *Foreign Language Annals* 25, 157–172.

Zimmerman, B.J. (1989) Theories of self-regulated learning and academic achievement. An overview and analysis. In B.J. Zimmerman and D.H. Schunk (eds) *Learning and Achievement: Theoretical Perspectives* (pp. 1–38). Berlin: Springer-Verlag.

Zimmerman, B.J. and Schunk, D.H. (2007) Motivation: An essential dimension of self-regulated learning. In D.H. Schunk and B.J. Zimmerman (eds) *Motivation and Self-Regulated Learning: Theory, Research and Applications* (pp. 1–30). New York: Lawrence Erlbaum.

Appendix A

Motivation Questionnaire for College and University Students in Hungary

We would like to ask you to help us by answering the following questions concerning foreign language learning. This is not a test so there are no 'right' or 'wrong' answers, and you don't even have to give your name. We are interested in your personal opinion. Please give your answers sincerely as only this will guarantee the success of the investigation. Thank you very much for your help.

I. In the following section we would like you to answer some questions by simply giving marks from 1 to 5.

5 = very much, 4 = quite a lot, 3 = so-so, 2 = not really, 1 = not at all.

For example, if you like 'apples' very much, 'bean soup' not very much, and 'spinach' not at all, write this:

How much do you like apples?	⑤	4	3	2	1
How much do you like bean soup?	5	4	3	②	1
How much do you like spinach?	5	4	3	2	①

Please put one (and only one) whole number in each box and don't leave out any of them. Thanks.

5 =very much, 4 =quite a lot, 3 =so-so, 2 =not really, 1 =not at all.

1. How much do you like the TV programmes made in the United States?	5	4	3	2	1
2. How much do you like the people who live in the United States?	5	4	3	2	1
3. How much do you think knowing English would help your future career?	5	4	3	2	1
4. How important a role do you think the United Kingdom plays in the world?	5	4	3	2	1
5. How much do you like English?	5	4	3	2	1
6. How much do you like the films made in the United States?	5	4	3	2	1
7. How much would you like to travel to the USA?	5	4	3	2	1
8. How much do you think knowing English would help you if you travelled abroad in the future?	5	4	3	2	1
9. How rich and developed do you think the United Kingdom is?	5	4	3	2	1
10. How important do you think learning English is in order to learn more about the culture and art of its speakers?	5	4	3	2	1
11. How much do you like the pop music of the USA?	5	4	3	2	1
12. How much do you like the people who live in the United Kingdom?	5	4	3	2	1
13. How important do you think English is in the world these days?	5	4	3	2	1
14. How rich and developed do you think the United States is?	5	4	3	2	1
15. How much would you like to become similar to the people who speak English?	5	4	3	2	1
16. How much do you like the magazines made in the United States?	5	4	3	2	1
17. How much do you like meeting foreigners from English-speaking countries?	5	4	3	2	1

18. How much do you think knowing English would help you to become a more knowledgeable person?	5	4	3	2	1
19. How important a role do you think the United States plays in the world?	5	4	3	2	1
20. How much would you like to travel to the UK?	5	4	3	2	1

II. Now there are going to be statements some people agree with and some people don't. We would like to know to what extent they describe your own feelings or situation. After each statement you'll find five boxes. Please put an 'X' in the box which best expresses how true the statement is about your feelings or situation. For example, if you like skiing very much, put an 'X' in the last box:

	Absolutely true	Mostly true	Partly true partly untrue	Not really true	Not true at all
I like skiing very much.	X				

There are no right or wrong answers – we are interested in your personal opinion.

	Absolutely true	Mostly true	Partly true partly untrue	Not really true	Not true at all
21. I am sure I will be able to learn a foreign language well					
22. I would feel uneasy speaking English with a native speaker					
23. People around me tend to think that it is a good thing to know foreign languages					

	Absolutely true	Mostly true	Partly true partly untrue	Not really true	Not true at all
24. It embarrasses me to volunteer answers in our English class.					
25. My parents really encourage me to study English.					
26. Learning English is really great.					
27. The things I want to do in the future require me to speak English.					
28. For me to be an educated person I should be able to speak English.					
29. I am willing to work hard at learning English.					
30. If I could speak English well, I could get to know people from other countries. (Not just English-speaking countries.)					
31. I think I am the type who would feel anxious and ill at ease if I had to speak to someone in a foreign language.					
32. I would get tense if a foreigner asked me for directions in English.					
33. I think that foreign languages are important school subjects.					
34. I always feel that the other students speak English better than I do.					

	Absolutely true	Mostly true	Partly true partly untrue	Not really true	Not true at all
35. My parents encourage me to practise my English as much as possible.					
36. I really enjoy learning English.					
37. Whenever I think of my future career, I imagine myself being able to use English.					
38. Nobody really cares whether I learn English or not.					
39. It is very important for me to learn English.					
40. Studying English will help me to understand people from all over the world. (Not just English-speaking countries.)					
41. Learning a foreign language is a difficult task.					
42. If there was an opportunity to meet an English speaker, I would feel nervous.					
43. My parents consider foreign languages important school subjects.					
44. I get nervous when I am speaking in my English class.					
45. My parents have stressed the importance English will have for me in my future.					

	Absolutely true	Mostly true	Partly true partly untrue	Not really true	Not true at all
46. I find learning English really interesting.					
47. I like to think of myself as someone who will be able to speak English.					
48. A knowledge of English would make me a better educated person.					
49. In the future, I really would like to communicate with foreigners.					
50. The job I imagine having in the future requires that I speak English well.					
51. I would like to be able to use English to communicate with people from other countries.					
52. I am worried that native speakers of English would find my English strange.					
53. Learning foreign languages makes me fear that I will feel less Hungarian because of it.					
54. I am afraid the other students will laugh at me when I speak English.					
55. My parents feel that I should really try to learn English.					
56. I always look forward to our English classes.					

	Absolutely true	Mostly true	Partly true partly untrue	Not really true	Not true at all
57. For people where I live learning English is not really necessary.					
58. If an English course was offered in the future, I would like to take it.					
59. In the future, I imagine myself working with people from other countries. (Not just English-speaking countries.)					
60. If my dreams come true, I will use English effectively in the future.					
61. If I fail to learn English, I'll be letting other people down.					
62. When I hear an English song on the radio, I listen carefully and try to understand all the words.					
63. I can imagine speaking English with international friends.					
64. Learning English is necessary because it is an international language.					
65. I can honestly say that I am really doing my best to learn English.					
66. When I think about my future, it is important that I use English.					

	Absolutely true	Mostly true	Partly true partly untrue	Not really true	Not true at all
67. If I could have access to English-speaking TV stations, I would try to watch them often.					
68. I am determined to push myself to learn English.					
69. Learning English is one of the most important aspects of my life.					

III. Finally, please answer these few personal questions.

70. If you could choose, which foreign languages would you choose to learn next year at school (or work)? Please mark three languages in order of importance.

        1)....................
        2)....................
        3)....................

71. Your gender? (Please underline): male   female

72. How old are you?

73. What foreign languages are you learning besides English?

74. What college/university you attend?

75. What do you study?

76. How old were you when you started learning English?

Have you answered all the questions? Thank you!

Chapter 6

Self and Identity in L2 Motivation in Japan: The Ideal L2 Self and Japanese Learners of English

STEPHEN RYAN

Introduction

The origins of this study can be traced back to my earliest experiences as a relatively young language teacher first arriving in Japan. Although I had experience of language teaching in other (European) contexts, I was immediately intrigued and more than a little confused by what seemed to be occurring in my classrooms in Japan. In my classes, I was regularly encountering an apparently contradictory mixture of raw enthusiasm and extreme apathy that seemed at variance with expectations nurtured in other learning environments.

As a practising teacher, I had two basic templates of language learning to turn to for guidance at that time. One was the one-size-fits-all model of second language education promoted by the international ELT industry and the other was a notion of Japanese exceptionalism prevalent within the Japanese education system, which held that the Japanese context was unique and that theories developed elsewhere were of little relevance. Neither of these seemed satisfactory; one appeared to deny the particularities of local context whereas the other placed too great an emphasis on them, rejecting the possibility of commonality with other cultural settings.

It was these early frustrations that prompted my initial interest in second language learning motivation theory. However, this avenue soon directed me towards that familiar feeling of a significant gap between theory and my own classroom reality. Initially, my uncritical approach led me to believe that the problem was with my classes rather than with theory but, over time, a gradual accumulation of experience and familiarity with theoretical developments convinced me of the possibility and necessity of a model of second language learning motivation robust enough to account for commonalities across cultural settings yet sensitive enough to allow for the idiosyncrasies of local context.

In this chapter, I intend to consider one approach to the study of L2 motivation – Dörnyei's L2 motivational self system (Dörnyei, 2005; see also this volume) – that presents a potential framework for achieving these goals. The concept of an L2 self is not merely concerned with reconciling generalities of the language learning experience with the particularities of local cultural context; it offers the possibility of moving the research agenda forward in a whole range of other exciting new directions, but I mention it here because it was this aspect that first attracted me to the theory and the dimension that forms the foundations of this chapter.

Still in its theoretical infancy, it is vital that the concept of an L2 self system is not allowed to mature into yet another dichotomous, reductionist model of language learning motivation, distinguishable only by its fashionable terminology. My purpose here is not so much to elaborate on the theory of the L2 self concept – this is covered elsewhere in the current volume (see chapter by Dörnyei) – but to empirically test its central component, the ideal L2 self, as a suitable base for reinterpreting efforts made to learn a language – in this case, specifically English. I do this in a manner consistent with the methods developed by Dörnyei and his associates (Csizér & Dörnyei, 2005a, 2005b; Dörnyei & Csizér, 2002; Dörnyei *et al.*, 2006) in Hungary as I believe it is vital to maintain an element of continuity with previous research and validate the approach within the parameters of existing paradigms as a necessary step to moving the research agenda forward.

My principal concern (Ryan, 2006: 23) is with understanding those learners who make 'extraordinary efforts to learn a language that holds out little immediate prospect of material reward and offers scarce opportunity to establish direct contact with its speakers'. Though firmly located in the Japanese educational setting, I believe this study to be of relevance to other contexts, especially those where there exists a feeling of being isolated from, or ignored by, not only the English-speaking world but also mainstream second language learning theory.

The Need for Change

As MacIntyre (2007: 566) observes, 'Gardner's (1985) socioeducational model, with its focus on integrative motivation, has been considered the dominant model in the field for many years'. This model has come under repeated challenge in recent years, a challenge initiated by an intense theoretical debate that began in the 1990s (see Crookes & Schmidt, 1991; Dörnyei, 1994; Oxford & Shearin, 1994). As the scope and intensity of these challenges escalated, major questions have arisen regarding the role and relevance of integrativeness within the current research framework.

On the one hand, there are those such as Kim (2005), who make a convincing case for a clean break, developing alternative paradigms, and rejecting the sequence of constant modifications to existing models, forcefully arguing:

this process is a vicious circle and will perpetuate in L2 motivation research if we rely on the current positivistic paradigms in L2 motivation theories. Whatever potential concepts are included in the current L2 motivation paradigm would have inherent limitations from the start. (Kim, 2005: 307)

On the other, there is a persuasive counter-argument in favour of preserving and building on the valuable insights obtained from over 30 years of research within the social psychological tradition. MacIntyre *et al.* (Chapter 3, this volume) advise caution in abandoning the social psychological foundations of L2 motivation research in favour of currently fashionable concerns, which for the most part remain untested in the field. The danger in uprooting the research agenda is that L2 motivation research may stray into areas where it can only hope to scratch the surface of already established fields; expanding the research agenda may result in a wider yet ultimately shallow theory of language learning motivation.

In this study, I adopt the view that it is only through a meaningful engagement with the field's social psychological roots that L2 motivation researchers can move the agenda forward into new and unexplored directions. The strengths of the social psychological approach must be acknowledged, utilised and addressed on their own terms before the legitimacy of alternative approaches can be fully established. I see this study – firmly based in the quantitative methodology of the social psychological tradition – as serving as part of a bridge between established concepts within the socio-educational framework and possible future directions suggested by a self based interpretation. In this chapter, I will problematise two aspects of the concept of integrativeness – its cultural generalisability and the nature of an English-speaking community within the context of globalisation – with a view to demonstrating how the affective dimension to language learning associated with a sense of emotional identification with a language and its speakers is in urgent need of a thorough and convincing reassessment.

Integrativeness and Cultural Context

Gardner's (1985) initial conceptualisation of integrativeness was based on a body of meticulous, empirically grounded research conducted in the unique Canadian educational environment, and this setting had a profound influence on some of the theoretical conclusions drawn from the data. This raises questions regarding the relevance of these theoretical constructs when applied to other fundamentally different sociocultural settings.

Dörnyei (1990) questioned the applicability of the concept of integrativeness in EFL learning contexts where learners have little direct contact with an L2 community. In such learning environments, distinctions between integrativeness and instrumentality tend to be blurred, as notions of contact with the L2 community take on new meanings. For example, to a learner in rural China the notion of interacting with other English speakers is not purely integrative in the Gardnerian sense of the term – nor in any other generally accepted meaning of the verb to integrate; it is likely to overlap with a range of other factors some of which may be regarded as instrumental in other contexts, such as career or academic advancement and overseas travel.

Dörnyei's concerns have been echoed by numerous Japan-based studies (McClelland, 2000; Nakata, 1995; Sawaki, 1997; Yashima, 2002) summarised by Irie (2003) as finding 'positive attitudes to TL communities without a desire to assimilate into them', and by studies in other EFL contexts (see Coetzee-Van Rooy, 2006; Warden & Lin, 2000). On the other hand, evidence of an affective dimension to L2 learning similar to integrativeness has been identified in several other studies (see Dörnyei & Clément, 2001; Gardner & MacIntyre, 1993). Perhaps the situation is best summed up by Noels *et al.* (2000: 60) who argue that the socio-educational model as proposed by Gardner 'has relevance only in specific sociocultural contexts'.

This apparent contradiction has been referred to (Dörnyei, 2005) as the 'integrativeness enigma'. It was the exploration of this 'enigma' that led to the most consistent and convincing empirical probing of the concept of integrativeness, carried out by Dörnyei and a number of colleagues in a series of studies based in Hungary (Csizér & Dörnyei, 2005a, 2005b; Dörnyei & Csizér, 2002; Dörnyei *et al.*, 2006). In a large-scale longitudinal study of secondary school learners of English in Hungary, integrativeness was found to dominate all other motivational variables. It dominated as a factor in language choice: the correlation figure for integrativeness and the criterion measures was consistently only marginally lower than the multiple correlations for all the other motivational variables used in the study. That this finding was obtained in a context where the possibility of integration did not exist did not make any sense, demanding that the concept of integrativeness undergo some form of substantial reinterpretation. The theoretical directions proposed by those Hungarian studies – that what has previously been interpreted as integrativeness would be better understood as part of an L2 motivational self system – represent the starting point for my own study.

Learners of English and an English-speaking Community

MacIntyre (2007: 566) argues that '[t]he major motivation to learn another language is to develop a communicative relationship with people from another cultural group'. An early definition of an integrative orientation was the desire 'to learn more about the language group'

(Gardner & Lambert, 1959: 267), also characterised as 'a willingness to be like valued members of the language community' (Gardner & Lambert, 1959: 271). At first sight these definitions appear very similar, but upon closer inspection MacIntyre's 'another cultural group' appears more inclusive, allowing for greater flexibility and possibilities than Gardner's insistence on the definite article ('the language group'/'the language community'), implying a clearly defined and visible L2 community tied to fixed locations, with which the language learner can identify, and ultimately integrate. It may be the case that for some languages and in certain learning situations such recognisable L2 communities exist, but in an era of global flows of people, trade, and information, this is surely no longer true for most learners of English. Though the international ELT industry sometimes appears to believe otherwise, a portrayal of the English-speaking community as essentially Anglo-American is becoming increasingly irrelevant to many learners. A study of Indonesian learners of English carried out by Lamb (2004) found the following:

> In the minds of learners, English may not be associated with particular geographical or cultural communities but with a spreading international culture incorporating (inter alia) business, technological innovation, consumer values, democracy, world travel, and the multifarious icons of fashion, sport and music. (Lamb, 2004: 3)

The static characterisation of language communities presented by Gardner's socio-educational model appears incompatible with the dynamic, fluid reality of the global English-speaking community of which many young people from all over the world believe themselves to be an integral part. The concept of integrativeness is predicated on a clearly identifiable and available L2 community, but for vast numbers of learners around the world not only are notions of contact with an English-speaking community dissimilar to those envisaged by Gardner, but the concept of that community itself is an altogether more vague, abstract entity.

The challenge for learners of English in an era of globalisation is to somehow transcend barriers of time and space to engage with other members of an English-speaking community for, as Giddens (1991: 21) argues, 'the concept of globalisation is best understood as expressing fundamental aspects of time-space distanciation'. The use of the term integrativeness does not seem to do justice to the complexities of these processes.

Language Learning Motivation in the Japanese Context

The literature on language learning in Japan presents a fascinating, though often depressing picture. Nakata (2006: 166) observes: 'There is a general consensus that the educational system has resulted in Japanese learners with weak English communication ability and low motivation to learn the language'. Hayes (1979: 366) identifies one possible cause as being that 'Japanese do not want to learn English or, for that matter, any foreign language'. In my own case, one of the earliest papers I recall reading (Berwick & Ross, 1989) referred to Japan's 'motivational waste-land'. Though these descriptions represent something of a simplification or overstatement, they do raise intriguing questions as to why such perceptions persist.

Without going into a detailed analysis of the Japanese education system, I would like to draw attention to a major distinction in the nature of English education provision between the pretertiary and tertiary levels. I restrict my comments to English, for as Kubota (2002: 19) points out, 'English is *de facto* the only option ... students learning languages other than English account for less than 1 per cent of the enrolment'. For most secondary students in Japan, English has a clearly defined instrumental function, stripped of any communicative function, as content for a series of examinations that have profound consequences for future academic or career prospects (see Benson, 1991; Berwick & Ross, 1989; Brown & Yamashita, 1995). In contrast, McVeigh (2002) presents English at the tertiary level as lacking any obvious purpose, merely functioning as an inversion of what has gone before at the secondary level, leading to students 'exoticising' English. He uses the term 'fantasy English' to describe a situation in which English serves as a hollow vessel conducive to the fantasies of young people seeking something meaningful, fulfilling, practical and fun from their university education. At the secondary level, English is uncompromisingly prag-matic but at the university level, removed of this pragmatic function, it becomes an altogether more fuzzy and exotic entity. This distinction has far-reaching implications for how learners approach learning the language.

International posture

Perhaps the most important theoretical construct emerging from the Japanese context is Yashima's (2002; Yashima *et al.*, 2004; see also Yashima, this volume) notion of international posture. Yashima devel-oped the notion of international posture as a means of explaining how learners in contexts lacking meaningful direct contact with the speakers of a target language manage to relate to an L2 community. The main characteristics of international posture are described as an 'interest in foreign or international affairs, willingness to go overseas to stay or work, readiness to interact with intercultural partners, and, one hopes, openness or a non-ethnocentric attitude toward different cultures' (Yashima, 2002: 57).

International posture undoubtedly represents a major contribution to our understanding of second language learning motivation but I discuss it here for another reason. The development of the concept of international posture illustrates how the conclusions we as researchers can draw are inhibited by our methodologies. Professional researchers immersed in academia struggle with the complexities of identity and language learning, so how are we to expect young people – most of Yashima's research has been concerned with secondary students – to articulate a phenomenon that they are unlikely to have the words for? In many respects, the concept of international posture emerges from, and is ultimately limited by, a meta-language of language education familiar to young learners in Japan.

It might be rewarding to speculate on how the constituent elements of the concept of international posture could be reinterpreted as part of an altogether more powerful L2 self system. However, that would be beyond the remit of this chapter. Instead I will restrict my interest here to these central areas of investigation:

(1)   An attempt to validate Dörnyei's proposal of regarding the concept of an ideal L2 self as equivalent to integrativeness through a replication of elements of his Hungarian studies.
(2)   A consideration of the relative strengths of the ideal L2 self and integrativeness as a means of explaining motivated language learning behaviour.
(3)   A comparison of how the ideal L2 self and integrativeness perform across some of the mains sub-groups of the sample with a view to establishing the greater effectiveness of the ideal L2 self as a base for the study of language learning motivation.

The Study

This chapter reports on data obtained as part of a large-scale, nationwide study. That study had two fundamental aims. The first was to empirically test the concept of the ideal L2 self as suggested by the work of Dörnyei and his associates in Hungary (Csizér & Dörnyei, 2005a, 2005b; Dörnyei & Csizér, 2002; Dörnyei et al., 2006), and the second was to explore the concept within the Japanese educational setting. In order to achieve these twin goals, two parallel research instruments were designed: an ambitious, comprehensive 'Motivational Factors Questionnaire' (MFQ) that retains an essential link with previous research in the social psychological tradition, and a series of interviews with learners and users of English in Japan that aimed to explore some of the issues arising out of the quantitative data. Due to space limitations I will address only those aspects of the quantitative research instrument that are directly relevant to the research aims stated above.

Questionnaire participants

A total of 2397 learners of English participated in the main questionnaire study, which was conducted in two stages, the first occurring in December 2005 and the second in May 2006. Of these, 1177 (49.1%) were males and 1082 (45.1%) females. There was missing gender information for 138 (5.8%) participants. Participants were drawn from nine educational institutions across Japan, five tertiary institutions and four secondary institutions.

Instrument

Since many of the ideas informing this research were suggested by Dörnyei and colleagues' longitudinal study in Hungary (Csizér & Dörnyei, 2005a; Dörnyei & Clément, 2001; Dörnyei & Csizér, 2002; Dörnyei *et al.*, 2006), that study was employed as a base for the design of the principal research instrument.

The complete questionnaire consisted of a total of 100 six-point Likert type items ranging across 18 motivational variables, covering a broad spectrum of theoretical issues (see Appendix A for a list of variables and items in English). These variables were developed from previously published sources and adapted to the Japanese context by means of thorough piloting. (A complete list of all the variables used is provided in Table 6.1.) However, since many of these issues are not of immediate relevance to the current discussion and space is limited, I will confine my comments to seven main motivational factors identified and validated in the Hungarian research (see Table 6.2) and two new scales developed for the study: *ideal L2 self* and *intended learning effort*. This ideal L2 self scale represents the key theoretical construct in the study and consists of six items designed to explore individuals' visions of themselves as users of English and the relative strength or intensity of those visions. The original Hungarian studies used both language choice and intended effort as criterion measures but neither of these variables was entirely appropriate for the Japanese learning context. Therefore a new scale was created and labelled *intended learning effort*, based on the Hungarian *intended effort* scale, and employed as the principal measurement of motivated behaviour.

The overriding challenge in designing the principal research instrument was to achieve an accommodation between the twin aims of validating the theoretical approach suggested by the Hungarian research through a replication of those studies, and creating an instrument that

Table 6.1 Motivational variables ordered according to the strength of correlation with intended learning effort, with internal reliability coefficients

	Intended learning effort (a =0.86)	
	Cronbach alpha	Correlation
Attitudes to learning English	0.88	0.86**
Ideal L2 self	0.85	0.77**
Interest in foreign languages	0.70	0.65**
International empathy	0.74	0.65**
International contact	0.87	0.60**
Cultural interest	0.79	0.59**
Travel orientation	0.77	0.58**
Instrumentality	0.87	0.49**
Attitudes to L2 community	0.83	0.47**
Parental encouragement	0.79	0.42**
Milieu	0.66	0.20**
Self-confidence	0.57	0.20*
L1 willingness to communicate	0.87	0.17**
Fear of assimilation	0.67	0.09**
English anxiety	0.81	0.05*
Ethnocentrism	0.63	0.03

$*p < 0.01; **p < 0.001$ level

adequately addressed the needs of the Japanese context. In order to achieve this a compromise was reached in which items from the original Hungarian scales – carefully translated and piloted – were embedded into the Japanese questionnaire in a manner that allowed them to be extracted and analysed separately as elements of scales specifically designed for the Japanese case. In practice, this meant that an item such as *How much would you like to travel to English-speaking countries?* could function simultaneously as an element of two separate scales: in the first instance as part of the original *direct contact with L2 speakers* scale when used to replicate the Hungarian study, and secondly as part of a *travel orientation* scale employed in the subsequent exploration of the specific Japanese situation.

Table 6.2 Internal reliability of the variables imported from the Hungarian studies

	Number of items	Cronbach alpha
Cultural interest	4	0.73
Direct contact with L2 speakers	4	0.80
Instrumentality	4	0.78
Vitality	4	0.75
Integrativeness	3	0.58
Milieu	3	0.60
Linguistic self confidence	3	0.53

Results

Commonality between the Japanese and Hungarian data

The initial aim of this research was to test the findings of the large-scale longitudinal research programme carried out by Dörnyei and his colleagues in Hungary – and by extension the significant theoretical advances associated with that line of research – when applied to the Japanese English language learning context. Table 6.3 shows how the main motivational dimensions used in the Hungarian studies correlate with intended learning effort in Japan.

Analysis of Table 6.3 reveals both similarities and differences between the two sets of data. I will address the differences a little later but the strength of some of the similarities suggests that some of the key Hungarian findings are not peculiar to the local Hungarian context but are indicative of common patterns to be observed in learning environments where contact with the L2 target community is not immediately available. This is especially important in light of criticisms that models of motivation are culture specific and not generalisable; it also serves as a timely reminder that there is still much to learn from understanding better some of the generalities of the language learning experience that cut across nationality and culture.

The L2 community

There are marked differences in the correlation values for four of the scales: *milieu, direct contact with L2 speakers, cultural interest* and *vitality*. It is possible to categorise these variables as two sets of social relationships: one set involving the learner's social relationships with people immediately around them, and the other set concerning the learner's

Table 6.3 Correlations of the motivational variables imported from the Hungarian studies with intended learning effort, also showing the original Hungarian results

	Intended learning effort	
	Japanese results	*Hungarian results*[†]
Integrativeness	0.65	0.65
Instrumentality	0.42	0.47
Direct contact with L2 speakers	0.53	0.30
Vitality	0.30	0.18
Cultural interest	0.52	0.10
Milieu	0.13	0.33
Linguistic self-confidence	0.31	0.31
Multiple correlations	0.71	0.69

Note: All correlations significant at the $p < 0.001$ level
[†]Refers to the results reported for English/US in 2004 (Dörnyei, personal communication)

relationships – often imagined – with the speakers of the L2. In the Japanese study the correlation between milieu and effort is much lower than that found in Hungary, which suggests that there are important differences in the role the learner's immediate social relationships play in the language learning process. This is a major issue which, unfortunately, remains beyond the scope of this chapter; here I will restrict my comments to a consideration of the notions of an L2 community suggested by the data.

The correlation values in Table 6.3 for *direct contact with L2 speakers, cultural interest* and *vitality* show the Japanese figures to be much higher than the Hungarian. If *cultural interest* can be considered a form of indirect contact with speakers of the L2 and *vitality* represents the perceived ethnolinguistic vitality of the culture associated with the language, then these sets of figures are pointing to differences in attitudes towards contact with the L2 community.

In the Hungarian study, the items connected the L2 community specifically to the UK and US, whereas piloting showed that this UK association did not work well in the Japanese context and some items were rewritten accordingly. The UK dimension was completely removed and there is a strong possibility that this redefinition of the L2 community, which recognises the international nature of the English-speaking world, affected the results.

Table 6.4 Correlations of attitudes towards the L2 community with intended learning effort

	Intended learning effort
Attitudes towards English speakers (US)	0.31
Attitudes towards L2 speakers (English an international language)	0.51

Correlations significant at the $p < 0.001$ level

In order to investigate this a little further, I separated those items in the MFQ that referred to a specific, national (US) aspect of the L2 community from those that signified an English-speaking community with no specific national ties. Table 6.4 shows the correlations of these two differing notions of the L2 community with intended learning effort.

The correlation for the US-based English-speaking community is almost identical to that of the Hungarian study shown in Table 6.3, but when the element of nationality is removed from the notion of an English-speaking community, the correlation with learning effort is much higher. This is a particularly important finding, which suggests that learners of English in Japan regard the notion of an English-speaking community freed from the ties of nationality and locality to be a more powerful motivating factor than the static notion of a target language community implied in conventional interpretations of integrativeness. The case for integrative motivation is undermined by data showing that attitudes towards a vague, undefined L2 community correlate more highly with effort than attitudes to a fixed and readily identifiable L2 community. It may be that this vague conception of an English-speaking community is a more effective motivator because it presents to learners the possibility of legitimate, full membership of that community. In contrast, an L2 community defined by either geographical location or cultural tradition situates the learner as an outsider looking in, the impostor struggling to establish a legitimate claim to membership.

Integrativeness and ideal L2 self

Perhaps the most remarkable of all the results shown in Table 6.3 is the stability of the integrativeness correlations. As with the Hungarian study, integrativeness in the Japanese dataset is almost equal to the multiple correlation figures for all the variables. In the Hungarian study, this led to the conclusion that only integrativeness had a direct path to effort, and that other factors were mediated by integrativeness (which was then tested and verified using structural equation modelling by Csizér & Dörnyei, 2005b), and that therefore, in order to develop a more meaningful

Table 6.5 Correlation: Integrativeness and the ideal L2 self

	Ideal L2 self
Integrativeness	0.59

$p < 0.001$

understanding of language learning motivation, the concept of integrativeness needed to be reconsidered from a self perspective.

Table 6.5 shows a remarkably high correlation between integrativeness and ideal L2 self, which suggests that the two concepts may in fact be tapping into the same pool of emotional identification that learners feel towards the values of the language and its speakers.

The strength of this correlation, even though the individual items on the relative scales were ostensibly very different, lends support to the view that what was interpreted as integrativeness in early Canada-based research was simply one local manifestation of a wider sense of affiliation with the values associated with a language and the language community; in other contexts the same sense of affinity exists but may take other forms. This helps to explain the 'integrativeness enigma' (Dörnyei, 2005), whereby numerous studies have found integrativeness or something equivalent to be a significant factor in the motivation to learn a second language, yet many others have found the concept problematic. If we regard integrativeness as a specific local variation of a wider sense of emotional identification with a language, this both expands and clarifies the research agenda. On the one hand, there is an obvious need to explore distinct local conditions, yet on the other, there clearly exists a requirement to develop a comprehensive understanding of the affective dimension to language learning motivation. The strength of the correlation presented in Table 6.5 in conjunction with the behavioural impacts of notions of an English-speaking community implied by Table 6.4 suggest that the ideal L2 self represents a better base for doing so than integrativeness.

Ideal L2 self and effort

If the ideal L2 self variable can be equated with integrativeness, this poses a very basic follow-up question: Which of the two variables represents a more effective means of explaining motivated behaviour?

Table 6.6 presents the correlations of *integrativeness* and the *ideal L2 self* with *intended learning effort* for both the whole sample and the various academic status groups (the academic status groups are explained in the next section). These figures presented in Table 6.6 offer a simple method of measuring which variable represents the more authentic predictor of efforts to learn English. Although the strength of all the *integrativeness*

Table 6.6 Correlations of integrativeness and the ideal L2 self with intended learning effort

	Total sample	University students (non-English majors)	University students (English majors)	Secondary school pupils
Ideal L2 self	0.77	0.74	0.71	0.75
Integrativeness	0.65	0.61	0.54	0.71

$p < 0.001$ level

correlations is consistently high, the *ideal L2 self* values surpass these for all the sub-groups as well as the whole sample. Analysis of the values for the various academic status sub-groups reveals that this difference is most noticeable for the university English majors, the group that we would expect to be the most highly motivated. In contrast, the difference between the two variable values for the secondary pupils remains relatively slight.

Academic status

The finding that the ideal L2 self clearly represents a better indicator of learning effort than integrativeness for the university English majors, though less so for secondary school learners, requires further investigation. For the purposes of analysis, the sample was divided into three separate categories of learners: secondary school students, university non-English majors, and university English majors. It is possible to broadly characterise these three groups as follows: (1) university majors are those who have made an active decision to study English, therefore we may expect them to display higher levels of motivation to learn; (2) non-English majors are generally studying English as a compulsory element of their university studies, with no great investment in the success of that learning; (3) falling somewhere in between the extremes are the secondary students for whom English would primarily exist as a school subject, though an important subject for those seeking to proceed to higher education.

One-way analysis of variance (ANOVA) tests were conducted to explore how the variables differ across academic status groupings. The results are presented in Table 6.7. Perhaps the most fundamental characteristic of Table 6.7 is that the university English majors have consistently higher scores than the other two groups. This was anticipated and supports the assumption that this group of learners is likely to be more highly motivated than the other groups.

Table 6.7 Variation across academic status

	Secondary students		Non-English majors		University English majors		F	Effect size[†]	Sequence[a]
	M	SD	M	SD	M	SD			
Ideal L2 self	3.43	1.13	3.31	1.05	4.46	1.02	165.27***	0.12	2,1/3
Integrativeness	4.00	1.06	3.71	0.99	4.53	0.87	101.25***	0.08	2/1/3
Intended learning effort	3.38	0.92	3.15	0.92	4.09	0.82	149.94***	0.11	2/1/3

***$p < 0.001$

[†] = eta squared

[a]Post hoc SNK comparison. Numbers refer to the academic status groups: 1 = secondary students; 2 = non-English major university students; 3 = English major university students and are presented with the lowest value coming first. A comma between numbers indicates non-significant differences between two values and a slash indicates significance

A crucial challenge in researching language learning in the Japanese educational context is establishing a cut-off point for what counts as language learning in any meaningful sense of the term. As mentioned earlier, much of what passes for English education in Japan's secondary schools is primarily concerned with the need to pass important examinations, with language being presented in a form that often has more in common with convoluted mathematical formulae than a system of human communication. Table 6.7 shows no significant difference for *ideal L2 self* between the secondary pupils and the university non-English majors but significance between the English majors and the other groups. This can be interpreted as showing that the ideal L2 self works best as a predictor of motivated behaviour in cases where language is regarded as a means of personal fulfilment and engagement with others, as opposed to a purely academic pursuit. A considerable amount of research is based on the assumption of equivalence between 'the subject taken at school and known as English' and language learning. I would argue that the two are not always the same and that the results shown here appear to indicate that the ideal L2 self is capable of distinguishing between them in a way that eludes the integrativeness variable.

Gender differences

In addition to academic status, the other main sub-division of the sample was based on gender, examining any significant differences in the responses provided by male and female participants. There is a common perception of foreign languages as 'feminine' subjects, with research studies repeatedly reporting higher levels of motivation and effort for females. The figures in Table 6.8 reveal an overall pattern of significantly higher scores for females than males. This was anticipated and consistent with previous findings from other studies.

Closer analysis of Table 6.8 reveals that when these gender differences are compared directly across the relative academic status categories, the *ideal L2 self* and *integrativeness* variables perform very similarly. This tells us that the concept of the ideal L2 has no particular gender bias, its behaviour being consistent with other established concepts in the field of language learning, and provides further verification of the earlier finding that the two variables share many common properties and tap into the same affective dimension to language learning. Nevertheless, the earlier finding that *ideal L2 self* distinguishes between the university English majors and the other groups confirms that the two variables are not entirely the same and that the ideal L2 self variable represents the more finely tuned instrument, crucially able to discriminate between different forms of learning effort.

Table 6.8 Gender differences

		Male		Female		*t*	*df*	Effect size[†]
		Mean	SD	Mean	SD			
Ideal L2 self	Whole	3.26	1.01	3.76	1.18	−10.60***	2140.92	0.46
	Secondary	3.24	0.97	3.52	1.20	−2.44*	311.57	0.26
	Non-major	3.23	1.00	3.47	1.09	−4.39***	1107.57	0.23
	Major	4.04	1.10	4.53	0.97	−3.22**	322	0.47
Integrativeness	Whole	3.61	1.00	4.15	0.97	−13.01***	2257	0.54
	Secondary	3.80	1.10	4.10	1.03	−2.60*	360	0.28
	Non-major	3.56	0.97	3.97	0.95	−8.02***	1571	0.42
	Major	4.21	1.06	4.59	0.82	−2.80**	322	0.39
Intended learning effort	Whole	3.11	0.92	3.56	0.95	−11.32***	2247	0.48
	Secondary	3.20	0.85	3.47	0.95	−2.62**	360	0.30
	Non-major	3.06	0.92	3.31	0.91	−5.17***	1569	0.27
	Major	3.80	0.94	4.14	0.78	−2.72**	320	0.39

*p < 0.05; **p < 0.01; ***p < 0.001
[†]Cohen's d

As an interesting sidenote, it is worth remarking that the least significant gender differences are observed at the secondary level. This supports the earlier assertion that there are important differences between English in the secondary and tertiary sectors. The clearly defined role of English classes in Japan's secondary schools – to help pass examinations that may have little connection to any use of the language – does not appear to contain the same degree of gender-based associations as learning at university. The absence of significant gender variation amongst secondary pupils suggests greater uniformity of attitudes at this level. The implication seems to be that young people really start to diverge in their attitudes at the tertiary stage, with attitudes to learning English and its implied values forming an important part of this process for many young people.

Summary

I began by identifying a need for greater awareness of those aspects of language learning that can be generalised across learning cultures and those that are specific to local context. Following on from Dörnyei's Hungarian research, I argued that an interpretation of language learning motivation based on the concept of integrativeness is fundamentally flawed in this respect as it is based on the representation of a culture-specific variable as generalisable construct. One aim of this chapter was to propose an interpretation of L2 motivation based on the concept of the ideal L2 self, as suggested by Dörnyei and his associates, as a possible means of developing an understanding of language learning motivation that is comprehensive and robust enough to be applicable to a wide range of language learning contexts yet with the capacity to remain sensitive to specific situations and individual idiosyncrasies.

Perhaps the most important of the findings from the study is that the data provide strong empirical backing for calls to reinterpret L2 motivation from a self perspective. The ideal L2 self variable demonstrates itself to be equivalent to integrativeness, strengthening the argument that integrativeness is simply one local manifestation of a much more complex, powerful construct, and explaining why it has been found lacking in many studies. What has been identified as integrativeness in numerous studies is simply one element of a much greater whole. Crucially, the study also finds that it is the ideal L2 self that has the more direct relationship with motivated behaviour. Integrativeness may indeed exist in many contexts but it does so as part of a broader L2 self concept.

A further area of inquiry concerned the notions that learners of English in Japan hold of the English-speaking community and how they affect efforts to learn. The idea of an L2 community tied to location and nationality – which is implicit in a conventional interpretation of the concept of integrativeness and consistently propagated through the Japanese English education system – is not as powerful a motivating factor as a vaguely defined English-speaking community which allows the young Japanese learner the possibility of membership and participation in the events of that community.

Finally, analysis of how the two variables perform across some of the sub-groups within the sample suggests that the ideal L2 self is a more precise measurement. In many situations, what is presented in the classroom as 'English' is not necessarily compatible with a view of language as a system of communication between people and language learning as based on a desire to engage with other speakers of the language. Learners may indeed make efforts to learn both these forms of 'language' but the nature of these efforts is surely different; the ideal L2 self appears to do a much better job at distinguishing between these forms of 'language learning'. For those involved in learning contexts where the function and purpose of second language education is not always about communication with the L2 community, this represents an important breakthrough.

References

Benson, M.J. (1991) Attitudes and motivation towards English: A survey of Japanese freshmen. *RELC Journal* 22 (1), 34–48.

Berwick, R. and Ross, S. (1989) Motivation after matriculation: Are Japanese learners of English still alive after exam hell? *JALT Journal* 11 (2), 193–210.

Brown, J.D. and Yamashita, O.S. (1995) English language entrance examinations at Japanese universities: What do we know about them? *JALT Journal* 17 (1), 7–30.

Coetzee-Van Rooy, S. (2006) Integrativeness: Untenable for world Englishes learners? *World Englishes* 25 (3/4), 437–450.

Crookes, G. and Schmidt, R.W. (1991) Motivation: Reopening the research agenda. *Language Learning* 41, 469–512.

Csizér, K. and Dörnyei, Z. (2005a) Language learners' motivational profiles and their motivated learning behavior. *Language Learning* 55 (4), 613–659.

Csizér, K. and Dörnyei, Z. (2005b) The internal structure of language learning motivation and its relationship with language choice and learning effort. *The Modern Language Journal* 89 (1), 19–36.

Dörnyei, Z. (1990) Conceptualizing motivation in foreign-language learning. *Language Learning* 40 (1), 45–47.

Dörnyei, Z. (1994) Understanding L2 motivation: On with the challenge. *The Modern Language Journal* 78 (4), 515–523.

Dörnyei, Z. (2005) *The Psychology of the Language Learner: Individual Differences in Second Language Acquisition*. Mahwah, NJ: Lawrence Erlbaum.

Dörnyei, Z. and Clément, R. (2001) Motivational characteristics of learning different target languages: Results of a nationwide survey. In Z. Dörnyei and R.W. Schmidt (eds) *Motivation and Second Language Acquisition* (pp. 399–432). Honolulu, HI: University of Hawaii Press.

Dörnyei, Z. and Csizér, K. (2002) Some dynamics of language attitudes and motivation: Results of a longitudinal nationwide survey. *Applied Linguistics* 23, 421–462.

Dörnyei, Z., Csizér, K. and Németh, N. (2006) *Motivation, Language Attitudes, and Globalisation: A Hungarian Perspective.* Clevedon: Multilingual Matters.

Gardner, R.C. (1985) *Social Psychology and Second Language Learning: The Role of Attitudes and Motivation.* London: Edward Arnold.

Gardner, R.C. and Lambert, W.E. (1959) Motivational variables in second-language acquisition. *Canadian Journal of Psychology* 13, 266–272.

Gardner, R.C. and MacIntyre, P.D. (1993) A student's contribution to second language learning. Part ii: Affective variables. *Language Teaching* 26, 1–11.

Giddens, A. (1991) *Modernity and Self-Identity: Self and Society in the Late Modern Age.* Stanford, CA: Stanford University Press.

Hayes, C.W. (1979) Language contact in Japan. In W.F. Mackey and J. Ornstein (eds) *Sociolinguistic Studies in Language Contact: Methods and Cases* (pp. 363–375). New York: Mouton Publishers.

Irie, K. (2003) What do we know about the language learning motivation of university students in Japan? Some patterns in survey studies. *JALT Journal* 25 (1), 86–101.

Kim, T.Y. (2005) Reconceptualizing L2 motivation: Vygotskian activity theory approach. *English Teaching* 60 (4), 299–322.

Kubota, R. (2002) The impact of globalization on language teaching in Japan. In D. Block and D. Cameron (eds) *Globalization and Language Teaching* (pp. 13–28). London: Routledge.

Lamb, M. (2004) Integrative motivation in a globalizing world. *System* 32, 3–19.

MacIntyre, P.D. (2007) Willingness to communicate in the second language: Understanding the decision to speak as a volitional process. *Modern Language Journal* 91 (4), 564–576.

McClelland, N. (2000) Goal orientations in Japanese college students learning EFL. In S.D. Cornwell and P. Robinson (eds) *Individual Differences in Foreign Language Learning: Effects of Aptitude, Intelligence, and Motivation* (pp. 99–115). Tokyo: Japanese Association for Language Teaching.

McVeigh, B.J. (2002) *Japanese Higher Education as Myth.* Armonk, NY: M.E. Sharpe.

Nakata, Y. (1995) New attitudes among Japanese learners of English. In K. Kitao, S.K. Kitao, J.H. Miller, J.W. Carpenter and C.C. Rinnert (eds) *Culture and Communication* (pp. 173–184). Kyoto: Yamaguchi Shoten.

Nakata, Y. (2006) *Motivation and Experience in Foreign Language Learning.* Bern: Peter Lang.

Noels, K.A., Pelletier, L.G., Clément, R. and Vallerand, R.J. (2000) Why are you learning a second language? Motivational orientations and self-determination theory. *Language learning* 50, 57–85.

Oxford, R.L. and Shearin, J. (1994) Language learning motivation: Expanding the theoretical framework. *The Modern Language Journal* 78 (1), 12–28.

Ryan, S. (2006) Language learning motivation within the context of globalisation: An L2 self within an imagined global community. *Critical Inquiry in Language Studies* 3 (1), 23–45.

Sawaki, Y. (1997) Japanese learners' language learning motivation: A preliminary study. *JACET Bulletin* 28, 83–96.

Warden, C. and Lin, H.J. (2000) Existence of integrative motivation in Asian EFL settings. *Foreign Language Annals* 33, 535–547.

Yashima, T. (2002) Willingness to communicate in a second language: The Japanese EFL context. *The Modern Language Journal* 86 (1), 54–66.

Yashima, T., Zenuk-Nishide, L. and Shimizu, K. (2004) The influence of attitudes and affect on willingness to communicate and second language communication. *Language Learning* 54 (1), 119–152.

Appendix A

Items and Composite Variables Used in the MFQ

CULTURAL INTEREST

2   Do you like the pop music of English-speaking countries?
5   Do you think that it is important to learn English in order to learn more about the culture and art of its speakers?
6   Do you like Hollywood films?
14   Do you like English magazines? (*Write 'X' if you don't know any.*)
19   Do you like English TV programmes?
32   I often wish I could read newspapers and magazines in another language.

ATTITUDES TOWARDS L2 COMMUNITY

3   Do you like the people of the United States?
4   Do you think that English-speaking countries (besides the USA) have an important role in the world?
8   Do you think that English-speaking countries (besides the USA) are advanced and developed nations?
11   Do you think that the United States has an important role in the world?
12   Do you like the people who live in English-speaking countries (besides the USA)?
15   Do you like meeting people from English-speaking countries?
16   Do you think that the United States is an advanced and developed nation?
17   Would you like to become similar to the people of English-speaking countries?

INSTRUMENTALITY

1   Do you think English is important in the world these days?
10   Do you think English would help you if you travelled abroad in the future?
13   Do you think knowing English would help you to become a more knowledgeable person?
18   Do you think English would help your future career?
29   For me to become an educated person I should learn English.
33   English ability would help me get a better paying job.
44   Studying English will help me get into better schools.
56   A knowledge of English would make me a better educated person.
90   Learning English is necessary because it is an international language.
98   Studying English will help me get a good job.

INTERNATIONAL CONTACT
41 I think that English will help me meet more people.
62 I would like to be able to use English to get involved with people from other countries.
78 I would like to be able to use English to communicate with people from other countries.
80 If I could speak English well, I could get to know more people from other countries.

INTEREST IN FOREIGN LANGUAGES
55 If I planned to stay in another country, I would study the local language.
66 I think I would study a foreign language even if it weren't compulsory.
85 I would like to learn a lot of foreign languages.
92 If I were visiting a foreign country I would like to be able to speak its language.
97 If I made the effort, I could learn a foreign language.

INTERNATIONAL EMPATHY
46 Studying English will help me to get to know English-speaking people.
50 Studying English will help me to understand people from all over the world, not just English-speaking countries.
87 Studying English is important to me because I would like to become close to other English speakers.

FEAR OF ASSIMILATION
42 As a result of internationalisation, there is a danger Japanese people may forget the importance of Japanese culture.
57 Using English in front of people makes me feel like I will be thought of as less Japanese.
74 As internationalisation advances there is a danger of losing the Japanese language and culture.
82 As a part of international society Japanese people must preserve the Japanese language and culture.

ETHNOCENTRISM
30 I don't trust people with different customs and values to myself.
47 I respect the values and customs of other cultures.
67 I find it difficult to work together with people who have different customs and values.
88 I find it difficult to comprehend the values and customs of other cultures.
99 I am not very interested in the values and customs of other cultures.

TRAVEL ORIENTATION
7   Would you like to travel to English-speaking countries?
51   Studying English will be useful when I travel overseas.
54   Learning English is important to me because I would like to visit English-speaking countries.
89   Learning English is important to me because I would like to travel internationally.

ENGLISH ANXIETY
38   I am worried that other speakers of English would find my English strange.
43   If I met an English speaker, I would feel nervous.
52   I get nervous and confused when I am speaking in my English class.
69   I'm not very good at volunteering answers in our English class.
71   I would feel uneasy speaking English with a native speaker.
84   I would get tense if a foreigner asked me for directions in English.

ATTITUDES TO LEARNING ENGLISH
9   Do you like English?
37   Learning English is really great.
60   I really enjoy learning English.
73   I'm always looking forward to my English classes.
86   I find learning English really interesting.
95   Learning English is one of the most important aspects in my life.

MILIEU
35   Most people around me tend to think that learning a foreign language is a waste of time.
40   Hardly anybody really cares whether I learn English or not.
63   Few people around me think that it is such a good thing to learn foreign languages.
75   For people where I live learning English doesn't really matter that much.
77   My parents do not consider foreign languages important school subjects.
96   I don't think that foreign languages are important school subjects.

PARENTAL ENCOURAGEMENT
34   I am often told by my parents that English is important for my future.
58   My parents encourage me to study English.
72   My parents think that I should really try to learn English.
81   My parents encourage me to practise my English as much as possible.

IDEAL L2 SELF

39 The things I want to do in the future require me to speak English.
45 Whenever I think of my future career, I imagine myself being able to use English.
59 I often imagine myself as someone who is able to speak English.
83 If my dreams come true, I will use English effectively in the future.
93 I can imagine speaking English with international friends.
100 When I think about my future, it is important that I use English.

L2 SELF-CONFIDENCE

28 I am sure I will be able to learn a foreign language.
36 I worry that the other students will laugh at me when I speak English.
48 Learning a foreign language is a difficult task for me.
70 I think I am the type who would feel anxious and ill at ease if I had to speak to someone in a foreign language.
91 I always feel that my classmates speak English better than I do.

WILLINGNESS TO COMMUNICATE (L1/in English)

How likely would you be to initiate communication in Japanese/English in the following situations?
20/28 Making a presentation in front of a large group.
21/29 Talking with an acquaintance while standing in line.
22/30 Talking with a salesperson in a store.
23/31 Talking in a small group of strangers.
24/32 Talking with a friend while standing in line.
25/33 Talking with a stranger while standing in line.
26/34 Talking in a small group of acquaintances.
27/35 Talking in a small group of friends.

INTENDED LEARNING EFFORT

31 I am working hard at learning English.
49 It is extremely important for me to learn English.
53 If an English course was offered in the future, I would like to take it.
61 When I hear an English song on the radio, I listen carefully and try to understand all the words.
65 I can honestly say that I am really doing my best to learn English.
68 If I could have access to English-speaking TV stations, I would try to watch them often.
76 I am the kind of person who makes great efforts to learn English.
79 If English were not taught in school, I would try to go to English classes somewhere else.

Chapter 7
International Posture and the Ideal L2 Self in the Japanese EFL Context

TOMOKO YASHIMA

Introduction

If you were asked to coach a high school baseball team of novices, what is the first thing you would do? Would you give a lecture on the history and rules of the game, or would you take the students to a stadium to watch a championship tournament? If students have an image of would-be great players responding to the cheers and roars of the audience imprinted in their minds, students are less likely to require much of an explanation for why they must undertake a hard daily training routine – e.g. running, muscle-building exercise, practice swings, and fielding practice – so long as they see these activities linked to what they want to be in the future, i.e. their ideal selves.

In the field of English education, nationwide efforts are being made to improve the level of English competency of Japanese learners in response to calls from the government, but often without a vision of where they lead learners to. It seems to me that increasing competency in English has become the ultimate goal. It may be useful to focus on the concept of ideal self to find an answer to the challenge we face in EFL contexts, of showing visions of a game English learners are playing and having them play the game well, or of motivating learners to study English when they do not perceive immediate need of it. In this framework, 'learning' implies becoming someone different from the present self, moving toward the ideal self.

'Learning an L2' is somewhat more complicated as it involves 'the adoption of new social and cultural behaviors and ways of being' (Williams, 1994: 77). Consequently, the efforts to create people with L2 competency inevitably involve the issue of social identity and the development of an L2 self. Language identity has traditionally been a concern of social psychological research on L2 learning and communication (e.g. Clément, 1986; Gardner & Lambert, 1972). Yet, the recent focus on L2 learning motivation as a self-system, instigated by Dörnyei and Csizér (2002) (See also Dörnyei, 2005, and this volume), provides us with a theoretical framework to deal with the issue of identity in a foreign language context. In this chapter, I will conceptually and empirically discuss the possible and ideal L2 self in relation to 'international posture', the concept postulated for EFL contexts as an alternative to the Gardnerian concept of integrativeness. I will first introduce the concept of international posture, and then discuss how international posture conceptually links to the possible and ideal L2 self as well as motivation to learn and communicate in an L2. Next, an educational initiative creating an imagined international community will be introduced with a review of studies, to illustrate how possible L2 selves can mediate L2 learning and communication behaviours. Finally, I will report on my recent empirical investigations conducted to explore the construct of international posture and its relations with the ideal self, as well as to examine how international posture and the ideal self relate to the way learning is internalised. In doing this, I will use two different research perspectives (that are not usually combined): (1) the individual differences research tradition to capture the patterns of changes and relations observed among proficiency, international posture, L2 WTC, and other psychological constructs; and (2) a community of practice perspective to understand how L2 communication is developed. The second aspect is deemed necessary because communication and language learning are fundamentally social.

International Posture and its Relevance to EFL Contexts

Gardner's well-known construct, *integrativeness,* reflects a positive affective disposition toward the L2 community as well as a desire to interact and identify with its members. In his socioeducational model, integrativeness supports the individual's motivation to learn an L2, which in turn is responsible for achievement in the language (e.g. Gardner, 1985, 2001; Masgoret & Gardner, 2003).

While influenced by integrativeness, *international posture,* on the other hand, tries to capture a tendency to relate oneself to the international community rather than any specific L2 group, as a construct more pertinent to EFL contexts. As English gains power as a world language, it has become increasingly more difficult for Japanese EFL learners to identify a clear target group or culture. English is something that connects us to foreign countries, and people with whom we can communicate in English, including Asians and Africans.[1] Even though many Japanese learners wish to interact with native speakers of English, they are not particularly interested in identifying with them. Of the many reasons given for studying English, identification with Americans/ British was among the least endorsed items in an earlier study of my own (Yashima, 2000).

Some other considerations were made in conceptualising international posture. To make a distinction between integrativeness and instrumentality is not easy with a language of such huge ethnolinguistic vitality (Giles *et al.*, 1977) and cultural capital (Bourdieu, 1977) as English. It is not realistic to talk about integrativeness as an attitude toward learning English without being influenced by its utilitarian value. In my study on reasons to learn English conducted with Japanese EFL learners (Yashima, 2000), I found that the correlation between instrumental and integrative orientations was 0.60. The same study delineated a factor labelled 'intercultural friendship orientation', capturing the tendency to learn English to have interaction with different cultural groups. In a subsequent path analysis, intercultural friendship orientation together with instrumental orientation significantly predicted motivational intensity to learn English, which in turn led to higher proficiency (Yashima, 2000).

Openness to foreignness or non-ethnocentric attitudes, which, according to Gardner (2001) is part of integrativeness, has relevance to the psychology of EFL learners, as I assume English relates us to something foreign or to different cultures in general. These attitudes can be partly explained using a multi-faceted concept, 'intercultural competence' postulated by Gudykunst (1991) and Kim (1991), which includes cognitive, affective and behavioural characteristics of an individual, including openness to different perspectives, adaptability, empathy, tendency to approach people who are different and non-ethnocentric attitudes.

Yashima *et al.* (2004) acknowledged the dual goals of learning English prevalent among Japanese EFL learners. Some learners are concerned with their immediate goals, such as tests, grades, and academic achievement, and others seem to feel international-communication goals to be personally relevant. Although one can have both goals to a greater or a lesser degree, the focus of international posture is on the individual differences in the latter. It captures a tendency to see oneself as connected to the international community, have concerns for international affairs and possess a readiness to interact with people other than Japanese. It seizes both integrative and instrumental aspects of motivation. In Yashima *et al.* (2004), international posture was operationalised to include three subcomponents based on reviews of intercultural communication/ social psychological research as I partly discussed above. The following are the three aspects with item examples. The rationales for choosing items are discussed in Yashima (2002).

(1) Intergroup approach tendency *e.g. I wouldn't mind sharing an apartment or room with international students.*
(2) Interest in international vocation and activities *e.g. I'd rather avoid the kind of work that sends me overseas frequently.*
(3) Interest in foreign affairs *e.g. I often read and watch news about foreign countries.*

International Posture, Willingness to Communicate, and Possible L2 Selves

MacIntyre *et al.*'s (1998) willingness to communicate (WTC) model represents the complexity of communicating using a second language. It does not place communicative competence as a goal of learning an L2 per se, but rather positions it as a means to achieve a communicative goal. This model has since stimulated research in various learning contexts with different L1 groups (Baker & MacIntyre, 2003; Cao & Philp, 2006; Kang, 2005; Yashima, 2002; Yashima *et al.*, 2004) with the aim of identifying factors that influence willingness to communicate in an L2. Yashima (2002), hoping to explain Japanese learners' motivation and willingness to communicate in English, combined Gardner's motivational theory and MacIntyre's (1994) WTC model with the concept of international posture into a structural equation model (SEM) to be tested. The results revealed that international posture is a valid construct that relates to motivation to learn and willingness to communicate among Japanese university learners of English. The model shows that international posture affects learners' motivation, which leads to proficiency as well as self-confidence, which, in turn, accounts for L2 WTC. It confirmed that L2 WTC is not simply the result of increased proficiency. Yashima *et al.* (2004) confirmed with a younger population (high school students) that international posture leads to motivation and L2 WTC as well as frequency of self-initiated communication inside and outside the school context.

Drawing on the theory of possible L2 selves, Yashima *et al.* (2004) argued that those who are conscious of how they relate themselves to the world tend to be motivated to study and communicate in English as they probably visualise 'English using selves' clearly. According to Dörnyei and Csizér (2002), possible selves (based on Markus & Nurius's, 1986, work) 'provide a conceptual link between cognition and motivation' because one tries to narrow the gap between one's present self-perceived status and what one should ideally be (Dörnyei & Csizér, 2002: 454). Markus and Nurius (1986: 954) state that possible selves are 'the cognitive manifestation of enduring goals, aspirations, motives, fears, and threats'. They are cognized in concrete imagery or semantic representation in the same way as the here-and-now self. The question raised here is what types of possible selves are in operation in learners with higher international posture that function as incentives to study and/or communicate in English. Those students with a higher level of international posture might generate possible selves (maybe based on experience) speaking with international students, helping foreigners lost on the street, reading English language newspapers. Furthermore, beyond those relatively familiar images, they might envision their ideal selves pursuing an international career, working in a foreign country, or conducting business negotiations in English. These ideal selves require proficiency in English as a necessary component and therefore function as incentives for L2 related actions.

On the other hand, Japanese students' ideal selves are typically formed without an L2 component. For a teenager who is striving to be a doctor and envisions herself treating a patient in a hospital, the ideal self is an incentive to make her study English as well as other subjects very hard because they are required for passing entrance examinations to competitive medical schools. For her, studying and getting a higher score in English tests generates an exchange value for her ideal self that does not necessarily require L2 competence. But developing international posture might help her produce possible selves attending international medical conferences or working in developing parts of the world, thus linking her achievement-focused possible selves to the L2 self. Based on what I found in my research with SEM, we could say that international posture is conducive to generating English-using possible selves giving rise to communication behaviours. International posture also stimulates one's English-studying possible selves (e.g. 'a high achiever who does well in English composition') that result in learning behaviours.

To imagine yourself communicating in English in the real world, it is natural that you also envision some kind of (often social) context in which you participate by using English. In this sense having a study abroad experience or other types of international/intercultural communication experiences make it easier for a person to situate her possible self in an English speaking environment. Often visions of using English are visions of participation in an English-speaking community. We could say international posture and visions of themselves using English reflect students' interest in participating in an 'imagined international community'. This concept is based on the notion of a community of practice developed by Lave and Wenger (1991) and Wenger (1998), and later adapted by Norton (2000, 2001) into her idea of imagined communities. For Wenger, imagination 'concerns the production of images of the self and images of the world that transcend engagement' (Wenger, 1998: 177), and it is a 'process of expanding our self by transcending our time and space creating new images of the world and ourselves' (Wenger, 1998: 176). To illustrate this, Wenger (and also Lantolf & Thorne, 2006) cites a story about two stonecutters: asked what they are doing, one stonecutter responds 'I am cutting the stone in a perfectly square shape' while the other says 'I am building a cathedral'. When a learner is memorising an English dialogue, is she memorising the sentences accurately or is she conducting a conversation as a participant of an imagined community? In other words, is the English-studying self here and now linked to the self participating in an L2 using community? Are the dual goals I mentioned above interconnected?

For ideal L2 selves to develop in an EFL context, where L2 communities do not visibly exist or are not readily accessible, we might need an educational initiative to help make an imagined community visible or create one for learners, in which learning new words and sentences can be linked to an imagined international community. In the next section I introduce studies conducted in a content-based English language teaching context representing such an attempt. I will discuss how international/global content can influence the development of international posture and the production of possible selves that mediate learners' interest in learning English and the L2 using ideal self.

An Imagined International Community and the L2 Possible Self

To explore how international posture, willingness to communicate and proficiency can be developed in different learning contexts, studies were conducted at a high school where content-based English teaching is carried out and where students are generally motivated to learn English (Yashima, 2007b; Yashima & Zenuk-Nishide, in press). The curriculum of the school is comprised of several thematic units that are covered over the three years. The Model United Nations (MUN) is one of the units students study in their third year, in which each student represents a country and does research so that she/he can discuss a topic (usually a human rights issue, e.g. child labour) from the country's perspective in English. Through cognitively and emotionally involving content, students are encouraged to form opinions and express themselves in English. They also prepare delegate speeches to make and collaboratively write drafts of resolutions to be discussed during the MUN sessions. All through the curriculum learners learn to use English to mediate their participation in 'an imagined international community', and the MUN is an occasion when the imagined community becomes visible and concrete (Yashima, 2007b).

In Yashima and Zenuk-Nishide's (in press) investigation comparing study abroad and 'at home' groups, questionnaires were administered to 165 students at the high school twice in their first and third years. The number included 16 (14 girls and two boys) students who participated in an academic year abroad in English speaking countries and came back to join the rest, as well as 149 (131 girls, 14 boys and four unknown) who stayed home and studied in Japan. The latter consisted of two groups of students who chose to enrol in programme options with slightly different focuses within the same theme based curriculum: Group A ($N = 62$) who take a substantially larger number of content-based classes, and Group B

($N = 84$) who take a smaller number of content-based classes together with grammar translation classes in preparation for entrance examinations to universities. There were small but significant differences in proficiency in favour of the study abroad group (SA) and Group A over Group B in their first year. During the next two and a half years, SA showed a larger gain than the two at home (AH) groups in proficiency (TOEFL scores), international posture, and frequency of communication. In proficiency, SA's mean score in their third year was significantly higher than both of the AH groups and the gap between SA and AH widened. Regarding international posture, SA's gain was larger than those of the AH groups, though it did not differ significantly from that of Group A students. All three groups communicated significantly more in their third year than in their first year. But the gap between the SA and AH groups widened in the amount of learner-initiated communication in the third year.[2,3]

In a subsequent cluster analysis that delineated three distinct developmental profiles among the at home population, one of the clusters (Cluster 3: $N = 31$) displayed a profile similar to the study abroad group in the development of the three parameters. Another cluster (Cluster 1: $N = 43$) exhibited an equally large proficiency gain but not as great a gain in international posture or frequency of communication. Cluster 1 consisted of more than twice as many learners from Group B who selected the curriculum option that prepares them for entrance examinations than Cluster 3. On the other hand Cluster 3 was represented by twice as many learners who were more heavily immersed in the content-based curriculum.

Overall results can be summarised as follows: although the advantage of study abroad over staying home was clear not only in proficiency but in the development of international posture and willingness to communicate, the differential profiles between learners in A and B programme options indicated that a higher exposure to a content-based curriculum resulted in a higher level of international posture and willingness to communicate in L2.

If I explore the results theoretically from a community of practice perspective, students who most fully participated in the community of practice of global studies developed proficiency, international posture and grew to be more active communicators as they were enculturated into the community, learned to share the values and developed a behavioural tendency encouraged in the community. Probably, these students were engaged in daily practices that included memorising words for quizzes and doing homework as a way to approximate their current selves to ideal imagined selves. These students showed developmental profiles similar to students who participated in a year abroad in terms of proficiency, international posture and self-initiated amount of communication. SA's gain can be accounted for by their participation in the actual L2 community, but AH's progress is a result of participation in an imagined community. It might be also possible that these learners envision English-using ideal selves as a representation of their career goals, while for others who were not equally involved in the activity, possible selves that represent the immediate goals of getting into university might have been more active.

In a descriptive questionnaire administered to a second cohort of both SA and AH students in their third year, qualitative analysis (open-coding) of students' comments on one of the questions (How have your attitudes/affect toward speaking English changed?) yielded five main categories. The first category is labelled 'English becoming natural part of life/self' exemplified by comments such as 'English comes out of my mouth naturally', 'I use English in my conversation with my friends without thinking so much about it'. The second category concerns the development of positive affect reflected in learners' comments such as 'I became less anxious in speaking English', 'I learned to enjoy speaking English'. Thirdly, learners learned to value the importance of communication in English as they know it allows them to communicate with varied people in the world. The fourth category was enhanced motivation. Having more chances to speak caused them to feel a desire to communicate well and feel a need to be fluent users of English. The fifth category shows that there were a handful of students for whom learning to communicate in English seemed more difficult than before. These results indicate that, as a whole, the meaning of 'speaking English' has become somewhat more personalised and realistic through the educational process.

In the MUN learners are given chances to form and express opinions from the perspective of the country they are representing, as well as negotiate genuinely to reach agreements that represent the country's interests to the maximum. From these kinds of realistic L2 experiences for language learners, they may well begin to visualise their future ideal L2 selves as linked to what they do in the here and now. Further, as Yashima (2007b) argued based on qualitative data analyses, engagement in global issues and doing research for the MUN makes what learners want to communicate clearer. (For example, some students learned about children killed in dangerous work and maintained that the resolution should include some clause addressing this issue.) This leads to a more intense desire to communicate. When they try to communicate for negotiation and collective knowledge creation, they strongly feel that they need to acquire accuracy and fluency in the L2 to make their voices clearer. Based on this, Yashima presented a model of a content-based approach (Yashima, 2007b) in which what we have to communicate based on our interest in and knowledge of the issue, our willingness to communicate, and our means of communication (L2 proficiency) are viewed as interacting and developing together rather than separately.

A Bridge of Self Representations toward the Ideal Self

I have shown an empirical study in which international posture with English-using ideal selves can lead to higher proficiency and more frequent communication through educational efforts toward creating an imagined international community. But how do the ideal L2 self images mediate learning behaviours? A learner who envisions herself giving a presentation in an international conference also needs to learn vocabulary, learn to write grammatical sentences and practise pronunciation. According to Markus and Ruvolo (1989: 212), 'global possible selves enable the construction or retrieval of related but more focused task-relevant possible selves'. This may mean that to the extent that the ideal self image is clear, one also develops possible selves that are task relevant and instrumental (e.g. I memorise the list of words to get a high score in a quiz. I practise pronunciation and read the text aloud.) To connect these task-related possible selves to ideal communicating selves, imagination is called for, and this is where educational and teacher intervention, such as the MUN, is required. MUN participants' comments from last year show that, after completing the session schedules, they can clearly state what they need to improve (e.g. pronunciation, grammar, research and preparation, WTC) to contribute more to the decision making process.

Dörnyei (2005: 100) writes '[t]he more vivid and elaborate the possible self, the more motivationally effective it is expected to be'. For this, possible selves need to be 'something you can touch and feel, or you are afraid of' (Dörnyei, personal communication, December 7, 2005)**. He also writes:

> The possible self needs to be associated with relevant procedural knowledge. A desired end-state will have an impact on behavior only if the individual can personalize it by *building a bridge of self-representations* between one's current self and the hoped for self. (Dörnyei, 2005: 117, emphasis added)

How is a self-representation that builds a bridge to the future L2-using self created and personalised? I believe, first of all, that the learner needs to have an embodied experience of using the language, or having the feeling of mediating one's thoughts or interpersonal relations using the language. Becoming involved in the collective decision making in the Model UN can give a feeling of using the language for some meaningful knowledge creation, which generates a representation of oneself using English and become the basis of a future possible self. In an open-ended questionnaire described earlier as part of Yashima and

Zenuk-Nishide's (in press) study, a student mentions, 'English has become a language just like Japanese for me', while another says 'English is easy as a school subject but very difficult to use as a language'. I got a sense that there was a critical moment in these students' learning experience when English, which had been just another subject to study at school to be tested and graded, had become 'a language' to be used for communication and I believe that the learners came to that realisation through an embodied experience.

Once a college student told me 'a native speaker is too remote a goal. I can never identify with them. But Japanese teachers are more accessible goals'. In this sense, a teacher and learners more advanced than oneself might offer personalised models of ideal selves. This point has been raised by other researchers (Cook, 1999; Murphey & Arao, 2001). Cook comments that we should establish 'a positive image of L2 users rather than seeing them as failed native speakers' (Cook, 1999: 185), while Murphey and Arao say L2 users are easier to identify with, suggesting the value of near peer role modelling in ELT, in which learners observe 'their peers succeeding in the task which carries information that they themselves also have the potential abilities' (Murphey & Arao, 2001: 2). Learners see in them their 'future selves' and become motivated about this potential. In the MUN I described earlier, third year students participated as delegates representing different nations in the MUN as part of the curriculum, and first and second year students also participated peripherally (but legitimately) as pagers whose responsibilities were to pass notes between delegates, secretaries and chairs. While they worked as pagers they witnessed the activity and might have seen in the third year students their immediate future selves. (In the MUN we find a number of scaffolding opportunities, including formulaic use of language, clear rules for floor-taking, and well-prepared drafts of resolutions (Yashima, 2007b), which could facilitate the development of the procedural knowledge of English using self-representations.) In this sense Japanese teachers' and classmates' roles in the classroom to present living images of English users are crucial. As Murphey and Arao (2001) show, 'near peer modelling' helps learners' beliefs and attitudes toward learning become more positive. This indicates that well-designed collaborative classroom activities utilising learners' zone of proximal development will help learners function as one another's future selves. When such immediate future selves are linked to an imagined community and an imagined ideal self or 'a desired end-state', they might become 'a bridge of self-representations'.

Figure 7.1 is drawn based on empirical studies I have conducted so far (Yashima, 2002, 2007a; Yashima *et al.*, 2004) and what I have discussed in this chapter. It indicates that international posture (including engagement in international issues), willingness to communicate resulting in

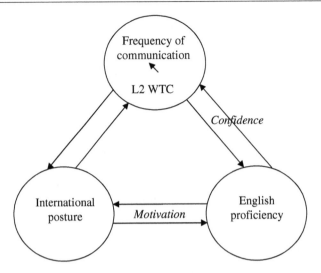

Figure 7.1 A schematic representation of the interaction between L2 WTC, international posture and English proficiency

frequency of communication, and English proficiency interact with each other and develop together in an EFL context. For this interaction or circulation to occur, new slightly more-advanced-than-current L2 self-representations should emerge and keep on emerging.

Exploring International Posture and the Ideal Self: Empirical Investigations

This final section reports on an empirical study I recently conducted to explore the constructs of international posture and the ideal self with two purposes: (1) to revise the construct of international posture and investigate its relations to the ideal L2 self as a social psychological construct, and (2) to investigate how international posture, WTC, and ideal self relate to the internalisation of learning into the self concept. In addition, I hope the report will partially confirm what I have discussed in relation to Figure 7.1 above.

Theoretical rationale

The international posture scales were originally designed to capture multi-dimensions under the broad attitudinal category as discussed earlier in this chapter. When international posture was applied to studies on content-based teaching (as well as an ongoing study with participants involved in international volunteer work), another important dimension arose as pertinent, that is, whether or not a person has things to say to an (imagined) international community. Based on students' comments in interviews and questionnaires, it was found that unless one has something to say about a topic or opinions to express about an agenda, one does not have an urge to communicate. For possible selves to be concrete in a situation like the MUN, they also need semantic representations of what is to be stated. For this reason international posture was expanded to include the dimension of 'having things to communicate to the world'.

In addition, as I discussed in the previous section, the image of oneself exerting day to day effort in learning should be linked to the image of oneself communicating in an international arena. In order to see how these learning selves develop and relate to the ideal L2 communicating self, I also investigated the relations between those psychological constructs and intrinsic as well as extrinsic motivations (i.e. the hypothesised continuum of internalisation – see below) in the framework of self-determination theory (SDT) by Deci and Ryan (1985). According to Dörnyei (2005), the application of SDT to L2 learning by Noels (2003) has contributed to the theoretical development of the L2 self system (see also Noels, this volume).

In SDT, intrinsic motivation refers to doing something because it is inherently interesting or enjoyable. In addition, SDT proposes that there are varied types of extrinsic motivation, from externally controlled forms of motivation, i.e. external regulation, to types of motivation which are more internalised within the self. A partially internalised type of extrinsic motivation is introjected regulation, capturing self-induced pressure. Identified regulation, somewhat further internalised, refers to carrying out an activity because it is important to attaining a valued goal for the person, such as learning English to become an 'international lawyer'. Finally, integrated regulation is a state where regulation is integrated into one's self-concept, so that doing something has become almost a natural part of being oneself. An important claim of this theory is that, over time, an externally regulated activity may become more internally regulated to the extent that students feel that they have freely chosen to participate in the learning process, that their skills or competence are improving, and that they are supported in these activities by significant others. The continuum is hypothesised as subcategories within extrinsic motivation but external regulations do not necessarily tranform into intrinsic motivation (Deci & Ryan, 1985). To clarify the conceptual relations among international posture, communication behaviour, and the ideal self, correlations were calculated among the scales designed to measure each of the constructs. In addition, relations between these and different types of motivation proposed in self-determination theory were explored.

Preparation of the scales

For the purpose of this study many scales used in previous research were adapted or updated. Regarding SDT scales, a preliminary study was conducted by translating the SDT scales adapted for L2 learning by Noels *et al.* (2000). A factor analysis of the Japanese version did not clearly represent the seven subscales hypothesised in SDT, so some items were replaced and others were rephrased to better fit the EFL context. The resulting SDT scales show clearer distinctions among subscales representing regulations and the expected simplex pattern[4] relationships (Yashima, 2006). In addition, a shorter version of the WTC scale consisting of eight items was adapted from Ryan (this volume: 143), with three of the items changed to fit the Japanese EFL classroom situation. Frequency of communication items were also changed to reflect realistic learning situations in EFL contexts. For assessing the ideal self, I adopted a scale of five items from Ryan (this volume: 143) that assesses the extent to which a learner identifies with the future self using the L2.

To update the international posture scale, first, two extra items were added to the *international interest* subsection, in order to make a more stable total of four as Dörnyei (2003) suggests. For the reason discussed above, a subcategory 'Having things to communicate to the world' with four items was also tentatively added to the scale in this study. Some of the revised measures with new items used in this study are shown with Cronbach alphas in Appendix A).

The study

Participants in this study were 191 students (156 girls and 31 boys, four unreported) at the same high school in which the study discussed earlier was conducted. A questionnaire including measures of international posture, L2 WTC, frequency of communication, ideal self, and SDT scales was administered in February, 2007.

Figure 7.2 shows the result of a confirmatory factor analysis of the four subscales of international posture and its hypothetical conceptual relationship with the ideal self. The four subscales represent different manifestations of international posture that are broadly classified into (1) attitudinal/behavioural propensity and (2) knowledge orientation. The former includes a tendency to approach and interact with foreigners (openness to foreignness), interest in going abroad to work or participating in international activities, while the latter reflects interest in foreign affairs and international news, and having opinions on international matters. Table 7.1 shows correlation coefficients calculated between international posture, WTC, frequency of communication and different types of motivation based on SDT. Also shown are correlations between the ideal self and SDT regulations, international posture, WTC and

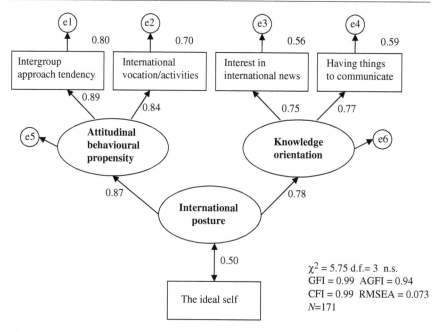

Figure 7.2 A confirmatory factor analysis of four subscales of international posture and its hypothesised relationship with the ideal self

frequency of communication.[5] The results of the correlational analyses show that the types of extrinsic motivation with a higher level of self-determination (identified and integrated regulations) correlate most strongly with international posture, L2 WTC, and frequency of communication as well as with the ideal self.

Intrinsic motivation does not correlate with these variables as strongly as the two types of extrinsic motivation. Since international posture theoretically and operationally captures both integrativeness and instrumentality, it is quite reasonable that it reflects self-determined types of extrinsic motivation more than genuinely intrinsic motivation. As I discussed before, international posture reflects the possible selves of a future English-using participant in an international community. Thus, the strongest relation to identified regulation in the continuum seems reasonable. In addition, the correlation between ideal self and integrated regulation indicates the following: as internalisation of learning progresses, the tendency to visualise an ideal L2 self intensifies and the current self gradually approximates toward the ideal self. When learning an L2 is integrated as a natural part of the person's self concept, learning and using an L2 has become a habitual activity. Those who show a higher level of international posture and frequency of communication

Table 7.1 Correlations between international posture, L2 WTC, frequency of communication in L2 with motivational regulations in SDT as well as ideal self

Cronbach's α	Amotivation (0.76)	Extrinsic motivation				Intrinsic motivation (0.64)	Ideal self
		External (0.58)	Introjected (0.76)	Identified (0.82)	Integrated (0.68)		
International posture (α = 0.90)	− 0.40**	− 0.23**	0.06	0.49**	0.47**	0.40**	0.43**
WTC (α = 0.86)	− 0.24**	− 0.13	0.10	0.29**	0.35**	0.28**	0.25**
Frequency of communication (α = 0.85)	− 0.19**	− 0.03	0.11	0.41**	0.41**	0.28**	0.33**
Ideal self (α = 0.79)	− 0.35**	− 0.11	0.14	0.47**	0.48**	0.44**	

*p < 0.05; **p < 0.01. N = 191

tend to endorse the vision of ideal selves more strongly. These findings lend partial support to what I discussed in relation to Figure 7.1 – that is, the hypothesised link between international posture, willingness to communicate, and proficiency mediated by English-using self concepts.

Conclusion

In this chapter, I have discussed the L2 self in relation to international posture and an imagined international community. I have illustrated an approach to education in EFL contexts in which students expand their self by creating new images of themselves linked to global concerns, and through the process find meaning in learning English while learning to use the language. Often in Japanese EFL learners' minds, studying English (e.g. memorising words, reading texts aloud) is unconnected to the ideal L2 self. An alternative approach shown here is to create a situation in which task-related possible selves are linked to the English using ideal self. For this, communication and learning take place for knowledge creation that itself is meaningful. Learners learn to think critically and form opinions while learning English. Recently from a sociocultural theoretical (Vygotskian) perspective, Lantolf and Thorne (2006) maintain that learning a second language gives us new tools to mediate our interaction with the world and with our own psychological functioning. From this perspective learning another language should help us to change the way we relate to the world as well as how we conceptualise ourselves. The visions of learners as ideal L2 users can be created through educational initiatives. For this, however, the content and themes that are dealt with are critical as they shape the ideal L2 selves that can be created. It is my hope that the content of English education will allow learners to take a global outlook, enhance critical thinking and enable multiple perspectives, because a fundamental goal of L2 learning is to empower learners to deal with an increasingly more complex globalising world.

Acknowledgements

I would like to thank Mark Sawyer, Miyuki Sasaki, and Linda Viswat for their invaluable comments on an earlier draft.

Notes

1. It is true that the Japanese public tend to associate English with westerners or whites rather than non westerners, as confirmed, for example, in Lee's (2007) critical review of the tendency of commercial language schools to preferentially hire western-looking teachers.
2. What is shown here is a summary of Yashima and Zenuk-Nishide (in press) that investigates contextual influence on changes in proficiency, attitudes, and communication behaviours. To compare the three groups (and four groups in

the second investigation with a cluster analysis) a mixed model repeated measures ANOVA (2×4) was performed for each of the four indicators, using time as within-subjects factor and group as the between subject factor. When the main effect of time-by-group interaction was significant, one-way ANOVA with Welch's adjustment was performed to compare the means between the groups at Time 1 and 2. Subsequently t-tests were performed to examine whether the amount of change was significant for each indicator in each group.

3. The students who participated in an academic year abroad had also enrolled in the A or B programme, but they were treated as one group in this study. 'At home' students also participated in a short homestay programme abroad.

4. According to Noels *et al.* (2000), the simplex pattern is hypothesised in SDT, which means that more self-determined types of motivation should be inversely related to those that are less self-determined

5. For each of the constructs the mean of the item scores was calculated for the analyses.

References

Baker, S.C. and MacIntyre, P.D. (2000) The role of gender and immersion in communication and second language orientations. *Language Learning* 50, 311–341.

Bourdieu, P. (1977) *Outline of a Theory of Practice* (R. Nice, Trans.). Cambridge: Cambridge University Press.

Cao, Y. and Philp, J. (2006) Interactional context and willingness to communicate: A comparison of behavior in whole class, group and dyadic interaction. *System* 34, 480–493.

Cook, V. (1999) Beyond the native speaker in language teaching. *TESOL Quarterly* 33, 185–209.

Clément, R. (1986) Second language proficiency and acculturation: An investigation of the effects of language status and individual characteristics. *Journal of Language and Social Psychology* 5, 271–290.

Deci, E.L. and Ryan, R.M. (1985) *Intrinsic Motivation and Self-Determination in Human Behavior.* New York: Plenum Press.

Dörnyei, Z. (2003) *Questionnaires in Second Language Research.* Mahwah, NJ: Lawrence Erlbaum.

Dörnyei, Z. (2005) *The Psychology of the Language Learner: Individual Differences in Second Language Acquisition.* Mahwah, NJ: Lawrence Erlbaum.

Dörnyei, Z. (2005) Personal communication, December 7.

Dörnyei, Z. and Csizér, K. (2002) Some dynamics of language attitudes and motivation: Results of a longitudinal nationwide survey. *Applied Linguistics* 23, 421–462.

Gardner, R.C. (1985) *Social Psychology and Second Language Learning: The Role of Attitudes and Motivation.* London: Edward Arnold.

Gardner, R.C. (2001) Integrative motivation and second language learning: Practical issues. *Kansai University Journal of Foreign Language Education and Research* 2, 71–91.

Gardner, R.C. and Lambert, W.E. (1972) *Attitudes and Motivation in Second Language Learning.* Rowley, MA: Newbury House.

Giles, H., Bourhis, R.Y. and Taylor, D.M. (1977) Towards a theory of language in ethnic group relations. In H. Giles (ed.) *Language, Ethnicity, and Intergroup Relations* (pp. 307–348). London: Academic Press.

Gudykunst, W.B. (1991) *Bridging Differences*. Newbury Park, CA: Sage.

Kang, S.J. (2005) Dynamic emergence of situational willingness to communicate in a second language. *System* 33, 277–292.

Kim, Y.Y. (1991) Intercultural communication competence: A systems-theoretic view, In S. Ting-Toomey and F. Korzenny (eds) *Cross-Cultural Interpersonal Communication* (pp. 259–275). Newbury Park, CA: Sage.

Lantolf, J.P. and Thorne, S.L. (2006) *Sociocultural Theory and the Genesis of Second Language Development*. Oxford: Oxford University Press.

Lave J. and Wenger, E. (1991) *Situated Learning: Legitimate Peripheral Participation*. Cambridge: Cambridge University Press.

Lee, S.I. (2007) Eigono atarashi yakuwari [A new role of English as a lingua franca connecting Asian countries]. *Ryukoku Daigaku Keizai Ronshu* 46, 207–223.

MacIntyre, P.D. (1994) Variables underlying willingness to communicate: A causal analysis. *Communication Research Reports* 11, 135–142.

MacIntyre, P.D., Clément, R., Dörnyei, Z. and Noels, K.A. (1998) Conceptualizing willingness to communicate in a L2: A situated model of L2 confidence and affiliation. *Modern Language Journal* 82, 545–562.

Markus, H. and Nurius, P. (1986) Possible selves. *American Psychologist* 41, 954–969.

Markus, H. and Ruvolo, A. (1989) Possible selves: Personalized representations of goals. In L.A. Pervin (ed.) *Goal Concepts in Personality and Social Psychology* (pp. 211–241). Hillsdale, NJ: Lawrence Erlbaum.

Masgoret, A.M. and Gardner, R.C. (2003) Attitudes, motivation, and second language learning: A meta-analysis of studies conducted by Gardner and associates. *Language Learning* 53, 123–163.

Murphey, T. and Arao, H. (2001) Reported belief changes through near peer role modeling. *TESL-EJ* 5(3). Online at http://tesl-ej.org/ej19/a1.html (Retrieved on October 31, 2007).

Noels, K.A. (2003) Learning Spanish as a second language: Learners' orientations and perceptions of their teachers' communication style. In Z. Dörnyei (ed.) *Attitudes, Orientations, and Motivations in Language Learning* (pp. 97–136). Oxford: Blackwell.

Noels, K.A., Pelletier, L.G., Clément, R. and Vallerand, R.J. (2000) Why are you learning a second language? Motivational orientations and self-determination theory. *Language Learning* 50, 57–85.

Norton, B. (2000) *Identity and Language Learning: Gender, Ethnicity and Educational Change*. Harlow: Longman/Pearson Education.

Norton, B. (2001) Non-participation, imagined communities and the language classroom. In M.P. Breen (ed.) *Learner Contributions to Language Learning: New Directions in Research* (pp. 159–171). Harlow: Longman.

Wenger, E. (1998) *Communities of Practice: Learning, Meaning, and Identity*. Cambridge: Cambridge University Press.

Williams, M. (1994) Motivation in foreign and second language learning: An interactive perspective. *Educational and Child Psychology* 11, 77–84.

Yashima, T. (2000) Orientations and motivation in foreign language learning: A study of Japanese college students. *JACET Bulletin* 31, 121–133.

Yashima, T. (2002) Willingness to communicate in a second language: The Japanese EFL context. *Modern Language Journal* 86, 54–66.

Yashima, T. (2006) A factor analysis of translated SDT items in a preliminary data collection. Unpublished raw data.

Yashima, T. (2007a) SEM analyses to confirm the relationships among variables including international posture, proficiency and L2 WTC. Unpublished raw data.

Yashima, T. (2007b) Autonomy and willingness to communicate: Development of an English-using ideal self. Paper presented at the Independent Learning Association October 2007 Japan conference, Kanda University of International Studies, Chiba, Japan.

Yashima, T. and Zenuk-Nishide, L. (in press) The impact of learning contexts on proficiency, attitudes, and L2 communication: Creating an imagined international community. *System* 36 (4).

Yashima, T., Zenuk-Nishide, L. and Shimizu, K. (2004) The influence of attitudes and affect on willingness to communicate and second language communication. *Language Learning* 54, 119–152.

Appendix A

Scales Used to Explore International Posture and WTC

*negatively-worded items

International Posture (an updated version)
Intergroup Approach-Avoidance tendency (α =0.80)

1) I want to make friends with international students studying in Japan.
2) *I try to avoid talking with foreigners if I can.
3) I would talk to an international student if there was one at school.
4) I wouldn't mind sharing an apartment or room with an international student.
5) I want to participate in a volunteer activity to help foreigners living in the surrounding community.
6) *I would feel somewhat uncomfortable if a foreigner moved in next door.

Interest in International Vocation or Activities (α =0.79)

1) *I would rather stay in my hometown.
2) I want to work in a foreign country.
3) I want to work in an international organisation such as the United Nations.
4) I'm interested in an international career.
5) *I don't think what's happening overseas has much to do with my daily life.
6) *I'd rather avoid the kind of work that sends me overseas frequently.

Interest in International News (α =0.76)

1 I often read and watch news about foreign countries.
2) I often talk about situations and events in foreign countries with my family and/or friends.
3) I have a strong interest in international affairs.
4) *I'm not much interested in overseas news.

Having Things to Communicate to the World ($\alpha = 0.78$)
1) I have thoughts that I want to share with people from other parts of the world.
2) I have issues to address with people in the world.
3) I have ideas about international issues, such as environmental issues and north-south issues.
4) *I have no clear opinions about international issues.

L2 WTC *($\alpha = 0.86$)*
How much would you choose to communicate in each of the following situations in English?
1) When you have a chance to make a presentation in front of a large group?
2) When you find your acquaintance standing before you in a line?
3) When you have a group discussion in an English class?
4) When you have a chance to talk in a small group of strangers?
5) When you are given a chance to talk freely in an English class?
6) When you find your friend standing before you in a line?
7) When you have a chance to talk in front of the class in an English class?
8) When you have a discussion in a small group of friends?

Frequency of communication *($\alpha = 0.85$)*
1) Did you volunteer to respond to or ask questions in English classes?
2) Did you talk to international students or teachers in English at school?
3) Did you try to talk during classroom activities such as pairwork?
4) Did you ask questions to your teachers in English outside class?
5) Did you talk with friends or acquaintances in English outside school?
6) Did you try to talk when you had a chance to speak English in English classes?

Chapter 8

Motivation and Vision: The Relation Between the Ideal L2 Self, Imagination and Visual Style

ABDULLAH S. AL-SHEHRI

Introduction

This chapter reports on a study to investigate the relationship between visual learning style, imagination, ideal language selves and motivated behaviour among language learners. My hypothesis was that learners with a marked visual learning style preference are likely to exhibit a strong capacity for visual imagery and imagination, and that therefore such learners are likely to develop a more potent ideal language self, given the prominent imagery content of the ideal self. In the first part of the chapter I will explain this hypothesis by discussing its key variables in the context of recent theoretical developments in the literature. Much of this literature is reviewed at length in Dörnyei's detailed account of the L2 motivational self-system (Dörnyei, this volume). Therefore, the discussion here will be brief since my purpose is merely to contextualise my hypothesis. Then, I will report on a study I conducted to investigate this hypothesis, drawing on survey data gathered from 200 Arab students studying English.

Theoretical Overview

Dörnyei's L2 Motivational Self-System (Dörnyei, 2005; this volume) presents a new approach to conceptualising the motivation to learn a second/foreign language within a 'self' framework. Essentially, it draws on the theory of 'possible selves' developed in the field of personality psychology through the 1980s. According to Markus and Nurius (1986: 954), possible selves 'represent individuals' ideas of what they might become, what they would like to become, and what they are afraid of becoming, and thus provide a conceptual link between cognition and motivation'. As Markus and Nurius (1986: 181) argue, possible selves thus represent future imagined self-states, including hoped for and dreaded outcomes. Drawing on the work of Higgins (1987), Dörnyei characterises these future imagined self-states as *ideal* and *ought* selves in his L2 Motivational Self-System, where the *ideal* self represents an ideal vision of oneself in the future, while the *ought* self represents a vision of oneself bearing attributes one feels one should possess.

As Oyserman and Markus (1990: 113) explain, possible selves can function as strong incentives in regulating behaviour. But for possible selves to have the power to direct behaviour, it is argued that they need to be vivid, specific and well-elaborated (Markus & Cross, 1994: 424; Markus & Nurius, 1986: 954). This point is reiterated by Dörnyei (2005: 100) who suggests that the more vivid and elaborate the possible self, the more motivationally effective it is likely to be. In this connection, Oyserman and Markus (1990: 113) further propose that 'specific and vivid senses' are involved as key components of possible selves and are instrumental in the motivational and goal-setting process. In particular, power of imagination has been emphasised as critical to the process of visualising possible or ideal selves (Cameron, 1999; Markus & Nurius, 1986; Leondari *et al.*, 1998). In this connection, Taylor *et al.* (1998) suggest that we harness imagination by means of effective mental simulations, constituting visualised representations of an event or series of events. As they remark (Taylor *et al.*, 1998: 430), mental simulations make events seem real and almost tangible since they usually operate within the constraints of reality, and thus can function as powerful motivators to self-regulate behaviour. As Dörnyei (this volume) emphasises, it is this power of *imagined reality* that is critical to our understanding of how possible selves are formed and how they harness motivation. An important empirical question, therefore, is whether a link can be identified between imaginative capacity, ideal self and motivation.

However, my hypothesis includes one further variable: visual style preference. Studies on visual style preferences have a long history, dating back to the 1960s (e.g. Rimm & Bottrell, 1969). Visual learners rely heavily on the visual channel when processing and internalising experience. According to Kinsella (1995: 227), such learners exhibit the following key characteristics:

- They relate to words such as *see, look, pictures, observe, show, imagine.*
- They understand better and retain information most efficiently by looking at visually stimulating objects such as pictures, diagrams and charts.
- They prefer modelling and observation to verbal explanation.
- They enjoy a powerful visual memory and can remember, for example, faces, locations, signs.

An interesting question is whether such preference for the visual channel in processing information and experience might also reflect a marked capacity for visualisation or imagination. From a neurological perspective, research has shown that vision and visual imagination may utilise similar neural circuitry (Modell, 2003), suggesting a simultaneous functionality between the visual and imaginative capacities in the human brain. If so, might it be possible to find a relationship between visual style and imagination, and consequently a relationship between these visual and imaginative capacities and the ideal self and motivation? Put simply, my assumption is that visual learners will have a better chance of imagining more vivid ideal selves, which in turn will generate stronger motivation to attain such ideal selves.

Therein lies my hypothesis, which the study described in the next section attempted to investigate.

Method

Participants

The sample consisted of 200 participants, who were recruited in two phases. Ninety-eight of them took part in the first phase of the study; of these, 20 participants were Saudi university students studying English as a second language in Saudi Arabia, and 78 were Arab students studying English as a second language in the UK as a prerequisite to their subsequent university studies. The second phase of the data collection took place in Saudi Arabia, involving 102 Saudi high school graduates who studied English as a second language and were about to complete a one-year English language course sponsored by a governmental training programme.

Instrument

Data were collected by means of a self-report questionnaire. The final version contained a total of 41 items that focused on four main variables: (1) *Motivated behaviour and effort* (18 items), which was the criterion measure; (2) *ideal L2 self* (eight items); (3) *visual learning style* (10 items); and (4) *imagination* (five items). The items for the *motivated behaviour and effort*, the *ideal L2 self* and the *imagination* scales were developed in cooperation with the researcher's supervisor, Zoltán Dörnyei, for the purpose of this study. The items for the *visual learning style* were based on Cohen *et al.*'s (2002) *Learning Style Survey* and Kinsella's (1995) *Perceptual Learning Preference Survey*. The instrument was submitted to a brief piloting phase, as a result of which the scales were fine-tuned. All variable items were measured by a five-point Likert-scale, ranging from 'strongly agree' to 'strongly disagree'. The questionnaire was in Arabic; the English translation of the final version is included in Appendix A.

Procedure

Finding participants for the survey was carried out following several strategies. First, a snowball sampling strategy was used at Nottingham

University, where the researcher studied, involving various acquaintances and their friends. Second, an electronic copy of the questionnaire was posted on an online internet forum for Arab students studying in the UK (this forum offered a facility to help researchers recruit participants). Third, copies of the questionnaire were emailed to Saudi Arabia, where the researcher's friends distributed them to university students. Finally, the second phase of data collection involved manual distribution of the questionnaire by the researcher to students in Saudi Arabia.

Data analysis

Data were analysed using SPSS 12.0. First a reliability analysis was run to check the Cronbach alpha internal consistency reliability coefficients of the four sets of items measuring the main variables, and based on a *post hoc* item analysis some items were excluded from further analyses. The reliability of the final scales was satisfactory: *motivated behaviour and effort:* 0.89, *ideal L2 self:* 0.85, *visual learning style:* 0.80, *imagination:* 0.65. These scales were then submitted to correlation analysis and regression analysis (to compute multiple correlations).

Results and Discussion

Table 8.1 presents the descriptive statistics of the four variables measured in the survey, and Table 8.2 presents their intercorrelation matrix.

As can be seen in Table 8.2, there is a strong correlation between the *ideal L2 self* and the criterion measure, accounting for 61% of the variance. This confirms that the ideal language self is indeed a major motivational factor. My second hypothesis was that visual learners would be better suited to develop well-defined ideal selves, and the strong correlation between *visual style* and *ideal L2 self* proves that this hypothesis was also correct. This link might explain Bailey *et al.*'s (2000) finding that visual learners usually outperform tactile/kinaesthetic learners. The imagery aspect of the ideal language self is further evidenced by the significant positive correlation between *imagination* and *ideal L2 self*.

Table 8.1 Descriptive statistics of the variables in the survey ($N = 200$)

	Min.	*Max.*	*M*	*SD*
Motivated behaviour	1.00	4.24	1.83	0.57
Ideal L2 self	1.00	4.75	1.60	0.68
Visual style	1.00	4.56	1.91	0.62
Imagination	1.00	5.00	2.20	0.79

Table 8.2 Pearson correlations of the variables

	Motivated behaviour	*Ideal L2 self*	*Visual style*	*Imagination*
Motivated behaviour	–			
Ideal L2 self	0.78	–		
Visual style	0.69	0.65	–	
Imagination	0.39	0.46	0.40	–

Note: All correlations are significant at the $p < 0.01$ level

Table 8.2 also reveals that one's imaginative capacity is positively related to one's visual style. This confirms the findings of Davis *et al.* (1970), according to which visual imagers enjoy a capacity to access a richer domain of imagination. In addition, Modell (2003) has also highlighted the interface between vision and visual imagery. These studies suggested a simultaneous functionality between the visual capacity and one's ability to imagine and my data supported this link. In order to measure the composite impact of these two variables on the ideal language self, I computed multiple correlations between the variables. The obtained multiple correlation coefficient of 0.69 meant that *visual style* and *imagination* together explained 47% of the variance in *ideal L2 self*, which is a surprisingly high proportion. This confirms that individuals with a more developed visual/imaginative capacity can develop a more potent ideal language self.

Conclusion

The ultimate aim of the present study was to examine the relationship among the learners' visual learning style, imagination, ideal language selves and motivated behaviour. My expectation was that learners with a visual style preference are more likely to access a richer domain of imagination, and that because of the prominent imagery content of the ideal self, the learners' overall visual/imaginative capacity will be positively related to their ideal language selves. The significant correlations confirmed this hypothesis, indicating that visual learners are more capable of perceiving a vivid representation of their ideal selves, which in turn is reflected in heightened motivated effort and behaviour.

Although the findings of this study are promising, we must not overstate the significance of a relatively small-scale correlational study. Further research that employs a more elaborate measure of various aspects of imagery will be needed to test the validity of the above claims.

It is hoped, nonetheless, that the intriguing results of this study will inspire further investigations in this area to shed light on the nature of the sensual element of the ideal self.

References

Bailey, P., Onwuegbuzie, A. and Daley, C. (2000) Using learning style to predict foreign language achievement at the college level. *System* 28, 115–133.

Cameron, J.E. (1999) Social identity and the pursuit of possible selves: Implications for the psychological well-being of university students. *Group Dynamics: Theory, Research, and Practice* 3 (3), 179–189.

Cohen, A.D., Oxford, R.L. and Chi, J.C. (2002) *Learning Style Survey: Assessing Your Own Learning Styles*. Minneapolis, MN: Center for Advanced Research on Language Acquisition, University of Minnesota. Online document – http://www.tc.umn.edu/~adcohen/publications.html#strategies. Accessed 30 July 2008.

Davis, D., McLemore, C. and London, P. (1970) The role of visual imagery in desensitization. *Behaviour Research and Therapy* 8, 11–13.

Dörnyei, Z. (2005) *The Psychology of the Language Learner: Individual Differences in Second Language Acquisition*, Mahwah, NJ: Lawrence Erlbaum.

Higgins, E.T. (1987) Self-discrepancy: A theory relating self and affect. *Psychological Review* 94, 319–340.

Kinsella, K. (1995) Perceptual learning preferences survey. In J. Reid (ed.) *Learning Styles in the ESL/EFL Classroom* (pp. 221–238). Boston: Heinle & Heinle.

Leondari, A., Syngokllitou, E. and Kiosseoglou, G. (1998) Academic achievement, motivation and possible selves. *Journal of Adolescence* 21, 219–222.

Markus, H. and Nurius, P. (1986) Possible selves. *American Psychologist* 41, 954–969.

Markus, H. and Cross, S. (1994) Self-schemas, possible selves, and competent performance. *Journal of Educational Psychology* 86 (3), 423–438.

Modell, A. (2003) *Imagination and the Meaningful Brain*. Cambridge, MA: MIT Press.

Oyserman, D. and Markus, H. (1990) Possible selves and delinquency. *Journal of Personality and Social Psychology* 59 (1), 112–125.

Rimm, D. and Bottrell, J. (1969) Four measures of visual imagination. *Behaviour Research and Therapy* 1, 63–69.

Taylor, S., Pham, L., Rivkin, I. and Armor, D. (1998) Harnessing the imagination: Mental simulation, self-regulation, and coping. *American Psychologist* 53 (4), 429–439.

Appendix A

Questionnaire to Measure Motivation, Ideal L2 Self, Visual Learning Style and Imagination

Items and composite variables in the questionnaire (5-point Likert scales)

Imagination

- When I read an interesting story, I imagine its events and characters.
- When someone tells me about an interesting place, I imagine what it would be like to be there.

- I avoid running into problems by imagining how they might happen in future.
- When I feel distressed, I imagine things that make me feel happy.
- I get drifted away by imagination.

Visual Learning Style

- I remember something better if I write it down.
- I like to take notes during lectures
- When I listen, I can visualise pictures, numbers, or words in my head.
- I underline or highlight the important information I read.
- Charts, diagrams, and maps help me understand what someone says.
- I use colour-coding to help me as I learn or work.
- Illustrations and charts make it easier for me to remember information.
- I understand lectures better when teachers write on the board.
- I make drawings in my notes to remember important material.
- I am better at remembering peoples' faces but not their names.

Ideal Self

- I like to think of myself as someone who will be able to speak English.
- Whenever I think of my future career I imagine myself being able to speak English.
- Whatever I do in the future, I think I will be needing English.
- If my dreams come true, I will speak English fluently in the future.
- If everything goes well, I see myself speaking English fluently some day.
- I can imagine a time when I can speak English with native speakers from other countries.
- The things I want to do in the future require me to speak English.
- The job I imagine having in the future requires that I speak English well.

Motivated Behaviour and Effort

- If my teacher wanted someone to do an extra English assignment, I would certainly volunteer.
- If an English course was offered in the future, I would like to take it.
- I frequently think over what we have learnt in my English class.
- I am prepared to expend a lot of effort in learning English.
- If English were not taught in school, I would try to obtain lessons in English somewhere else.
- When it comes to English homework, I work very carefully, making sure I understand everything.
- I have a very strong desire to learn English.

○ Considering how I study English, I can honestly say that I really try to learn English.
○ Learning English is one of the most important aspects in my life.
○ After I get my English assignment, I always rewrite them, correcting my mistakes.
○ I am determined to push myself to learn English.
○ When I am in English class, I volunteer answers as much as possible.
○ If I could have access to English-speaking TV stations, I would try to watch them often.
○ I am willing to work hard at learning English.
○ When I hear an English song on the radio, I listen carefully and try to understand all the words.
○ It is very important for me to learn English.
○ If I had the opportunity to speak English outside of school, I would do it as much as I can.
○ When I have a problem understanding something we are learning in English class, I immediately ask the teacher for help.

Chapter 9

Links between Ethnolinguistic Affiliation, Self-related Motivation and Second Language Fluency: Are They Mediated by Psycholinguistic Variables?

NORMAN SEGALOWITZ, ELIZABETH GATBONTON and
PAVEL TROFIMOVICH

Introduction

Since the early 1970s, a great deal of literature has documented the intimate link between language and ethnic group identity (Fought, 2006; Giles, 1967; Gumperz & Cook-Gumperz, 1982; Labov, 1972; Pavlenko & Blackledge, 2004; Ricento, 2005) and ethnic group affiliation (Gatbonton, 1975; Gatbonton *et al.*, 2005). For this reason, a number of scholars have hypothesised that this language and identity link would have consequences for the level of skill attained in a second language (L2) (Gatbonton *et al.*, 2005; Lambert, 1967; Taylor, 1977; Taylor *et al.*, 1977). Ellinger (2000) presents empirical evidence of this in her study of a group of Russian and Hebrew learners of English as a lingua franca in Israel. Participants who had strong identification with their respective ethnolinguistic groups had higher levels of achievement in English as measured through classroom achievement tests, teacher evaluations, and other measures. Coupland *et al.* (2005) also found, in a multiple regression analysis of the responses of high school students in Wales, that students' strong sense of identification and personal engagement with the Welsh language and community contributed significantly to explaining the levels of competence they attained in Welsh.

Recently, Gatbonton and Trofimovich (2008) provided similar evidence of a complex relationship between identity variables on the one hand and measures of L2 proficiency on the other. These researchers showed that a group of Québec Francophones' sense of belonging and loyalty to their primary group (Québécois) and to a target language group (English speakers) had both positive and negative consequences for the levels of English proficiency they attained. The positive consequences were that participants with a strong sense of identification

172

both with their primary ethnolinguistic group and their target language group had significantly higher levels of proficiency in English than those who showed only strong identification with their primary group. This result complements the findings of studies on the role of attitudes and motivations showing that a positive orientation towards the target language group leads to higher levels of L2 proficiency attained (Dörnyei, 2003, 2005; Gardner & Lambert, 1972). The negative consequences were found for participants who had strong beliefs in the role of language in maintaining the identity of their primary group as well as for those who showed support for its political aspirations. These participants were seen to have lower levels of proficiency in their L2 compared to those with a weaker degree of affiliation and support for the political agendas of their group. The question of interest in this chapter is how best to explain the connection between what is presumably a social cognition (ethnolinguistic affiliation) and a psycholinguistic skill (L2 proficiency).

At least two possible explanations come to mind. One is that L2 speakers with a strong sense of affiliation to their primary ethnolinguistic group may deliberately 'hold back' some aspects of their L2 use in order to avoid sounding too much like members of a different ethnolinguistic group. Bourhis and Giles (1977) provide evidence for this deliberate strategy used by L2 users in order to differentiate themselves from their interlocutors. When challenged by an interlocutor speaking in a clear English accent about the usefulness of learning Welsh, the integratively motivated learners in the group broadened their Welsh accent in English in an apparent move to show their disapproval of the challenger's position. These interlocutors thus used a more Welsh-accented English speech than the speech they employed when talking about a more neutral topic just prior to the challenge.

Such deliberate manipulation of one's speech to create a social distance from an interlocutor from a different target language community has also been shown in Labov's (1972) classic study of residents of Martha's Vineyard in the United States (see also Blake & Josey, 2003, for an update of this study). Long-term inhabitants of Martha's Vineyard who wished to affirm their claim as the true residents of this fishing community differentiated themselves from non-residents (who invaded the place in the summer) by pronouncing their vowel sounds differently from non-residents. It has also been shown that speakers switch languages (e.g. Bailey, 2000), retain traces of an accent or non-native-like prosodic features (e.g. Boberg, 2004; Schilling-Estes, 2004), or use vocabulary (e.g. Doran, 2004) to set themselves apart from speakers of other language communities.

However, although such examples demonstrate that deliberate speech *distancing* can occur, it seems unlikely that such distancing is the only explanation for the existence of an ethnolinguistic affiliation–proficiency link. This is because, as will be seen later in this chapter, affiliation is also linked to L2 speech patterns that differ from nativelike speech in ways that are far too subtle to reflect conscious efforts to sound non-nativelike.

A second possible explanation for an affiliation–proficiency link, one possibly complementary to the first given above, may be that a sense of ethnolinguistic affiliation shapes the social niche one inhabits and this in turn determines the type and range of experiences a person might have in hearing and using the target language. For example, if a person's sense of ethnolinguistic affiliation leads him or her to limit contact with members of another ethnolinguistic group, then it follows that he or she would have fewer occasions to be exposed to the language and thus experience fewer opportunities to increase his or her proficiency. This shaping of L2 experiences would impact, in turn, on a number of *psycholinguistically* relevant cognitive variables (e.g. ability to perceive important phonetic distinctions in the L2 or to discern recurrent, formulaic sequences in the L2) that normally would contribute to L2 development. This chapter explores the feasibility of the explanation that the affiliation–proficiency link may be mediated by psycholinguistic variables.

Anchor Question

A useful way to start this discussion is to identify an anchor question to keep in mind throughout the rest of this chapter. This anchor question could be formulated as follows: *Does ethnolinguistic affiliation (language identity) impact on some critical aspects of language learning motivation in such a way as to shape individual differences in L2 acquisition outcomes?*

In addressing this question, we will draw on re-analyses of data from three recent studies in our lab (Gatbonton & Trofimovich, 2008; Gatbonton *et al.*, 2007; Trofimovich *et al.*, 2007). These studies were not conceived with the above anchor question in mind. Nevertheless, we believe that the data from these studies shed interesting light on issues raised by that question. These three studies focused on adult Francophone users of English in Québec, the majority of whom were no longer involved in instructed language learning at the time of the studies. There were considerable individual differences among the participants in two areas of focus in this chapter – level of L2 attainment and feelings of affiliation to a primary ethnolinguistic group. Many of the participants considered themselves to be members of an ethnolinguistic group (Québécois) which they considered to be 'distinct' from other ethnolinguistic groups (namely, those who speak English or some other [non-French] language) but who nevertheless live together with them in the same province (Québec).

The studies reported here address motivational issues linked to group identity and affiliation. However, these studies contrast with much of the motivational research in L2 acquisition. Unlike most such studies, our research is not concerned with how motivation impacts on choices made in the classroom (e.g. whether or not to study another language, which language to study and why). Instead, it is concerned with language use *outside* the classroom (see, for example, MacIntyre, 2007, for a discussion of willingness to communicate as a psycholinguistic construct) and individual differences in attainment, once acquisition has most likely stabilised with low probability of much more learning taking place.

Figure 9.1 presents a graphical view of the anchor question that will serve as an overview of the issues as they unfold in this chapter. The figure shows that an L2 user's sense of ethnolinguistic affiliation influences L2 proficiency through L2 acquisition motivation and other mediating variables. The data reviewed here do not speak directly to the specific nature of the motivational system. However, they fit into the framework of an L2 Motivational Self System for L2 use proposed by Dörnyei (2005, see also this volume; Csizér & Dörnyei, 2005) and discussed below. Thus, the focus of this chapter can be stated as an attempt to understand how the affiliation–proficiency link can be viewed in terms of psycholinguistic variables implicated in the association between the L2 motivational self-system and proficiency.

The studies reported below involved a group of 59 adult French speakers (aged from 18 to 72; 37 females, 22 males) living in Montréal (Québec) and the surrounding region. All participants reported having Francophone parents and Québec French as their first language. All but two were born in Québec; with no exception, all were raised in Québec. They spoke French at home and had attained different levels of proficiency in English as an L2. All participants reported using English to a greater or lesser extent in their daily transactions at work and/or in their neighbourhoods (with merchants, etc.).

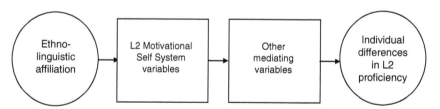

Figure 9.1 Graphical representation showing that a second language (L2) users' feeling of ethnolinguistic affiliation contributes to an L2 Motivational Self System, which in turn impacts on L2 proficiency through some as yet unidentified mediating variables, resulting in observable individual differences in performance

Study 1: Establishing the Ethnolinguistic Affiliation–Proficiency Link

The first step in discussing the link between L2 proficiency and ethnolinguistic affiliation is to establish operational definitions for the proficiency and affiliation constructs and then to investigate what kinds of general relationships exist between them in this population. Gatbonton and Trofimovich (2008) accomplished this in their study as follows.

L2 proficiency. The 59 participants were recorded reading aloud a special story text. This text contained 70 exemplars of the voiced interdental fricative /ð/. This phoneme is often rendered as the voiced alveolar /d/ by French Canadian speakers and is considered a strong phonological marker of the speaker's origin (Blake & Josey, 2003; Labov, 1972). The recordings of the full reading of the story were then presented to a panel of 10 native English speakers for rating on seven features of proficiency. In addition, the participants also filled out questionnaires detailing their history of learning English as an L2, filled out scales on 12 self-rated measures of L2 proficiency, and scales on the amount of English used in their daily lives. As a group, they rated their daily use of English as being at about 26.8%, ranging from 0% to 100%.

Ethnolinguistic affiliation. An Ethnic Group Affiliation (EGA) questionnaire was specifically developed to measure language identity in ways that were appropriate to the historical, political and social context of Québec where the participants lived. This questionnaire consisted of 21 9-point Likert-type scales of the following types: label preference (Québécois, Canadian, French Canadian), beliefs in the importance of language in defining personal and group identity, emotional reactions to their own ethnic group, and willingness to engage in political action in defense of the group (e.g. supporting French unilingualism, promoting display of the Québec flag, favouring political independence). The rating scale data were subjected to an exploratory factor analysis and four clear factors emerged involving 20 of the items (accounting for 58% of the variance; all factor loadings ≥ 0.52). These were subsequently labeled as follows:

(1) *Core EGA* (nine items retained): These items addressed basic feelings towards the participant's own ethnic group (e.g. pride in its history and accomplishments, in displaying its symbols, in knowing its language, in defending it).

(2) *Group Identity EGA* (four items retained): These items addressed willingness to be identified as 'Canadian' and emotional reactions to this identification. While there was some variation in willingness to be identified as 'Québécois', most participants scored high on this

item; consequently, this item did not load on any factor. The term 'French Canadian' turned out to be ambiguous and so was dropped.

(3) *Language EGA* (three items retained): These items addressed the importance of language in defining group identity.

(4) *Political EGA* (four items retained): These items addressed political issues related to language and identity (e.g. Québec independence, language of commercial signs, schooling in French for immigrants).

The question about whether there exists an ethnolinguistic affiliation–proficiency link was investigated by submitting each of the four EGA factors (Core, Group Identity, Language and Political EGA) to a correlational analysis with the 12 features of self-rated proficiency and with the measures of native speaker rated proficiency. All the significant correlations reported below yielded Spearman rho-values between 0.42 and 0.48, with $p < 0.002$ (after Bonferroni corrections for the large number of correlations were applied). The principal results were the following:

- *Group Identity EGA* correlated significantly with self-rated global ability. Those participants scoring high on Canadian identity rated the quality of their English to be higher than did those scoring low on Canadian identity. Gatbonton and Trofimovich (2008) looked more closely at this factor. Of the 59 participants, they found that 25 scored very high on the 9-point scale for Québécois identity (nine on the scale). Of these, 12 indicated strong willingness to also be identified as Canadian (scoring eight or nine on the scale) and 13 indicated strong unwillingness to be identified as Canadian (scoring one or two on the scale). Those people embracing the double Québécois-Canadian identity rated their own global ability in L2 English to be significantly higher than those embracing only the Québécois identity.

- *Language EGA* correlated significantly with native speaker ratings of proficiency. Those scoring high on beliefs about the importance of language for identity were rated as less comprehensible by native speaking judges than those scoring low on this belief.

- *Political EGA* correlated significantly with the native speaker ratings and with self-rated global measure of proficiency. Those scoring high on beliefs supportive of their ethnolinguistic group's political aspirations (independence from Canada for the Province of Québec) were perceived to be more highly accented, less fluent, and less comprehensible by native speakers; they also rated themselves globally to be lower on English ability.

- No EGA factor correlated with self-rated accentedness and *Core EGA* correlated with none of the proficiency measures.

In sum, these results provided evidence for a strong relationship between various social measures of ethnolinguistic affiliation and L2 proficiency.

Unfortunately, at the time the research was conducted, there was no direct assessment of these participants' sense of an L2 self as described by Dörnyei (2005). However, given Dörnyei's (2005: 106) discussion of the L2 Motivational Self System, the following account seems plausible. Those embracing the double identity may be said to have possessed an *ideal L2 self* (Dörnyei, 2005: 102–104) in which they saw themselves speaking the other language (English) in addition to their native language as an inherent aspect of their overall identity. This ideal self reflects a sense of inclusiveness extending to the larger Canadian population, including speakers of English. That is, for them, speaking English as an L2 was not necessarily negative nor did it imply that they were serving as an 'ambassador' to another group. Rather, it meant that they were speaking the language of another part of their own group, as defined by them to include all Canadians regardless of native language. In other words, being Canadian was part of these participants' identity too, along with being Québécois, and this inclusive identity entailed the need to speak English in order to communicate with other members of this larger community. In contrast, this aspect of ideal L2 self was absent in those who held the more exclusive sense of identity (Québécois only).

Dörnyei also identifies an *ought-to L2 self*, which refers to the duties and obligations one has in order to *avoid* possible negative outcomes (Dörnyei, 2005: 106). Here, Dörnyei appears to have in mind instrumental motivations such as speaking the L2 in order to avoid unemployment. Perhaps, however, this understanding of the *ought-to self* should be extended to include duties and obligations to *avoid* activities that could lead to negative outcomes. For example, people scoring high on the Political EGA factor could be described as holding certain political aspirations as part of the belief system underlying their sense of ethnolinguistic affiliation. These beliefs might entail obligations not to do anything that might compromise their political goals, including not speaking too well the language of what they perceive to be a competitor group.

Finally, Dörnyei (2005) identifies a component of the L2 Motivational System he calls *L2 learning experience*. This refers to 'situation specific motives related to the immediate learning environment and experience' (Dörnyei, 2005: 106). Gatbonton and Trofimovich (2008) did not inquire into the beliefs the participants had in this category, but it is not difficult to imagine why it might be fruitful to do so. For example, it could be that people will differ in terms of whether they think it would be desirable from an L2 acquisition perspective to immerse themselves in particular kinds of environments, and these beliefs may well be associated with different L2 proficiency outcomes.

In light of these speculations, one can imagine a more fine-grained version of Figure 9.1 to reflect the results of this first analysis. The attempt to measure ethnolinguistic affiliation yielded four factors, here labeled Core, Group Identity, Language and Political EGA. Three of these – Group Identity, Language and Political – appeared to be significantly associated with individual differences in L2 proficiency in one way or another. Moreover, the group identity factor encompassed two possibilities – an inclusive identity that was more positively associated with L2 proficiency and an exclusive identity that was less positively associated with L2 proficiency.

It is not clear, however, through what mechanisms the four postulated L2 self elements might impact on L2 proficiency. One possibility, mentioned earlier, is that speakers with the more inclusive L2 self are more likely to avail themselves of opportunities to use the target language in order to learn and practise those nuances that signal acceptance and membership in the target language community. In a similar vein, those with the less inclusive L2 self or with a strong ought-to self might avoid such opportunities to use the language or, when necessary, might even modify their speech in ways that ensure their primary linguistic identity is clearly marked (e.g. Appel & Schoonen, 2005; Bailey, 2000; Schilling-Estes, 2004). Gatbonton and Trofimovich (2008) were able to explore the hypothesis that *language use* mediates the link between language identity, as reflected in the different types of L2 self, and L2 proficiency. They computed Spearman rank correlations between the self-reported use of the L2, the various EGA measures, and the proficiency features. The chief findings were the following:

- L2 use did not correlate significantly with Core or with Group Identity EGA.
- L2 use did correlate significantly and negatively with Language EGA, indicating that the less important language was believed to be a factor in identity, the greater the use of the L2.
- L2 use did correlate significantly and negatively with Political EGA, indicating that the lower the support for the primary group's political aspirations, the greater the use of the L2.
- L2 use did correlate significantly and positively with all features of proficiency.

The most important finding, however, was the following:

- All the significant correlations reported earlier between the various measures of ethnolinguistic affiliation (EGA) and L2 proficiency vanished when the amount of L2 use was statistically controlled for through partial correlations.

This result indicates that the association between the social variable ethnolinguistic affiliation and L2 proficiency was mediated by L2 use and that the social variable had only an *indirect* association with L2 proficiency.

Study 2: Measuring L2 Proficiency

The measures of L2 proficiency presented so far were only subjective self-reports made by the participants themselves and subjective ratings by native speakers of English. More objective measures of L2 proficiency could be useful in allowing one to pinpoint more precisely the locus of impact from social variables via language use on proficiency. Trofimovich *et al.* (2007) provide such an analysis in an examination of the data from 40 of the original pool of 59 participants reported on in Gatbonton and Trofimovich (2008).

Trofimovich *et al.* (2007) focused on one phonological target in the English speech of French speaking Quebecers, one that is known to be a reliable marker of the ethnolinguistic origin of the speaker. The target phoneme was the interdental fricative (/ð/), typically difficult for French Canadian speakers of English and typically rendered as /d/. There are usually strong individual differences in how frequently /ð/ is pronounced or mispronounced. The major focus of the study was to identify the factors that determine the nature of these individual differences.

As mentioned earlier, the participants had been given a special story text to read aloud. This text contained 70 target instances of /ð/ embedded in seven different phonetic contexts with 10 exemplars in each environment (originally eight environments were used but for reasons described in Trofimovich *et al.*, only seven were included in the final analyses). To explain the logic of the analysis conducted in that study, it will be helpful to refer to Table 9.1. Table 9.1 shows participants (Subject #1–40) in the rows and the seven different phonetic contexts as the columns.

As expected, there were individual differences in the ability to produce native-like renditions of /ð/; some people were good at it while others were poor. The numbers in the column marked Total Correct reflect these individual differences, shown here as the total out of the 70 exemplars attempted that were accurately pronounced. The numbers in the Total Correct column can, in principle, serve as a measure of each individual's level of phonological attainment with respect to /ð/, under the assumption that the more accurately a person pronounces /ð/ the greater the level of phonological attainment achieved. As can be seen in Table 9.1, the participants are shown as ranked approximately in order of mastery of the /ð/ (the reason for the less than perfect ranking will be evident in a moment).

Table 9.1 Matrix showing the gradual diffusion of accurate pronunciation of English /ð/ by 40 French speakers across seven phonetic environments, revealing an implicational scale pattern (see text for explanation)

S#	Total correct: max=70	#1 Voiced fricative/affricate, e.g. was there	#2 Sentence initial, e.g. The...	#3 Inter-vocalic, e.g. father	#4 Voiceless stop, e.g. took the	#5 Voiceless fricative/affricate, e.g. off the	#6 Nasal, e.g. on the	#7 Voiced stop, e.g. wanted the	Stage
31	5	0	0	0	0	0	0	0	1
18	7	0	0	0	0	0	0	0	1
29	8	0	0	0	0	0	0	0	1
4	8	0	0	0	0	0	0	0	1
20	13	0	0	0	0	0	0	0	1
21	12	01	0	0	0	0	0	0	2
3	15	01	0	0	0	0	0	0	2
14	14	0*	01	0	0	0	0	0	3
10	12	0*	01	0	0	0	0	0	3
19	13	01	01	0	0	0	0	0	3
12	15	01	01	0	0	0	0	0	3
23	18	01	01	0	0	0	01*	0	3
13	13	01	01	0	01*	0	0	0	3

Table 9.1 (Continued)

S#	Total correct: max=70	#1 Voiced fricative/affricate, e.g. was there	#2 Sentence initial, e.g. The...	#3 Intervocalic, e.g. father	#4 Voiceless stop, e.g. took the	#5 Voiceless fricative/affricate, e.g. off the	#6 Nasal, e.g. on the	#7 Voiced stop, e.g. wanted the	Stage
32	20	01	01	0	01*	0	01*	0	3
7	17	01	01	01	01	0	0	0	5
6	16	01	01	0*	01	0	0	0	5
5	26	01	01	01	01	01	0	0	6
1	22	01	01	01	0*	01	01	0	7
11	27	01	01	0*	01	01	01	0	7
34	28	01	01	01	01	01	01	0	7
37	24	01	01	01	01	01	01	0	7
30	21	01	01	01	01	01	01	0	7
36	26	01	01	01	01	01	01	01	8
35	22	01	01	0*	0*	01	01	01	8
38	26	01	01	01	01	01	01	01	8
26	32	01	01	01	01	01	01	01	8
15	37	01	01	1*	01	01	01	01	8

Table 9.1 (*Continued*)

8	41	01	01	01	01	01	01	01	8
2	41	1	01	01	01	01	01	01	9
22	37	01*	1	01	01	01	01	01	10
28	43	01*	1	01	01	01	01	01	10
25	58	1	1	1	1	01*	1	1	15
33	58	1	1	1	1	01*	1	1	15
17	61	1	1	1	1	01*	1	1	15
39	66	1	1	1	1	1	1	1	15
16	67	1	1	1	1	1	1	1	15
24	69	1	1	1	1	1	1	1	15
9	69	1	1	1	1	1	1	1	15
40	69	1	1	1	1	1	1	1	15
27	70	1	1	1	1	1	1	1	15

*Entries that depart from the expected implicational scale pattern. The cell entry '0' indicates 20% accuracy or worse. '1' indicates 80% accuracy or better. '01' indicates 21–79% accuracy.

By focusing only on the Total Correct, however, some important features of the data are missed. This becomes clear when one looks more closely at the performance of each individual with /ð/ in each of the phonetic environments. Following a proposal by Gatbonton (1975), the cells corresponding to each phonetic environment contain the codes '0' and/or '1'. The code '0' indicates that this speaker rarely achieved native-like pronunciation of /ð/ in the corresponding phonetic context (20% accuracy or worse). A '1' indicates that this speaker (nearly) always achieved a native-like pronunciation of /ð/ in the corresponding phonetic context (80% accuracy or better). A '01' indicates that both accurate and inaccurate forms co-existed in this context (21–79% accuracy level). Table 9.1 also shows the stage to which the speaker could be assigned. For this, each pattern can be thought of as representing a 'stage' of phonological development with respect to the target phoneme. Seven environments will yield a set of 15 distinct possible patterns that fit into an implicational scale (out of a potential $7^3 = 343$ possible patterns). A pattern of all '0' (all or most inaccurate) represents the lowest stage (Stage 1), a pattern of all '1' (all or most accurate) represents the highest stage (Stage 15), and various mixtures of '0', '01' and '1' represent intermediate stages.

There is something interesting about the pattern of results that appeared in the matrix when the data were coded in this way. One might have expected that accurate and inaccurate forms would be randomly scattered across the environments and that the speakers would be differentiated only by the total number of correct productions. This is not, in fact, what occurred. With appropriate ordering of the columns, an *implicational scale* emerged. This scale indicates that the native-like forms of /ð/ emerge across levels of phonological attainment in a systematic way, with the native-like typically appearing (with very few exceptions) in certain environments before others. Moreover, the pattern exhibited a systematic and gradual 'diffusion' of the native-like forms. Thus, there were some speakers who were generally inaccurate (all '0' for their entries). There were others whose accurate rendition of the target sound appeared alongside inaccurate forms in a few environments (coded as '01'). In fact, it was possible to put the environments into an order that reflected an implicational pattern (if environment X contained an accurate form, then so did environment Y, etc.). Had the distribution been truly random across environments, this would not have been possible. See Trofimovich *et al.* (2007) for details about how this ordering was arrived at. Thus, if we think of the individuals as lying along a continuum of individual differences in phonological attainment, then it appears that the appearance of the correct forms emerge in various phonetic contexts in a systematic pattern.

Examination of the matrix also shows that where some speakers were coded as '01' in some environment, other speakers were coded as '1', to indicate that, for these speakers, mostly correct forms appeared. An implicational pattern emerged here as well; that is, if someone had a correct form in environment Y then they also had it in environment Z. In other words, there appears to be a similar systematic gradual elimination of variable forms, replaced by correct forms, as there was for the appearance of variable forms in place of incorrect ones. These results replicated and extended the findings of Gatbonton (1978) who first proposed the idea of implicational scaling for understanding L2 phonological development (in Gatbonton, 1975). See Trofimovich *et al.* (2007) for full details of these analyses.

The emergence of the gradual diffusion pattern just described depends on the way the phonetic environments (the columns in Table 9.1) are ranked according to their ease of accommodating accurate production of /ð/. For example, the voiced fricative environment most easily admitted accurate /ð/ while voiced stop least easily admitted accurate /ð/. The question arises, then, what are the factors responsible for this ordering of the environments leading to the observed pattern of individual differences? The analyses reported in Trofimovich *et al.* (2007) pointed to two important psycholinguistic processing variables. The first variable was the perceptual similarity between the target English voiced /ð/, when that target was embedded in a given phonetic environment, to other sounds in French with which it might be confused. The idea here is that the more perceptually similar an L2 (English) target sound is to a specific native language (French) sound, the harder it will be for a native French speaker to avoid 'assimilating' the L2 target to a French sound (e.g. Baker *et al.*, 2008; Guion *et al.*, 2000). The result will be an inaccurate pronunciation of those L2 sounds that closely resemble similar, but not necessarily phonetically identical, sounds in the native language. For example, instead of producing a nativelike English /ð/ in a given phonetic context, the speaker will more likely produce a sound that is perceptually similar to it in French (e.g. the English /ð/ in 'wanted the' will likely be assimilated to, and consequently produced as, French /d/).

The second psycholinguistic processing variable proposed in Trofimovich *et al.* (2007) was the frequency with which the target voiced /ð/ occurred in English in the various phonetic environments. The idea here is that the more frequently a target sound occurred in that environment, the easier it would be for L2 users to master that sound in that environment.

Trofimovich *et al.* (2007) determined independently the L1–L2 similarity and the frequency characteristics for each of the target environments, and used the results to order the environments to construct Table 9.1. The outcome was that when the environments were ordered in this way, the participants' data filled the cells in a manner consistent with the gradual diffusion pattern described above far greater than was possible by chance alone (that is, assuming random, nonsystematic distribution across environments), $\chi^2(1) = 262.58$, $p < 0.01$.

The result of this analysis is strongly consistent with the previous conclusion that *language use* is the factor that has the direct impact on L2 proficiency, and not directly associated with the social variable as such. This is because the implicational scale patterning of the individual differences in L2 proficiency could not possibly be shaped by a social factor directly – the patterning is too subtle for speakers to deliberately modify their speech to produce such an effect. Moreover, the evidence is now overwhelming that this implicational scale results from the operation of at least two psycholinguistic processing variables – L1–L2 similarity and frequency of occurrence of the target elements. These are precisely the kinds of factors that would be influenced by the amount of language use.

The fine-grained analysis of proficiency provided by Trofimovich *et al.* (2007) allowed for a rather nuanced ranking of L2 users according to their proficiency on a single, socially relevant, phonological marker (here, voiced /ð/). It may be fruitful to consider a whole range of other psycholinguistic processing variables having to do with individual differences in the nature and efficiency of the cognitive system under-lying L2 use. Of particular importance, for instance, is to study how the cognitive system becomes more efficient or automatic over time as a function of experience using the target language and how this efficiency or lack thereof results in particular speech patterns. It is beyond the scope of this chapter to discuss the details, but given the present results, it would appear that this is likely to be an important consideration for fully understanding the way psycholinguistic processes mediate the ethno-linguistic affiliation–proficiency link (see for example, Segalowitz, 1997 and Segalowitz & Hulstijn, 2005, for a discussion of psycholinguistic processing issues in individual differences in L2 attainment).

The results reported so far raise an important new question: How does the social variable of ethnolinguistic affiliation relate to this phonological measure of L2 proficiency? That is the focus of the next section.

Study 3: Ethnolinguistic Affiliation, the L2 Self and L2 Proficiency

In a final set of analyses, Gatbonton *et al.* (2007) examined the relationship between ethnolinguistic affiliation and the L2 proficiency measure based on the implicational scale analysis. For this purpose, the data from 50 of the 59 participants in the Gatbonton and Trofimovich (2008) study were retained for analysis. Data from nine of the participants were dropped because these nine were still enrolled in language classes and it was considered that their phonological skills were likely to be developing as a result of the explicit instruction they were receiving. In contrast, the other 50 (40 of whom were the participants in Trofimovich *et al.*, 2007) had, for all intents and purposes, reached a plateau (for now at least) in their development and used English in their daily activities without formal instruction.

The voiced /ð/ data from the 50 participants were subjected to the same analysis described earlier, resulting in placement for each participant in a table similar to Table 9.1. Each of the 50 participants in this analysis was assigned a stage number according to the distribution of their correct and incorrect renditions of the voice /ð/ in the different environments. These stage assignments were then submitted as the criterion measure to multiple regression analysis with the four EGA factors identified earlier (*Core, Group Identity, Language* and *Political EGA*) as the predictor variables. L2 use was entered as a control variable prior to entering the main predictor variables. The results are summarised in Table 9.2.

Several things stood out from these analyses. First, the four EGA factors together accounted for 20.0% of the variance of the stage assignment variable (adjusted $R^2 = 0.124$). Of the four EGA factors, however, only *Political EGA* yielded a significant association with stage ($\beta = -0.401, p = 0.028$). This result indicates that the higher the support for political policies to favour the primary ethnolinguistic group, the lower the stage of phonological attainment in the L2. However, when the analyses were recomputed with L2 use entered first as a control variable, none of the β values remained significant (all $p > 0.18$), indicating that the relationship between Political EGA and level of phonological attainment that had been observed before had, in fact, been mediated by L2 use. Analyses between L2 use and Political EGA in this larger sample again

Table 9.2 Summary of multiple regression analyses for ethnolinguistic affiliation measures entered simultaneously as predictors of stage of L2 phonological attainment with /ð/, with and without L2 use entered as a control predictor

Variable	R^2	Adjusted R^2	R^2 change	F change	df	Sig. of change
Without L2 use entered first						
EGA	0.200	0.124	0.200	2.630	4, 42	0.048
With L2 use entered first						
L2 use	0.063	0.042	0.063	2.911	1, 43	0.095
EGA	0.236	0.138	0.172	2.199	4, 39	0.087

revealed a significant correlation ($rho = -0.514$, $p < 0.001$).[1] Together these results indicate that L2 use mediates connections between ethnolinguistic affiliation and proficiency, consistent with the earlier results in which subjective measures of L2 proficiency had been used.

Discussion

This chapter opened with the anchor question – does ethnolinguistic affiliation (language identity) impact on some critical aspects of language learning motivation in such a way as to shape individual differences in L2 acquisition outcomes? The question was originally represented in a simplified, schematic form in Figure 9.1. In light of the presented findings, this figure can now be modified as shown in Figure 9.2. This figure shows the following chain of relationships and associations. Aspects of ethnolinguistic affiliation are psychologically realised in terms of a multi-component, socially based L2 Motivation Self System. This system, inspired by Dörnyei (2005), consists of an Ideal L2 Self, an Ought-to Self, and an L2 Experience component (and possibly other components as well). These motivation system components affect the amount of L2 use a person will engage in. Presumably (although this merits further study), motivation affects L2 use by modulating in some way the selection of communicative experiences the individual allows him or herself to engage in. These experiences in using the L2, in turn, have particular, psycholinguistically relevant consequences. Among these consequences is the fine-tuning of the speaker's perceptual and cognitive systems with respect to the processing of target language elements. For example, this fine-tuning will reflect some awareness (as reflected in a speaker's comprehension and production accuracy or fluency) of the patterning that exists in the language. This patterning that can be described as the frequency with which particular elements exist (e.g. how frequently a particular phonological target occurs), as regularities of co-occurrence of elements (e.g. the occurrence of particular targets in specific phonetic environments), and as the similarities and differences between L1 and L2 elements (e.g. aspects of phonetic similarity that will lead to perceptual assimilation).

Thus, taken together, the results of Gatbonton and Trofimovich (2008), Trofimovich *et al.* (2007) and Gatbonton *et al.* (2007) indicate that there is a link between ethnolinguistic affiliation and attained L2 proficiency. At the same time, they suggest a plausible scenario for how this link may be mediated by language use and psycholinguistic processing considerations.

The research reported here suggests that the components of the L2 Motivation Self System can be operationalised in terms of a person's core feelings about their primary ethnolinguistic group, identity factors

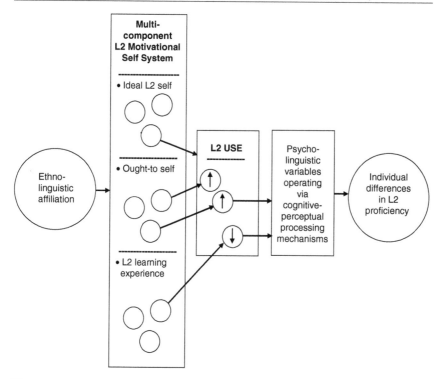

Figure 9.2 Generic representation showing the pathways through which a second language (L2) users' ethnolinguistic affiliation (language identity) can result in individual differences in L2 proficiency. Language identity contributes to the emergence of several components of L2 acquisition motivation. These components affect language use (by increasing and/or decreasing different aspects of use [up and down arrows]), in possibly more than one way. Some but not all of these different uses of the L2 impact on the psycholinguistic processing mechanisms that ultimately affect the development of L2 proficiency, resulting in measurable individual differences in particular aspects of performance

that may be inclusive or exclusive, political beliefs, and beliefs about the role of language in identity. Further studies in other social contexts may uncover yet other ways the Motivation Self System may be expressed (e.g. Clément, 1986; MacIntyre & Charos, 1996; Noels *et al.*, 2000; Ushioda, 2006; Yashima, 2002). As the data indicated, some of the components associated with language identity and ethnolinguistic affiliation will impact on L2 use by increasing or decreasing amounts of language use speakers engage in, whereas other components may have no effect. Finally, in some cases, increasing or decreasing L2 use will have an impact on proficiency development, by acting through the individual's cognitive-perceptual processing mechanisms. Thus, ethno-linguistic affiliation can be seen to affect L2 proficiency, and it can be seen to do so through the mediation of language use which in turn shapes how cognitive-perceptual psycholinguistic variables will impact on skill acquisition.

Although the studies discussed in this chapter point to possible psycholinguistic bases of the links between L2 proficiency on the one hand and ethnolinguistic affiliation and the L2 Motivation Self System on the other, the nature of such links clearly needs to be investigated in future research. For example, there is a need to understand whether the different facets of ethnolinguistic language identity and of the L2 Motivation Self System are specific to a language-learning context or whether at least some of these facets may be 'universal', common to a variety of language teaching and learning situations. Likewise, it is important to understand whether the relationship between L2 proficiency and ethnolinguistic affiliation is particular to a linguistic feature being investigated. That is, are ethnolinguistic affiliation–L2 proficiency links obvious only for L2 proficiency measures that are identity laden (i.e. /ð/ for Francophone learners of English) but not for other, perhaps more general L2 proficiency measures (e.g. speech rate as an indicator of general L2 speaking fluency)? Last but not least, it is important to isolate the cognitive-perceptual psycholinguistic mechanisms that sustain the relationship between social cognition (ethnolinguistic affiliation) and a psycholinguistic skill (L2 proficiency). We have broadly outlined plausible mechanisms of this kind (see Trofimovich *et al.*, 2007), drawing on two-representation connectionist models of spoken word processing and learning (e.g. Gupta & Dell, 1999; Luce *et al.*, 2000). What remains to be seen, however, is how these and similar cognitive-perceptual psycholinguistic mechanisms can be conceptualised *outside* a psycholinguistic laboratory, in real-world socio-cultural contexts of language learning and use.

Note

1. L2 use correlations with the other EGA factors were: Core–$rho = 0.165$, ns; group identity–$rho = 0.314$, $p = 0.032$; and language–$rho = -0.397$, $p = 0.006$.

References

Appel, R. and Schoonen, R. (2005) Street language: A multilingual youth register in the Netherlands. *Journal of Multilingual and Multicultural Development* 26, 85–117.

Bailey, B. (2000) Language and negotiation of ethnic/racial identity among Dominican Americans. *Language in Society* 29, 555–582.

Baker, W., Trofimovich, P., Flege, J.E., Mack, M. and Halter, R. (2008) Child-adult differences in second-language phonological learning: The role of cross-language similarity. *Language and Speech* 51 (4).

Blake, R. and Josey, M. (2003) The /ay/ diphthong in a Martha's Vineyard community: What can we say 40 years later after Labov? *Language in Society* 32, 451–484.

Boberg, C. (2004) Ethnic patterns in the phonetics of Montreal English. *Journal of Sociolinguistics* 8, 538–568.

Bourhis, R. and Giles, H. (1977) The language of intergroup distinctiveness. In H. Giles (ed.) *Language, Ethnicity, and Intergroup Relations* (pp. 119–135). London: Academic Press.

Clément, R. (1986) Second language proficiency and acculturation: An investigation of the effects of language status and individual characteristics. *Journal of Language and Social Psychology* 5, 271–290.

Coupland, N., Bishop, H.A., Williams, A., Evans, B. and Garrett, P. (2005) Affiliation, engagement, language use and vitality: Secondary school students subjective orientations to Welsh and Welshness. *The International Journal of Bilingual Education and Bilingualism* 8, 1–24.

Csizér, K. and Dörnyei, Z. (2005) The internal structure of language learning motivation and its relationship with language choice and learning effort. *The Modern Language Journal* 89, 19–36.

Doran, M. (2004) Negotiating between *bourge* and *racaille*: Verlan as youth identity practice in suburban Paris. In A. Pavlenko and A. Blackledge (eds) *Negotiation of Identities in Multilingual Contexts* (pp. 93–124). Clevedon: Multilingual Matters.

Dörnyei, Z. (ed.) (2003) *Attitudes, Orientations, and Motivations in Language Learning*. Oxford: Blackwell.

Dörnyei, Z. (2005) *The Psychology of the Second Language Learner: Individual Differences in Second Language Acquisition*. Mahwah, NJ: Lawrence Erlbaum Associates.

Ellinger, B. (2000) The relationship between ethnolinguistic identity and English language for native Russian speakers and native Hebrew speakers in Israel. *Journal of Multilingual and Multicultural Development* 21, 292–307.

Fought, C. (2006) *Language and Ethnicity: Key Topics in Sociolinguistics*. New York: Cambridge University Press.

Gardner, R.C. and Lambert, W.E. (1972) *Attitudes and Motivation in Second Language Learning*. Rowley, MA: Newbury House.

Gatbonton, E. (1975) Systematic variations in second language speech: A sociolinguistic study. Unpublished doctoral dissertation. McGill University.

Gatbonton, E. (1978) Patterned phonetic variability in second language speech: A gradual diffusion model. *Canadian Modern Language Review* 34, 335–347.

Gatbonton, E. and Trofimovich, P. (2008) The ethnic group affiliation and L2 proficiency link: Empirical evidence. *Language Awareness* 17 (13).

Gatbonton, E., Trofimovich, P. and Segalowitz, N. (2007) Language and identity: Does ethnic group affiliation affect L2 performance? Paper presented at the International Symposium on Bilingualism (ISB6), June 2007. Hamburg, Germany.

Gatbonton, E., Trofimovich, P. and Magid, M. (2005) Learners' ethnic group affiliation and L2 pronunciation accuracy: A sociolinguistic investigation. *TESOL Quarterly* 39, 489–511.

Giles H.G. (ed.) (1967) *Language, Ethnicity, and Intergroup Relations*. London: Academic Press.

Guion, S.G., Flege, J.E., Akahane-Yamada, R. and Pruitt, J.C. (2000) An investigation of current models of second language speech perception: The case of Japanese adults' perception of English consonants. *Journal of the Acoustical Society of America* 107, 2711–2724.

Gumperz, J. and Cook-Gumperz, J. (1982) Introduction. In J. Gumperz (ed.) *Language and Social Identity*. New York: Cambridge University Press.

Gupta, P. and Dell, G.S. (1999) The emergence of language from serial order and procedural memory. In B. MacWhinney (ed.) *The Emergence of Language* (pp. 447–481). Mahwah, NJ: Lawrence Erlbaum Associates.

Labov, W. (1972) On the mechanism of language change. In J.J. Gumperz and D. Hymes (eds) *Directions in Sociolinguistics* (pp. 312–338). New York: Holt, Rinehart and Winston.

Lambert, W.E. (1967) A social psychology of bilingualism. *Journal of Social Issues* 23, 91–109.

Luce, P.A., Goldinger, S.D., Auer, E.T. and Vitevitch, M.S. (2000) Phonetic priming, neighborhood activation, and PARSYN. *Perception and Psychophysics* 62, 615–625.

MacIntyre, P.D. (2007) Willingness to communicate in the second language: Understanding the decision to speak as a volitional process. *Modern Language Journal* 91, 564–576.

MacIntyre, P.D. and Charos, C. (1996) Personality, attitudes, and affect as predictors of second language communication. *Journal of Language and Social Psychology* 15, 3–26.

Noels, K.A., Pelletier, L.G., Clément, R. and Vallerand, R.J. (2000) Why are you learning a second language? Motivational orientations and self-determination theory. *Language Learning* 50, 57–85.

Pavlenko, A. and Blackledge, A. (eds) (2004) *Negotiation of Identities in Multilingual Contexts*. Clevedon: Multilingual Matters.

Ricento, T. (2005) Considerations of identity in L2 learning. In E. Hinkel (ed.) *Handbook of Research in Second Language Teaching and Learning* (pp. 895–910). Mahwah, NJ: Lawrence Erlbaum Associates.

Schilling-Estes, N. (2004) Constructing ethnicity in interaction. *Journal of Sociolinguistics* 8, 163–195.

Segalowitz, N. (1997) Individual differences in second language acquisition. In A. de Groot and J. Kroll (eds) *Tutorials in Bilingualism* (pp. 85–112). Hillsdale, NJ: Lawrence Erlbaum Associates.

Segalowitz, N. and Hulstijn, J. (2005) Automaticity in bilingualism and second language learning. In J.F. Kroll and A.M.B. De Groot (eds) *Handbook of Bilingualism: Psycholinguistic Approaches* (pp. 371–388). Oxford: Oxford University Press.

Taylor, D.M. (1977) Bilingualism and intergroup relations. In P.A. Hornby (ed.) *Bilingualism: Psychological, Social, and Educational Perspectives* (pp. 67–75). New York: Academic Press.

Taylor, D.M., Meynard, R. and Rhéault, E. (1977) Threat to ethnic identity and second-language learning. In H. Giles (ed.) *Language, Ethnicity, and Intergroup Relations* (pp. 98–118). London: Academic Press.

Trofimovich, P., Gatbonton, E. and Segalowitz. N. (2007) A dynamic look at L2 phonological learning: Investigating effects of cross-language similarity and input frequency. *Studies in Second Language Acquisition* 29, 407–448.

Ushioda, E. (2006) Language motivation in a reconfigured Europe: Access, identity, autonomy. *Journal of Multilingual and Multicultural Development* 27, 148–161.

Yashima, T. (2002) Willingness to communicate in a second language: The Japanese EFL context. *Modern Language Journal* 86, 54–66.

Chapter 10

Toward the Development of a Scale to Assess Possible Selves as a Source of Language Learning Motivation

PETER D. MACINTYRE, SEAN P. MACKINNON and
RICHARD CLÉMENT

Introduction

Motivation has been a central concept in SLA since the seminal work of Gardner and Lambert (1959) developed into the socio-educational model, with integrative motivation as its centerpiece (Gardner, 1985, 2001). The close links among language, culture, identity, and the self clearly suggest, however, that we need to know more about the self-concept as it relates to language learning. A small number of studies in the SLA literature have used the concept of self as a basis for their findings (Clément *et al.*, 2001; Csizér & Dörnyei, 2005a, 2005b; Yashima *et al.*, 2004). Recently, Dörnyei (2005) has proposed a conceptual scheme called the 'L2 Motivational Self System' that features possible selves as a bridge between research into the self and studies of language learning motivation. The purpose of the present study is to create a quantitative measure of L2-related possible selves and to examine the links between possible selves and core elements of Gardner's (2001) integrative motive.

The conceptualisation of motivation in SLA has undergone rapid expansion in the past two decades, but empirical research has not kept pace (MacIntyre *et al.*, 2001). For many years, the central concept in the study of motivation in the SLA literature has been the integrative motive from Gardner's (1985) socio-educational model. The integrative motive has two key defining features: integrativeness and motivation. Integrativeness refers to openness and positive attitudes toward a target cultural/linguistic group. It refers to a desire to take on attributes of that other group, such as their language (Gardner, 2005), though not necessarily to become a group member. Motivation reflects a combination of positive attitudes, desire to learn, and effortful behaviour directed toward the target language.[1]

The conceptualisation of the self in psychological research also has undergone substantial change over the years, moving toward a

193

multifaceted conceptualisation of the self (Greenwald & Pratkanis, 1984). The self, indeed, has been used as a framework to understand a variety of motivational processes, such as academic achievement (Leondari *et al.*, 1998; Marsh & Craven, 1997), adolescent delinquency (Oyserman & Markus, 1990) and work motivation (Leonard *et al.*, 1999). Several chapters in the present volume (see, for example, the chapters by Csizér & Kormos; Dörnyei; Kim; Noels; Ryan; Segalowitz *et al.*; Taguchi *et al.*; Yashima) advance theory and research applications specifically for SLA.

Dörnyei (2005), in fact, argues that at the core of the integrative motive is a psychological and emotional identification with social and cultural material associated with the target language. Specifically, he refers to the concept of possible selves, which was designed to provide a link between self-related cognition and affect (Markus & Nurius, 1986: 958). In commenting on the notion of possible selves, Gardner (2005) noted:

> It is quite possible that individuals who are high in integrativeness may have different perceptions of their self and their ideal self, particularly as they relate to the second language ... (I)n any event, research will be needed to establish whether there is any relation between the two conceptualizations. (Gardner, 2005: 8)

It is, therefore, in the spirit of reconciling these two frameworks that the following is proposed.

Possible Selves in SLA

Possible selves create a link between self-related cognition and motivation by synthesising the relevance of various incentives for future behavior. From the perspective of a researcher, linking the literature on the self with the SLA literature appears to be a daunting task (see MacIntyre *et al.*, Chapter 3, this volume). The literature on the self is expansive, with both a rich historical tradition and extensive current interest. In particular, current research argues for reciprocal causal links among self-concept, academic interest, and achievement (Marsh *et al.*, 2005).

Marsh and colleagues have published numerous studies on the self concept in conjunction with academic achievement (Marsh, 1992, 1993; Marsh *et al.*, 2005, 2006; for a review, see Marsh & Craven, 1997). Generally, Marsh and colleagues' research shows that not all aspects of the self concept play a role in academic achievement and motivation. Self-concepts can be developed in different domains, such as academic, social and physical selves, and they are not necessarily related to each other (Marsh & Craven, 1997). Moreover, Marsh and colleagues' research has revealed that academic self-concept, while substantially related to academic achievement, does not show a strong relationship with non-academic self-concepts (Marsh, 1992), global measures of self-esteem (Marsh, 1993), or the Big Five personality characteristics (Marsh *et al.*, 2006). In sum, it appears that a domain-specific self concept plays a significant role in predicting academic achievement, serving as a more consistent predictor than personality traits and non-differentiated models of the self. Given the strong links among language, culture, identity and self-concept, SLA researchers should consider ways in which concepts of the self change when learning a second language, and the motivational implications of those changes.

Dörnyei's (2005) L2 Motivational Self System provides the conceptual basis for the study of self in the second language domain. Dörnyei argues that 'possible selves offer the most powerful, and at the same time the most versatile, motivational self-mechanism, representing the individuals' ideas of what they might become, what they would like to become, and what they are afraid of becoming' (Dörnyei, 2005: 99). Drawing on Higgins's (1987, 1998) work on the promotion and prevention functions of self-regulation, Dörnyei (2005) proposes three key dimensions of the L2 Self System: Ideal L2 self, Ought-to L2 self, and L2 learning experience. The Ideal L2 self is the language speaker that one would like to become; it represents the promotion of a hoped-for future self. The Ought-to L2 self serves a prevention function, that is, it represents our vision of what we should become in the future in order to avoid undesirable or feared future outcomes. Motivation stemming from the ought-to or feared self drives the behaviour that we feel we should do out of duty or obligation. The third element of the system, L2 Learning Experience, reflects situation-specific motives that regulate the immediate environment and guide the learner through the present learning experience. This dimension of the L2 self is qualitatively different from the other two in that (1) its focus lies in the present, not future, by reflecting the evaluation of past success at language learning, and (2) it requires an ongoing language learning activity of some sort to trigger the situation-specific motives.

L2 Self System and the Integrative Motive

The L2 Self System approach differs in phrasing from Gardner's Integrative Motive but Dörnyei (2005: 107) has argued that the two approaches share 'striking similarities' and 'correspond closely'. If this claim can be supported empirically, the results would be quite encouraging for the study of motivation in SLA because:

(1) The extensive work on integrative motivation and social identity could be used to inform future development of the L2 Self System without repeating those studies;

(2)   future research on the motivational properties of reducing the discrepancy between present and future self would be a novel research trajectory derived from Dörnyei's L2 Self System, yet still informed by extensive work on discrepancy as the cognitive basis for motivation (see Reeve, 2005);

(3)   cross-cultural differences in the conceptualisation of the Self in general, and the L2 Self in particular, could be taken explicitly into account in the development of new research tools and measures;

(4)   research that focuses on the multifaceted nature of motivation and how language learners prioritise between competing motives would be a significant advance, and would complement prior research on the integrative motive.

Typically, the research on possible selves takes a distinct qualitative bent, often asking participants to spontaneously generate possible selves in open-ended surveys (Carver & Sakina, 1994; Leondari *et al.*, 1998; Norman & Aron, 2003; Oyserman & Markus, 1990; Oyserman *et al.*, 2002). This approach has been used to examine possible selves within various domains. It would be both useful and practical to complement this qualitative approach with quantitative measures that allow for an empirical assessment of the links with Gardner's Integrative Motive (see Dörnyei, 2005). This is the major purpose of the present study.

Developing the Scale

Our approach to developing the possible selves measure centres on Markus and Nurius's (1986) research which makes it clear that it is important to know whether or not respondents think the self in question (1) is a potential future self and/or (2) a self that describes them presently. There are four possible combinations of answers, two of which hold the potential to enhance motivation. If a characteristic of the present self is envisioned to continue being relevant to the future self, this reflects ongoing development in that area (as when incipient language skills are acquired and then developed; see for example Tomlinson, 2007). Also, some characteristics might not currently be part of the self-concept, but conceivably could be added in the future. In this case, a person would feel motivated to achieve congruence between his or her present and future self by adding a new element to their self-concept.

In contrast, there are two response patterns that do not endorse future L2 possible selves and therefore seem far less likely to support motivated behaviour. A person whose present self is not expected to continue might reflect the end of action in that area, as when a person drops out of school. This type of responding is likely to be quite rare. Moreover, a language learner who neither recognises the qualities mentioned in our scale item as an element of the present self nor contemplates them as part of their future self is likely to be unmotivated. In this case, the component of the self is irrelevant and there exists little motivation for its development.

With this in mind, the core of the measure being developed is whether a potential personal characteristic is part of the present self (yes or no) and part of possible future self (yes or no). To assess the motivational qualities of these items, three additional issues will be considered, each at the item level. First, it is important to know if the possible self in question is *desirable* or not, because a possible self that is not supported by the emotion system – that is, a self that might be a nice idea but has no emotional investment – will not likely be motivating (Lewis, 2005). Oyserman *et al.* (2004) postulate that there are two types of possible selves: (1) possible selves that simply promote feeling good, with no plan of action, and (2) possible selves that promote self-regulation of behaviour. Their research showed that for a possible self to have an impact on academic outcomes, the possible self must include a plausible plan of action; merely placating oneself with a pleasant possible self with no specific plan is not related to academic outcomes. Thus, it is also important to find out how *likely* participants consider a possible self to be; a highly unlikely possible self probably will have little relation to motivation. Finally, Norman and Aron's (2003) research suggested that people will be more motivated by, and therefore likely to achieve or avoid a possible self that is easily constructed in the mind, more easily brought into conscious awareness and under one's perceived control. For this reason, it may also be interesting to obtain a rating of *how often a possible self is thought about*; the easier it is to bring a possible self into awareness, and the more often it is thought about consciously, the more likely it will impact motivation.

The Present Research

Following the above, the present research pursues three goals.

(1) We will develop and assess the reliability and dimensionality of a scale measuring present and possible future selves in domains relevant to L2 acquisition.
(2) We will assess the predictive validity of both possible selves and Gardner's motivational constructs by examining correlations with perceived L2 competence (see Baker & MacIntyre, 2000).
(3) We will examine empirically the relationship between the new possible selves measure and key elements of Gardner's integrative motive.

Method

Participants

The sample consisted of high school students ($N = 135$) from an all-girls school in a small, predominately English speaking city.

Materials

The following instruments were administered to all participants:

- *Possible selves.* As an initial step in developing an approach utilising possible selves, we created 18 items related to the French Language and French Canadians (see Appendix A for the items), based on items from Gardner's (1985) AMTB. Each item generated five responses. The first two responses had dichotomous options to the prompts: (1) Describes me now (yes/no) and (2) Describes possible future (yes/no). These two responses are of primary interest in assessing present and future selves. Three additional questions tapped how desirable the future self is, how likely it is, and how often the respondent has thought about it. These latter three variables were measured on a 5-point scale. We will examine the reliability and factor structure of the responses to the dichotomous items, and use the three 5-point responses to assess the motivational quality of each item.
- *Integrativeness* ($\alpha = 0.94$). This was measured by combining three scales from Gardner's Attitude/Motivation Test Battery (Gardner, 1985; 2000): (1) *integrative orientation* which examines reasons for learning the other language based on attraction to the other group; (2) *interest in foreign languages* which examines the level of appeal held by other languages in general; and (3) *attitudes toward French Canadians* which examines the degree of positive evaluation of the language group (French Canadians in the present research).
- *Motivation* ($\alpha = 0.96$). This is the second key element of the integrative motive shown to be relevant across cultures, which was also measured by combining three subscales from Gardner's AMTB: (1) *motivational intensity* which represents the amount of effort expended in language learning, (2) *desire to learn French* which examines how much the learner wants to acquire the language, and (3) *attitudes toward learning French* which examines the beliefs that the learner holds about the language itself.
- *Perceived competence/fluency in French* ($\alpha = 0.95$). This four item measure asked participants to rate their overall ability to perform the following tasks: read French, write French, speak French, and understand spoken French. Participants place a mark on a continuum that ranged from 1 (not at all) to 7 (fluently) for each of the four tasks.

Results

Reliability and dimensionality of the possible selves scale

The first research question addresses the development of a quantitative measure for possible L2 selves. The measure has two key response vectors, Present L2 Self and Future L2 Self. To determine the underlying factor structure of the new items, two separate principal components analyses were conducted, one for present self responses and the other for future self responses. In order to determine the number of factors to retain, we examined (1) all the eigenvalues that were greater than one; (2) the scree plot of the eigenvalues; and (3) all factor loadings that were $\geq |0.30|$. Analyses were conducted using SPSS 12.0, and missing values were replaced with the mean.

The initial extraction on each of the Principal Components Analyses (PCAs) resulted in a varying number of factors when using the eigenvalue greater than one rule, with a different number of factors for Present L2 Self (seven factors) and Future L2 Self (four factors). However, when the scree plots for each analysis were examined (see Figure 10.1), in both cases there was a single clear break in the scree plot occurring after the first factor. Given the notorious unreliability of the eigenvalues-greater-than-one rule (Cliff, 1988), we selected the one factor solutions based on the scree plots. Having determined a preference for a one-factor solution, the PCAs were run again extracting one factor in each without rotation, because solutions with one factor cannot be rotated. The factor loading matrices resulting from these analyses are shown in Table 10.1 and the reliabilities for both 18-item scales are located in Table 10.2. Overall, these results indicate that

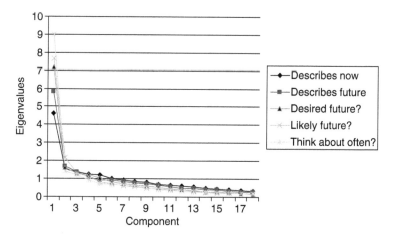

Figure 10.1 Scree plots from all five scales on the French Canadian Possible Selves Questionnaire

Table 10.1 Factor loadings for all five Possible Selves scales when one factor was extracted

	Component				
	Describes now	*Describes future*	*Likely future?*	*Desired future?*	*Think about often?*
Variance accounted for:	25.7%	32.4%	42.7%	40.0%	50.0%
Understand French Canadians' views	0.603	0.666	0.747	0.733	0.692
Think like French Canadians	0.299	0.487	0.682	0.589	0.612
Be a knowledgeable person	0.211	0.422	0.485	0.378	0.499
Be a cultured person	0.528	0.463	0.601	0.592	0.606
Understand French literature	0.676	0.681	0.769	0.812	0.841
Appreciate French art and literature	0.603	0.637	0.764	0.716	0.833
Feel at ease with French Canadians	0.308	0.542	0.654	0.634	0.742
Friendships with French Canadians	0.465	0.455	0.686	0.615	0.802
Feel respected because I speak French	0.676	0.579	0.689	0.707	0.798
Enjoy speaking French	0.664	0.697	0.710	0.711	0.812
Want to learn many languages	0.380	0.524	0.620	0.508	0.594
Participate freely in activities of other cultural groups	0.336	0.452	0.671	0.531	0.691
Act like French Canadians	0.211	0.398	0.386	0.424	0.573
Meet and converse with French Canadians	0.706	0.693	0.770	0.761	0.821

Table 10.1 (*Continued*)					
Work at a job using French	0.475	0.653	0.627	0.632	0.645
Travel to French-speaking areas/countries	0.389	0.479	0.609	0.554	0.650
Go to French films in the original language	0.534	0.597	0.539	0.640	0.639
Read newspapers and magazines in French	0.592	0.664	0.622	0.670	0.750

Table 10.2 Reliability coefficients for possible selves questionnaire

	Cronbach's alpha	*Variable type*
Describes me now	$\alpha = 0.82$	Dichotomous
Describes possible future	$\alpha = 0.88$	Dichotomous
Is this an undesirable or desirable future?	$\alpha = 0.91$	5-point Likert
How likely is this in the future?	$\alpha = 0.92$	5-point Likert
How often have you thought about this future?	$\alpha = 0.95$	5-point Likert

these response vectors of present and future selves are internally consistent and unidimensional.

At the scale level, the total scores for the 18 items for present and future selves correlated highly with the ratings of desirability, likelihood and how often the self was thought about. All correlations were within the range of 0.61 to 0.75 and were all significant at the $p < 0.001$ level. At the item level, the pattern was consistently replicated. Of the 108 correlations between present and future selves with desirability, likelihood and how often the self was thought about, 96 (89%) were significant at $p < 0.001$.

The reliability and unidimensionality of the scale allow us to examine the content of the items to assess the content of present and future L2 selves, as reflected in the items used (see Table 10.3). The most frequently endorsed (> 70%) present selves include being a knowledgeable person who wants to learn many languages and feeling at ease with

Table 10.3 Possible selves frequencies and means

Item no.	Describes me now? (% yes)	Describes possible future? (% yes)	Frequencies (%)				Means (SD)		
			Now and a possible future	Not now, but is a possible future	Not now, and not a possible future	Now, but not a possible future	Desired future?	Likely future?	Think about the future often?
1	37	70	36	36	27	<1	3.6 (1.4)	3.2 (1.4)	2.1 (1.3)
2	9	31	9	22	69	0	2.8 (1.5)	2.5 (1.4)	1.7 (1.2)
3	78	94	79	15	6	0	4.7 (0.8)	4.1 (1.2)	3.7 (1.5)
4	66	87	65	21	13	<1	4.4 (1.1)	3.9 (1.4)	3.3 (1.5)
5	34	54	33	21	44	2	3.6 (1.4)	3.1 (1.5)	2.5 (1.5)
6	66	76	62	14	21	4	3.8 (1.2)	3.4 (1.4)	2.3 (1.3)
7	70	87	70	17	13	0	4.1 (1.27)	3.8 (1.3)	2.4 (1.5)
8	63	88	61	27	11	2	4.3 (1.0)	3.7 (1.3)	2.6 (1.5)
9	31	50	31	19	49	2	3.4 (1.6)	3.0 (1.6)	2.4 (1.5)
10	58	65	56	9	33	2	3.6 (1.6)	3.4 (1.6)	2.7 (1.5)
11	76	84	74	10	14	2	4.3 (1.3)	3.7 (1.5)	3.6 (1.5)
12	49	72	47	25	26	2	3.8 (1.4)	3.5 (1.4)	2.5 (1.5)
13	5	15	6	9	85	0	2.1 (1.3)	2.2 (1.4)	1.5 (0.9)

Table 10.3 (*Continued*)

14	50	77	48	29	22	2	3.7 (1.3)	3.5 (1.4)	2.5 (1.5)
15	13	51	13	38	49	0	3.3 (1.6)	3.1 (1.6)	2.8 (1.5)
16	51	82	50	31	18	<1	4.2 (1.3)	3.9 (1.3)	3.4 (1.6)
17	20	47	20	27	53	0	2.9 (1.6)	2.9 (1.5)	2.2 (1.4)
18	20	38	17	21	60	23	2.9 (1.7)	2.9 (1.6)	2.1 (1.4)

Items: (1) Understand French Canadians' views; (2) Think like French Canadians; (3) Be a knowledgeable person; (4) Be a cultured person; (5) Understand French literature; (6) Appreciate French art and literature; (7) Feel at ease with French Canadians; (8) Friendships with French Canadians; (9) Feel respected because I speak French; (10) Enjoy speaking French; (11) Want to learn many languages; (12) Participate freely in activities of other cultural groups; (13) Act like French Canadians; (14) Meet and converse with French Canadians; (15) Work at a job using French; (16) Travel to French-speaking areas/countries; (17) Go to French films in the original language; (18) Read newspapers and magazines in French

French-speakers. The least frequently endorsed (< 20%) were thinking and acting like a Francophone, and working at a job requiring French. The most frequently endorsed (> 80%) future selves include being a knowledgeable and cultured person who wants to learn many languages, who feels at ease with Francophones, and has friendships with French Canadians. The least frequently endorsed future selves (< 50%) were thinking and acting like French Canadians and using media in French (newspapers, magazines, and films).

Correlations among possible selves and Gardner's measures

The two components from the AMTB, motivation and integrativeness, are significantly, highly correlated ($r = 0.74$, $p < 0.01$) with each other, consistent with previous findings (Masgoret & Gardner, 2003). Moreover, correlations between the possible selves measures and the integrativeness and motivation scales ranged from 0.54 to 0.76, and were consistently significant (see Table 10.4).

Predicting L2 perceived competence

To examine the predictive validity of the possible selves measure and Gardner's measures, each was correlated with the overall perceived competence score. As can be seen in Table 10.4, correlations with possible selves were moderate-to-strong, ranging from 0.51 to 0.70. As well, perceived competence correlates strongly with Motivation and Integrativeness (0.76 and 0.51, respectively).

Item-level: Present–future discrepancy

In order to assess the relationship of discrepancies between present and future selves with Motivation, Integrativeness and Perceived Competence, a series of ANOVAs was done, one for each of the PS scale items. There are four possible combinations of responses to the items 'describes me now' and 'describes me in the future' (group 1: yes/yes; group 2: no/yes; group 3: no/no; and group 4: yes/no). Being in Group 1 indicates that the possible self describes the individual now and in the future; in other words, she/he is developing one aspect of the L2 self, a response pattern we will call *developing aspects of self*. Group 2 indicates that the self does not possess the item's properties now but expects to do so in the future, indicating that she/he is adding to the L2 self, which we will call *expanding future aspects of self*. Group 3 indicates that the respondent does not currently possess the attribute and is not contemplating adding this to the self, indicating that the item is viewed as *extraneous to self*. The last of these possibilities (yes/no, indicating the item describes me now but not in the future) did not occur frequently enough to be included in the following analysis (see Table 10.3). This is

Table 10.4 Correlations between possible selves, the AMTB and perceived competence

	PS now	PS future	PS desired	PS likely	PS often	MOTIV	INEG	Perceived competence
PS now	1							
PS future	0.70	1						
PS desired	0.65	0.75	1					
PS likely	0.65	0.69	0.67	1				
PS often	0.60	0.65	0.61	0.64	1			
MOTIV	0.69	0.71	0.69	0.65	0.57	1		
INEG	0.59	0.76	0.62	0.57	0.54	0.74	1	
Perceived competence	0.70	0.57	0.57	0.59	0.51	0.76	0.51	1

Note: PS = Possible self; MOTIV = motivation; INEG = integrativeness. All correlations are significant at $p < 0.001$ (2-tailed)

understandable because a person who, for example, indicates that they presently understand French Canadian views but will not do so in the future is in an unusual state of mind and might experience motivational deprivation.[2]

Motivation

A series of one-way ANOVAs were conducted comparing the mean motivation scores for the three groups using Tukey's HSD method for post hoc tests ($p < 0.01$). Significant differences among the PS categories were observed for 14 of 18 items. Most of these item-level differences involved contrasts with the *extraneous* group who did not envision development of the L2 self in the area described by the item. Among the 14 cases where differences were found, all showed that the *developing* group was higher in motivation than the *extraneous* group. Further, in ten cases, significant differences showed that the *expanding* group was higher in motivation than the *extraneous* group. In only six cases were differences observed between the *developing* and *expanding* groups. In these cases, the *developing* group was higher in motivation than the *expanding* group. Thus, as an overall pattern, we can see that the *developing* group is highest in motivation overall, followed by the *expanding* group, while the *extraneous* group is lowest in motivation.

Integrativeness

With respect to the variable integrativeness, the results are similar. Most of the significant item-level differences ($p < 0.01$) involved contrasts between the *extraneous* group and both the *developing* group (16 of 18 comparisons were significant) and the *expanding* group (15 of 18 contrasts were significant). In only two cases was a significant difference observed between the *developing* and *expanding* groups. We observe the same overall pattern as last time; the *developing* group was highest in integrativeness, followed by the *expanding* group, with the *extraneous* group remained lowest in integrativeness.

Perceived competence

Finally, perceived competence showed a slightly different pattern. Significant differences ($p < 0.01$) were observed between the *extraneous* group and the *developing* group on 12 of 18 items. Only three of 18 comparisons between the *extraneous* group and the *expanding* group were significant indicating a greater degree of similarity between the level of perceived competence than was observed for motivation or integrativeness. Further, less than half (seven of 18) of the comparisons between the *developing* and *expanding* groups were significant. These results show that the level of perceived competence is consistently highest within the *developing* self group and lowest in the *extraneous* group. The other group, *expanding*, is not consistently similar to either of the other two groups in current levels of perceived competence.

Discussion

The pattern of results provides encouragement for further pursuing the motivational basis of possible selves for language learning. In examining the research questions, we find that (1) the new possible selves measure shows strong reliability and a simple, unitary factor structure that provide information about the content of the L2 self; (2) possible selves show strong and consistent correlations with key elements of integrative motivation and perceived L2 competence; and (3) discrepancies between present and future selves are related to integrativeness, motivation and perceived L2 competence.

The factor structure and strong internal consistency of the possible selves scale is encouraging. At the scale-level, scores for future selves correlate strongly with scores for the present selves and, despite the different areas of experience covered by the 18 items, a single factor structure appears to emerge. To the extent that these items cover the domain of Possible L2 Selves, the conceptualisation appears to be unitary and tends to reflect a cohesiveness among items. Whereas the integrative motive has 11 variables contributing to its three major factors, we found that the possible selves data can be represented by a single-factor structure. This is due in part to having only 18 possible selves items, compared with the 72-item AMTB. However, it may also suggest that an idealised view of the L2 self tends to be cohesive and integrated (Csizér & Dörnyei, 2005a), though future work in this area is required to better understand the structure of the L2 self.

The pattern of results for the present L2 self at the item level paints an interesting picture. The most frequently endorsed items, receiving approval from at least two-thirds of learners, include: being knowledgeable, cultured, interested in learning many languages, at ease with L2 speakers, and appreciative of their art and literature. The already high percentages of learners endorsing these items increased with reference to future selves. The largest increases were observed for working at a job using French and understanding French Canadian views. These items include elements of both the classic instrumental and integrative orientations (and intrinsic and extrinsic motives). Although they can be grouped separately and distinctions drawn between them, the present data show that endorsing one set of reasons for language learning tends to predict endorsing the others as well, results mirroring those obtained elsewhere (e.g. Clément *et al.*, 1994; Clément & Kruidenier, 1985).

Similarly, scores on Gardner's measures of integrativeness and motivation correlate with scores on the possible selves scale. This provides some empirical evidence for Dörnyei's (2005) claim that the two conceptual schemes share common ground. The correlations are not so high as to preclude differential predictions of language learning outcomes, so the scales are not necessarily alternate forms of the same test. Rather, this suggests a relationship between the two frameworks which may link a process represented in the socio-educational model and a structure represented by the L2 self.

The structure of the new possible L2 selves lends itself to application in educational settings. The contrast between present and future selves may be interesting when students indicate that the item does not describe them now or in the future. This pattern would be indicative of amotivation or the absence of motivational support for language learning (Noels, 2005). Teachers might be able to use this information with their students to identify learning activities that might strengthen the notion of possible future selves.

Teachers might also consider ways of enhancing motivation when respondents indicate that the possible self describes them in the future. In cases where the present self does not include the item but the future self does, the motivation implications are to acquire the item, if it is a desirable future. In contrast, when the self describes a respondent both now and in the future, motivation for language learning and main-tenance of the L2 self likely would come primarily from the feared self. Oyserman and colleagues have suggested that students need both a hoped-for self and a countervailing feared self in the same domain in order to stimulate motivation (Oyserman & Markus, 1990; Oyserman *et al.*, 2002). The sense of losing what one has achieved can be a powerful motivator if the loss is salient to the self. In its present configuration, our possible L2 selves scale does not test feared futures per se, but feared selves could be interesting especially to study in language learning contexts among minority group members.

The possible selves framework provides interesting forays into less studied domains. The nature of the self-concept differs among various cultural groups and the development of variations of the scale using other conceptual schemes holds promise. In future research, items could be added or modified to be appropriate to the context in which the study is being conducted. It should be recognized that using differing methodol-ogies will make comparisons among studies more difficult. However, it is more important that the concept of self be used in culturally appropriate ways, and differences among views of the self can be documented as part of the research. Future research in this vein could map areas of cross-cultural similarities and difference in the role of the self-concept in language learning, and elaborate on the development of the present scale.

One of the advantages of using a possible selves framework is looking at the integration of present and future selves and how various elements of those selves work together for an individual. The psychological demands for such integration would be far greater with self-relevant items than for items reflecting attitudes or beliefs where inconsistencies among specific beliefs are more easily tolerated. Implicating the self by contemplating one's future increases the demands for the various aspects of self to make sense together, especially if the learner has thought seriously about his or her language learning future.

In the present study we have not attempted to capture directly the notions of ideal and ought-to self (Dörnyei, 2005) or desired and feared future selves (Oyserman & Markus, 1990) that are central to understanding the multifaceted nature of the self. Future development of the new scales along those lines would allow for examination of the differentiation among aspects of self-functioning, and their roles in second language acquisition and development. By testing learners in an all-girls school, in a social milieu where majority group members are learning the language of a high ethnolinguistic vitality minority group, we must not assume that the results will be generalisable. However, this study has produced evidence that the development of possible selves links with existing work on language learning motivation and provides potential new directions for future research into present-future self discrepancies.

Conclusion

The development of possible selves represents a new approach to language learning motivation that draws upon a widely studied concept in psychology. The present study shows that elements of the integrative motive (Gardner, 2001) correlate consistently and strongly with possible selves (Dörnyei, 2005), providing evidence that the concepts share conceptual ground. We believe that the potential advantage of using a possible selves approach lies in the comparison of present and future states, highlighting the discrepancy between them to understand the sources of language learning motivation. This idea might be used systematically by teachers to tailor motivational strategies to aspects of individual students' developing and expanding selves, or in some cases to search for potential motivational loss.

Notes

1. A third element of the integrative motive, attitudes toward the learning situation, is specific to language classrooms (teacher and course) and is not included here because it does not have clear parallels to the L2 Self System.
2. This might occur in situations of subtractive bilingualism or language dropouts, neither of which is the case in the present sample.

References

Baker, S. and MacIntyre, P.D. (2000) The role of gender and immersion in communication and second language orientations. *Language Learning* 50, 311–341.

Carver, C.S. and Sakina, R.L. (1994) The possible selves of optimists and pessimists. *Journal of Research in Personality* 28, 133–141.

Clément, R., Noels, K.A. and Deneault, B. (2001) Interethnic contact, identity, and psychological adjustment: The mediating and moderating roles of communication. *Journal of Social Issues* 57, 539–577.

Clément, R., Dörnyei, Z. and Noels, K.A. (1994) Motivation, self-confidence and group cohesion in the foreign language classroom. *Language Learning* 44, 417–448.

Clément, R. and Kruidenier, B.G. (1985) Aptitude, attitude and motivation in second language proficiency: A test of Clément's model. *Journal of Language and Social Psychology* 4, 21–37.

Cliff, N. (1988) The eigenvalues-greater-than-one rule and the reliability of components. *Psychological Bulletin* 103, 276–279.

Csizér, K. and Dörnyei, Z. (2005a) Language learners' motivational profiles and their motivated learning behaviour. *Language Learning* 55 (4), 613–659.

Csizér, K. and Dörnyei, Z. (2005b) The internal structure of language learning motivation and its relationship with language choice and learning effort. *The Modern Language Journal* 89 (1), 19–36.

Dörnyei, Z. (2005) *The Psychology of the Language Learner: Individual Differences in Second Language Acquisition*. Mahwah, NJ: Lawrence Erlbaum Associates.

Gardner, R.C. (1985) *Social Psychology and Second Language Learning: The Role of Attitudes and Motivation*. London: Edward Arnold.

Gardner, R.C. (2000) Correlation, causation, motivation, and second language acquisition. *Canadian Psychology* 41, 10–24.

Gardner, R.C. (2001) *Integrative Motivation: Past, Present and Future*. Temple University Japan, Distinguished Lecturer Series, Tokyo, February 17, 2001; Osaka, February 24, 2001. Retrieved from http://publish.uwo.ca/~gardner/GardnerPublicLecture1.pdf.

Gardner, R.C. (2005) Integrative motivation and second language acquisition. Canadian Association of Applied Linguistics Joint Plenary Talk, London, Ontario, May 30, 2005. Retrieved from http://publish.uwo.ca/~gardner/caaltalk5final.pdf.

Gardner, R.C. and Lambert, W.E. (1959) Motivational variables in second language acquisition. *Canadian Journal of Psychology* 13, 266–272.

Greenwald, A.G. and Pratkanis, A.R. (1984) The self. In R.S. Wyer and T.R. Srull (eds) *Handbook of Social Cognition* (Vol. 3) (pp. 129–178). Hillsdale, NJ: Erlbaum.

Higgins, E.T. (1987) Self-discrepancy: A theory relating self and affect. *Psychological Review* 94 (3), 319–340.

Higgins, E.T. (1998) Promotion and prevention: Regulatory focus as a motivational principle. In M.P. Zanna (ed.) *Advances in Experimental Social Psychology* (Vol. 30) (pp. 1–46). New York: Academic Press.

Leonard, N., Beauvais, L. and Scholl, R. (1999) Work motivation: The incorporation of self-concept based processes. *Human Relations* 52 (8), 969–998.

Leondari, A., Syngollitou, E. and Kiosseoglou, G. (1998) Academic achievement, motivation and future selves. *Educational Studies* 24 (2), 153–164.

Lewis, M.D. (2005) Bridging emotion theory and neurobiology through dynamic systems modeling. *Behavioral and Brain Sciences* 28, 169–245.

MacIntyre, P.D., MacMaster, K. and Baker, S. (2001) The convergence of multiple models of motivation for second language learning: Gardner, Pintrich, Kuhl and McCroskey. In Z. Dörnyei and R. Schmidt (eds) *Motivation and Second Language Acquisition* (pp. 461–492). Honolulu, HI: University of Hawaii Press.

Markus, H. and Nurius, P. (1986) Possible selves. *American Psychologist* 41 (9), 954–969.

Marsh, H. (1992) The content specificity of relations between academic self-concept and achievement: An extension of the Marsh/Shavelson model. ERIC NO: ED349315.

Marsh, H.W. (1993) Academic self-concept: Theory measurement and research. In J. Suls (ed.) *Psychological Perspectives on the Self* (Vol. 4) (pp. 59–98). Hillsdale, NJ: Erlbaum.

Marsh, H.W. and Craven, R. (1997) Academic self-concept: Beyond the dustbowl. In G. Phye (ed.) *Handbook of Classroom Assessment: Learning, Achievement and Adjustment* (pp. 131–198). Orlando, FL: Academic.

Marsh, H., Trautwein, U., Köller, O. and Baumert, J. (2005) Academic self-concept, interest, grades and standardized test scores: Reciprocal effects models of causal ordering. *Child Development* 76 (2), 397–416.

Marsh, H., Trautwein, U., Köller, O. and Baumert, J. (2006) Integration of multidimensional self-concept and core personality constructs: Construct validation and relations to well-being and achievement. *Journal of Personality* 74 (2), 403–456.

Masgoret, A.M. and Gardner, R.C. (2003) Attitudes, motivation and second language learning: A meta-analysis of studies conducted by Gardner and associates. In Z. Dörnyei (ed.) *Attitudes, Orientations, and Motivations in Language Learning* (pp. 167–210). Oxford: Blackwell.

Noels, K.A. (2005) Orientations to learning German: Heritage language learning and motivational substrates. *Canadian Modern Language Review* 62, 285–312.

Norman, C.C. and Aron, A. (2003) Aspects of possible self that predict motivation to achieve or avoid it. *Journal of Experimental Social Psychology* 39, 500–507.

Oyserman, D., Bybee, D., Terry, K. and Hart-Johnson, T. (2004) Possible selves as roadmaps. *Journal of Research in Personality* 38, 130–149.

Oyserman, D. and Markus, H.R. (1990) Possible selves and delinquency. *Journal of Personality and Social Psychology* 59 (1), 112–125.

Oyserman, D., Terry, K. and Bybee, D. (2002) A possible selves intervention to enhance school involvement. *Journal of Adolescence* 25, 313–326.

Reeve, J. (2005) *Understanding Motivation and Emotion* (4th edn). Hoboken, NJ: Wiley.

Tomlinson, B. (2007) *Language Acquisition and Development: Studies of Learners of First and Other Languages.* New York: Continuum.

Yashima, T., Zenuk-Nishide, L. and Shimizu, K. (2004) The influence of attitudes and affect on willingness to communicate and second language communication. *Language Learning* 54 (1), 119–152.

Appendix A

French Canadian Possible Selves Questionnaire

Probably everyone thinks about the future to some extent. When doing so we often think about the kinds of experiences that are in store for us. Some of these experiences are probably quite likely to occur while others are much less likely. Some of these future experiences are very much desired and hoped for while others are worried about or feared. As we think about the future we also think about the kind of people we might become. Again, we may look forward to some of these 'future selves' but we may be quite concerned about others. In short, given the proper circumstances, we can probably all imagine a number of possible futures for ourselves in terms of the kind of people we might become, the way we might feel, or the acts we might commit. Some of these possible selves may be also achieved or quite likely to be achieved and some may only be very vague or fanciful ideas for the future. Some of us may have a larger number of 'possible selves' in mind as we think about the future while others may have only a few.

Listed below are a number of possibilities of 'future selves' that have been provided by other people. We are interested in what 'possible selves', both positive and negative, that you may have considered for yourself.

Column 1: The first question asks whether this possible self actually characterizes you right now. If it does, mark 'yes', if not, mark 'no'.

Column 2: Next we are concerned with whether this possible self will characterize you in the future. If you think that it describes a future self, mark 'yes', if not, mark 'no'.

Column 3: The third question asks whether you want this as a possible self for you in the future; is it desirable? If you see this possible self as very undesirable, write 1. But if you really want to achieve this possible self in the future, write 5. You can use the numbers 2 (somewhat undesirable), 3 (neutral), or 4 (somewhat desirable) to indicate how much you want to become this possible self.

Column 4: The next one asks, 'for you, how likely is this possible self?' If a possible self is very likely to occur in the future such that you are very certain that you will become this way, mark 'extremely likely'. If, on the other hand, you have considered this as a possibility for you, but you are very uncertain if you will become this way, mark 'extremely unlikely'. You should mark the numbers in between to indicate less extreme judgments of how often you have considered a particular possible self.

Column 5: The last question asks, 'how often do you think of this as a possible self for you?' If you have spent a lot of time thinking about this self as a possible future self for you, mark 'very often'. If you have not spent any time thinking about this, mark 'never'. If you have at one time or other considered this self as a possible self, use the numbers in between to indicate less extreme judgments.

Please work very rapidly on this questionnaire. We are interested in your first thoughts about your future selves. Try to be honest. Do not mull over your answer – answer with the first responses that come to mind. Do not worry about contradictions, inconsistencies, or uncertainties.

		Describes me now	Describes possible future	Is this desired or undesirable future? (1=undesired 5=desired)	How likely is this in the future? (1=not likely 5=very likely)	How often have you thought about this future (1=never 5=a lot)
1.	Understand French Canadians' views	Yes | No	Yes | No			
2.	Think like French Canadians	Yes | No	Yes | No			
3.	Be a knowledgeable person	Yes | No	Yes | No			
4.	Be a cultured person	Yes | No	Yes | No			
5.	Understand French literature	Yes | No	Yes | No			
6.	Appreciate French art and literature	Yes | No	Yes | No			
7.	Feel at ease with French Canadians	Yes | No	Yes | No			
8.	Friendships with French Canadians	Yes | No	Yes | No			
9.	Feel respected because I speak French	Yes | No	Yes | No			
10.	Enjoy speaking French	Yes | No	Yes | No			

		Describes me now	Describes possible future	Is this desired or undesirable future? (1=undesired 5=desired)	How likely is this in the future? (1=not likely 5=very likely)	How often have you thought about this future (1=never 5=a lot)
11.	Want to learn many languages	Yes | No	Yes | No			
12.	Participate freely in activities of other cultural groups	Yes | No	Yes | No			
13.	Act like French Canadians	Yes | No	Yes | No			
14.	Meet and converse with French Canadians	Yes | No	Yes | No			
15.	Work at a job using French	Yes | No	Yes | No			
16.	Travel to French speaking areas/countries	Yes | No	Yes | No			
17.	Go to French films in the original language	Yes | No	Yes | No			
18.	Read newspapers and magazines in French	Yes | No	Yes | No			

Chapter 11

A Person-in-Context Relational View of Emergent Motivation, Self and Identity

EMA USHIODA

Introduction

In this chapter, I would like to put forward what I call a person-in-context relational view of language motivation. By this, I mean a view of motivation as emergent from relations between real persons, with particular social identities, and the unfolding cultural context of activity. As a way in to exploring this perspective, I shall begin by unpacking key concepts in this phrase – person, in context, relational – and examine how they contrast sharply with concepts in more established approaches to language motivation. In this respect, I shall present an ontological position that is at odds with and inevitably critical of the more positivist positions underpinning the bulk of the papers in this volume.

Person versus Individual Difference

Simplifying somewhat, it is probably true to say that the study of language motivation over the past 40 years or so has been shaped by two successive though overlapping research traditions – North American social psychology, and cognitive motivational psychology. Both traditions share a common root in psychometric approaches to the measurement of individual traits or differences. This means that they deploy measurement techniques and statistical procedures that make certain assumptions about the normal distribution of particular traits in a given population. As Atkinson (2002: 536) argues of such quantitative methodologies, 'because they neutralize by design what is variable and individual (in human behaviour or otherwise), [they] produce epiphenomenally uniform accounts'. In essence, one might say that research on individual differences focuses not on differences between individuals, but on averages and aggregates that group together people who share certain characteristics, such as high intrinsic motivation or low self-efficacy. Such research can therefore tell us something about these individual difference characteristics and the kinds of learning behaviour they may lead to. Such research may also be able to tell us something about certain types of learner in an abstract collective sense. But individual difference research can tell us very little about particular students sitting in our classroom, at home, or in the self-access centre, about how they are motivated or not motivated and why. Research on motivation as individual difference has, in this sense, depersonalised learners so that, as Bandura (2001: 2) puts it, 'it is not people but their componentized subpersonal parts that are orchestrating courses of action'.

Hence, I argue here for a focus on people or 'persons', rather than on learners or individual differences in an abstract theoretical sense. My argument does not stem from some kind of humanistic whole-person approach to language learners. Rather, if our aim in this themed collection of papers is to examine how L2 motivation relates to self and identity, I contend that we should not position the central participants in our research simply as language learners, since this is just one aspect of their identity. Following Lantolf and Pavlenko (2001), I argue instead that we need to understand second language learners as people, and as people who are necessarily located in particular cultural and historical contexts.

Person-in-Context versus Context as Independent Variable

This brings me to the critical issue of context in language motivation research. Context has always been ascribed an implicit and now increasingly explicit role in the study of language motivation, and contextual factors are usually integrated into the major theoretical models. However, as I shall argue, when incorporated into these models, context is generally defined as an independent background variable which is theorised to influence motivation, but over which learners have no control.

Let us consider, first of all, the role of context in models of motivation developed in the Gardnerian social-psychological tradition. In this connection, it is worth noting that, although we call it 'social' psychology, the focus in social psychology is on the individual (as social being), rather than on the social or cultural collective (as in sociology). As Dörnyei (1999) points out, Gardner and Lambert's (1972) original social-psychological model of L2 learning is essentially a theory of individual, rather than socially or culturally constituted, motivation; and social and cultural factors are reflected only through the individual's attitudes, measured through self-report instruments. Although the influence of the socio-cultural environment is implicit in this and later versions of the model, in the form of 'cultural beliefs' in the social milieu which are assumed to shape an individual's attitudes (Gardner, 1985: 146–147), the model sustains the basic Cartesian dualism between the mental and material worlds, between the inner life of the individual and the surrounding culture and society.

With the transition from social-psychological towards more cognitive perspectives in the 1990s, research on language motivation also sharpened its focus on contextual factors, partly in response to Crookes and Schmidt's (1991) call for more classroom-based concepts of motivation. Thus Dörnyei (2005: 74–83) has christened this phase the 'cognitive-situated' period of language motivation research, with its sharper focus on features of the micro-context in which learning is situated, such as teaching methods or communicative styles, task design or participation structures.

Yet when we examine studies that take a more 'situated' approach, we find there is a tendency to rely on students' self-reported perceptions of their learning environment (e.g. student perceptions of teachers' communicative styles in Noels *et al.*, 1999, or of instructional activities in Jacques, 2001). On one level, we might argue that how students construe relevant features of the social context is more illuminating than any objective measure of these contextual features. However, on another level, we might also argue that this more 'situated' approach to language motivation continues to sustain the Cartesian distinction between the inner mental world of the individual, and the surrounding social environment. Each learner interprets and reacts to her environment, yet remains essentially distinct from it – as Harré and Gillett (1994: 22) put it, hermetically sealed in her own individual and self-contained subjectivity. Moreover, despite the focus on contextual variables, the researchers' aim in such studies is, of course, to uncover rule-governed psychological laws that explain how context affects motivation, rather than to explore the dynamic complexity of personal meaning-making in social context.

Another contextual dimension that is attracting increasing attention in this cognitive-situated period is the cultural one. In particular, an emerging argument seems to be that motivation models and constructs developed in Western cultural contexts may not sit easily within East Asian educational cultures. For example, Chen *et al.* (2005) factor analyse survey data from over 500 learners of English in Taiwan and find evidence to support the notion of a 'required motivation' construct which, they argue, is conceptually different from Western notions of extrinsic motivation. Labelled the 'Chinese imperative', this construct reflects culturally valued and internalised motivation to meet societal, parental and educational expectations and examination requirements. The claim is that such non-individualistic motivation may be specific to Chinese Confucian culture.

The cross-cultural perspective is undoubtedly an interesting and valuable line of inquiry, and is informed by a long tradition of comparative research in general education examining differences in achievement motivation among different cultural and ethnic groups (e.g. Salili *et al.*, 2001). However, in pursuing generalisable claims about one cultural group compared to another, this line of inquiry inevitably goes for broad brushstrokes only, so that the notion of 'context' is often isomorphic with national culture. In the search for differences between national cultures, we seem to lose sight of variation at local and individual levels, or variation at the level of what Holliday (1999) 'small cultures'.

To summarise my arguments about the role of context, it seems that in much existing research on language motivation, context or culture is located externally, as something pre-existing, a stable independent background variable, outside the individual. It is either the object of our attitudes and perceptions, or a determinant of our behaviour. The unique local particularities of the person as self-reflective intentional agent, inherently part of and shaping her own context, seem to have no place in this kind of research. Hence, I argue here for a focus on 'person-in-context', rather than on context as independent variable, to capture the mutually constitutive relationship between persons and the contexts in which they act – a relationship that is dynamic, complex and non-linear.

Relational versus Linear Approaches to Motivation

This brings me to the issue of relational versus linear approaches in language motivation research, for it is without question the linear approach that dominates the field. Primarily, SLA researchers have been interested in motivation because it seems to play such an important role in whether learners learn or not, how much effort they put into learning, how long they persist at learning, and how successfully they learn a language. It is worth reminding ourselves that Gardner and Lambert's (1972) original interest in motivation was prompted by the search for possible causes of successful learning, other than cognitive factors such as ability or language aptitude. This search for cause-effect patterns has largely defined research perspectives on language motivation. Of course, this is very much in keeping with the positivist psychometric tradition of this kind of research. The aim is to make generalisable predictions about what kinds of motivation might lead to what kinds of learning behaviour in what kinds of context, and thus to identify what kinds of pedagogical intervention might be needed to change maladaptive patterns of motivation, and so improve learning behaviours and outcomes.

But how helpful are such linear cause–effect models when it comes to understanding how a particular student might think and feel about language learning? Let me illustrate this point with reference to a particular student I interviewed many years ago during my doctoral research on motivation (Ushioda, 1996, 2001). Sean (not his real name) was studying French at university in Dublin. When I first interviewed him (when he was in his first year), he told me, amongst other things, about his French girlfriend and how his relationship with her was having a rather healthy effect on his motivation to study French – a classic case of integrative orientation par excellence! However, a year later when I interviewed him again, it transpired that Sean and his French girlfriend had experienced a rather bitter and acrimonious break-up. Now, while Gardner's socio-educational model does not explicitly predict what happens when integrative orientation dramatically turns sour, logically one would expect rather negative consequences for Sean's motivation to study French and his learning progress. After all, linear models of this kind always hypothesise relations between variables in positive or negative terms, conventionally represented as positive or negative correlation coefficients or path coefficients. In fact, however, Sean told me that the whole experience was motivating him even more to work on his French and really master the language. It seemed that, out of personal pride and even a sense of spite, he wanted to prove to himself (and to his French ex-girlfriend) that he could be as proficient as she or anyone else at the language. (The reader may like to know that Sean successfully completed his degree and subsequently went on to achieve a PhD in French Studies.)

Obviously I am simplifying and telescoping events greatly, and I do not wish to imply that Sean's ultimate long-term success in French was somehow 'caused' by the experiences related here. Indeed, my whole argument is that we cannot and should not simplify events in terms of cause-effect relations like this. The point about Sean's story is that is illustrates very clearly the complexity and idiosyncrasy of a person's motivational response to particular events and experiences in their life. To adapt that earlier quotation from Bandura (2001: 2), we must recognise that it is people, and not their componentised subpersonal parts, who are orchestrating course of action in the unique and complex system of social relations they inhabit and are inherently part of. Linear models of motivation which reduce learning behaviour to general commonalities cannot do justice to the idiosyncrasies of personal meaning-making in social context. As Allwright (2006: 13) suggests, a gradual shift from 'commonalities' to 'idiosyncrasies' seems to be a significant hallmark of current thinking in applied linguistics.

A Person-in-Context Relational View: A Summary

Let me summarise then what I mean by a person-in-context relational view of motivation. I mean a focus on real persons, rather than on learners as theoretical abstractions; a focus on the agency of the individual person as a thinking, feeling human being, with an identity, a personality, a unique history and background, a person with goals, motives and intentions; a focus on the interaction between this self-reflective intentional agent, and the fluid and complex system of social relations, activities, experiences and multiple micro- and macro-contexts in which the person is embedded, moves, and is inherently part of. My argument is that we need to take a relational (rather than linear) view of these multiple contextual elements, and view motivation as an organic process that emerges through the complex system of interrelations.

Fundamentally, of course, the argument I am making about linear versus relational approaches reflects deeper philosophical and ontological tensions in our field, or what Zuengler and Miller (2006) call 'the two parallel SLA worlds' of cognitive and sociocultural perspectives, or the positivist and relativist paradigms (see also Firth & Wagner, 1997, 1998; also Seidlhofer, 2003). To cut a long story short, there is now a considerable body of opinion in our field which suggests that we should view language learning as a sociocultural and sociohistorically situated process, rather than as primarily a cognitive psycholinguistic process (see for example, Johnson, 2004). However, it seems to me that what Block (2003) calls the current 'social turn' in SLA has yet to make significant inroads into the study of motivational aspects of language learning, which remains largely anchored in traditional linear models. This may not be surprising given that the same largely holds true for motivation research in general educational psychology. As Turner (2001: 88) argues, sociocultural and situated perspectives on general learning theory are far in advance of such developments in motivation theory in education, though at least two important edited volumes suggest that the tide may be turning (McInerney & Van Etten, 2004; Volet & Järvelä, 2001).

Some Theoretical and Analytical Frameworks

In the final part of this chapter, I should like to identify some theoretical and analytical frameworks which may usefully inform a more contextually embedded relational view of motivation and identity. I should like to begin this discussion by acknowledging and emphasising the multiplicity of socially and contextually grounded theoretical frameworks now shaping insights in SLA since the 'social turn'. These include, for example, Vygotskian sociocultural theory (Lantolf & Thorne, 2006), language socialisation (Watson-Gegeo, 2004), ecological perspectives (van Lier, 2004), theories of situated learning and communities of practice

(Toohey, 2000), sociocognitive approaches (Atkinson, 2002), social theory (Sealey & Carter, 2004), and poststructuralist and critical perspectives (Norton, 2000; Pavlenko & Blackledge, 2004). It is beyond the scope of this chapter to examine the distinctive and interrelated features of the various theoretical frameworks, since each has significant potential to illuminate a contextually grounded relational analysis of language motivation. In this connection, a point I should like to make is that a person-in-context relational view of motivation need not privilege any particular theoretical framework over another, but may usefully build on different theoretical perspectives in an integrated though not indiscriminate way. Elsewhere, I have already begun to explore the contributions of sociocultural theory and poststructuralist critical perspectives to the analysis of language motivation in this respect (Ushioda, 2006, 2007a). Here, by way of illustration, I should like to focus on Sealey and Carter's (2004) social realist approach to research in applied linguistics, for the specific insights they bring to bear on language motivation.

In applying contemporary social theory to contextualise language as social practice, Sealey and Carter highlight the dynamic interplay between agency and social structure. As they explain, one of the major issues in social theory has always been the relationship between human beings and the social context within which we seek to realise our intentions, aspirations, needs and desires (Sealey & Carter, 2004: 5). As they point out (Sealey & Carter, 2004: 205), it is a distinctive characteristic of human beings that we have reflexivity – that is, we have the ability, through self-consciousness, to attain a degree of objectivity towards ourselves in the world, and to make decisions among a range of possible choices, rather than simply be determined by the world and our instincts (or, we might add, by our componentised subpersonal parts). However, our agency or human intentionality must always contend with the properties of social structure which act to constrain or facilitate our intentions. Motivation is thus conceptualised not as an individual difference characteristic, but as emergent from relations between human intentionality and social structure (Sealey & Carter, 2004: 206). As Sealey and Carter point out, we need therefore to take account of the 'specificity of time, place and social location' (Sealey & Carter, 2004: 195) of participants, and take account of the relational nature of social phenomena, including linguistic and motivational phenomena.

It seems to me that Sealey and Carter's social realist perspective points to a focus of analysis that has received curiously little attention in language motivation research – the analysis of discourse. Admittedly, a focus on discourse practices in relation to motivation and ethnic identity has long been a feature of social psychological research on second language communication (e.g. Clément *et al.*, 2001; Giles & Byrne, 1982). In general, however, the analytical focus in such research is on styles or patterns of speech or features of the linguistic code, rather than on the situated process of how discourse practices, motives and identities are locally constructed in face-to-face encounters. In the last decade, of course, pioneering work by Norton (2000, 2001) has drawn attention to the micro level of communication encounters between native and non-native speakers in the analysis of motivation, identity and power relations from a poststructuralist angle, and has helped to shape critical research perspectives on motivation in particular communication set-tings (Kinginger, 2004; Pavlenko, 2002). At the same time, a small but growing body of research has begun to analyse language motivation in the context of classroom or non-classroom interactions from a socio-cultural activity theory perspective (Kim, 2007, and this volume; Lantolf & Genung, 2002). In terms of methodology and analysis, however, communication encounters in critical or activity-theoretic studies on motivation tend to be filtered through retrospective participant inter-views, narratives, diaries, or other forms of reconstruction. As I have argued elsewhere (Ushioda, 2007b), very few studies have focused on the analysis of discourse itself in relation to emergent motivation and identity (though promising work using conversation analysis is being developed by Preston, 2006, 2007). Recent discussions of 'emergentism' as a growing theoretical perspective in applied linguistics (Ellis & Larsen-Freeman, 2006) suggest that such an approach to exploring the organic development of motivation and identity emergent through discourse may be especially timely and have much to offer.

Analysing Discourse Data: Emergent Motivation and Identity

To conclude, I should like to mention very briefly three studies which illustrate the potential value of analysing discourse data in this regard. None of the studies was explicitly focused on motivation, yet it is interesting to observe how participant motivation emerges as an important feature of the analysis and is inextricably bound up with the engagement of identities.

Coughlan and Duff (1994) analyse recorded data gathered from non-native speakers engaged in a picture description task with an interviewer. They identify marked differences in how participants conceptualised the pragmatic purpose of the discourse event and in how they saw themselves in relation to the interviewer. These differences were reflected in differences in the amount and quality of language they produced, and in the degree to which they sought to involve the interviewer in the task and establish interpersonal bonds through dialogic interaction. Thus, though participants were ostensibly engaged in the same task of picture description, they were each engaged in a different 'activity', where activity is understood in its sociocultural theoretic sense to comprise the behaviour that is actually produced when a task is performed (Engeström *et al.*, 1999; Leontiev, 1981). In the context of my arguments in this chapter, analysis of the discourse sheds light on participants' emergent motives and social identities in terms of how they constructed the purpose of the task and their relationship with the interviewer and her motives, and in terms of how the interviewer contributed to shaping this unfolding process.

More recently, Richards (2006) has applied Zimmerman's (1998) model of discoursal and social identities to the analysis of language classroom talk, in an effort to explore whether 'real conversations' are possible in this institutionalised setting. Following Zimmerman, Richards makes a distinction between three aspects of identity. Firstly, there are 'situated identities' which are explicitly conferred by the particular context of communication, such as doctor versus patient in the context of a health clinic, or what Richards calls the default position of teacher versus student identity in the context of a classroom. Secondly, there are associated 'discourse identities' as participants orient themselves to particular discourse roles in the moment-by-moment organisation of the interaction (e.g. initiator, listener, questioner, challenger). Thirdly, there are 'transportable identities' which are latent or implicit and can be invoked during the interaction for particular reasons. For example, during a lesson a teacher might allude to the fact that she is also a mother of two, or an avid science fiction fan. In an illuminating analysis of verbal exchanges between teachers and students in different language class-rooms, Richards shows very convincingly the powerful motivational impact of invoking and orienting to students' own transportable identities in the classroom talk, in terms of stimulating a much higher level of personal involvement and effort in the interaction than in traditional teacher-student talk, where students are invariably positioned as students or language learners. In this respect, Richards' analysis provides valuable data-based evidence to support Norton's critique of traditional communicative methodologies which 'do not actively seek to engage the identities of language learners' or 'their sense of who they are and how they relate to the social world' (Norton, 2000: 139).

From a pedagogical point of view, a key strategy may lie in classroom approaches underpinned by principles of learner autonomy. As Riley (2003: 239) observes, a significant characteristic of writing on learner autonomy is its concern with the learner as a fully rounded person, with a social identity, situated in a particular context. In language classrooms that seek to promote autonomous learning, it seems that this concern is translated into pedagogical practices which encourage students to develop and express their own identities through the language they are learning – that is, to be and become themselves. In this connection, I should like to refer here to an interesting study of language learner conversations by Legenhausen (1999). The study constitutes part of a longitudinal programme of research comparing the English language development of students from traditional textbook-based communicative classrooms in German Gymnasium and comprehensive schools, and students socialised in a more autonomous learning environment in a Danish comprehensive school (see for example, Dam & Legenhausen, 1996). In his 1999 study, Legenhausen compares free conversation practice among students in the two kinds of pedagogical environment. His analysis of the conversation data shows that students in traditional communicative classrooms seem unable or unwilling 'to speak as themselves' (Legenhausen, 1999: 181) when invited to converse with one another. They invariably fall back instead on memorised routines and content from textbook dialogues (such as asking one another where they live, what their telephone number is, how many brothers and sisters they have). In sharp contrast, students socialised in the autonomous learning environment invariably engage their own motivation, personal interests and identities in their conversations. Moreover, as Legenhausen demonstrates through his analysis of turn-taking structures, interactional moves, responsivity and Gricean principles, these autonomous students' conversations develop in a far more natural and organic fashion than the 'pseudo-communication' practised by students in traditional communicative classrooms.

As is clear from my brief summaries of these three illustrative studies, they have in common a focus on actual discourse data in particular communication settings, yet they vary considerably in the conceptual frameworks and modes of analysis they adopt (sociocultural activity theory, conversation analysis, Gricean pragmatics). This brings me back to my earlier point that a person-in-context relational view of motivation need not (and perhaps should not) privilege any particular theoretical framework over another, and that different approaches to the analysis of relevant discourse data are possible and potentially illuminating. For example, while relations of power between participants are perhaps implicit rather than explicit aspects of the analyses developed by Coughlan and Duff (1994) and Richards (2006), a more critically oriented analysis of the same data may well bring to the fore relational patterns of power and resistance in the discursive construction of motivation and identities. In this connection, it is worth noting that Richards' (2006) paper is itself built on a conceptual re-analysis of examples of classroom talk from other studies.

Emergent Motivation and Possible Selves

By the same token, analysis of emergent motivation at the micro-level of spoken interactions might equally be grounded in the notion of 'possible selves' which dominates theoretical perspectives in this volume. Possible selves represent people's ideas of 'what they might become, what they would like to become, and what they are afraid of becoming' (Markus & Nurius, 1987: 157), and thus are theorised to function as an interface between the self-concept and motivation. In this sense, possible selves are defined with explicit reference to *future* self-states, characterised by Dörnyei (2005, this volume) in relation to language learning motivation as the 'ideal L2 self' and the 'ought-to self' – that is, future self-states that one may aspire to achieve or feel under pressure to achieve.

Yet, as Dörnyei (this volume) argues, these future self-states can have strong psychological reality in the *current* imaginative experience of learners, as they try to envision or see themselves projected into the future as competent L2 users. In other words, these future self representations or possible selves are entirely continuous with language learners' current selves. To the extent that language learners (are enabled to) engage their current selves in their L2 interactions with other people, 'speak as themselves' (Legenhausen, 1999: 181) with their 'transportable identities' (Richards, 2006), and engage 'their sense of who they are and how they relate to the social world' (Norton, 2000: 139), one can argue that such learners are also enabled to engage directly with their possible selves as users of the L2, but within the scope and security of their current communicative abilities, interests and social contexts. In short, a person-in-context relational view of motivation may, through the analysis of relevant discourse data, help to illuminate how language learners' current experiences and self-states (characterised broadly as 'L2 learning experience' in Dörnyei's L2 Motivational Self System; see Dörnyei, this volume), may facilitate or constrain their engagement with future possible selves.

Conclusion

In her seminal discussion of constructivist challenges for applied linguistics, McGroarty (1998: 600) argued for a strategy of inquiry that examines motivation 'as it is constructed and expressed in and through interaction'. A similar concern has been voiced in motivation research in education by Turner (2001: 90–92) who argues for a multi-method analysis of motivation in context from multiple angles and multiple participant perspectives. By integrating a range of relevant theoretical frameworks to inform our analysis of interaction processes and relational contextual phenomena, we may enrich and diversify our understanding of how motivation shapes and is shaped through engagement in L2-related activity and the engagement of identities and engagement with possible selves.

References

Allwright, D. (2006) Six promising directions in applied linguistics. In S. Gieve and I.K. Miller (eds) *Understanding the Language Classroom* (pp. 11–17). Basingstoke: Palgrave Macmillan.

Atkinson, D. (2002) Toward a sociocognitive approach to second language acquisition. *Modern Language Journal* 86 (iv), 525–545.

Bandura, A. (2001) Social cognitive theory: An agentic perspective. *Annual Review of Psychology* 52, 1–26.

Block, D. (2003) *The Social Turn in Second Language Acquisition.* Edinburgh: Edinburgh University Press.

Chen, J.F., Warden, C.A. and Chang, H.T. (2005) Motivators that do not motivate: The case of Chinese EFL learners and the influence of culture on motivation. *TESOL Quarterly* 39 (4), 609–633.

Clément, R., Noels, K.A. and Deneault, B. (2001) Interethnic contact, identity, and psychological adjustment: The mediating and moderating roles of communication. *Journal of Social Issues* 57, 559–577.

Coughlan, P. and Duff, P. (1994) Same task, different activities: Analysis of SLA task from an activity theory perspective. In J.P. Lantolf and G. Appel (eds) *Vygotskian Approaches to Second Language Research* (pp. 173–193). Westport, CT: Ablex Publishing.

Crookes, G. and Schmidt, R. (1991) Motivation: Reopening the research agenda. *Language Learning* 41, 469–512.

Dam, L. and Legenhausen, L. (1996) The acquisition of vocabulary in an autonomous learning environment – the first months of beginning English. In R. Pemberton, E.S.L. Li, W.W.F. Or and H.D. Pierson (eds) *Taking Control – Autonomy in Language Learning* (pp. 265–280). Hong Kong: Hong Kong University Press.

Dörnyei, Z. (1999) Motivation. In J. Verschueren, J.O. Östmann, J. Blommaert and C. Bulcaen (eds) *Handbook of Pragmatics 1999* (pp. 1–22). Amsterdam: John Benjamins.

Dörnyei, Z. (2005) *The Psychology of the Language Learner. Individual Differences in Second Language Acquisition.* Mahwah, NJ: Lawrence Erlbaum.

Ellis, N. and Larsen-Freeman, D. (2006) Language emergence: Implications for applied linguistics – introduction to the Special Issue. *Applied Linguistics* 27 (4), 558–589.

Engeström, Y., Miettinen, R. and Punamäki, R.L. (eds) (1999) *Perspectives on Activity Theory.* Cambridge: Cambridge University Press.

Firth, A. and Wagner, J. (1997) On discourse, communication, and (some) fundamental concepts in SLA research. *The Modern Language Journal* 81, 285–300.

Firth, A. and Wagner, J. (1998) SLA property! No trespassing! *The Modern Language Journal* 82, 91–94.

Gardner, R.C. (1985) *Social Psychology and Second Language Learning: The Role of Attitudes and Motivation.* London: Edward Arnold.

Gardner, R.C. and Lambert, W.E. (1972) *Attitudes and Motivation in Second Language Learning.* Rowley, MA: Newbury House.

Giles, H. and Byrne, J.L. (1982) An intergroup approach to second language acquisition. *Journal of Multilingual and Multicultural Development* 3, 17–40.

Holliday, A. (1999) Small cultures. *Applied Linguistics* 20 (2), 237–264.

Harré, R. and Gillett, G. (1994) *The Discursive Mind.* Thousand Oaks, CA: Sage.

Jacques, S.R. (2001) Preferences for instructional activities and motivation: A comparison of student and teacher perspectives. In Z. Dörnyei and R. Schmidt (eds) *Motivation and Second Language Acquisition* (pp. 185–211). Honolulu, HI: University of Hawaii Press.

Johnson, M. (2004) *A Philosophy of Second Language Acquisition*. New Haven, CT: Yale University Press.

Kim, T.Y. (2007) Second language learning motivation from an activity theoretic perspective: Case studies of Korean ESL students and recent immigrants in Toronto. PhD thesis, University of Toronto.

Kinginger, C. (2004) Alice doesn't live here anymore: Foreign language learning and identity reconstruction. In A. Pavlenko and A. Blackledge (eds) *Negotiation of Identities in Multilingual Contexts* (pp. 219–242). Clevedon: Multilingual Matters.

Lantolf, J.P. and Genung, P. (2002) 'I'd rather switch than fight': An activity-theoretic study of power, success and failure in a foreign language classroom. In C. Kramsch (ed.) *Language Acquisition and Language Socialization* (pp. 33–46). London: Continuum.

Lantolf, J.P. and Pavlenko, A. (2001) (S)econd (L)anguage (A)ctivity theory: Understanding second language learners as people. In M.P. Breen (ed.) *Learner Contributions to Language Learning: New Directions in Research* (pp. 141–158). Harlow: Pearson Education.

Lantolf, J.P. and Thorne, S.L. (2006) *Sociocultural Theory and the Genesis of Second Language Development*. Oxford: Oxford University Press.

Legenhausen, L. (1999) Autonomous and traditional learners compared: The impact of classroom culture on attitudes and communicative behaviour. In C. Edelhoff and R. Weskamp (eds) *Autonomes Fremdsprachenlernen* (pp. 166–182). Ismaning: Hueber.

Leontiev, A.N. (1981) The problem of activity in psychology. In J. Wertsch (ed.) *The Concept of Activity in Soviet Psychology* (pp. 37–71). Armonk, NY: Sharpe.

Markus, H. and Nurius, P. (1987) Possible selves: The interface between motivation and the self-concept. In K. Yardley and T. Honess (eds) *Self and Identity: Psychosocial Perspectives* (pp. 157–172). Chichester: John Wiley & Sons.

McGroarty, J. (1998) Constructive and constructivist challenges for applied linguistics. *Language Learning* 48 (4), 591–622.

McInerney, D.M. and Van Etten, S. (eds) (2004) *Big Theories Revisited: Research on Sociocultural Influences on Motivation and Learning* (Vol. 4). Greenwich, CO: Information Age Publishing.

Noels, K.A., Clément, R. and Pelletier, L.G. (1999) Perceptions of teachers' communicative style and students' intrinsic and extrinsic motivation. *The Modern Language Journal* 83 (i), 23–34.

Norton, B. (2000) *Identity and Language Learning: Gender, Ethnicity and Educational Change*. Harlow: Longman.

Norton, B. (2001) Non-participation, imagined communities and the language classroom. In M.P. Breen (ed.) *Learner Contributions to Language Learning* (pp. 159–171). Harlow: Longman.

Pavlenko, A. (2002) Poststructuralist approaches to the study of social factors in second language learning and use. In V. Cook (ed.) *Portraits of the L2 User* (pp. 277–302). Clevedon: Multilingual Matters.

Pavlenko, A. and Blackledge, A. (eds) (2004) *Negotiation of Identities in Multilingual Contexts*. Clevedon: Multilingual Matters.

Preston, A. (2006) Re-locating L2 motivation in classroom interaction: A new methodology? Paper presented at BAAL-IRAAL Conference, 7–9 September 2006, University College, Cork.

Preston, A. (2007) Suis-je bovvered, though? Measuring L2 motivation at the classroom level. Paper presented at BAAL Language Learning and Teaching SIG 3rd Annual Conference, Towards a Researched Pedagogy, 2–3 July 2007, University of Lancaster.

Richards, K. (2006) 'Being the teacher': Identity and classroom conversation. *Applied Linguistics* 27 (1), 51–77.

Riley, P. (2003) Drawing the threads together. In D. Little, J. Ridley and E. Ushioda (eds) *Learner Autonomy in the Foreign Language Classroom: Teacher, Learner, Curriculum and Assessment* (pp. 237–252). Dublin: Authentik.

Salili, F., Chiu, C.Y. and Hong, Y.Y. (eds) (2001) *Student Motivation: The Culture and Context of Learning*. New York: Plenum.

Sealey, A. and Carter, B. (2004) *Applied Linguistics as Social Science*. London: Continuum.

Seidlhofer, B. (2003) *Controversies in Applied Linguistics*. Oxford: Oxford University Press.

Toohey, K. (2000) *Learning English at School: Identity, Social Relations and Classroom Practice*. Clevedon: Multilingual Matters.

Turner, J. (2001) Using context to enrich and challenge our understanding of motivational theory. In S. Volet and S. Järvelä (eds) *Motivation in Learning Contexts: Theoretical Advances and Methodological Implications* (pp. 85–104). Amsterdam: Pergamon-Elsevier.

Ushioda, E. (1996) Language learners' motivational thinking: A qualitative study. PhD thesis, University of Dublin, Trinity College.

Ushioda, E. (2001) Language learning at university: Exploring the role of motivational thinking. In Z. Dörnyei and R. Schmidt (eds) *Motivation and Second Language Acquisition* (pp. 93–125). Honolulu, HI: University of Hawaii Press.

Ushioda, E. (2006) Language motivation in a reconfigured Europe: Access, identity, autonomy. *Journal of Multilingual and Multicultural Development* 27 (2), 148–161.

Ushioda, E. (2007a) Motivation, autonomy and sociocultural theory. In P. Benson (ed.) *Learner Autonomy 8: Teacher and Learner Perspectives* (pp. 5–24). Dublin: Authentik.

Ushioda, E. (2007b) Motivation and language. In J.O. Östman and J. Verschueren (eds) *Handbook of Pragmatics Online (2007)*. Amsterdam: John Benjamins.

van Lier, L. (2004) *The Ecology and Semiotics of Language Learning: A Sociocultural Perspective*. Boston, MA: Kluwer Academic.

Volet, S. and Järvelä, S. (2001) *Motivation in Learning Contexts: Theoretical Advances and Methodological Implications*. Amsterdam: Pergamon-Elsevier.

Watson-Gegeo, K.A. (2004) Mind, language, and epistemology: Toward a language socialization paradigm for SLA. *The Modern Language Journal* 88 (iii), 331–350.

Zimmerman, D.H. (1998) Discoursal identities and social identities. In C. Antaki and S. Widdicombe (eds) *Identities in Talk* (pp. 87–106). London: Sage.

Zuengler, J. and Miller, E.R. (2006) Cognitive and sociocultural perspectives: Two parallel SLA worlds? *TESOL Quarterly* 40 (1), 35–58.

Chapter 12
Situating the L2 Self: Two Indonesian School Learners of English

MARTIN LAMB

Introduction

While the concept of identity has a long history in second language learning (McNamara, 1997) it has recently been dominated by post-structuralist approaches (e.g. Norton, 2000; Pavlenko & Blackledge, 2004; Toohey, 2000). These have yielded important insights, but Block (2007) has argued that a concept potentially so fundamental to personal well-being and successful learning merits examination from a psychological point of view too. Dörnyei's (2005; see also this volume) L2 self-system model has the potential to meet this need, drawing on the insights of self psychology (Boyatzis & Akrivou, 2006; Higgins, 1998) to propose that learners who envision their future selves as L2-users (i.e. have an 'ideal L2 self') will be strongly motivated to work towards becoming L2-users in order to reduce the discrepancy between this vision and their current state; others may ostensibly share the same goal of L2 proficiency but feel it as an obligation, imposed by others or society in general (i.e. have an 'ought-to L2 self'), and this engenders a more defensive stance where the individual's main focus is on preventing failure rather than striving towards achievement. The constructs of 'ideal' and 'ought-to L2' selves may prove to be a valuable 'psychological substrate' (Bendle, 2002: 8) underlying the more fluid and fragmented notion of identity presented in poststructuralist writing, and help explain the differential exercise of agency by learners.

At the same time it is important not to lose sight of the social dimension that is implied by the term 'identity'. The formation of self-guides occurs in and through the social domains in which the individual moves – 'the pool of possible selves derives from the categories made salient by the individual's particular sociocultural and historical context' (Markus & Nurius, 1986: 954) – and Boldero and Francis (1999) point out that the effects of self-guides are by no means uniform or predictable: although ideal and ought-to selves represent distinct self-regulatory systems, their actual impact on behaviour is mediated by several factors, for example the relevance of a particular context to the ideals being aspired to. Just as constructs from achievement motivation theory are now being viewed less as stable personality traits than as dynamic and highly context-sensitive states (e.g. Bempechat & Boulay, 2001; Volet & Järvelä, 2001), so the development and motivational impact of 'ideal' and 'ought-to' L2 selves will need to be explored at levels of analysis beyond the self, including the situated activity in which learners engage, their home and institutional settings and the wider context of society and global regions. This in turn means supplementing the large-scale quantitative research that is being carried out to validate the L2 self-system model (see for example chapters in this volume by Csizér & Kormos; Taguchi *et al.*; Ryan) with case studies which investigate the L2 self-guides of specific individuals over time, in their various contexts of learning.

Like the poststructuralist studies cited above, such case studies may benefit from utilising 'middle-range' theories which attempt to explain how individual agency and social structure are mutually shaped and constrained. Two such theories are Lave and Wenger's situated learning theory (Lave & Wenger, 1991; Wenger, 1998) and Bourdieu's (1991) social theory. As in other neo-Vygotskian perspectives such as language socialisation (Kramsch, 2002) and activity theory (Lantolf, 2000), Lave and Wenger view learning as a fundamentally social activity, whereby knowledge and understandings are negotiated in interaction with other people, and skills develop as changing forms of situated practice entailing changed relations with others. Lave and Wenger contend that learning occurs in, or in relation to, 'communities of practice', with learners gradually moving from a position of 'legitimate peripheral participation' toward fuller participation through their engagement in community activities, interaction with more experienced members, and the gradual alignment of their practice with those of these 'experts'. With new forms of participation comes a transformed identity. Communities of practice may be 'as broad as a society or culture, or as narrow as a particular language classroom' (Lantolf & Pavlenko, 2001: 148); they may be a 'real' community in which a person has regular involvement (e.g. a school) or an 'imagined community' – defined by Kanno and Norton (2003: 241) as 'groups of people not immediately tangible and accessible, with whom we connect through the power of the imagination'.

As several writers have recently pointed out (e.g. Murphey *et al.*, 2005; Ryan, 2006) for many learners of English as a foreign language the global community of English users is more 'imagined' than 'real', in that their actual contact with users might be quite limited. Dörnyei (2005) himself sees a connection between Lave and Wenger's notion of imagination, as an important way of belonging to a community, and his own notion of the 'ideal L2 self', which relies on the individual having a powerful vision of him/herself as a future user of the new language. Kramsch

(2006) has recently elaborated on the power of imagination in potentially motivating language learners, especially in adolescence when identity formation is a central concern:

> Like rap and hip hop, a foreign language can reveal unexpected meanings, alternative truths that broaden the scope of the sayable and the imaginable... Seduced by the foreign sounds, rhythms and meanings, and by the 'coolness' of native speakers, many adolescent learners strive to enter new, exotic worlds where they can be, or at least pretend to be, someone else, where they too can become 'cool' and inhabit their bodies in more powerful ways. (Kramsch, 2006: 102)

One further important aspect of situated learning theory is the way identity can be a site of struggle, for a learner's aspirant identity may not be recognised by other community members, or may conflict with his/ her aspirations towards membership of other communities. Individual learners may not have equal access to the resources of a community, nor be granted 'legitimate' status. Lave and Wenger's ideas are therefore often linked (e.g. in Norton, 2000; Block, 2006) to the social theory of Bourdieu (1991), which offers tools for analysing the way that agency is constrained, in an arguably non-deterministic way, by social structure. The key notions are those of *capital*, *field* and *habitus*. By the time they enter school, children have inherited (through background and early experience) different amounts of social, economic and cultural capital, and have acquired a habitual way of understanding the world and a predisposition to act in certain ways, i.e. a 'habitus'. The combination of capital and habitus in each individual makes certain 'fields' of social activity (e.g. school) more congenial than others; successful practice within those fields then further shapes the habitus and endows different forms of capital, which Bourdieu argues contributes in the long-term to the reproduction of social classes. Agency is thus constrained both externally 'by the framework of opportunities and constraints the person finds him/herself in', and also internally 'by an internalized framework that makes some possibilities inconceivable, others improbable, and a limited range acceptable' (Reay, 2004: 435), a formulation which neatly overlaps with the psychological notion of 'possible selves' (see above).

In the rest of this chapter I will report on a study of Indonesian junior high school pupils' motivation to learn English as a foreign language. The main research aim was to track their motivation over the first two years of formal study of the language in school, to see how it changed and what factors were associated with the change. It was not specifically targeted at investigating Dörnyei's L2 self-system model, but this emerged as one useful theoretical framework for interpreting the data, particularly, as I shall argue, when linked with the two social theories described above.

The chapter therefore offers a description of L2 motivation in specific individuals in a particular cultural context, and suggests a possible way of deploying the constructs of 'ideal' and 'ought-to' L2 self in concert with other more socially-oriented constructs to explain L2 motivation.

The Case Study Research

The research site was a provincial Sumatran town called Ajeng,[1] where I had worked during the 1990s. The school itself (JHS 70) was situated in a relatively prosperous emerging middle-class neighbour-hood, though the intake was socially mixed, the facilities themselves extremely basic by western standards, and the most common teaching methodology was traditional teacher-centred 'chalk and talk' based on a mainly grammatico-lexical national syllabus (see Lamb & Coleman, 2008). The research employed a mixed-method strategy, combining surveys of the whole year cohort at the beginning and end of the period with three phases of semi-structured interviews (in Indonesian or English according to preference) and class observations of 12 'focal learners', chosen for having diverse motivational profiles on the basis of their survey responses and teacher comments. All eight English teachers in the school were also interviewed.

Broadly speaking, the survey results demonstrated very high levels of motivation in the school year cohort (Lamb, 2007). Many claimed to learn or use the language outside of school (over half took private courses in English during this period) and, although there was a slight drop in the pleasure which pupils took in their school English lessons, almost everyone considered the language either 'important' or 'very important', with a statistically significant shift towards the latter response after 20 months of formal study.

In this second questionnaire an open item asked pupils to offer reasons for the importance of English. Just under half ($n = 88$) responded, and analysis of their comments revealed a distinction between those which associated English with a personal *aspiration*, either immediate (such as enabling them to play computer games) or distant (such as future study abroad), and those which linked it more to a *requirement.* 42 comments could be identified as falling into the former category, some very general:

> English is important, my dreams are connected to English.[2]
> Because English is the international language. My father used to teach English, and I want to become like my father.

and others with a slightly more specific goal:

> Because I dream of being able to set foot in Europe...and I would like to play football there.

> I'm learning English so I can go to neighbouring countries and because I want to make my family and school proud.
> Because English is an international language. And, I can speak with my idol wherever am I (Japan, Taiwan etc.)! [original]

This latter statement can be contrasted to the following one:

> Maybe because English is the international language and has to be known and understood.

25 comments can be placed in this 'requirement' category, including those which use the auxiliary verb *harus* ('should' or 'have to') and others which suggest an element of wariness or fear:

> So I'm not shy if I'm called to speak with someone, and if my teacher directs a question or problem at me.
> Because in my country there's going to be a free market and we won't be made fools of by foreigners.
> With English we can face up to the era of globalisation which confronts the young generation. And it becomes my responsibility to learn the universal language of this time – English.
> To protect ourselves!

This broad classification appears to mirror the distinction made by Higgins (1998) between a 'promotion' and a 'prevention' regulatory focus, and which is the basis for the distinction in Dörnyei's L2 motivational self-system between 'ideal' and 'ought-to' L2 self. I am not suggesting that single comments like these are sufficient evidence of an individual disposition, but collectively they indicate that the distinction between these two regulatory foci may be conceptually useful in this context. The rest of this chapter explores this further by concentrating on two individuals who seem to exemplify these two different stances towards the English language. Dewi and Munandar were both aged 11 on entry to the school, and were 13 by the time of my last field visit. I will begin by presenting evidence for their L2 self-guides, and link them to their biographies. I will then look at how each responded to me as researcher, the way they appear to regulate their learning over this period, and their attitude towards their school English lessons, using the theoretical frameworks mentioned above. Finally I will consider the implications of their differing learning trajectories – for themselves, for local pedagogy, and for future research.

Two Learners

Very early in her first interview, Dewi let me know an unusual fact about herself – she was born in the USA. Although she had only spent a year there, while her father had a scholarship to study for a Masters

Degree, this quirk of biography evidently had meaning for her because in her third interview, when asked to say something about herself, she began with the words 'I am from Fayetteville, Texas'. After a period living in the capital Jakarta, her parents were now both lecturers at Ajeng University, and Dewi lived with them and her four younger siblings in the pleasant suburb of T_, near the school.

Before entering JHS 70 she had studied English for four years at one of the best primary schools in Ajeng and her initial questionnaire responses suggest she had very positive attitudes towards English – she gave the highest possible responses for the importance of English, her satisfaction with progress and confidence in ultimate success. In her first interview she also expressed a desire to live abroad:

> I: What's your opinion of westerners, of western countries?
> D: Ooh very good, self-disciplined, and if you want to chat to them, they're very friendly.
> I: What about living there one day?
> D: I'd really like to
> I: Or would you prefer to live in Indonesia?
> D: Mmm...over there!
> I: And do you have any ambitions?
> D: Yes, for example, if I could get to study abroad, then I could become really fluent in English.

Dewi's final comment is interesting in the way it inverts the traditional 'instrumental' motive for learning English – it suggests that, for her, it is fluency in English which is the real goal. During this period, Dewi's goals appeared to become slightly more focused. At her second interview she said she wanted to become a businesswoman: 'so I can help build Indonesia, so it isn't left behind'; her hero, she said, was ex-President Habibie, a multilingual who had spent much of his career in the German aero-industry before returning to serve in government in Indonesia. In her final interview, when asked where she would be in 10 years' time, she replied:

> I really want to go to my birthplace, Fayetteville, because I am from Fayetteville so I have to go to my birthplace...maybe I will be a journalist so I can go everywhere, maybe businesswoman.........
> maybe I want to have two *tempat tinggal* (homes), in foreign and in Indonesia [original]

She sounds as if she is imagining her future self as a global professional, a responsible Indonesian citizen yet also comfortable in international settings. English was not the only language that Dewi showed enthusiasm for: 'beside America, I really want to go to Japan', she said, and she enjoyed taking Japanese and Chinese lessons because 'they are very important too...and I think this very unique, maybe my friends will say oh Dewi you are so great because you know Japanese, Chinese...!' [original].

When I first met him, Munandar had just arrived in Ajeng from a rural area of the province. He was unusual among his peers in never having studied English before, either in primary school or in a private course. His father worked in forestry, though Munandar was careful to say that he himself did not chop down trees – a comment that may have been aimed at soothing environmental concerns on my part, but more likely was intended to signal that he was 'in business' rather than working with his hands. His parents had decided to send Munandar to school in the provincial capital, where he lived with his extended family (grandmother, uncle, aunt and cousins), none of whom spoke any English.

From the start he recognised English as important, changing his assessment in the survey to 'very important' at the end of the 20-month period. When elaborating on this importance, he consistently referred to a *need* to learn, as in this extract from his second interview:

> **M:** You know in B_ [a rural area of the province], over there we didn't have any English lessons but in Ajeng we need English, if you don't have English, it's difficult. Wherever we go here we need English.
> **I:** For example, where do you need it?
> **M:** What I mean is, if we've already progressed, got success, started working, we need to be tested in English, everywhere our English is tested.

He makes exactly the same point in his third interview: 'Everywhere, including school, English is examined, it's important.'

Compared to Dewi, Munandar's expressed ambitions were vague, and had no international element. In his first interview he simply said his goal was 'studying well, getting ahead'; in his second interview, he said he had not considered a possible career as he was 'still studying, the important thing is to study first, before thinking about that'. When I asked him in his third interview to imagine himself 10 years ahead, he replied:

> **M:** Yeah, after this JHS, I'll go to senior high school, after that, study, high school, study, university...
> **I:** You want to go to University?
> **M:** Yes
> **I:** Any particular area of study, do you know?
> **M:** Not yet.
> **I:** Ambitions? For work?

M: My ambition is....be a successful businessman and a footballer, that's my hobby.

I: ...and in 10 years' time, where will you live, B_, Ajeng, where?

M: Yeah it depends, if the school's in Ajeng, then I'll live here, if in Jakarta, then there.

Although I have no precise psychometric assessment, Munandar's talk over the three interviews suggests that he has a strong sense of obligation to learn English, an ought-to L2 self, but lacks Dewi's vision of a future English-using self, the key component of an ideal L2 self. Growing up in a small rural town Munandar would have had minimal exposure to English and contact with outsiders of any sort (he told me that I was the first foreigner he had met face-to-face). However, he would have been regularly exposed to official discourses stressing the importance of learning English, as one of the major subjects on the school curriculum. By contrast, Dewi entered JHS 70 with considerable cultural capital – four years of primary school English lessons (albeit brief and sporadic), English-speaking parents, and a house containing plenty of English-language resources – 'story books in English, Encyclopaedias in English, what's more the internet...', as she reported. The way these resources fed her imagination was neatly encapsulated in a joke in her final interview:

D: I ever go to Arab.

I: You have been to Saudi?

D: Yes, by my book! [original]

In other words, by reading about Saudi Arabia in a book she felt she had already been there.

Participation in the Research

Both Dewi and Munandar willingly agreed to take part in my research, but they differed hugely in the way they interacted with me. Dewi seemed eager to exploit her participation to generate opportunities for interaction in English. For example, in both questionnaire open items and in the interviews, she was ready to depart from my agenda and ask *me* questions. Although in the first interview she used little English, her use of occasional interjections such as 'cool!' hinted at a deeper facility in oral language and an eagerness to participate in authentic communication. In the second interview approximately half of her utterances began in English, and there was further deft use of short interjections, such as 'sure', 'really?', 'of course', and times when she talked to her co-interviewee, a friend, in English. At her third interview, all but six of her 78 contributions were in English (though 13 of them included code-mixing with Indonesian). She felt confident enough to joke with me too, accusing me of being a 'workaholic' for example, and asked numerous personal questions about my family. A liking for spoken idiom revealed itself in other ways too. In her initial questionnaire responses she said her favourite activities were expressing words in English 'so they sounded really good'; in her second interview she showed her enthusiasm for slang:

> D: You know, I also have a magazine that contains slang language.
> I: What magazine is that?
> D: *CNS...Cool 'n Smart...* do you know it, do you know it Mister?

She also reported picking up English phrases from listening to pop music and watching Hollywood films. Finally, Dewi appeared proud of her involvement with me in front of her peers – for instance, she attached an institutional badge that I had given them as a gift to her school bag.

By contrast, my interviews with Munandar were all in Indonesian. In his second interview he said that he could now say some things in English in class, but not 'in conversations', and when I began the final interview by inviting him in simple English to give some personal information about himself, he replied with a smile 'oh I don't know English yet!' as if such a possibility were inconceivable. Although he was always amiable with me, he appeared to be slightly embarrassed by his association with me; for example, he never made any attempt to talk to me outside of class, and when I visited him in class, he was teased by his friends. Uniquely among the focal learners in the study, when I asked him what advice he might give to a new pupil at the school about how they could learn English, he declined to give any, saying that it would make him appear 'different' and 'intellectually arrogant'.

It is possible to explain these differing reactions in terms of their ideal and ought-to L2 selves. To Dewi, my presence in the school represented a rare chance to participate in the wider English-speaking community. When the encounters went well, it ratified her evolving identity as an English-speaker. To Munandar, though his ought-to L2 self made him feel duty-bound to participate in the research once invited, he may have projected an evaluative function onto my role which persuaded him to 'play safe' – his interviews were shorter than average, and he hardly ever volunteered contributions but merely responded to my own prompts or questions. Although he consistently recognised the importance of the language, he evidently did not see it as a legitimate form of self-expression.

Again, home background may partly account for their contrasting positions. While Munandar lacked any prior contact with the language, Dewi had heard it and even used it occasionally with her parents (see later). She also had regular exposure to the spoken language through a variety of media, including films on TV and video, radio programmes

('BBC London'), and songs on her Walkman, and read English for interest in books, magazines and on the internet. To Dewi, English was a living language which could make her, in the words of her teen magazine, simultaneously 'cool' and 'smart'. In Bourdieu's terms, her linguistic habitus, along with the cultural capital that she inherited, made her feel comfortable with the identity that English generated for her, and which she enacted through participation in my interviews.

Self-Regulation of Learning

Dewi and Munandar received roughly the same amount of instruction in English at school, but according to their own accounts supplemented that to quite different degrees. Outside of school Munandar apparently made little effort to find ways of learning or using English, though he said he always did his homework, which was grammar and vocabulary exercises in the class workbook. In his second interview he admitted that his school grades were low, and that 'I've been told to play less by my Aunt, she says I must play less and study more'. At the third interview he told me with pride that 'from yesterday I've started taking English lessons at *Ganesha Operation*, my parents told me to'. The limited time he did devote to learning English therefore seems to have been at the instigation of others rather than his own initiative. Further, when I visited him at the private institute, it turned out that this was a general tuition school for all school subjects, the main purpose of which was to boost pupils' state school scores.

As we have seen, Dewi had access to English conversations in the home and she actually saw these as learning experiences:

> D: I learn English with my parents.
> I: You mean, your parents teach you?
> D: It's me myself who wants to learn from them [1st interview].

In interview and questionnaire she also mentioned a number of other resources she was able to exploit for learning, including books, TV, radio, computer and Walkman. During her first year at JHS 70 she started to feel frustrated (see next section) and she also found opportunities to talk to her parents were fewer. As a result she began taking private lessons:

> D: I've started taking lessons, you know, at LIA [Indonesia-America Association].
> I: Oh, you're taking private lessons?
> D: Yes...So I get most of my practice at LIA now, not at home.
> I: Aha, and how are the lessons, are they different from here [i.e. school]?
> D: Mmm...they're more enjoyable.

LIA was one of the best private language institutes in Ajeng, and when I observed a lesson there, I noted that she was enjoying the classes and was a much more active oral participant than she was at school, for example exchanging jokey remarks with the teacher in English as part of a role-play:

T: Dewi, would you like to come to the cinema with me?
D: Yes, but what will your wife say? [original]

Moreover as she reported to me in interview, the institute, in return for the substantial course fee, also supplied her with:

> extra money for buying English books, and I read them over and over and if for instance there's a new word, I can immediately practice it there with friends who know English.

As Boyatzis and Akrivou point out, the 'ideal self', once activated, 'promotes the development of a person's learning agenda and then a more articulated learning plan, experimentation and practice with new behaviour, feelings and perceptions' (Boyatzis & Akrivou, 2006: 628). It is possible then that even at this relatively young age, Dewi's 'ideal L2 self' helped her to regulate her learning of English, pushing her to find alternative means when others broke down. With only an 'ought-to' self guide, Munandar may be less likely to put himself in situations where his lack of competence is exposed; hence, a general tutoring college with 40 pupils per class, and with a focus on exam preparation, suits his purpose well.

Of course, Dewi cannot rely exclusively on her own agency to develop her English skills. She needs access to economic capital to pay for her course. Once there, she benefits from legitimate peripheral participation in the community of practice that is the classroom. With a small number of pupils (12), she has regular opportunities for interaction with the teacher (as in the role-play cited above), who in turn is able, in these relatively well-resourced conditions of work, to organise communicative activities of various sorts that provide further oral practice. The knowledge practices of this community therefore mirror, to some extent, those of the wider community of global English users, so reaffirming the participants' aspirant membership of that wider community. Moreover, as Dewi indicates in the quotation above, they are able to draw on each other's expertise, as when trying out new language, and while there may be many personal differences among them, their shared enterprise over the many weeks of the course inevitably gives them a sense of shared identity as current or future English-users. This is exemplified in the following quotation from one of Dewi's friends at JHS 70 who also took a private course at LIA:

It's different [from school], the lessons are at a higher level there... because the competition is different, there we're all in one class, so we think of them as friends, whereas here in school...Maybe they're cleverer than we are, but we just make a big effort.

Judging from her interaction with myself over this period, Dewi's investment in learning outside of school is paying off in terms of an enhanced capacity for participation in English-mediated communication.

Experience of School English Lessons

Except for a period of about five months during her first year when Dewi was placed in a streamed elite class with a particularly popular teacher, the teaching methodology that she and Munandar experienced in their English lessons was very similar. My observation notes report teacher-dominated lessons based on a standard textbook with a grammatico-lexical syllabus and offering a set of traditional activities (cf. Lamb & Coleman, 2008), including teacher explanations of language, reading comprehension tasks, reading texts aloud, grammar and vocabulary exercises, and feedback sessions involving pupils writing their answers up on the blackboard. Oral work consisted mainly of teacher questions, plus some choral chanting. Dewi and Munandar's reaction to this experience was very different.

In her second interview, Dewi complained that her teacher during the first half of the year (whose name she had already forgotten) 'just asked to translate English words, just that, no practice at all'. When I observed her in school classes I noted her behaviour to be highly variable; she sat at the back and appeared disengaged for long periods, but when the teacher asked a genuine question about the pupils' school activity, she came alive, quickly volunteering an answer in English. When nominated to read aloud by the teacher, she visibly made an effort to do her best, reading fluently and with excellent pronunciation, but then quickly relapsed into distraction when the next student began. She also claimed not to care about the marks she received, saying 'my father doesn't hope I get a particular score...what's important is speaking not the grade you get'.

In her second year class, with the same teacher who had frustrated her at the beginning of her first year, she expressed further dissatisfaction:

I: How do you feel about studying English in this junior high school, now you're in your fourth semester?

D: I feel *senang apa*? [happy or what?] but now I don't like er *cara mengajar guru saya* [the teacher's way of teaching] because maybe I can't understand what does he say...

I: ...Have you talked to the teacher about this?

D: Never, because I am afraid. [original]

Later on in the same interview she complained again: 'don't say to her, her pronunciation is not clear' and agreed wholeheartedly with her co-interviewee when she said that 'with Ms TW we only study with book and *praktikum* [practice] very little...and we are in the class very... boring [original]'. In her final questionnaire she rated her progress as 'not satisfactory', though she was still confident of ultimate success, and rated English as very important for all reasons. When asked in interview whether English was more or less important to her, she replied 'sure, more important, but now I feel...so-so' [original], repeating the same comment later on, as if trying to emphasise the distinction between the objective importance of English to her future, and her feelings, which she knew were temporary and related to her class teacher.

Munandar stressed in each of his interviews that he was happy at JHS 70 – 'it's safe, there aren't any nasty friends, the lessons are calm and disciplined' – whereas at his previous rural primary school 'the teacher often didn't come, only when the sports classes were on, then he'd come'. In his English classes he said he was 'happy...I like it...so I learn'. He is equally consistent about what is important for him in school English lessons:

I need to understand what the teacher says. [1st interview]
In English classes and in other lessons we try our best to catch the meaning of the teacher. [2nd interview]
The teacher teaches what's in the book – I try to catch it. [3rd interview]

In the last two interviews he complains not about the teacher but about his peers, and the way they disturb him. However, when I actually observed him in class, Munandar appeared to be as much the cause of class disturbances as the victim. He was obviously a popular boy and sat with groups of friends at the back or at the far side of the class. Neither he nor his friends volunteered answers to the teacher's questions, and they were rarely called upon to contribute. And as the long 90-minute lessons progressed, their behaviour became rowdier. I wrote in my observation notes that Munandar 'seems incapable of sustained attention', though I also noted that he seemed to enjoy the experience, as he himself reported.

Clearly every child will have experienced the school lessons in a different way, but the stark contrast in Dewi and Munandar's experience might be interpreted with reference to their L2 self-guides and to the communities of practice they were engaging with. As Norton and Kamal point out, there may be no direct overlap between a learner's imagined community and the school classroom:

When learners begin a program of instruction, they may be invested in communities that extend beyond the four walls of the classroom.

If the language teacher does not validate these imagined communities, students may resist participation in learning. (Norton & Kamal, 2003: 303)

This may help to explain Dewi's frustration in her second year school class. By not speaking the language clearly herself, the teacher does not seem to represent a master practitioner in the wider English-speaking community; and by not providing her with opportunities for oral practice, she offers a very restricted set of knowledge practices that deny Dewi the legitimate peripheral participation she craves for the eventual realisation of her ideal L2 self. As a result she adopted a form of non-participation in which she gave selective attention to class activities, as I observed, and took a detached attitude towards the class community's forms of assessment. Furthermore, while normally the teacher would be accorded great respect in local society, she chose to depart from this script in her interviews with me by criticising her. If, as I have argued, she viewed me as a member of the wider English-speaking community, then voicing her concerns with me could be viewed, along with her non-participation in class, as 'acts of alignment to preserve the integrity of [her] imagined community' (Norton, 2001: 165).

Turning our attention to Munandar, his ought-to L2 self may predispose him to trust the system, since deviation from it is likely to bring trouble. Hence, as his interview comments above show, he at least intends to pay close attention to the teacher's words in class and to do his homework dutifully, and unlike Dewi he does not express concern with the lack of meaningful communication in the language. When I observed him in class he never offered any voluntary contributions himself, only speaking on the rare occasions when the teacher directly addressed him. As Chick (1996) has pointed out, tasks such as completing textbook exercises, choral chanting and sequential reading aloud are 'safe' practices in that they do not threaten the face of either teacher or pupil; they may therefore be popular with teachers whose own English is limited and with learners like Munandar who, with a dominant ought-to self, 'moves away from and protects himself/herself from threatening aspects of the present' (Boyatzis & Akrivou, 2006: 626). But because these activities are so dissimilar to the knowledge practices of expert English users – and the language itself a dry code rather than the value-laden expression of human meanings and intentions – pupils' classroom activity is actually a form of 'legitimate non-participation' in this wider L2 community of practice. Hickey and Granade (2004) comment that 'participants in collaborative learning activities can be completely disengaged from the larger community to which they are ostensibly being acculturated' (Hickey & Granade, 2004: 236). In the long-term such learners may, warn Lave and Wenger (1991), prioritise the 'exchange value' of learning over the 'use value', and thus focus mainly on passing tests and getting good qualifications, as Munandar already seems to do. Deprived of meaningful forms of identification inside class, he may also be susceptible to contrary youth identities that deny the value of educational achievement and encourage the sort of ill-discipline I observed in his class.

Some Implications

Not all the focal learners in my study had easily identifiable L2 self-guides. Even those who clearly had an 'ideal L2 self' and who seemed to share Dewi's broad learning trajectory had different background profiles and demonstrated different patterns of participation in English-learning activities. I am not intending to portray Dewi and Munandar as 'prototypical' of learners with ideal and ought-to L2 selves. Rather, the contrast between them helps to highlight the contextual influences on the formation of L2 selves, and their operation during early adolescence in a provincial suburb in a developing country.

I believe the study supports the view that ideal and ought-to L2 selves could be useful explanatory constructs in language learning motivation especially when combined with more sociologically-oriented theories such as those of Lave and Wenger (1991) and Bourdieu (1991). For example, in showing how the notion of community of practice can help explain Dewi and Munandar's differing experience of similar school English classrooms, the study supports Dörnyei's (2005) own contention that situated learning theory offers a 'possible promising inroad into understanding the interface of the Ideal L2 Self and the actional phase of motivation' (Dörnyei, 2005: 108). If Dewi has a strong 'ideal L2 self', this may underlie her ability to ride out the frustrations of school and to self-regulate learning outside of school, though Wenger reminds us that

> Understanding something new is not just a local act of learning. Rather, [it] is an event on a trajectory through which they [learners] give meaning to their engagement in practice in terms of the identity they are developing. (Wenger, 1998: 155)

Thus the precise nature of the identity they are aspiring to might help explain the choices that learners make in their independent learning. For instance, Dewi's vision of herself as a fluent speaker in the international community may partly account for her use of film and music to learn the language, and her interest in slang, as well as her enthusiastic participation in oral activities at the private language course (and in conversations with myself).

Similarly, Bourdieu's social theory helps us to see how individual agency is shaped, and either enabled or constrained, by context. I have suggested that Dewi's linguistic habitus was formed in the home, perhaps even in her American origins, and that it helped her feel comfortable using the language as a form of self-expression; further, her agency in appropriating the language for her use was enabled by the cultural and economic capital that she inherited, and which allowed her to gain social capital in the form of new English-proficient friends at the private language course. All this makes it more likely that she will ultimately acquire the important symbolic capital of English, which in turn will enable her to provide the family milieu and educational resources necessary for her own offspring to acquire the language. Over the long term English may therefore have a role in accentuating social class differences even in national contexts where it was not previously the colonial language.

Nevertheless, recent commentators on Bourdieu (e.g. Reay, 2004) have stressed the non-deterministic nature of his theory; habitus only becomes active in relation to particular 'fields' of practice, and since context is both multilayered and dynamic, individual agency is always unpredictable and has the potential to overcome social disadvantage, a view which Canagarajah (1999) points out is shared by many of the poststructuralist studies mentioned earlier in this chapter (e.g. Norton, 2000). In my study, the focal learner with the most auspicious background – the son of an internationally-trained Professor of Education at Ajeng University – did not (as yet) display much evidence of either an ideal or an ought-to L2 self over this period, and certainly made little effort to learn English; likewise, other focal learners who invested just as much as Dewi in learning English had quite distinct family backgrounds. As for the future, Dewi appears set on a learning trajectory towards 'full' participation in the wider English-speaking community, and towards actualising her ideal L2 self as a cosmopolitan Indonesian member of that community; though it is conceivable that repeated negative experiences in school English classes (an example of a particular 'field' to which her habitus was not suited) may dull her passion for the language, or failure in formal assessments may reduce her sense of self-efficacy, undermining her ideal self (and recalling George Bernard Shaw's comment about school being the only time his education was interrupted). Munandar's future is harder to discern because although his ought-to L2 self encourages him to adopt an identity of participation in the school classroom and he appears determined to do well in school assessments, the restricted set of knowledge practices do not engage his imagination. Just as he and his friends chose to sit on the physical margins of the classroom, their learning trajectory may also become increasingly marginal in relation to school as a whole.

From an educational policy perspective, it could be argued that Munandar's fate is critical, because his background and school experience is more typical of his compatriots. If they do not gain any practical competence in the language during their school years then a huge proportion of Indonesia's population are denied access to a major means of self-improvement, while the country's workforce lacks an important component skill. Even a relatively cursory look at individual learners in context, such as the one presented here, shows that motivation is implicated in this problem, and that identity issues are integral to understanding motivation. L2 self guides may prove to be valuable concepts for describing the way individuals identify with a foreign language, but their value for finding practical solutions to motivational problems will be much enhanced if we also explore their origins in, and impact on, the social settings and situated activity of language learning.

Finally, a research methodology issue. I have argued that Dewi and Munandar's interactions with myself as researcher were influenced by their ideal and ought-to L2 selves, respectively. On the one hand this indicates that talking to learners might be a valid way of eliciting active self-guides; on the other hand, if the researcher him/herself is perceived to be implicated somehow in the achievement of those ideal/ought-to selves, then this may distort respondents' accounts of what they do to reduce the discrepancy with their actual selves. Boldero and Francis (1999) point out a similar effect in quantitative research, where the test location affected the results of studies on the impact of ideal and ought-to selves – for example, testing for academic-related self guides in a university classroom produced different results from testing for them in a less relevant location. Identity is being 'performed' even when completing a questionnaire, in that people seek 'to control the reception of the subject positions they choose to adopt' (Block, 2007: 17); face-to-face interaction provides far more scope for identification processes to emerge, but demands a particularly high degree of reflexivity in the qualitative researcher.

Notes

1. I have changed all place and person names to protect the participants' anonymity.
2. All quotations from learners are translated from Indonesian unless otherwise specified.

References

Bempechat, J. and Boulay, B.A. (2001) Beyond dichotomous characterizations of student learning. In D. McInerney and S. Van Etten (eds) *Research on Sociocultural Influences on Motivation and Learning* (Vol. 1) (pp. 15–36). Greenwich, CT: IAP.
Bendle, M. (2002) The crisis of identity in high modernity. *British Journal of Sociology* 53 (1), 1–18.

Block, D. (2006) *Multilingual Identities in a Global City: London Stories*. London: Palgrave.

Block, D. (2007) *Second Language Identities*. London: Continuum.

Boldero, J. and Francis, J. (1999) Ideals, oughts, and self-regulation: Are there qualitatively distinct self-guides? *Asian Journal of Social Psychology* 2, 343–355.

Bourdieu, P. (1991) *Language and Symbolic Power* (G. Raymond and M. Adamson, trans.). Cambridge: Polity Press.

Boyatzis, R.E. and Akrivou, K. (2006) The ideal self as the driver of intentional change. *Journal of Management Development* 25 (7), 624–642.

Canagarajah, A.S. (1999) *Resisting Linguistic Imperialism in English Teaching*. Oxford: Oxford University Press.

Chick, J.K. (1996) Safe-talk: Collusion in apartheid education. In H. Coleman (ed.) *Society and the Language Classroom* (pp. 21–39). Cambridge: Cambridge University Press.

Dörnyei, Z. (2005) *The Psychology of the Language Learner: Individual Differences in Second Language Acquisition*. Mahwah, NJ: Lawrence Erlbaum Associates.

Hickey, D.T. and Granade, J.B. (2004) Theories of engagement and motivation. In D. McInerney and S. Van Etten (eds) *Big Theories Revisited* (pp. 223–247). Greenwich, CT: IAP.

Higgins, E.T. (1998) Promotion and prevention: Regulatory focus as a motivational principle. *Advances in Experimental Social Psychology* 30, 1–46.

Kanno, Y. and Norton, B. (2003) Imagined communities and educational possibilities: Introduction. *Journal of Language, Identity and Education* 2 (4), 241–249.

Kramsch, C. (ed.) (2002) *Language Acquisition and Language Socialization*. London: Continuum.

Kramsch, C. (2006) Preview article: The multilingual subject. *International Journal of Applied Linguistics* 16 (1), 97–110.

Lamb, M. (2007) The impact of school on EFL learning motivation: An Indonesian case-study. *TESOL Quarterly* 41 (4), 757–780.

Lamb, M. and Coleman, H. (2008) Literacy in English and the transformation of self and society in post-Suharto Indonesia. *International Journal of Bilingual Education and Bilingualism* 11 (2), 189–205.

Lantolf, J.P. (ed.) (2000) *Sociocultural Theory and Second Language Learning*. Oxford: Oxford University Press.

Lantolf, J.P. and Pavlenko, A. (2001) (S)econd (L)anguage (A)ctivity theory: Understanding second language learners as people. In M.P. Breen (ed.) *Learner Contributions to Language Learning* (pp. 141–158). Harlow: Pearson.

Lave, J. and Wenger, E. (1991) *Situated Learning: Legitimate Peripheral Participation*. Cambridge: Cambridge University Press.

Markus, H. and Nurius, P. (1986) Possible selves. *American Psychologist* 41 (9), 954–969.

McNamara, T. (1997) Theorizing social identity. *TESOL Quarterly* 31 (3), 561–567.

Murphey, T., Jin, C. and Li-Chi, C. (2005) Learners' constructions of identities and imagined communities. In P. Benson and D. Nunan (eds) *Learners' Stories* (pp. 83–100). Cambridge: Cambridge University Press.

Norton, B. (2000) *Identity and Language Learning: Gender, Ethnicity and Educational Change*. Harlow: Longman/Pearson Education.

Norton, B. (2001) Non-participation, imagined communities, and the language classroom. In M. Breen (ed.) *Learner Contributions to Language Learning* (pp. 159–171). Harlow: Pearson.

Norton, B. and Kamal, F. (2003) The imagined communities of Pakistani school children. *Journal of Language, Identity and Education* 2 (4), 301–317.

Pavlenko, A. and Blackledge, A. (eds) (2004) *Negotiation of Identities in Multilingual Settings*. Clevedon: Multilingual Matters.

Reay, D. (2004) 'It's all becoming a habitus': Beyond the habitual use of habitus in educational research. *British Journal of Sociology of Education* 25 (4), 431–444.

Ryan, S. (2006) Language learning motivation within the context of globalization: An L2 self within an imagined global community. *Critical Inquiry in Language Studies: An International Journal* 3 (1), 23–45.

Toohey, K. (2000) *Learning English at School: Identity, Social Relations and Classroom Practice*. Clevedon: Multilingual Matters.

Volet, S. and Järvelä, S. (eds) (2001) *Motivation in Learning Contexts: Theoretical Advances and Methodological Implications*. Oxford: Pergamon.

Wenger, E. (1998) *Communities of Practice: Learning, Meaning and Identity*. Cambridge: Cambridge University Press.

Chapter 13
Imagined Identity and the L2 Self in the French Foreign Legion

ZACHARY LYONS

Introduction

The research reported in this chapter was part of a larger four-year investigation into L2 identity and L2 motivation in the French Foreign Legion (henceforth Legion). The researcher's own experience of learning French as a young volunteer in the Legion classroom and Noels and Clément's (1996) findings that language competence has been found to correlate positively with positive adaptation encouraged him to investigate the Legion's instructional environment and the relationships between motivation, self-confidence, attitudes (particularly ethnocentrism), and L2 achievement.

Initially, given the unique aspects of the Legion learning environment, a socio-educational approach to this investigation seemed appropriate. Gardner and Lambert (1972) and Gardner's (1983) integrative motive hypothesis take the position that an integrative motive is positively related to L2 achievement. It has been argued that the Gardnerian paradigm with its integrative/instrumental dichotomy (Riemer, 2001; Shedivy, 2004) is pertinent to the Canadian L2 perspective where English and French L1 speakers are in sociolinguistic competition in different domains. Gardner (2001), in addressing the criticism that the socio-educational model may only be applicable to the Canadian bilingual context, makes the point that the two languages are not necessarily available in every individual's environment across Canada. A similar perspective pertains within the Legion, where not only do many English L1 learners of French not integrate with the wider Francophone community but they actively give voice to separatist messages of categorical identity differentiation, confrontation, and conflict (Lyons, 2004). Therefore, it was felt that the socio-educational model might be appropriate in this particular context.

As a first step, therefore, a two-year quantitative study was undertaken to critically examine the applicability of the socio-educational model to this unique socio-cultural context, and will be reported in the first part of this chapter. 257 English L1 recruits answered psychometric questionnaires assessing their motivation, self-confidence, attitudes towards learning French and the culture of the Legion and, in addition, were tested on their French L2 achievement. The relationships among these variables were used to assess the validity of a causal model suggested by Gardner *et al.*'s (1997) socio-educational model of SLA. However, the data suggested that the model failed to confirm any significant correlations between these variables and challenged the model's theoretical and methodological assumptions. As a second step, and to examine the deficiencies of the model, a qualitative study was undertaken involving in-depth interviews with 13 of the recruits. As will be reported in the second part of this chapter, the qualitative analysis suggests that motivation is context-dependent, multifaceted and dynamic, and that changes in individuals' motivation to learn L2 are better explained by reference to ongoing processes of identification, differentiation and the L2 learning experience, considered in the light of the new theoretical framework of ideal and ought-to selves suggested by Csizér and Dörnyei (2005).

Research Setting: The French Foreign Legion

Composed exclusively of male volunteers aged between 18 and 40, the present day Legion comprises about 7800 men who enlist initially for a period of five years. The Legionnaire[1] is constrained to serve the full five years unless he deserts, a common enough occurrence.[2] The Legion is remarkably multilingual and multinational, with volunteers comprising 117 nationalities (Lyons, 2005), though all instruction and interaction with superiors (the overwhelming majority of whom at officer-level are French nationals) is conducted through French and promotion through the ranks is contingent on L2 achievement. An aspect of the Legion that is seldom reported is that it is composed of approximately 60% French L1 speakers, who are mainly French nationals but include Canadian, Belgian, Swiss and African nationals (Lyons, 2000).

Little has changed in the motivations for joining since Merolli (1937: 21) identified four categories of recruits who found their way to the Legion:

- adventurers who joined to start a new life, and forget an unpleasant past;
- the chronically unemployed;
- very young men who sought adventure and/or were unhappy at home;
- soldiers who had deserted from other armies (or completed their service), and who, having been trained, wished to continue in their chosen profession.

The Legion is a complex institution that binds its adherents from the outside world, attracting a constant turnover of new recruits of many nationalities despite the discipline and hard treatment it is known to dispense (some nine out of 10 applicants are rejected in the first two weeks after enlisting). It is a peer-led, all-male environment exhibiting the potential for huge institutional and peer violence. However, separatist messages of categorical identity differentiation, confrontation and conflict are frowned upon by authority. The aim of the Legion is to create a disciplined and dependable armed force from the disparate elements that join, half of whom are non-Francophones when they enlist. Implicit to the notion of the imagined L2 community (Anderson, 1991; Kanno & Norton, 2003) constituted by the Legion is that it is a refuge and fellow Legionnaires are a band of brothers[3] who communicate and construct a common shared identity using French (Lyons, 2004).

The Legion's L2 Learning Environment

Unlike most L2 learning which normally takes place in a supportive environment, the process of L2 learning in the Legion occurs within a much less favourable ecology. As an L2 learning environment, the Legion has a number of characteristics which mark it as different in relation to other L2 environments. Prime amongst these is that L2 learner anxiety, which can have a deleterious effect on L2 achievement (e.g. Gardner *et al.*, 1997; MacIntyre *et al.*, 1997; Young, 1991), is augmented further by the heightened stressful and violent nature of the learning environment (Lyons, 2005). It is a commonplace for a recruit to receive a slap or disapproving punch in the head from the higher ranking officer or Legionnaire delivering the lesson. The classroom teaching of French in the Legion is conducted in an environment of extreme stress, maintaining the recruit in a highly *traumatisé* (traumatised, a very common word during training) state (Lyons, 2000, 2002).

The Legion stresses the use of the *binome* or Francophone training partner who is tasked with assisting the non-Francophone in acquiring the L2. The Francophone binome is constrained to work closely with his non-Francophone partner throughout the four months of training and not only in the L2 classroom. As an L2 learning environment, another unusual feature of the Legion and its L2 classroom is the emphasis placed on song to supplement L2 instruction as pertinent technical and formulaic expressions are conveyed to the new recruit. Singing, which forms an integral part of the Legion's tradition, can replace L2 classroom work altogether (the onus is then on the binomes and their non-Francophone partners to work together during mealtimes or on guard duty to understand the lyrics).

Loyalty and discipline characterise the Legion's identity (Lyons, 2004). A third element which characterises the shared identity of the Legion is its inaccessibility to outsiders which makes it a difficult environment to study. The Legion and Legionnaires in general have a negative view of outsiders (Geraghty, 1996). Once the recruit is accepted by the Legion (following a thorough investigation of his past background), he is offered the option of adopting a new name which he must then retain for the first five-year contract. Conveniently, this uses the recruit's actual initials and more or less his nationality – the exception to this practice being French nationals who are always recorded as being Canadian, Belgian or Swiss nationals (thus Michael Smith becomes Martin Short; Claude François becomes Charles Fauré, etc.). He may then re-assume his previous name, a process referred to as *Rectification*. The name change is designed to protect the recruit from any further enquiries arising from his past by either outside authorities or family. This is indicative of the Legion's desire to preserve the integrity of its communal isolation and refuge from the outside world as reflected by its motto: *Legio patria nostra* (the Legion is our country/home).

The Quantitative Study

The setting for this investigation was the French Foreign Legion's reception/transit/training base at Aubagne, just outside Marseilles. In this study, the main concerns were to investigate the effects of learners' orientation on language performance and to test the plausibility of a socio-educational model within the Legion's instructional environment context.

Research questions

The following research questions were considered:

(1) Could the identified language learning variables (motivation, self-confidence and attitudes) predict a Legionnaire's L2 achievement?
(2) What were the relationships among motivation, self-confidence, attitudes and L2 achievement in the English L1 learners of French in the Legion?

Participants and procedures

The researcher enlisted the help of three Non-Commissioned Officers (NCOs) at Aubagne who were in charge of the reception of new recruits and the transmission of these same *légionnaires* nearly 4 months later to their respective regiments around the globe. The three NCOs were all of the rank of Caporal-Chef, had over 15 years of service each, were permanently stationed at Aubagne and would have several hours of undisturbed access to the recruits during the average week, in between the recruits' identity, physical and psychometric testing. They would equally have access to the *légionnaires* returning from basic military and language training at Castelnaudary, as these NCOs would be in charge of assigning daily *corvée* duties (cleaning, etc.) to all *légionnaires* awaiting their *Affectation* (joining one of the French Foreign Legion's regiments around the world). It would also be to these NCOs that *légionnaires* would have to come if they wanted an evening's leave to go into the town of Aubagne or into Marseilles (15 km away). Two of the NCOs were former colleagues of the researcher.

Though the researcher was not present during the administration of the tests, in order to ensure that testing was carried out successfully, attention was concentrated on the following points:

(1) That informants were told that the questionnaire contained questions about their motivation in joining the Legion and in learning French, some anxiety measures and background information;
(2) that they understood the items contained on both the questionnaires and the French achievement test;
(3) that they felt they could answer the questions truthfully, without any pressure or fear of consequence;
(4) that they were aware that the answers they gave would have no bearing on their future careers within the Legion itself;
(5) that the tests would take approximately 40 mins.

The researcher was very conscious of two factors which could adversely impact on the questionnaire respondents' performance, as reported by Dörnyei (2001: 209): (1) failure to read the written instructions leading to the possible loss of important information; (2) the manner in which the questionnaire was presented. Those administering the questionnaire were made aware of these concerns and were directed to read out the instructions clearly and encourage the research participants by suggesting that the test was important and that consequently they should endeavour to do their best. Moreover, since explicit evaluation of competence and performance in the domains of professional activities (of which French language use is one within the Legion) is a regular feature of military life, this investigation of language abilities and attitudes appeared authentic and congruent with ongoing practices, thus ensuring that it did not create any disruption in the informants' day-to-day practices.

The initial sample consisted of 360 English-speaking (as determined by nationality) recruits. Each filled in a background information questionnaire, the affective measures instrument and completed a French achievement test. Due to a high rate of attrition in the ranks, by the time the same informants repeated the process after four months of basic training, this sample had reduced to 257 respondents. Though the sample size is comparatively small, it may plausibly be considered representative of Anglophone volunteers in the French Foreign Legion and sufficient for a multivariate analysis (Tabachnick & Fidell, 1989).

Instruments

Four factors were selected as the foci for this study: (a) motivation; (b) self-confidence; (c) attitudes; and (d) L2 achievement. The variables included have been operationally defined and evidence of their validity and reliability accepted and used in several studies (e.g. Gardner & MacIntyre, 1991; Gardner *et al.*, 1979; Masgoret *et al.*, 2001). The researcher compiled a pool of 58 items, some of which were chosen from existing research measures because of their discriminatory power in previous studies but were adapted to fit the particular circumstances of the Legion recruits. Modifications of and additions to the original items were made in order to make them relevant to the context of learning French within the Legion or to reduce the redundancy in the original scales. Dörnyei (2001) points out the importance of designing instrumentation with appropriate psychometric properties aligned with the population being studied.

Each index had five to nine questions that were answered on a five point Likert scale, anchored at one end by *disagree strongly* and at the other by *agree strongly*. Following expert judgement of individual items, negatively worded items were changed to positive items for clarity. The conceptual framework of each factor was defined originally for this research. There are some issues concerning the use of self-report questionnaires. In order to overcome these concerns, 18 research participants took part in semi-structured interviews which presented these constructs in depth and gave the research participants the opportunity to comment on issues raised by the instruments. The instruments were piloted and then revised, taking into account the research participants' comments.

The following measures were designed and piloted for the study (cf. Lyons, 2005 for a more extensive discussion):

Background Information Questionnaire

Research participants were asked to provide information regarding the following six demographic variables:

(1) Age, in years.
(2) Nationality.
(3) Was English their L1?
(4) Educational level. This item required the research participants to specify fully their previous educational background.
(5) Were they French speakers, for how long, and could they read/write French?

(6)   Other languages. Research participants were asked to indicate the number of languages, other than English and French, that they spoke and to what level.

Affective measures

These comprised the following:

- **Motivation**. This measure was developed from motivational and attitudinal measures previously elaborated by Gardner (1985) and consisted of Attitudes toward learning French, Desire to learn French and Motivational Intensity scales. This measure was designed to measure strength of motivation in terms of difficulty and preference for French in relation to other skills recruits have to learn in the Legion, the effort they actually expend in learning French, and future plans to use and study French.
- **Self-confidence**. This measure consisted of L2 anxiety, self-confidence and self-rating of French Achievement scales. The anxiety scale consisted of items which describe classroom situations within the Legion instructional environment in which a recruit might feel anxious or uncomfortable about learning or speaking French. Informants rated their French achievement using a modification of the CanDo measure developed by Clark (1984).
- **Attitude**. This factor comprised attitudes towards French Legionnaires, Interest in learning a language and Integrative Orientation scales. It also included an ethnocentric scale derived from Chen and Starosta's (2000) intercultural sensitivity scale, consisting of items which measure the subject's sensitivity to participating in other cultures (Fritz *et al.*, 2001). Following Lyons (2004), ethnocentrism was hypothesised to be a significant variable in the context of the Legion.

L2 achievement measures

Access to reliable and verifiable French language achievement tests conducted by the recruits was not possible, so an interactionalist vocabulary achievement test was designed for this study (for detailed justification, see Lyons, 2005). An interactionalist approach assesses vocabulary as a trait which is manifested in particular contexts of use. Some form of context dependence should be an essential feature of test design if learners are to demonstrate their ability to deal with vocabulary receptively. Validation of tests from an interactionalist perspective is likely to be multi-faceted, drawing on the various forms of validity enquiry identified by Messick (1996) and discussed in relation to vocabulary testing by Chapelle (1994, 1998). In addition, it is a receptive test and does not provide direct information about the ability to use the target words productively.

The test consisted of five sections with 37 items covering lexical and grammatical use. A sixth section consisted of identifying lexical items which are in daily use in the Legion. Each section had English instructions and the items were simple in format designed to make the test accessible to all research participants. This test was a revised version of more general vocabulary tests including the Vocabulary Levels Test (Nation, 1990) and the Vocabulary Knowledge Scale (Paribakht & Wesche, 1997). The revisions were intended to make the test somewhat easier and more applicable to both the test environment and the amount of time available in which to test the informants.

Drawing on research originally carried out by Meara (1994), the sixth section of the test included words which, though real, were highly unlikely to feature in any conceivable manner during the Legionnaires' first months of basic training (such as *Canot* and *Filleul*). The informants were asked to indicate any words they recognised and to leave blank those that they do not know well enough to say what they meant. Scoring was designed to correct for guessing (i.e. when informants indicated that they knew a pseudoword).

After three pilot studies, construct validity and internal consistency were estimated using Exploratory Factor Analysis (EFA) with Principle Axis Factoring, Oblimin, and Cronbach's α. The significance level for all tests was set at 0.05. All 58 items loaded on the expected factors (accounting for 57.01% of the variance) and yielded high communalities, with their h^2 between 0.711 and 0.459. Cronbach's α was 0.876. Based on these results, it was inferred that all the scale items had satisfactory construct validity.

Results of the quantitative study

The data discussed here refer to the questionnaires and achievement tests completed by 257 English L1 *légionnaires* upon their return to Aubagne, following four months of basic military and language training at Castelnaudary. The most important initial finding from the study was the significantly low test scores on the French Achievement Test ($M = 33.21$ [*scored out of 100*], SD $= 4.87$).

The following statistical procedures were conducted after gathering the data:

(a) All necessary steps were taken for data screening (Tabachnick & Fidell, 1996).
(b) Descriptive statistics were examined.
(c) Reliability for the items in each measure was estimated using Cronbach's α.
(d) Data reduction procedures were conducted using Principal Component Analysis (PCA) in order to determine the main sources of

variance underlying each set of indicants and to determine the underlying nature of each construct.

(e) The internal relationships among the factors found in the factor analysis and the relationships among the reduced indicants in the structural causal modelling were examined.

The relationships among these variables were used to assess the validity of a causal model suggested by Gardner *et al.*'s (1997) socio-educational model of SLA since structural equation modelling is one of the preferred statistical techniques used by researchers interested in the socio-educational model (Gardner, 2001). EQS 5.5 was used to assess the validity of this causal model and to assess how well it fitted any correlations obtained among the variables. In evaluating model fit, multiple indexes were used. The model obtained a chi-square of 371.11 with 437 df, $p > 0.05$ (p value $= 0.89$). Also, fit indexes showed Goodness-of-Fit Index (GFI) $= 0.91$, Non-Normed Fit Index (NNFI) $= 1.01$, Comparative Fit Index (CFI) $= 0.90$, and Root Mean Square Error of Approximation (RMSEA) $= 0.007$ (< 0.05), $p = 1.00$. Based on these fit indexes, the proposed model was a good fit for the data.

Figure 13.1 shows the proposed model of motivation, self-confidence, attitudes and L2 achievement. The model shows that the parameter coefficients to language Achievement from Motivation was 0.10 and from Self-Confidence was 0.19. Interestingly, the parameter coefficient

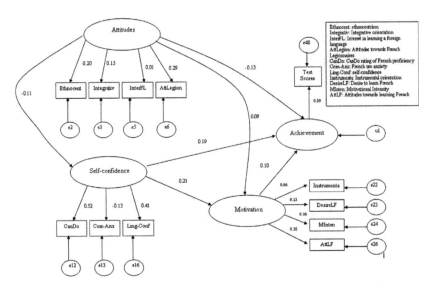

Figure 13.1 Model of motivation, self-confidence, attitudes and L2 achievement (after Gardner *et al.*, 1997)

estimate to Achievement from the Attitudes factor is negative (-0.13) but is not highly significant. There was no significant correlational relationship found between Attitudes and Self-confidence though it was found to be a negative correlation (-0.11). The latent factor Attitudes had a slight positive causal effect on Motivation (0.09). There was a slight negative correlation between Anxiety and Self-confidence (-0.13) and a positive correlation between Self-confidence and Motivation (0.21). In the model, neither Integrative Orientation nor Instrumental Orientation had any significant causal relationship with L2 achievement. The model shows that there were no statistically significant paths to language Achievement from Anxiety and Motivational Orientation and that the three constructs had only indirect effects. The role of Attitudes as a precursor of Motivation was confirmed but was not significant (0.09). Importantly, the effect of Motivation on L2 Achievement was much lower (0.10) than the Gardner *et al.* (1997) model would predict.

This is interesting, given that according to the descriptive statistics the research participants had high levels of integrative and instrumental orientations. That is, the recruits' interests towards the Legion's culture were strong and they equally felt a strong need to master French for their future in the Legion. However, the results of the causal model suggest that this did not affect their language achievement. These findings do not support the claim in Gardner *et al.*'s (1997) model that these orientations are significant factors in L2 acquisition. The model tested here failed to adequately address the two research questions outlined earlier.

Limitations of the socio-educational model in this context

Given that the Legion is an L2-immersed second language learning (SLL) rather than foreign language learning (FLL) environment with strong affiliative properties, why should the socio-educational model fail to clarify the interplay between linguistic confidence, anxiety, motivational intensity, orientations, ethnocentrism, attitudes, and L2 achievement? More fundamentally, why does the recruits' positive motivational orientation fail to impact positively on their language attainment?

One problem inherent in the model may lie with the construct of anxiety. Gardner *et al.* (1997) did not treat anxiety as a separate factor but as a negative component of self-confidence. However, the model's emphasis on the larger social milieu makes it difficult to adequately identify the role of situation-specific anxiety in the elucidation of motivational orientations towards L2 performance, or to ascertain what cognitive and emotive processes are involved on the part of the learner. The low L2 achievement of the recruits as evidenced by their Background Information Questionnaire, the French linguistic confidence CanDo measures and their scores on the French language test may have impacted negatively on their motivational orientation, though the model fails to elucidate this. In contrast to MacIntyre and Gardner (1991), Au (1988) and Sparks *et al.* (2000) suggest that motivation, self-confidence and anxiety are the result and not the cause of L2 achievement, while Ushioda (1996) suggests that L2 success engenders motivation. Could the recruits' lack of engagement with the L2 community, as a result of low self-confidence, be a factor in their low L2 achievement? If the recruits' confidence is high, they may be more likely to engage in cross-cultural interaction, exhibit Motivational Intensity, and make every effort to interact efficiently. This is supported by studies which suggest that self-confidence influences L2 achievement both directly and indirectly through the learners' attitudes and effort in learning the L2 (Clément *et al.*, 1994).

Another limitation of the socio-educational model may be that it is not sufficiently sensitive to the complexities of particular social settings. Most studies related to the socio-educational model, whether in SLL or FLL contexts, have been conducted with college students in structured, formal, and standard learning environments. Norton points out that conceptions of instrumental and integrative motivation 'which are dominant in the field of SLA, do not capture the complex relationship between relations of power, identity, and language learning' (Norton, 1995: 16). While recognising the importance of the social *milieu*, the socio-educational model may have a weak emic aspect and may not in fact be generalisable to other non-Canadian SLL contexts (Yashima, 2000). Pennycook (1994: 15) addressed this concern and pointed out that 'we cannot reduce questions of language to such social psychological notions as instrumental and integrative motivation, but must account for the extent to which language is embedded in social, economic and political struggles'. Ushioda (2006) echoes this view arguing that integrative motivation is part of an internal domain of self and shifting 'processes of engaging, constructing and negotiating' identities (Ushioda, 2006: 289).

Since the socio-educational model could not adequately address the research questions, it became apparent that a different strategy of inquiry and alternative theoretical framework were needed to examine issues of motivation, anxiety and L2 learning in the context of the Legion.

The Qualitative Study

A small-scale qualitative study conducted contemporaneously to the above quantitative investigation was undertaken as a means of examining these issues in greater depth. This is in keeping with studies which have used qualitative research methodology to examine motivational constructs (e.g. Nikolov, 1999; Syed, 2001; Ushioda, 2001; Williams & Burden, 1999; Williams *et al.*, 2001), and L2 anxiety (e.g. Bailey, 1983;

Gregersen & Horwitz, 2002; Pappamihiel, 2002; Phillips, 1992; Spielmann & Radnofsky, 2001). It was hoped that the qualitative study might shed light in particular on the second research question – namely, why does the recruits' positive motivational orientation fail to impact positively on their language attainment?

Procedure

Thirteen recruits who also participated in the questionnaire study were interviewed upon their return to Aubagne following four months of military and language training at Castelnaudary. Age ranged from 19 to 25 years old ($M = 20.1$). Nine were English, three Irish and one American. Informants are labelled S1–S13.

Semi-structured interviews were conducted to identify affective variables as articulated by the recruits. Specifically, the researcher's focus was on capturing instructional, affective and cultural factors assumed to influence Legionnaires' language achievement. All interviews were conducted in an informal environment outside the Legion camp at Aubagne, at the Hotel Estérel, Marseilles, and lasted between 40 and 70 mins each.

Each interview began with a few general questions in French about Legion life (e.g. How do you find Aubagne now that you are back from Castelnaudary? Not as scary as when you were a new recruit?) with a view to ascertaining the informant's level of spoken French. The results of each informant's CanDo rating and French language test were also available. A number of probe questions were used to guide the investigation, which were further clarified for the interviewees:

- Why did you enlist? Do you intend to desert? (Many disaffected recruits desert when they return from training at Castelnaudary and before they get sent to a regiment overseas as it is relatively easy to do so now without fear of capture.)
- What are your attitudes towards French L1 Legionnaires? And towards the Legion?
- Is a good level of French necessary for daily life in the Legion? And long-term?
- How good is your level of French? (Summarily tested by asking a number of related questions in French as illustrated above.)
- Is learning French seen by you as being important for integrating into the Legion? Is a fluent command of French necessary to becoming an integrated Legionnaire?
- What are your attitudes towards how you are taught French in the Legion?
- Were you ever anxious during French class? While speaking French to an officer (higher rank)? What made you anxious?

- Do you think this had an effect on your motivation to learn French? Be a model Legionnaire?
- Do you think you are still motivated to learn French?
- When you joined the Legion, who were your role models amongst the Legionnaires you met?
- Do you intend applying for French citizenship when it is time? (One of the carrots offered to Legionnaires after they finish their first five years of enlistment is the offer of French citizenship.)
- What do you think it means to be a Legionnaire as an English/ Irish/American, etc. citizen?

The interviews were conducted in English, recorded, transcribed and archived to digital MP3 format. A broad transcription approach was employed with standard orthographic full stops and commas used to mark pauses and grammatical phrase groups. Data analysis followed an inductive, grounded theory development process (Eisenhardt, 1989; Sutton, 1991). Interview data were searched for categories of motivational orientations, attitudinal variables and identity, and the transcripts were coded for evidence of each. An iterative process of moving back and forth between the data, relevant literature, and emerging concepts then took place to develop conceptual categories. Finally, as Ushioda (2001) recommends, qualitative findings were interpreted through the prism of an existing theoretical framework.

Discussion of some sample data

I will outline just a small sample of data which addresses aspects of the fluid, complex and context-dependent relationship between the Legionnaires' motivational orientations, anxiety and their low L2 achievement, and which may shed light on why the socio-educational model failed to adequately elucidate recruits' motivational orientations.

It was universally recognised by the informants that French was very necessary for daily life in the Legion, in addition to being important for integrating into the Legion. Motivational factors revealed strong instrumental and integrative orientations:

- If you want to get on you have to learn it – it makes you look stupid around the other guys if you can't get it. You won't be promoted if you don't get it. (S4)
- Yes, definitely. No one can command a unit if they can't speak French. (S7)
- If you can't speak French you're not considered a Legionnaire. I don't even know if you can stay here. (S2)
- Being a good soldier is important and being able to take orders also – if you can speak French as well you are well in. (S9)

- A good level of French is not just necessary, it's mandatory. To get food, to get from A–B, to speak to your mates – to get to know the ones from Portugal or Germany, you have to do it through French. There is no way around it. It really is the French [emphasis] Foreign Legion! (S12).
- French is important because there are people from all over the world here. If there is no common language, it would all be a shambles. (S4)

The harsh reality of the system as well as the sporadic manner of instruction are voiced by the next informants, while motivational orientations are still evident:

- In school if you didn't learn, no one cared but here if you don't learn French they hit you. It make[s] you try harder to learn just to avoid that. Sometimes I just shit myself before language class. (S9)
- They treat you like shit – like you're really dumb if you don't pick it up quickly. The classes are very tense as people are afraid of getting hit or humiliated. It can be hard to think never mind learn a different language. And just when you get used to it [*a particular language lesson*], you do something mad for the next three days – like marching through the mountains – and then they stick you back into the classroom and you're right back again at square one having lost all that you had learnt earlier in the week...[*in the classroom they then usually*] go on to do something completely different. (S4)
- The way they treat you is crazy but effective – none of these guys would make an effort if they weren't being threatened. It works I guess but it can scare the shit out of you when an officer talks to you as you're in for it if you get something wrong when you answer him. (S9)
- The way I see it is everyone is here for the same reason – some will make it through, a lot will not. The ones that make it will be wanting to do well and move up [*the ranks*]. That's my goal and probably with the language under my belt that will get easier and I will really feel more like a Legionnaire then. That's all I ever wanted and if it takes getting a few blows, well then I'll just have to put up with it – that's the system. (S2)

An interesting assumption of much L2 motivation and participation[4] literature is that in language classrooms, learners are there to learn the language. The conclusion which is inevitably drawn from this is that if they fail to learn, it is likely to be their motivation which is at fault. However, students' goals have been shown to be more complex (Gillette, 1994; Lantolf & Pavlenko, 2001). The informants in this study did not express any initial desire to learn French, nor did any suggest that they joined the Legion to learn French. Learning French is a by-product of a desire to become a Legionnaire. The realities of this required and supervised *lingua franca* are conveyed by the next informant:

– The hard part of becoming a Legionnaire is that even when you are talking to your English mates you have to do it in French. Stuff that you could say in two sentences in English can take 10 minutes in French by the time you make yourself understood and all the stuff that you wouldn't normally need to explain has to be put into a different language and then it's not the same – you don't feel like yourself when you're talking because you have to concentrate so hard on forming the sentence and getting it right, getting the accent, saying it, hoping it actually means something and then hoping you can understand what's said back to you. Most of the lads just don't bother. I know I don't usually. (S12)

So, after four months of L2 instruction and immersion, were the informants still motivated to learn French? The interplay of instrumental and integrative orientations is still much in evidence but the problematic nature of the co-construction of identity is introduced below in informant S4's observation on the French:

– I have never wanted to learn French but I have to so I can stay and get on. That's my only motivation. (S8)
– My motivation to learn French comes from wanting to be promoted as high as possible in the Legion. I love the life and want respect. (S5)
– I'm motivated to improve my level of French most of the time – I am here for as long as possible so you just have to get on with it. But sometimes I think why bother? (S13)
– Sure, it is a great language once you get the hang of it. I never had any problems with learning. The only problem is that the French speak it. (S4)

The term 'co-construction' refers to meaning as negotiated in interaction (Lantolf, 2000). The co-construction process belies the notion of fixed identities and has consequences for many aspects of language learning and teaching as well as for identity construction. L2 learners do not simply co-construct agreement through assimilation (Duff *et al.*, 2000). They can sometimes resist and reframe their participation in socialising interactions as well (e.g. Cole & Zuengler, 2003; Lantolf & Genung, 2002).

It has been argued that the Legion as a culturally and linguistically cohesive imagined community is undermined by categorical identity differentiation and confrontation (Lyons, 2004), just as this qualitative data suggest with many of the informants rejecting 'the desired integration into an imagined L2 community' (Dörnyei, 2005: 98). The development of individual self-identity is inseparable from the parallel development of collective social identity. This problematic relationship has been described as the internal-external dialectic of identification by Jenkins (1996), who maintains that self-identity must be validated through social interaction and that the self is embedded in social practices. Following De Cillia *et al.* (1999: 153), this communal identity can be 'conceived as specific forms of social identities – [which] are discursively, by means of language and other semiotic systems, produced, reproduced, transformed and destructed'. Informant S12 below problematises the construction of a self identity within an environment which stresses group cohesion and affiliation and the construction of a shared social identity:

> – You're not relaxed in yourself the way you are when you speak in your own language. It's the same for everyone – it's easier to stick with your own sometimes just so you don't have to work so hard to be understood. It feels great when you can speak English – like a little holiday – reminds you who you are – even the French are more relaxed when they are speaking amongst themselves. My *binome* is always ignoring me that way and my French is poor because of that – I can barely get him to explain the new words in the classroom. (S12)

Matsumoto and Obana (2001: 77) point out that 'the ultimate aim of learning a foreign language is to interact with the community of the language' even in interculturally problematic contexts (Donitsa-Schmidt *et al.*, 2004; Inbar *et al.*, 2001; Kraemer, 1993). What comes across from this data sample is that few of the informants are interacting 'with the community of the language' at more than a superficial level. This is an important point as Lemke (1995: 24–25) points out that L2 learners speak with the voices of their communities and 'to the extent that we have individual voices, we fashion them out of the social voices already available to us'. When the L2 is rejected, for whatever reason, then the L1 learner will take refuge in the L1:

> – Whenever I speak French to my *binome* or to the *caporal* [*corporal*] or even to a *képi noir* [*a higher rank indicated by a black kepi*], I feel a right prat. I do it ... then it's down to the *Foyer* [*a bar/shop*] for a beer with all the other Brits. (S6)

The construction of a successful L2 identity for these Legionnaires is put in jeopardy by attitudinal variables which evoke Schumann's (1978) concept of social distance (cf. Cook, 2001; Lybeck, 2002; Simpson, 1997 for studies which examine social distance and L2 orientations). Social distance may also explain the variability in motivation in informant S3 below, and in the response from S13 above who alludes to being 'motivated to improve my level of French most of the time'. Norton

(1995: 11) explains that a 'learner may sometimes be motivated, extroverted, and confident and sometimes unmotivated, introverted and anxious'.

> – There were times that I really felt like I fitted in. I could rabbit away [*in French*] but the Legion never let's you forget that you are a Brit and that you rule [*English-speakers are generally viewed favourably by Legion authorities (Young, 1998)*]... all in all, I just hate the language ... I really hate my *binome*. I do try [*to learn French*] sometimes and I really try. (S3)

L2 learning needs to be understood within complex and sometimes inequitable social structures (Norton, 1995, 2000) and as Briguglio (2000) points out the construction of L2 identities is rendered complex where learners resist the L2 and its culture. As Schumann (1978) argues, greater social distance engenders a bad language learning situation. A similar idea is captured in Clément's (1980) concept of ethnolinguistic vitality which suggests that the perceived status of the L2 determines whether the learner will display an integrative (or even assimilative) orientation. It is interesting to note that attitudes towards the French L1 Legionnaires (the informants were constrained to spend every moment of every day with their *binome*) reflected a high degree of animosity not only towards the French L1 Legionnaires but towards the French and French culture/ identity in general.

> – The French ones think they're it – they act superior because they don't have to waste time learning to speak the language – they look down on anyone who is struggling ... as I am. (S1)
> – The French are not helpful – in fact, they are the opposite. Right now they are in a superior position because they don't have to learn the language but that's not forever and when everyone speaks it, then things will even out. (S11)
> – They are pathetic, the way they prance around. (S1)
> – I don't really have much to do with them. They seem cocky bastards. (S4)
> – Some of them are ok, just cocky and arrogant in a French way. Bloody French, [*their*] plonk and Coquille St. Jacques! [*A lunchtime meal on Fridays invariably consists of Coquille St. Jacques*]. (S10)

The impact of this cultural and linguistic incommensurability on the co-construction of identity within imagined communities can lead to a situation where the L2 learning is constrained since 'to invest in a language is to invest in an identity' (Churchill, 2002: 3). Support for this proposition may be found in Siegal's (1996), LoCastro's (1996) and Cohen's (1997) examinations of learning Japanese. This constraint may be occasioned by the interplay of one or more various agents (e.g. learner, instructor, peers, L2 culture, learning environment, even characteristics of the L2 itself). The L2 may be learnt in a limited manner, according to perceptions of one's duty or responsibility, as determined by either the learner or a significant other. This is in accord with Norton's research suggesting that the L2 context may encourage resistance and non-participation if there is 'a disjuncture between the learner's imagined community and the ... goals' of language learning (Norton, 2001: 170).

It seems likely that integrative motivation is less strongly evident in the Legion context as compared to instrumental motivation, given the negative views that exist between English versus French native speakers and the fluid, complex and highly context-dependent co-construction of multiple identities and allegiances which characterise the Legionnaire's identity. However, there may also be a fundamental problem in the Gardnerian constructs of integrative and instrumental motivation which fails to adequately contextualise the orientations behind this co-construction. Within an SLL environment like the Legion, Gardnerian instrumental and integrative motivational orientations may play only minor roles since even Legionnaires with low motivational orientation are constrained to interact with the L2. These motivational orientations, along with the social context, may as Norton (2000: 5) contends, be 'possibly coexisting in contradictory ways.'

Siegal (1996), and Sharkey *et al.* (2003), highlight the need to consider the ways in which language learning opportunities and identities are co-constructed in interaction, reflecting not only the multiplicity and impermanence of identity as it is produced in interaction but also the impermanence and instability of attitudes and motivation. Norton (1995) proposed the notion 'investment' as better capturing the complex relationship between a learner's motivation and his/her willingness to use the L2. She uses the term to signal 'the socially and historically constructed relationship of learners to the target language, and their often ambivalent desire to learn and practice it' (Norton, 2000: 10), and suggests that a learner's imagined community is best understood within the context of his/her investment (Norton, 2001).

Ideal and ought-to L2 selves in the context of the Legion

The reinterpretation of integrative motivation from a self perspective by Csizér and Dörnyei (2005; see also Dörnyei, this volume) sees it overlapping with instrumental motivation as the L2 learner struggles to become his ideal and/or ought self (the Legionnaire he wants and/or thinks he should be, respectively). It may be that this offers a more useful prism than the Gardnerian model through which to view the motivations of these English L1 Legionnaires.

The research participants' responses suggest an integrative disposition towards the Legion and a somewhat lesser integrative disposition towards the L2. This reflects Dörnyei and Csizér's (2002; also Dörnyei, 2003; Csizér & Dörnyei, 2005) findings – albeit about a very different L2 context – that the source of integrativeness lies mainly within the confines of the learner's mind. I would posit that an ideal L2 self for the English L1 Legionnaires is conceptually similar to Yashima *et al.*'s (2004) English-speaking ideal L2 selves. Legionnaires who are conscious of how they relate to the Legion as an imagined L2 community tend to be motivated to improve their French as they visualise their French-using selves. A Legionnaire's ideal L2 self would reflect an integrative disposition towards this L2 community. This supports Csizér and Dörnyei's (2005: 29) assertion that 'it is difficult to imagine that one's ideal self would often be associated with competence in a L2 that is spoken by a community we despise'; or put another way, 'it is difficult to envisage that one can develop a potent ideal L2-speaking self while at the same time despising the people who speak the L2 in question' (Dörnyei, 2005: 102). Consequently, the Legionnaire's ideal L2 self is a 'member of an imagined L2 community whose mental construction is partly based on [his] real-life experiences of the community/communities speaking the particular L2 in question and partly on [his] imagination' (Dörnyei, 2005: 102).

However, this L2 community is not that of the French L1 officers or Legionnaires but rather French L2 speakers who also share a similar L1 and ethnic affiliation or nationality. So, an Irish Legionnaire will identify with longer-serving Irish (or English L1) Legionnaires, who will appear to the L2 novice as possessing strong Bourdieuian habitus by their proficiency[5] in using the L2 according to interactional norms. Habitus, a central Bourdieuian construct, aligns closely with identity. 'The habitus is a system of durable, transposable dispositions' which predispose the participant to act, think and behave in particular ways (Bourdieu, 1977: 641). Those who have more of the dispositions valued by relevant structuring practices are more likely to be positioned more favourably than those who do not have such dispositions. This is supported by the qualitative data. If there is a group characteristically associated with the L2 in the learner's closer social environment, his attitudes toward integration would be most likely related to this group – even though its members are not native speakers. As the L2 becomes associated with these groups who possess more social, cultural or material resources, individuals will tend towards reifying the L2 itself as a symbol of status. We may then consider L2 motivation and L2 selves as the investment (Norton, 1995) learners make which has the potential of increasing their capital, self-concept and identity.

The strongest possible self visualised and activated for the recruits was clearly the ought self as their L2 focus was on avoiding failure in all their dealing with the language (sample statements include: 'you had better learn ... French or you're in trouble'; 'after being shouted at enough, you have to learn the language'). This is in sharp contrast with the visualised ideal self which is reflected in the role models identified by the Legionnaires, who were predominantly English L1 speakers with five to seven years service in the Legion and perceived as being L2 proficient by the research participants. This ideal self was an ideal L2 self who spoke French 'like a native' and was 'good enough at the language to put the French to shame'. This view was also reflected in their comments of what it means to be a Legionnaire as an English L1 speaker, namely, being confident and proficient in the L2.

Conclusion

The quantitative research reported above permitted a critical interrogation of the socio-educational model challenging the model's theoretical and methodological assumptions. To highlight the inadequacy of the model, a qualitative study to flesh out the 'skeletal statistical models derived from questionnaires alone' (Spolsky, 2000: 163) was undertaken. While the small scale and exploratory nature of this qualitative study should be acknowledged, it has problematised the notion of identity, L2 motivation and the L2 self in the context of the Legion. The Legion's L2 Learning Experience presents an intriguing constellation of less than common executive motives relating to group dynamics, power relations and differentials, extreme 'socionormative influences of peer pressure' (Dörnyei, 2001: 250), and learner L2 self confidence, all of which the socio-educational model failed to capture. It also highlights the issue of power relations between the L2 learner and the L2 community, which echoes Norton's (1995: 3) view that 'power relations play a very crucial role in social interactions between language learners and target language speakers'.

The realisation of possible selves occurs in a social dialogic context (Leondari *et al.*, 1998), a view echoed by McGroarty (2001: 74) who states that 'self and social context are mutually influential; all selves are socially situated, including the selves of language learners', and by Ushioda (2006: 291) who describes social identity as 'subject to conditions and constraints imposed by surrounding social practices'. Identity cannot be separated from the context of the social interaction in which it originates (Goldberg & Noels, 2006) since language is used to socio-culturally construct an image or identity. However, it is important to note Delanty's view that, 'all identities are based on some kind of exclusion, as the identity of the self can be defined only by reference to a non-self' (Delanty, 2000: 115).

For our Legionnaires, this reference point seems to be French L1 speakers. So, a sense of what is possible and which possible self is viable are defined by and bounded by an individual's situated perspective.

However, the preponderance of the ought self undermines the recruit's sense of L2 investment and may explain the low L2 proficiency of the integratively disposed English L1 Legionnaires in this study, though Sideridis (2006) found, for his elementary school students, that strong oughts were not predictive of effort withdrawal. Our Legionnaires may persevere in co-constructing a supra-national identity as a Legionnaire and a vision of an ideal language-using self, regardless of whether the effort results in positive L2 achievement outcomes.

Notes

1. Throughout this paper, '*Legionnaire*' denotes any member of the force – '*légionnaire*' is the term used in the Legion for the rank of private soldier.
2. The Bureau Des Statistiques de la Légion Etrangère estimates that 30% of recruits try to quit or desert before their basic training is over – this figure is low in Legion terms simply because the recruit during training has absolutely no access to civilian clothes, maps, radios, identity cards or much money. The figure jumps above 30% by end of year one and above 41% before the first five-year contract expires. In addition to this high desertion rate other factors may cause recruits to be thrown out of the Legion, or leave on their own volition – physical or psychological injury or damage (attempting suicide), arrest by Interpol, incompatibility (rejection for homosexual activities, etc.) (Lyons, 2005).
3. Within the Legion, this fraternity in arms is embedded in the second tenet of the Legionnaire's Code d'honneur:'
   Chaque Légionnaire est ton frère d'arme, quelle que soit sa nationalité, sa race, sa religion. Tu lui manifestes toujours la solidarité étroite qui doit unir les membres d'une même famille.' (Every Legionnaire is your brother in arms, regardless of nationality, race or religion. You show him always the close solidarity which must unite the members of the same family).
4. In the context of co-construction of identity within imagined communities, the term 'participation' suggested by Sfard (1998) is of relevance since participation involves 'doing' and the ability to 'perform' as a part of new discourse communities (Pavlenko, 2000), whereas acquisition is about gains in knowledge of rules and codes.
5. Proficiency is 'contextualised, dynamic, and reciprocal, depending on the context in which it is learned and used, changing mood and need, and varying according to the person with whom it is used' (Spolsky, 2000: 165).

References

Anderson, B. (1991) *Imagined Communities*. New York: Verso.
Au, S.Y. (1988) A critical appraisal of Gardner's social-psychological theory of second-language (L2) learning. *Language Learning* 38, 75–100.
Bailey, K. (1983) Competitiveness and anxiety in adult second language learning: Looking at and through the diary studies. In H. Seliger and M. Long (eds) *Classroom Oriented Research in Second Language Acquisition* (pp. 67–103). Rowley, MA: Newbury House.

Bourdieu, P. (1977) The economics of linguistic exchanges. *Social Science Information* XVI, 637–668.

Briguglio, C. (2000) Language and cultural issues for English-as-a-second/foreign language students in transnational educational settings. *Higher Education in Europe* XXV, 3, 425–434.

Chapelle, C.A. (1994) Are C-tests valid measures for L2 vocabulary research? *Second Language Research* 10, 157–187.

Chapelle, C.A. (1998) Construct definition and validity inquiry in SLA research. In L.F. Bachman and A.D. Cohen (ed.) *Interfaces between Second Language Acquisition and Language Testing Research* (pp. 32–70). Cambridge: Cambridge University Press.

Chen, G.M. and Starosta, W.J. (2000) The development and validation of the intercultural communication sensitivity scale. *Human Communication* 3, 1–15.

Churchill, E. (2002) Interview with Bonny Norton. *The Language Teacher* 26 (6), 3–5.

Clark, J.L.D. (1984) *Language. A Survey of Global Understanding: Final Report.* New Rochelle, NY: Change Magazine.

Clément, R. (1980) Ethnicity, contact and communicative competence in a L2. In H. Giles, W.P. Robinson and P.M. Smith (eds) *Language: Social Psychological Perspectives* (pp. 147–154). Oxford: Pergamon Press.

Clément, R., Dörnyei, Z. and Noels, K.A. (1994) Motivation, self-confidence and group cohesion in the foreign language classroom. *Language Learning* 44, 417–448.

Cohen, A.D. (1997) Developing pragmatic ability: Insights from the accelerated study of Japanese. In H.M. Cook, K. Hijirida and M. Tahara (eds) *New Trends and Issues in Teaching Japanese Language and Culture* (pp. 137–163). Honolulu, HI: University of Hawaii, Second Language Teaching and Curriculum Center.

Cole, K. and Zuengler, J. (2003) Engaging in an authentic science project: Appropriating resisting, and denying scientific identities. In R. Bayley and S.R. Schecter (eds) *Language Socialization in Bilingual and Multilingual Societies* (pp. 98–113) Clevedon: Multilingual Matters.

Cook, V. (2001) *Second Language Learning and Language Teaching.* New York: Oxford University Press.

Csizér, K. and Dörnyei, Z. (2005) The internal structure of language learning motivation and its relationship with language choice and learning effort. *Modern Language Journal* 89 (1), 19–36.

De Cillia, R., Reisigl, M. and Wodak, R. (1999) Discursive construction of national identities. *Discourse and Society* 10 (2), 149–172.

Delanty, G. (2000) *Citizenship in a Global Age: Society, Culture, Politics.* Buckingham: Open University Press.

Donitsa-Schmidt, S., Inbar, O. and Shohamy, E. (2004) The effects of teaching spoken Arabic on students' attitudes and motivation in Israel. *Modern Language Journal* 88 (2), 217–228.

Dörnyei, Z. (2001) *Teaching and Researching Motivation.* Harlow: Longman.

Dörnyei, Z. (2003) Attitudes, orientations, and motivations in language learning: Advances in theory, research and applications. *Language Learning* 53 (1), 3–31.

Dörnyei, Z. (2005) *The Psychology of the Language Learner: Individual Differences in Second Language Acquisition.* Mahwah, NJ: Lawrence Erlbaum Associates.

Dörnyei, Z. and Csizér, K. (2002) Some dynamics of language attitudes and motivation: Results from a longitudinal nationwide study. *Applied Linguistics* 23 (4), 421–462.

Duff, P.A., Wong, P. and Early, M. (2000) Learning language for work and life: The linguistic socialization of immigrant Canadians seeking careers in healthcare. *Canadian Modern Language Review* 57, 9–57.

Eisenhardt, K.M. (1989) Building theories from case study research. *Academy of Management Review* 14, 532–550.

Fritz, W., Möllenberg, A. and Chen, G. (2001) Measuring intercultural sensitivity in different cultural contexts. Paper presented at the Biannual Meeting of the International Association for Intercultural Communication Studies, July 24–29, Hong Kong.

Gardner, R.C. (1983) Learning another language: A true social psychological experiment. *Journal of Language and Social Psychology* 2, 219–239.

Gardner, R.C. (1985) *Social Psychology and Second Language Learning: The Role of Attitudes and Motivation*. London: Edward Arnold.

Gardner, R.C. (2001) Integrative motivation and second language acquisition. In Z. Dörnyei and R. Schmidt (eds) *Motivation and Second Language Acquisition* (pp. 1–19). Honolulu, HI: University of Hawaii Press.

Gardner, R.C. and Lambert, W.E. (1972) *Attitudes and Motivation in Second Language Learning*. Rowley, MA: Newbury House.

Gardner, R.C. and MacIntyre, P.D. (1991) An instrumental motivation in language study: Who says it isn't effective? *Studies in Second Language Acquisition* 13, 57–72.

Gardner, R.C., Smythe, P.C. and Clément, R. (1979) Intensive second language study in a bicultural milieu: An investigation of attitudes, motivation and language proficiency. *Language Learning* 29, 305–320.

Gardner, R.C., Tremblay, P.F. and Masgoret, A.M. (1997) Towards a full model of second language learning: An empirical investigation. *Modern Language Journal* 81, 344–362.

Geraghty, T. (1996) *March or Die: A New History of the French Foreign Legion*. New York: Facts on File.

Gillette, B. (1994) The role of learner goals in L2 success. In J. Lantolf and G. Appel (eds) *Vygotskyan Approaches to Second Language Research* (pp. 344–362). Norwood, NJ: Ablex.

Goldberg, E. and Noels, K.A. (2006) Motivation, ethnic identity, and post-secondary education language choices of graduates of intensive French language programs. *The Canadian Modern Language Review* 63 (3), 423–447.

Gregersen, T.S. and Horwitz, E.K. (2002) Language learning and perfectionism: Anxious and non-anxious language learners' reactions to their own oral performance. *The Modern Language Journal* 86 (4), 562–570.

Inbar, O., Donitsa-Schmidt, S. and Shohamy, E. (2001) Students' motivation as a function of language learning: The teaching of Arabic in Israel. In Z. Dörnyei, and R.W. Schmidt (eds) *Motivation and Second Language Acquisition* (pp. 292–308). Honolulu, HI: University of Hawaii Press.

Jenkins, R. (1996) *Social Identity*. London: Routledge.

Kanno, Y. and Norton, B. (2003) Imagined communities and educational possibilities: Introduction. *Journal of Language, Identity and Education* 2 (4), 241–249.

Kraemer, R. (1993) Social psychological factors related to the study of Arabic among Israeli Jewish high school students: A test of Gardner's socio-educational model. *Studies in Second Language Acquisition* 15, 83–105.

Lantolf, J.P. (ed.) (2000) *Sociocultural Theory and Second Language Learning*. Oxford: Oxford University Press.

Lantolf, J.P. and Pavlenko, A. (2001) (S)econd (L)anguage (A)ctivity theory: Understanding second language learners as people. In M.P. Breen (ed.) *Learner Contributions to Language Learning* (pp. 141–158). Harlow: Pearson.

Lantolf, J.P. and Genung, P.B. (2002) I'd rather switch than fight: An activity-theoretic study of power, success, and failure in a foreign language classroom. In C. Kramsch (ed.) *Language Acquisition and Language Socialization* (pp. 175–196). London: Continuum.

Lemke, J. (1995) *Textual Politics: Discourse and Social Dynamics.* London: Taylor and Francis.

Leondari, A., Syngollitou, E. and Kiosseoglou, G. (1998) Academic achievement, motivation and possible selves. *Journal of Adolescence* 21, 219–222.

LoCastro, V. (1996) English language education in Japan. In H. Coleman (ed.) *Society and the Language Classroom* (pp. 40–58). Cambridge: Cambridge University Press.

Lybeck, K.E. (2002) The role of acculturation and social networks in the acquisition of second language pronunciation. PhD dissertation. University of Minnesota.

Lyons, Z. (2000) Legio Patois Nostra: A study of some motivational and attitudinal variables amongst English learners of French in the French Foreign Legion. Undergraduate thesis, Trinity College, Dublin.

Lyons, Z. (2002) Aspects of the French Foreign Legion classroom as language learning environment. *Journal of Postgraduate Research 2001–2002.* Dublin: Dublin University.

Lyons, Z. (2004) Under two flags: National conflicts and the reconstruction of identity in the French Foreign Legion. *Language and Intercultural Communication* 4 (1/2), 109–120.

Lyons, Z. (2005) Hollow vessels: A study of some attitudinal, motivational and affective variables and their impact on L2 proficiency of English-speaking learners of French in the French Foreign Legion. PhD thesis, Trinity College, Dublin.

MacIntyre, P.D., Noels, K.A. and Clément, R. (1997) Biases in self-ratings of second language proficiency: The role of language anxiety. *Language Learning* 47 (2), 265–287.

MacIntyre, P.D. and Gardner, R.C. (1991) Anxiety and second-language learning: Toward a theoretical clarification. *Language Learning* 39, 251–275.

Masgoret, A.M., Bernaus, M. and Gardner, R.C. (2001) Examining the role of attitudes and motivation outside of the formal classroom: A test of the mini-AMTB for children. In Z. Dörnyei and R. Schmidt (eds) *Motivation and Second Language Acquisition* (pp. 281–296). Honolulu, HI: University of Hawaii Press.

Matsumoto, M. and Obana, Y. (2001) Motivational factors and persistence in learning Japanese as a foreign language. *New Zealand Journal of Asian Studies* 3 (1), 59–86.

McGroarty, M. (2001) Situating second language motivation. In Z. Dörnyei and R. Schmidt (eds) *Motivation and Second Language Acquisition* (pp. 69–91). Honolulu, HI: University of Hawaii Press.

Meara, P. (1994) *LLEX: Lingua Vocabulary Tests v. 1.4.* Swansea: Centre for Applied Language Studies, University of Wales.

Merolli, A. (1937) *La Grenade Héroique.* Paris: Payot.

Messick, S.A. (1996) Validity and washback in language testing. *Language Testing* 13, 241–56.

Nation, I.S.P. (1990) *Teaching and Learning Vocabulary.* Boston, MA: Heinle and Heinle.

Nikolov, M. (1999) Why do you learn English? Because the teacher is short. A study of Hungarian children's foreign language learning motivation. *Language Teaching Research* 3 (1), 33–56.

Noels, K.A. and Clément, R. (1996) Communicating across cultures: Social determinants and acculturative consequences. *Canadian Journal of Behavioural Science* 28, 214–228.

Norton, B. (1995) Social identity, investment, and language learning. *TESOL Quarterly* 29, 9–31.

Norton, B. (2000) *Identity and Language Learning: Gender, Ethnicity and Educational Change*. Harlow: Longman/Pearson Education.

Norton, B. (2001) Non-participation, imagined communities, and the language classroom. In M. Breen (ed.) *Learner Contributions to Language Learning* (pp. 159–171). Harlow: Pearson.

Pappamihiel, N.E. (2002) English as a second language students and English language anxiety: Issues in the mainstream classroom. *Research in the Teaching of English* 36, 327–356.

Paribakht, T.S. and Wesche, M. (1997) Vocabulary enhancement activities and reading for meaning in second language vocabulary acquisition. In J. Coady and T. Huckin (eds) *Second Language Vocabulary Acquisition* (pp. 174–200). Cambridge: Cambridge University Press.

Pavlenko, A. (2000) New approaches to concepts in bilingual memory. *Bilingualism: Language and Cognition* 3 (1), 1–36.

Pennycook, A. (1994) *The Cultural Politics of English as an International Language*. New York: Longman.

Phillips, E. (1992) The effects of language anxiety on students' oral test performance and attitudes. *Modern Language Journal* 76, 14–25.

Riemer, C. (2001) Zur Rolle der Motivation beim Fremdsprachenlernen. In C. Finkbeiner and G. Schnaitmann (eds) *Lehren und Lernen im Kontext empirischer Forschung und Fachdidaktik* (pp. 376–398). Donauwörth: Ludwig Auer.

Schumann, J.H. (1978) The acculturation model for second language acquisition. In R.C. Gingras (ed.) *Second Language Acquisition and Foreign Language Teaching* (pp. 27–50). Washington, DC: Center for Applied Linguistics.

Sfard, A. (1998) On two metaphors of learning and the dangers of choosing just one. *Educational Researcher* 27 (2): 4–13.

Sharkey, J., Shi, L., Thompson, B. and Norton, B. (2003) Dialogues around social identity, investment and language learning, by Bonny Norton Peirce (1995). In J. Sharkey and K. Johnson (eds) *The TESOL Quarterly Dialogues: Rethinking Issues of Language, Culture and Power* (pp. 55–74). Alexandria VA: TESOL Inc.

Shedivy, S.L. (2004) Factors that lead some students to continue the study of foreign language past the usual 2 years in high school. *System* 32 (1), 103–119.

Sideridis, G.D. (2006) Goal orientations and strong oughts: Adaptive or maladaptive forms of motivation for students with and without suspected learning disabilities? *Learning and Individual Differences* 16, 61–77.

Siegal, M.S. (1996) The role of learner subjectivity in second language socio-linguistic competency: Western women learning Japanese. *Applied Linguistics* 17 (3), 356–382.

Simpson, B.L. (1997) Social distance as a factor in the achievement of pragmatic competence. CLCS Occasional Paper No: 47. Dublin: Centre for Language and Communication Studies, Trinity College.

Sparks, R.L., Ganschow, L. and Javorsky, J. (2000) Déjà vu all over again. A response to Horwitz, Saito, and Garza. *Modern Language Journal* 84 (2), 251–255.

Spielmann, H. and Radnofsky, M.L. (2001) Learning language under tension: New directions from a qualitative study. *Modern Language Journal* 85, 259–278.

Spolsky, B. (2000) Language motivation revisited. *Applied Linguistics* 21 (2), 157–169.

Sutton, R.I. (1991) Maintaining norms about expressed emotions: The case of bill collectors. *Administrative Science Quarterly* 36, 245–268.

Syed, Z. (2001) Notions of self in foreign language learning: A qualitative analysis. In Z. Dörnyei and R. Schmidt (eds) *Motivation and Second Language Acquisition* (pp. 127–148). Honolulu, HI: University of Hawaii Press.

Tabachnick, B.G. and Fidell, L.S. (1989) *Using Multivariate Statistics*. New York: Harper Collins.

Tabachnick, B. and Fidell, L. (1996) *Using Multivariate Statistics*. New York: Harper Collins.

Ushioda, E. (1996) Developing a dynamic concept of L2 motivation. In T. Hickey and J. Williams (eds) *Language, Education and Society in a Changing World* (pp.239–45). Dublin and Clevedon: IRAAL/Multilingual Matters.

Ushioda, E. (2001) Language learning at university: Exploring the role of motivational thinking. In Z. Dörnyei and R. Schmidt (eds) *Motivation and Second Language Acquisition* (pp. 93–125). Honolulu, HI: University of Hawaii Press.

Ushioda, E. (2006) Motivation and autonomy in language learning. In M. Kötter, O. Traxel and S. Gabel (eds) *Investigating and Facilitating Language Learning. Papers in Honour of Lienhard Legenhausen* (pp. 283–295). Trier: Wissenschaftliger Verlag Trier.

Williams, M., Burden, R.L. and Al-Baharna, S. (2001) Making sense of success and failure: The role of the individual in motivation theory. In Z. Dörnyei and R. Schmidt (eds) *Motivation and Second Language Acquisition* (pp. 171–184). Honolulu, HI: University of Hawaii Press.

Williams, M. and Burden, L. (1999) Students' developing conceptions of themselves as language learners. *Modern Language Journal* 83, 193–201.

Yashima, T. (2000) Orientations and motivation in foreign language learning: A study of Japanese college students. *JACET Bulletin* 31, 121–134.

Yashima, T., Zenuk-Nishide, L. and Shimizu, K. (2004) The influence of attitudes and affect on willingness to communicate and second language communication. *Language Learning* 54, 119–152.

Young, D. (1991) Creating a low-anxiety classroom environment: What does language anxiety research suggest? *Modern Language Journal* 75, 426–437.

Young, J.R. (1998) *The French Foreign Legion* (2nd edn). London: Thames and Hudson.

Chapter 14

The Sociocultural Interface between Ideal Self and Ought-to Self: A Case Study of Two Korean Students' ESL Motivation

TAE-YOUNG KIM

Introduction

The purpose of this case study is to make theoretical refinements by re-interpreting Dörnyei's (2005, 2006, this volume) *ideal L2 self* and *ought-to L2 self* from the perspective of Vygotskian Sociocultural Theory (SCT) and Activity Theory (AT). To date, the exact nature of and the interrelationship between ideal L2 self and ought-to L2 self have not been fully investigated. This study aims to explore this neglected area by analysing two adult Korean English as a second language (ESL) students' L2 learning experiences.

SCT and Activity Theory

As Dörnyei (2006) and Skehan (1989) point out, L2 learning motivation is one of the most widely investigated fields in L2 research, but the SCT-based research in this area is in its infancy. Even though Vygotsky's (1978, 1979a, 1979b) theory has influenced motivation research in general education (e.g. Rueda & Dembo, 1995; Rueda & Moll, 1994; Sivan, 1986; Turner, 2001) and also in applied linguistics (e.g. Block, 2003; Johnson, 2004; Lantolf, 2000; Lantolf & Thorne, 2006; Swain & Deters, 2007), to date, only a few studies (Kim, 2005, 2007; Ushioda, 2003, 2007) have applied Vygotskian theory to the analysis of L2 motivation. Therefore, it is timely to explore L2 motivation from an SCT perspective and investigate the compatibility of this perspective with *the L2 Motivational Self System*.

This chapter is guided by AT (Engeström, 1987, 1999a; Leont'ev, 1978), which owes its theoretical lineage to SCT. AT focuses on the reciprocal relationship between a subject (or an L2 learner) and an object (or the L2 to be acquired). An L2 learner's (or a subject's) acquisition of the L2 (an object) is a mediational procedure. Lantolf and Thorne (2006: 79) state that 'mediation is the process through which humans deploy culturally constructed artefacts ... to regulate (i.e. gain voluntary control over and transform) the material world'. The culturally constructed artefacts (or tools) include physical tools (e.g. pencil and paper, cassette recorder, computer); symbolic tools (e.g. written or spoken language systems, visual signs, gestures); mental tools (e.g. L2 learner beliefs, cf. Alanen, 2005; L2 learning strategies such as mnemonics and phonics); and significant others (e.g. L2 teachers, more capable peers). Defining activity as 'a specific form of the societal existence of humans consisting of purposeful changing of natural and social reality', Davydov (1999) emphasises the following:

> any activity carried out by a subject includes goals, means, the process of molding the object, and the result. In fulfilling the activity, the subjects also change and develop themselves. (Davydov, 1999: 39)

Since (L2) learning is a series of purposive cognitive and social behaviours, it is understood as an activity, and L2 learning motivation relates to this activity.

In this chapter, the analyses are based on Engeström's (1999a) AT framework (see Figure 14.1), which locates the subject, the object, and the instrument (or the mediational artefact) as three core elements. The community (i.e. those who share the same general object; see Cole, 1996), the rules (i.e. explicit norms and conventions that constrain actions within the activity system), and the division of labour (i.e. the division of object-oriented actions among members of the community) are included as well because human activity is always influenced by these elements. In L2 learning, Figure 14.1 serves as an explanatory framework, where an

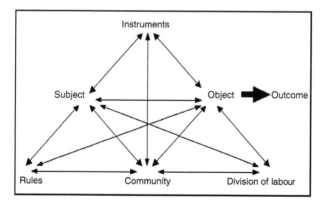

Figure 14.1 A complex model of activity system (Engeström, 1999a)

We are grateful to the following for permission to reproduce copyright material: Cambridge University Press from 'Activity theory and individual and social transformation' by Y. Engeström, in *Perspectives on Activity Theory* (1999), edited by Y. Engeström, R. Miettinen and R.L. Punamäki.

L2 learner (*subject*), who wants to acquire sufficient L2 skills (*object*), needs to use various mediational artefacts (*instrument*). The learner, as a social being, lives in a variety of language communities such as L2 schools, (homestay) family, peer networks, and workplaces (*community*), conforms to unique rules of learning and using the L2 (*rules*), and collaborates with other L2 learners or users (*division of labour*). The double arrows in the relational lines in Figure 14.1 imply that elements may potentially oppose one another and in such cases tensions may arise. From a longitudinal perspective, L2 learning is the process of experiencing and overcoming tensions; if tensions persist, L2 learning stagnates, whereas if the L2 learner can solve the tensions, he or she can achieve a higher level of L2 proficiency.

AT and the L2 Motivational Self System

I believe that the AT perspective on L2 learning can usefully contribute to theoretical refinement of Dörnyei's (2005, 2006, this volume) L2 Motivational Self System. The concept of the ideal L2 self has the potential to overcome the distinction between integrativeness and instrumentality (Gardner, 1985), often (mis)understood as dichotomous (e.g. Brown, 2000). Dörnyei (2005, 2006) considers the ideal L2 self as dynamic and including both integrative and instrumental dispositions. As an image of the ideal L2 self, L2 learners may dream of being a person competent in the L2. This image may reflect a desire to integrate into the L2 community (integrativeness) or the hope of working in an international company using the L2 (instrumentality), or the combination of both aspirations. In the era of globalisation, it does not seem so easy to maintain a clear distinction between integrative and instrumental orientations, and the concept of an ideal L2 self offers a more meaningful way of capturing this complexity.

The second concept, the ought-to L2 self, reflects a less-internalised type of instrumental disposition. In this connection Higgins (1998) draws an insightful distinction: the ideal self is *promotion* focused, whereas the ought-to self is *prevention* focused. In other words, the ought-to L2 self reflects the situation where learners feel pressured to learn an L2 in order to avoid the negative consequences of not learning it. For example, in many parts of the world, English is now regarded as a powerful tool for future success in a job or in the college entrance exam. Given this, ESL learners feel that they should or *ought to* possess at least a minimum level of English proficiency.

The third concept in Dörnyei's L2 Motivational Self System – L2 learning experience – deserves careful consideration as well. In the execution of L2 motivation, the learner's experiences in the L2 surroundings mediate the learner and the development of L2 proficiency. Through these L2 learning experiences in various, multiple L2 communities, the learner's initial motivation in the preactional stage may subsequently undergo significant changes. For this reason, in their Process Model of L2 Motivation, Dörnyei and Ottó (1998; see also Dörnyei, 2005) focus on the dynamic nature of L2 motivation during the actional stage of the L2 learning process.

The three concepts summarised above can be linked to Engeström's (1987, 1999a) AT framework. Since the ideal L2 self is more geared toward the positive aspiration to become a better person who commands good skills in the L2, this self image relates more to the subject rather than other elements in Engeström's (1987, 1999a) AT framework. The ideal L2 self represents uniquely internalised, personal aspirations. On the other hand, the ought-to L2 self originates from an L2 learner's apprehension of failure, which mirrors social pressure (e.g. fulfilling parents' aspirations for academic or career success). The ought-to L2 self, compared to the ideal L2 self, is less internalised in the subject. It rather reflects the external demands coming from other members of the community, another major element in the AT framework, and in this regard, there is a possibility that tension may exist between the subject and the community. As stated above, if tension arises among the AT elements and the L2 learner does not notice or overcome the tension, L2 learning may stagnate, which may lead to demotivation.

It should be noted that the object needs to be operationalised into a more manageable learning goal or set of goals. The object in L2 learning may vary but usually is the ultimate attainment of L2 skills to the satisfaction of the learner. However, an L2 learner needs to establish proximal, specific, and moderately difficult goals (cf. Locke & Latham, 1990) to attain the distal object. Regarding the nature of goal and object, Engeström (1999b) underscores the following:

> goals are attached to specific actions. Actions have clear points of beginning and termination and relatively short half-lives ... the object is never fully reached or conquered. (Engeström, 1999b: 381)

In this sense, although not illustrated in Figure 14.1, the subject and the object are mediated by L2 learning goals.

Goals also bear bidirectional relationships with other elements in AT, especially with the community. As Turner (2001) states, contexts perceived beneficial to L2 learners turn into affordances. For example, a considerate homestay owner who is fluent in the target language and gives appropriate L2 feedback in daily L2 conversations can afford an optimal L2 learning environment for the L2 learner. This may positively affect the learner's sense of ideal L2 self. In contrast, a teacher-fronted L2 classroom providing few opportunities for meaningful L2 interactions may conflict with the learning goal of an L2 learner who wishes to develop L2 communication skills (Lantolf & Genung, 2002). This may eventually lead to a less-internalised ought-to L2 self. The L2 learning in the former situation, from an SCT perspective, reflects the functioning of the L2 learner's self-image within the zone of proximal development (ZPD) (Vygotsky, 1978) through appropriate linguistic scaffolds (Wood *et al.*, 1976) from more capable other(s), and the L2 learner can maintain (or even enhance) L2 learning motivation. In contrast, the L2 learner's self-image in the latter situation does not function within the ZPD, and the learner's motivation may gradually decrease, resulting in demotivation.

The Study

The study reported in this chapter investigates the intricate relationship among subject, object, goal, and community. The general research question is: How can we understand the ideal L2 self and the ought-to L2 self in relation to Vygotsky's (1978, 1979a, 1979b) sociocultural theory of mind and Engeström's (1987, 1999a) AT framework? Specific research questions are: (1) To what degree can the internalisation of the ought-to L2 self contribute to L2 learning motivation and learning behaviour? (2) How does the learning goal (or how do the learning goals) influence the above two selves?

To address the research questions, I will analyse two cases of Korean ESL students. By presenting selected interview data, I will focus on the interface among the ideal L2 self, the ought-to L2 self, and L2 learning experiences through the lens of SCT. Based on Engeström's (1987, 1999a) AT framework, I will then highlight differences in the two students' ideal and ought-to L2 selves through illustrations of their activity system. I will conclude by analysing the relationship between the ideal and ought-to selves in terms of Vygotsky's (1979b) general law of cultural development.

Participants

Originally, I recruited a total of ten adult Korean ESL students in Toronto, Canada, for a larger longitudinal case study (Kim, 2007). However, for the sake of thick description (Geertz, 1973) and in-depth analysis from an SCT perspective, I will focus here on just two study-abroad ESL students, Joon and Woo (pseudonyms). Both were males in their mid-20s who had attended university and majored in economics-related fields in South Korea before coming to Toronto for the purpose of learning English (see Table 14.1). Despite these similarities, as my analysis will show, the two students differ considerably in terms of their ideal and ought-to L2 selves.

Joon wanted to get a job in which he could use English. He was not only interested in learning English in Toronto but very much interested

Table 14.1 Korean ESL visa student profiles

Name	Status	Age	University major	Arrival	Departure	# of interviews conducted	Courses taken in Toronto
Joon	Student visa	24	Business	September 2004	July 2005	7	General ESL → study group
Woo	Visitor	25	Accounting	September 2004	August 2005	8	General ESL → business English + private tutoring

in travelling and socialising with others in Canada. As such, Joon's data showed that his goals for learning English were to get a job in Korea and to socialise with members of L2 communities. His communication in L2 contexts was quite diverse. On many occasions, Joon also socialised with other Korean ESL students where communication in L1 prevailed. Woo, the other participant, expressed his goal to work at a steel company in South Korea in the future, and his motivation to learn English seemed clearly related to this practical goal. In his opinion, for application to the steel exporting company, excellent proficiency in English would be his strongest asset. From his first month, he had stayed in a Canadian homestay and built a solid relationship with the native English-speaking homestay owner.

Methods of data collection and analysis

For data triangulation (Denzin, 1978), I collected data from four complementary sources: interviews, ESL classroom observations, picture-cued recall tasks, and language learning autobiographies. Among these, the interviews received the most research attention and were conducted on a monthly basis. I conducted semi-structured interviews with my participants and used NVivo, a QDA computer program (Richards & Richards, 2002) to analyse them. After conducting a series of pilot studies, I developed core interview questions (see Kim, 2006a, for the interview questions) and used them throughout the interviews. Since I used qualitative thematic analysis, all the thematic categories emerged as the NVivo analysis proceeded. That is, I coded topics commented on by participants first. Then, by iteratively re-reading the interview transcripts and initial coding categories, I re-coded the data, and deleted or added categories. In doing so, I applied the constant comparison method of qualitative data analysis (Miles & Huberman, 1994).

I used meaning units (Ratner, 2002) for my unit of analysis. Ratner states:

> the meaning unit must preserve the psychological integrity of the idea being expressed. It must neither fragment the idea into meaningless, truncated segments nor confuse it with other ideas that express different themes. (Ratner, 2002: 169)

Thus, I coded coherent related comments in the interviews as one meaning unit. I always included the participants' comments in a meaning unit and, if necessary, included my clarifying questions or related comments as well. All the interviews were conducted in Korean and the data presented in this chapter have been translated into English. The inter-coder reliability (i.e. percentage of agreement) was 0.83.

Analysis of the Two Students

Joon: Instrumentality functioning in the ought-to L2 self

It is noteworthy that Joon, a third-year university student, had a very close relationship with an American living in Korea who was of Korean parentage but had been adopted by an American couple in infancy. To communicate with him and to build a personal relationship with him, Joon tried to learn English in Toronto. His close friendship is described in his language learning autobiography in Excerpt 1.

> *Excerpt 1 (Language learning autobiography, October 2004)*
> [In Korea,] I was in the same dormitory with him [his American friend]. Drinking beer together and travelling together, I think I learned lots of English from him. (...) My goal is not obtaining full scores on the TOEIC or TOEFL. It is simply to be able to have a nice, relaxing heart-to-heart talk with my American friend when I go back to Korea.

This is a typical expression of Joon's ideal L2 self in that Joon aspires to learn English to consolidate his friendship with the American peer by having 'a nice, relaxing heart-to-heart talk'. Even after his arrival in Toronto, Joon keeps communicating with his American friend in Korea through an Internet chatting program. Joon's ideal L2 self, however, is not limited to the continuation of the pre-existing friendship. He also actively participates in ESL student communities and in fact believes that the best way to learn English in ESL (not EFL) contexts is to make friends and to have various conversations with other English speakers.

In his daily communications with his friend in Korea and other ESL students in Canada, Joon cultivates his internalised ideal L2 self. Since 'the ideal L2 self is a powerful motivator to learn the L2 because of the desire to reduce the discrepancy between our actual and ideal selves' (Dörnyei, 2005: 106), we might expect to find in Joon's data utterances that relate his ideal L2 self to his L2 learning motivation such as 'I learn English to communicate with my American friend in Korea'.

However, contrary to expectation, when asked about his main motivation to learn English in Toronto, Joon's answers across six months were as follows:

> *Excerpt 2 (Second interview, November 2004)*[1]
> 2.69. Interviewer (I): Why are you interested in learning English?
> 2.70. Joon (J): **That's because I need to get a job in Korea. Also, I want to talk with the adoptee.** I mean, my [American] friend in Korea.

Excerpt 3 (Third interview, December 2004)

3.40. J: **Of course**, getting a job in Korea comes first. And then I want to communicate with my American friend. I mean without any hesitation.

Excerpt 4 (Seventh interview, April 2005)

7.72. J: Now, in Korea, uh, English has already become a world language, so **learning English is not a matter of personal interest but a must.** That's why I learn English.

It is important to note the order of sentences in Turn 2.70 in Excerpt 2. Even though Joon's desire to communicate with his American friend is firmly grounded in his past experiences in Korea and maintained by his current Internet chatting, he first mentions a different goal for learning English: to get a job in Korea. Similarly, in Turn 3.40 in Excerpt 3, he uses 'of course' to emphasise the Korean (or worldwide) belief that English will surely be key to employment in Korea.

Excerpt 4 shows the influence of the macro social discourse of English as *the* Global Language (EGL). Although Crystal (2003) talks of English as *a* global language, I prefer to say *the* global language. As Canagarajah (1999) and Phillipson (1992) point out, English is perceived as *the only* global language in many countries. Be it positive, negative, or value-neutral, English has gradually gained the status of *lingua franca* (cf. Dörnyei *et al.*, 2006; Jenkins, 2007). Excerpt 4 suggests strongly that Joon's job-related orientation to learn English is in fact generated from Korean societal demand, and reflects both Joon's concern about potential unemployment due to lack of English proficiency, and his desire 'to avoid possible negative outcomes' which is mentioned as an important characteristic of the ought-to L2 self (Dörnyei, 2005: 106).

However, by no means is it easy to reach an accurate understanding of whether or not Joon's comments in Excerpts 2, 3, and 4 reflect his ought-to L2 self. Much depends on the degree of internalisation of the EGL discourse wherein may lie the major distinction between the ideal L2 self and ought-to L2 self. That is, even though the job-oriented, utilitarian disposition is often categorised as instrumentality or as an instantiation of the ought-to L2 self as Dörnyei (2005, 2006) notes, ostensibly similar comments can be understood as evidence of the ideal L2 self. If an L2 learner internalises such reasons for needing to learn the L2 and can foresee a personally prosperous future in this way, such utilitarian reasons connect to the ideal L2 self.

In Joon's data, clues to define the nature of his self expressed above are provided in subsequent interview questions asking about his job prospects. The logic is, if he has internalised the EGL discourse so that it is transferred into his ideal L2 self, he must have elaborated on specific job plans by adding a personal rationale, and I should be able to find coherent comments about specific occupations requiring English. If such comments are not to be found in the data, the evidence points to a less-internalised ought-to L2 self. Excerpts 5, 6 and 7 are Joon's responses to the question about his future job.

Excerpt 5 (First interview, October 2004)
1.200. J: I'm not sure if this will come true, but, anyways, I would like to work in the New York Stock Exchange.

Excerpt 6 (Second interview, November 2004)
2.76. J: I think it may not be sufficient to learn English for only a year. I'm planning to apply for a Working Holiday Maker visa[2] and go to Australia. Maybe in two years?

Excerpt 7 (Fourth interview, January 2005)
4.195. J: Perhaps, international business. Or hotel management? Now I would like to get a job in a hotel. I'm trying to find some books on the hotel business or hotel management. I don't know what exactly I want to do for a living.

Excerpts 5, 6, and 7 all clearly demonstrate inconsistency in Joon's plans, and suggest that he does not seem to have developed a concrete future plan for using English with a specific job in mind. Regarding this kind of inconsistency, Ryan (2006) points out that without any concrete idea about future job prospects, ESL learners often expend extraordinary efforts, time, and money to learn English. Viewed in this light, it seems that Joon's ought-to L2 self, rather than ideal L2 self, is reflected in the above Excerpts 2, 3, and 4. Joon's ought-to L2 self takes its roots in the beliefs of the Korean community. Even before coming to Toronto, Joon came to be familiarised with the EGL discourse which is dominant in South Korea, and *ventriloquates* the externally-driven EGL discourse in Excerpt 4 (cf. Bakhtin, 1981).

From an AT perspective, it can be understood that Joon has formulated two distinctive learning goals to achieve the object. Joon's two learning goals are: to communicate with other L2 speakers (Goal 1), and to get a job in South Korea (Goal 2). These are relatively specific and proximal compared to the distal object, which can be broadly summarised as to acquire English proficiency. Excerpts 2, 3, and 4 show that the two goals influence Joon's L2 learning in Toronto. The first communicatively oriented goal reflecting his ideal L2 self is confirmed and internalised through his daily interactions with other L2 speakers. In this case, tension between subject and goal does not exist. On the other hand, the second EGL-based and job-oriented goal reflecting his ought-to L2 self is less internalised in Joon. This goal is not supported by other elements in Joon's activity system either. Since he attended ESL schools and not job preparation courses in Toronto, none of the community, rules, and division of labour relate to this externally-imposed goal. Therefore, tension arises between subject and goal. Figure 14.2 is the visual representation of the relationships among elements in Joon's activity system.

Note that Goals 1 and 2 are clearly separate. Goal 1 is more incorporated into Joon, the subject, whereas Goal 2 is located in Community 2 (L1 community) in Figure 14.2. On the one hand, Goal 1 stems from Joon's desire to reduce the discrepancy between his actual self and ideal self (see Excerpt 1), so this goal is closely related to Joon's ideal L2 self. Goal 2, on the other hand, resonates with the L1 community's dominant social discourse. Excerpts 5, 6, and 7 corroborate that Goal 2 is not fully internalised in Joon, which results only in inconsistent job plans. Goal 2 is an extrinsically stipulated one which

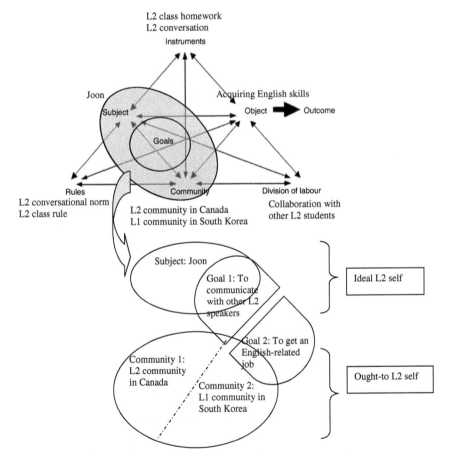

Figure 14.2 Joon's activity system

Joon does not perceive as imminently necessary since this goal does not stem from his life experiences. Goal 2 is related to Joon's ought-to L2 self.

In sum, for Joon, the ideal L2 self and the ought-to L2 self function on different planes. His ideal L2 self, supported by other elements in his activity system, is connected with Goal 1: to communicate with other L2 speakers; whereas his ought-to L2 self stems from the dominant EGL discourse in South Korea and is connected to Goal 2: to get a job in Korea. No interface between the ideal L2 self and the ought-to L2 self is found.

Woo: Incorporation of instrumentality into the ideal L2 self

In contrast to Joon who did not have clearly developed job plans, Woo, a fourth-year university student, consistently mentioned the importance of learning English in order to work at a steel exporting company in Korea. As shown in Excerpt 8, his goal in Toronto was to increase his job opportunities by enhancing his proficiency in English. Thus, he kept attending ESL schools and remained in a Canadian homestay, which he regarded as an optimal community of English practice.

Excerpt 8 (Language learning autobiography, October 2004)
In the future, I hope to meet many other people (...) And eventually to increase my English speaking and listening skills for my future job.

Since Woo, like Joon, came from South Korea where the EGL discourse prevails, we can assume that his job-related, utilitarian orientation towards learning English reflects the outer societal EGL discourse. As discussed in the previous section, even the same comments reflecting the EGL discourse can relate to either the ideal L2 self or the ought-to L2 self depending on the degree of internalisation. In Joon's case, as he did not fully internalise this goal and other elements in his AT system did not support the discourse, he showed no interface between the two selves. This is corroborated in his comments on qualitatively different learning goals and in his inconsistent job plans. To tap into the degree of internalisation, I compared Woo's comments on job plans with Joon's. Unlike Joon's inconsistent job plans, Woo expressed a specific, consistent career goal as Excerpts 9, 10, and 11 show.

Excerpt 9 (Second interview, November 2004)
2.284. Woo (W): What I'd like to do in the future is work in the field of steel manufacturing. The steel company, BOSCO [a pseudonym] is, for sure, the top producer of high quality steel [in Korea]. (...) It is not sufficient to sell the steel within Korea. So, I hope I can get a job in the international sales department of that company and be successful.

Excerpt 10 (Third interview, January 2005)
3.172. W: I'd like to devote myself to that field [steel manufacturing].
       I'd like to sell steel. We cannot sell everything only in Korea;
       we need to sell all over the world. In that sense, English skill is
       an important requirement.

Excerpt 11 (Eighth interview, June 2006)
8.142. W: Well, for my job. It is the best tool for my steel exporting job,
       I mean, employment. My major goal is to get the job.

Woo's future goal is very specific: to work at BOSCO. Woo's job-oriented L2 learning motivation is more internalised and firmly associated with his career goal. This differs from Joon. In this sense, despite the similarity in the job-oriented comments, Woo's comments in Excerpts 9, 10, and 11 confirm Woo's internalisation of the dominant EGL discourse of learning English in the Korean community. Without this internalisation, Woo's job plans expressed above could not show such consistency. Therefore, it would seem that Woo's comments, originating from the EGL discourse, represent the ideal L2 self.

Regarding the internalisation, his close contact with his girlfriend in Korea seems to be a contributing factor (see Excerpt 12). According to Woo, his girlfriend's low TOEIC (Test of English for International Communication) score posed a barrier for entry into the job market. Although there have been a few noticeable changes in the employment policies of public and private employers in South Korea, in general it is still widespread practice for each job applicant to submit an official test score (demonstrating that he or she has above-minimum English proficiency) in order to advance to the second round of job interviews.

Excerpt 12 (Third interview, January 2005)
3.104. W: I believe, if I can't speak English, I can't get a job. **Actually,
       my girlfriend in Korea is going to graduate from her college
       very soon, but her TOEIC score is really low. So, because of
       her poor English score, she has not been offered any job
       interviews yet.** The more I see this situation, the more I feel I
       need English.

In short, Woo's job-related motivation for learning English was confirmed through various channels, such as communication with his girlfriend above, whereas Joon's job motivation, which was ostensibly similar to Woo's, was not. Woo's job plans are firmly focused on the steel exporting company. Woo makes the EGL discourse (as succinctly expressed in 'if I can't speak English, I can't get a job' in Excerpt 12) personally meaningful by equating his friends' negative experiences with his own (as in 'The more I see this situation, the more I feel I need English' in Excerpt 12).

As stated above, Woo gradually built a strong relationship with his Canadian homestay owner, who clearly had a beneficial impact on Woo's English use. He had many opportunities to speak English at the dinner table and while watching TV with his 'homestay mom'. In Excerpt 13, Woo's relationship with the homestay owner is described as quite casual like 'an open-ended conversation' and intimate like 'a mother-and-son relationship', which is similar to the conditions of scaffolding (Bruner & Sherwood, 1976; Wood *et al.*, 1976). That is, in a non-threatening atmosphere, the caregiver or teacher provides necessary assistance to the novice.

Excerpt 13 (Second interview, November 2004)
2.224. W: Once I come back home, I can ask anything about English to my homestay mom [i.e. owner]. I ask her what she did that day, and she also asks me about my day. In this way, I can talk with her comfortably. This is really an open-ended conversation. It's like a mother-and-son relationship.

The scaffolding from the homestay owner is found in other interview data. In Excerpt 14, where Woo describes his Christmas card writing, the homestay owner demonstrates the role of skilful L2 teacher.

Excerpt 14 (Third interview, January 2005)
3.224. W: At Christmas time, I wrote two Christmas cards and gave one to my homestay mom and the other to her neighbour. Both of them were quite pleased. Of course, I wrote my greetings in English. You know what? She [the homestay mother] checked my English grammar!
3.225. I: (laugh) Oh, did she?
3.226. W: She said she would check whether or not I wrote properly. And she said everything was OK. I said thank you. I felt so happy, because I had this handy opportunity every day.

Excerpt 14 demonstrates that Woo and the homestay owner constitute the community in this activity system. As defined by Cole (1996: 141), the community comprises 'those who share the same general object'. If their general objects had been different, Woo might have perceived the situation above as unwanted criticism by a dominant person who holds both linguistic (native English speaker) and environmental (landlady in the guise of homestay mom) hegemony. However, Woo, instead of being embarrassed, is genuinely thankful to the owner and sees this as an opportunity. Their object was to increase his English proficiency and Woo's goal of getting a job is aligned with the object. For this reason, the unexpected scaffolding coming from the community in Excerpt 14 strengthens Woo's goal, object, and his ideal L2 self (working in the steel exporting company using English). In sum, Woo's L2 community afforded constant provision of optimal L2 input, which had a positive impact on Woo's ideal L2 self. This was not found in Joon's case.

Figure 14.3 illustrates Woo's activity system, which significantly differs from Joon's. The relationships among the subject, the goals, and the community show considerable overlap. Unlike Joon, Woo expressed only one goal: to get a steel exporting job in South Korea. This goal does not alter as shown in Excerpts 9, 10, and 11, which evidences the integrated nature of this goal for Woo. Accordingly, the goal overlaps with the subject. The community, represented mainly by Woo's homestay family, also overlaps with both subject and goal. The community constantly patrols and guides Woo's goal and maintains his (executive) L2 learning motivation. In terms of conceptual overlap, on the right hand side of Figure 14.3 the goal of learning English to get a job, which relates only to the ought-to L2 self in Joon's case, is subsumed into Woo's ideal L2 self.

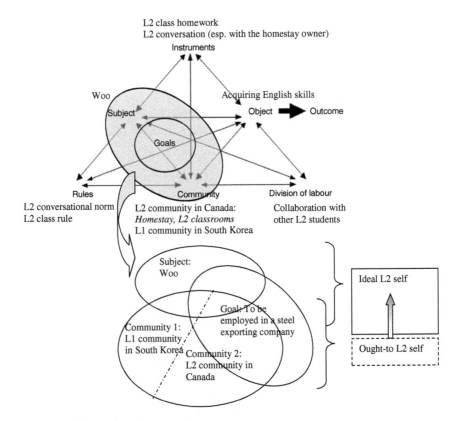

Figure 14.3 Woo's activity system

In sum, the English as the Global Language (EGL) discourse and L2 learning experiences influence the creation of both Joon's and Woo's ideal and ought-to L2 selves. For Joon, the EGL functions only in his less-internalised ought-to L2 self. Joon perpetuates the dominant social discourse without fully internalising its meaning into his personal life. The less-internalised nature of the ought-to L2 self is reflected in Joon's inconsistent remarks on future job plans. Joon's ideal L2 self is grounded in his previous and current L2 experiences in Korea and Canada. For Joon, the ideal L2 self and the ought-to L2 self do not share any interface. In contrast, for Woo, his instrumentality originating from the externally stipulated social discourse of EGL is subsumed into his ideal L2 self. The internalised nature of the EGL discourse is confirmed in his consistent comments on his job plan. Woo's goal of learning English for a job, which also mirrors the EGL discourse, is deeply rooted in Woo's L2 experiences, such as his girlfriend's negative experiences and his meaningful communication with his homestay owner, and significantly contributes to the expansion of his ideal L2 self.

Ideal L2 Self and Ought-to L2 Self: SCT Accounts

In analysing the two students' self systems, it is important to emphasise that their ideal L2 self and ought-to L2 self are not in entirely antithetical positions. What can be regarded as the typical instantiation of the ideal L2 self can sometimes be understood as that of the ought-to L2 self, or vice versa.

Using Structural Equation Modeling, Dörnyei *et al.* (2006) proposed a schematic model of the interrelationships between the motivational variables and the criterion measures. They argue that one of the immediate antecedents of the ideal L2 self is instrumentality. They state that 'depending on the extent of the internalisation of the extrinsic motives that make up instrumentality, the instrumentality can be either ideal L2 self or the ought-to L2 self' (Dörnyei *et al.*, 2006: 93). Put simply, if an L2 learner genuinely wishes to use the L2 for utilitarian purposes (e.g. job, academic advancement), the instrumental disposition becomes closely linked to the person's vocational or academic identity, which leads into a brighter future image of him/herself. In such a case, the instrumentality is internalised into the L2 learner and reflects a promotion-focused self-image. Since the instrumentality is internalised, it is natural for the learner to have personalised, contextualised reasons or meaning for learning the L2, and these reasons, often expressed explicitly as learning goals, should be specific and concrete. If not internalised sufficiently, however, the instrumentality reflects more the prevention side of external obligation. In this case, the L2 learner becomes passive and does not attribute a personal rationale and meaning to L2 learning. Although he or she may reiterate reasons mandated by others in a speech community, they do not emanate from an internalised, promotion-driven self-image. The L2 learner may want to learn the L2 because parents, teachers, friends, the education system and the media keep emphasising the importance of the L2 (in this study, English). Thus viewed, the less internalised instrumentality is prevention-focused, and the fear of having a negative future self-image prevails in this case.

Dörnyei *et al.*'s (2006) concept of instrumentality fits well with the AT analyses shown earlier. The important difference between Joon and Woo is the degree of internalising the instrumentality. Vygotsky (1979b: 163) states that human development appears twice, or on two different planes, first 'on the social plane, and then on the psychological plane'. Referring to this developmental process as *the general genetic law of cultural development,* he further states:

> First, [cultural development] appears between people as an inter-psychological category, and then within the child as an intrapsycho-logical category. This is equally true with regard to voluntary attention, logical memory, the formation of concepts, and the development of volition... [I]t goes without saying that internalization transforms the process itself and changes its structure and functions. (Vygotsky, 1979b: 163)

In L2 learning situations, L2 development stems from intermental functioning between the L2 learner and other L2 users, and through L2 interactions (or L2 instruction) the external social plane is gradually and creatively internalised, or taken up, by the learner. The ought-to L2 self and the ideal L2 self, interpreted from Vygotsky's (1979b) perspective, capture the developmental nature of self. As shown in Joon's data, the social discourse is mostly related to the social or inter-psychological plane, whereas in Woo, we can identify the transition from the inter- to intra-psychological plane and thus his ideal L2 self prevails. In other words, we might say that the ought-to L2 self reflects the inter-psychological plane, and the ideal L2 self reflects the intra-psychological plane in the development of the L2 self.

In this study, the EGL discourse is linked to the prevention-focused nature of instrumentality. Proficiency in English is understood as 'the social ladder' (Zeng, 1995) into the power-elite in Korean society (Kim, 2006b). Joon understood the external meaning of learning English for his job preparation, but did not fully internalise it into his ideal L2 self. In contrast, Woo internalised this discourse and it became subsumed into his ideal L2. If an L2 learner regards the EGL discourse as more closely related to his or her personal contexts, this discourse may provide a powerful motivator for learning English; if not, this may function only as a minimal role and remain only in the realm of the ought-to L2 self. Depending on how far they internalise the external social discourse, learners may transform their ought-to L2 self into their ideal L2 self. That is, they may imagine the situation of actively or even freely using English in their ideal job, which is associated with the aspiration of enhancing their life quality.

Summary

The cases reported in the study enrich our understandings of the ideal L2 self and ought-to L2 self in two important ways. First, instrumentality, or pragmatic orientations, in learning an L2 can be merged into either the ideal L2 self or the ought-to L2 self, depending on the degree of internalisation. In this study, the socially originated EGL discourse was aligned to the job-oriented comments of the two participants. Second, an L2 learner's ideal L2 self needs to be aligned to the learner's life experiences in a variety of communities. Without the support from the community and its related rules and division of labour as defined Engeström's (1987, 1999a) AT framework, the L2 learner cannot envisage a positive, competent, and promotion-based future L2 self-image. As Joon's data indicate, this may result in the prevention-focused ought-to L2 self.

Despite the findings, this case study has limitations. First, since an ESL proficiency test was not administered, it is hard to investigate the relationship between the ideal and/or ought-to L2 selves and the two students' linguistic gains during and after their stay in the ESL contexts. Second, as case studies do, this study has focused only on a selected population, which inherently makes the findings specific to particular phenomena and contexts. More extensive cases need to be researched to make conclusive arguments about the interface between the ideal L2 self and ought-to L2 self in a variety of contexts.

Acknowledgements

I would like to thank Ping Deters and Kim MacDonald at OISE/UT for their feedback on earlier versions of this manuscript. I am also grateful for the thoughtful comments from the editors.

Notes
1. '2' means the second interview session, '69' means the 69th turn. The bold face in Excerpts denotes an added emphasis by the author. Brackets mean the author's added phrases or comments for clarification. Three dots in parentheses indicate a deleted utterance.
2. The Working Holiday Maker Visa issued by the Australian Embassy in Korea combines a study permit and a work permit. Once issued, applicants can learn English as a second language for less than three months as well as work for a maximum of one year. They are often hired as interns or volunteers.

References

Alanen, R. (2005) A sociocultural approach to young language learners' beliefs about language learning. In P. Kalaja and M.F. Barcelos (eds) *Beliefs about SLA: New Research Approaches* (pp. 55–86). Dordrecht: Kluwer.

Bakhtin, M.M. (1981) *The Dialogic Imagination: Four Essays by M.M. Bakhtin.* Austin, TX: University of Texas Press.

Block, D. (2003) *The Social Turn in Second Language Acquisition.* Edinburgh: Edinburgh University Press.

Brown, H.D. (2000) *Principles of Language Learning and Teaching* (4th edn). White Plains, NY: Longman.

Bruner, J. and Sherwood, V. (1976) Peekaboo and the learning of rule structures. In J. Bruner, A. Jolly and K. Sylva (eds) *Play: Its Role in Development and Evolution* (pp. 277–285). New York: Basic Books.

Canagarajah, A.S. (1999) *Resisting Linguistic Imperialism in English Teaching.* Oxford: Oxford University Press.

Cole, M. (1996) *Cultural Psychology.* Cambridge, MA: Harvard University Press.

Crystal, D. (2003) *English as a Global Language* (2nd edn). Cambridge: Cambridge University Press.

Davydov, V.V. (1999) The content and unsolved problems of activity theory. In Y. Engeström, R. Miettinen and R.L. Punamäki (eds) *Perspectives on Activity Theory* (pp. 39–52). New York: Cambridge University Press.

Denzin, N.K. (1978) *The Research Act: A Theoretical Introduction to Sociological Methods* (2nd edn). New York: McGraw-Hill.

Dörnyei, Z. (2005) *The Psychology of the Language Learner: Individual Differences in Second Language Acquisition.* Mahwah, NJ: Lawrence Erlbaum.

Dörnyei, Z. (2006) Individual differences in second language acquisition. *AILA Review* 19, 42–68.

Dörnyei, Z., Csizér, K. and Németh, N. (2006) *Motivation, Language Attitudes and Globalisation.* Clevedon: Multilingual Matters.

Dörnyei, Z. and Ottó, I. (1998) Motivation in action: A process model of L2 motivation. *Working Papers in Applied Linguistics* (Thames Valley University, London) 4, 43–69.

Engeström, Y. (1987) *Learning by Expanding: An Activity-Theoretical Approach to Developmental Research.* Helsinki: Orienta-Konsultit.

Engeström, Y. (1999a) Activity theory and individual and social transformation. In Y. Engeström, R. Miettinen and R.L. Punamäki (eds) *Perspectives on Activity Theory* (pp. 19–38). New York: Cambridge University Press.

Engeström, Y. (1999b) Innovative learning in work teams. In Y. Engeström, R. Miettinen and R.L. Punamäki (eds) *Perspectives on Activity Theory* (pp. 377–404). New York: Cambridge University Press.

Gardner, R.C. (1985) *Social Psychology and Second Language Learning: The Role of Attitudes and Motivation.* London: Edward Arnold.

Geertz, C. (1973) *The Interpretation of Cultures.* New York: Basic Books.

Higgins, E.T. (1998) Promotion and prevention: Regulatory focus as a motivational principle. *Advances in Experimental Social Psychology* 30, 1–46.

Jenkins, J. (2007) *English as a Lingua Franca: Attitude and Identity.* Oxford: Oxford University Press.

Johnson, M. (2004) *A Philosophy of Second Language Acquisition.* London: Yale University Press.

Kim, T.Y. (2005) Reconceptualizing second language motivation theory: Vygotskian activity theory approach. *English Teaching* 60 (4), 299–322.

Kim, T.Y. (2006a) Interview method development of qualitative study on ESL motivation. *Foreign Languages Education* 13 (2), 231–256.

Kim, T.Y. (2006b) Motivation and attitudes toward foreign language learning as socio-politically mediated constructs: The case of Korean high school students. *The Journal of Asia TEFL* 3 (2), 165–192.

Kim, T.Y. (2007) Second language learning motivation from an activity theory perspective: Longitudinal case studies of Korean ESL students and recent immigrants in Toronto. PhD dissertation, University of Toronto.

Lantolf, J.P. (ed.) (2000) *Sociocultural Theory and Second Language Learning*. Oxford: Oxford University Press.

Lantolf, J.P. and Genung, P.B. (2002) 'I'd rather switch than fight': An activity theoretic study of power, success, and failure in a foreign language. In C. Kramsch (ed.) *Language Acquisition and Language Socialization: Ecological Perspectives* (pp. 175–196). London: Continuum.

Lantolf, J.P. and Thorne, S. (2006) *Sociocultural Theory and the Genesis of Second Language Development*. Oxford: Oxford University Press.

Leont'ev, A.N. (1978) *Activity, Consciousness, and Personality*. Englewood Cliffs, NJ: Prentice-Hall.

Locke, E.A. and Latham, G.P. (1990) *A Theory of Goal Setting and Task Performance*. Englewood Cliffs, NJ: Prentice-Hall.

Miles, M.B. and Huberman, A.M. (1994) *Qualitative Data Analysis: An Expanded Sourcebook* (2nd edn). Thousand Oaks, CA: Sage.

Phillipson, R. (1992) *Linguistic Imperialism*. Oxford: Oxford University Press.

Ratner, C. (2002) *Cultural Psychology: Theory and Method*. New York: Plenum.

Richards, L. and Richards, T. (2002) *NVivo (Version 2.0)*. Thousand Oaks, CA: Sage.

Rueda, R. and Dembo, M.H. (1995) Motivational processes in learning: A comparative analysis of cognitive and sociocultural frameworks. In P.R. Pintrich (ed.) *Advances in Motivation and Achievement: Culture, Motivation and Achievement* (Vol. 9) (pp. 255–289). Connecticut, CT: JAI Press.

Rueda, R. and Moll, L.C. (1994) A sociocultural perspective on motivation. In M. Drillings (ed.) *Motivation: Theory and Research* (pp. 117–140). Hillsdale, NJ: Lawrence Erlbaum.

Ryan, S. (2006) Language learning motivation within the context of globalization: An L2 self within an imagined global community. *Critical Inquiry in Language Studies* 3 (1), 23–45.

Sivan, E. (1986) Motivation in social constructivist theory. *Educational Psychologist* 21 (3), 209–233.

Skehan, P. (1989) *Individual Differences in Second-Language Learning*. London: Edward Arnold.

Swain, M. and Deters, P. (2007) 'New' mainstream SLA research: Expanded and enriched. *The Modern Language Journal* 91 (5), 818–834.

Turner, J.C. (2001) Using context to enrich and challenge our understanding of motivational theory. In S. Volet and S. Järvelä (eds) *Motivation in Learning Contexts: Theoretical Advances and Methodological Implications* (pp. 85–104). Amsterdam: Elsevier.

Ushioda, E. (2003) Motivation as a socially mediated process. In D. Little, J. Ridley and E. Ushioda (eds) *Learner Autonomy in the Foreign Language Classroom: Teacher, Learner, Curriculum and Assessment* (pp. 90–103). Dublin: Authentik.

Ushioda, E. (2007) Motivation, autonomy and sociocultural theory. In P. Benson (ed.) *Learner Autonomy 8: Teacher and Learner Perspectives* (pp. 5–24). Dublin: Authentik.

Vygotsky, L.S. (1978) *Mind in Society: The Development of Higher Psychological Processes*. Cambridge, MA: Harvard University Press.

Vygotsky, L.S. (1979a) The development of higher forms of attention in childhood. In J.V. Wertsch (ed.) *The Concept of Activity in Soviet Psychology* (pp. 189–240). Armonk, NY: M.E. Sharpe.

Vygotsky, L.S. (1979b) The genesis of higher mental functions. In J.V. Wertsch (ed.) *The Concept of Activity in Soviet Psychology* (pp. 144–188). Armonk, NY: M.E. Sharpe.

Wood, D., Bruner, J. and Ross, G. (1976) The role of tutoring in problem-solving. *Journal of Child Psychology and Psychiatry* 17, 89–100.

Zeng, K. (1995) Japan's Dragon Gate: The effects of university entrance examinations on the educational system and students. *Compare* 25, 59–83.

Chapter 15

The Internalisation of Language Learning into the Self and Social Identity

KIMBERLY A. NOELS

Introduction

In recent years, scholarly interest in the role of identity and the self in language learning has grown, such that, as is evident in the current volume (see also Noels & Giles, in press, for overview), there is a multitude of perspectives and hence potential for new insights. In this chapter, I would like to talk a bit about my own interest in this theme, by addressing two questions to which many people besides me have long endeavoured to provide answers. The first question has been posed in one form or another for almost 50 years: 'How can we better support students' motivation to learn a new language?' A good answer to this question would presumably help us to facilitate students' engagement in the learning process and thereby improve not only their capabilities in a new language but also opportunities in their social world. A second question concerns the implications of such volitional engagement in the learning process, particularly for feelings of identification with ethno-linguistic groups. I think that there is a good argument to be made for the importance of learner autonomy in motivation, and that a sense of autonomy in relation to one's social world is central for developing the sense that a new language is one's own language and that one could become an active participant in another language community. But while I appreciate its importance, I am also concerned that we not forget other concerns that people have that may be as important as autonomy in supporting self-regulated learning.

Self-Determination Theory as a Humanistic/Existential-Phenomenological Theory

The self

My understanding of the social psychological processes involved in language learning has been informed, in part, by Self-Determination Theory (SDT; Deci & Ryan, 1985, 2002), which is a theory rooted in existential and humanistic philosophies. As an organismic theory, SDT assumes that human beings (indeed, all animate beings) have an innate tendency to explore and master new situations in their environment, and to assimilate the newly acquired knowledge into their existing cognitive structures, including their sense of self. This integration of the old with the new continues throughout the lifespan (Ryan & Powelson, 1991), such that development of the self is characterised by the simultaneous processes of, on the one hand, becoming increasingly differentiated and refined as a result of new experiences, and, on the other hand, becoming more and more coordinated and cohesive as a result of the synthetic process.

This process of assimilation and accommodation is assumed to be directional. SDT maintains that all persons have an innate predisposition to regulate their own behaviour in line with their 'true' or 'authentic' self. Ryan and Deci's (2004) use of the term 'authenticity' is derived from Kierkegaard, who maintained that the self is continually 'relating itself back to itself', such that with each new experience, the self considers possible actions in light of its present interests and beliefs, and then acts in a way that reflects the best correspondence with these interests. This assumption suggests that the self mindfully appraises and evaluates choices of action, and in the process organises and regulates behaviour in a way that benefits the person as a whole (cf. Dworkin, 1988). An authentic action is characterised by a sense of authorship, in the sense that one endorses and takes responsibility for one's actions. When endorsed by the whole self, actions are experienced as congruent with other values and commitments that the person holds. The emotional tone of such reflective synthesis is 'eudaimonic', involving a feeling of fulfilment of potential and a sense of flourishing by acting in a meaningful manner (Ryan & Deci, 2006; Ryan *et al.*, 2008).

Although the authentic self is assumed to be a natural endowment, the self is also in a continuous, dialectical relationship with the social and physical worlds. If these environments provide the appropriate 'nutriments' (which I will describe in greater detail later), then growth and synthesis of the self can readily take place. However, everyday life is full of obstacles that confound the easy realisation of the self, and we are often compelled to pursue courses of action that do little to support, or indeed that run counter to, our innermost beliefs and values. At such times, we experience a sense of inauthenticity and despair. Thus, the process of self-synthesis involves a dynamic in which a person struggles to realise her potential while attending to the social and physical constraints inherent to everyday life.

The motivational orientations

This perspective on the self as engaged in an ongoing process of integration suggests a motivational typology which can describe the varying degrees of synthesis of an activity into the self. Deci and Ryan (1985; Ryan & Deci, 2002) differentiate two broad categories of motivation, which they term 'intrinsic' and 'extrinsic' motivation, along with a sort of antithesis to motivation termed 'amotivation'. Intrinsic motivation comes from the enjoyment felt while performing in an inherently interesting activity, as in the case of a learner who experiences a spontaneous sense of satisfaction in mastering linguistic and communicative challenges and elaborating her capacities in the new language.

Extrinsic motivation refers to any sort of regulation that is external to the enjoyment of the activity itself. Although many goals may be described as extrinsic, they vary in the extent to which they are under the control of the person or under the control of other people or situational circumstances that lie outside the person. For convenience, these goals are described as four separate types, but it is important to remember these types represent points along a continuum, not categorically different motivational orientations. The implication is that a student may endorse multiple reasons for language learning, tending usually to indicate reasons that are similar in degree of self-regulation.

The form of regulation that is least under personal control is external regulation. External regulation refers to the case in which one performs an activity because of an interpersonal demand or a situational contingency (e.g. working for a monetary incentive, or studying to achieve a course credit). The cause of the action is removed from the person's own wishes, and is experienced as a form of control. As long as that contingency is present, a student would engage in language learning; once removed, that engagement would desist. A second, somewhat more personally controlled, form of extrinsic motivation is introjected regulation. In this case there still exists contingencies to learn the language, but these pressures come from the person herself, rather than directly from other people or the general context. With this intrapsychic form of regulation, the rationale for performing the activity is based less on the person's own sense of priorities than on a desire to maintain self-esteem by living up to evaluative standards that are often derived from without. With such introjects, a student generally feels that she 'should' or 'ought to' learn the language, and does so in order to demonstrate that she can live up to her own and others' expectations.

Two other forms of extrinsic motivation are more self-regulated. With identified regulation, one consciously engages in an activity because it is consistent with a goal that is personally important. A student might identify with language learning because she 'consciously evaluates that activity as important and meaningful to herself' (Ryan & Deci, 2003: 258). Integrated regulation is the most internalised and self-determined form of regulation; in this case, the activity fits in with other goals, beliefs and activities that a person already endorses, such that performing the activity is a realisation and expression of the self.

As noted earlier, these motivational orientations can be contrasted with the experience of amotivation. When amotivated, people either do not engage at all in the activity, or they act passively, going through the motions to carry out an activity that makes no sense to them until they can escape it. Amotivation arises under various, related conditions: when a person does not value the activity or the outcomes it could yield; when one feels a sense of incompetence in performing the activity; and/or when one feels that their actions are irrelevant for bringing about the desired consequences. Although amotivation generally connotes passive disinterest, it is not far removed from the active resistance that some students demonstrate when they feel that others are imposing an activity or identity on them (Norton, 2007; see also Ushioda, 2003).

Motivational Orientations and Language Learning Contexts

I have argued elsewhere that such a model of motivation captures well the experiences of many language learners across a variety of contexts (cf. Noels, 2001a). It is, however, tenable that groups of learners differentially internalise language learning depending upon the exigencies of their social environment. In some circumstances, learning a new language may involve a certain 'urgency', in the sense that the language is necessary to sustain basic necessities. For instance, immigrants to a new country may be faced with the very immediate necessity of developing English competence in order to get a job, find appropriate accommodation, and so on. This utilitarian focus, possibly combined with discriminatory encounters with the target language community, can potentially under-mine the learner's desire to engage in a more personal way with that community (cf. Norton, 2000). Under such circumstances, the learner may only slowly and perhaps reluctantly take on the language as part of her identity. In other contexts, learning a language may be less pressing; although developing skill in the language may garner certain practical benefits, the pursuit is primarily enjoyed as an engaging hobby. And in yet other contexts, learning the language may be neither particularly useful nor particularly enjoyable, but may serve as a touchstone for one's identity and sense of belongingness to an esteemed community.

Some preliminary findings from a study of 103 ESL, heritage language (HL), and modern language (ML) students point to systematic differences between groups of learners (Noels *et al.*, in preparation). University-level students registered in a language course answered the open-ended question 'What are your reasons for learning (your heritage language/a second language/English)?' Students generally provided extensive and well articulated responses to this question, often including multiple reasons for language learning. In a preliminary analysis, participants' responses were coded (by coders blind to the purpose of the study) with regard to the major theme evident in the answer, using a coding scheme that reflected the types of orientations outlined by SDT, as well as Gardner's (1985) integrative orientation and a general 'other' category.

The results of this content analysis raise two important points. First, the findings underscored that SDT usefully contributes to our theoretical framework representing the experiences of language learners across different contexts. Almost 95% of the responses had a major theme that could be classified within the typology outlined by Self-Determination Theory (see Table 15.1 for examples of responses) or the integrative orientation category. Across the full sample, the theme of external regulation was particularly evident in 32.0% of the cases, introjected regulation in only 1.0%, identified regulation in 13.6%, integrated regulation in 20.4%, intrinsic motivation in 14.6%, and integrative orientation in 12.6% of the cases. Only 5.8% of the responses reflected themes that did not fit well within the scheme.

Second, the results indicated that features of the context of acquisition can have quite profound implications for the experience of language learning. As seen in Figure 15.1, there were clear differences between the groups in terms of the endorsed reasons ($\chi^2 = 56.91$, df $= 12$, $p < 0.001$). Inspection of the adjusted standardised residuals (Haberman, 1978) showed that, as the main theme, integrated regulation was reported more frequently by HL learners and less frequently by ESL and ML learners than would be expected by chance alone. External regulation was a main theme for more ESL learners and fewer HL learners than would be expected by chance. Finally, intrinsic regulation was a main theme for ML students marginally more frequently than would be expected by chance.

It seems, then, that students in dissimilar circumstances can have quite different foci in learning. The importance of the context of learning for motivation has been noted by many others, who have suggested that we need to be more attentive to the student's network of interpersonal contacts, the relative status of ethnolinguistic groups under considera- tion, the opportunities for direct contact with the language community, the heritage background of the learner, among other dimensions (cf. Clément & Kruidenier, 1983; Clément *et al.*, 2007). It is my opinion that a comparative perspective can most constructively reveal how these aspects of context shape the learner's experience, and, reciprocally, how the learner shapes the context to meet her needs and aspirations.

Table 15.1 Examples of responses to the open-ended question 'What are your reasons for learning (your second language/your heritage language/English)?'

Student's background	Response
Modern language	
Japanese	'I have always had an interest in Asian art, culture, etc. I had the opportunity to begin studying Japanese (I had time) at the [name of university and department]. I have always liked language, having studied German, Russian, etc. I have continued to study Japanese.'
French	'I am learning French because I enjoy it and I believe a second language is valuable for working in Canada and traveling overseas, which is what I hope to do, and have been doing, in my life.'
Heritage language	
Dene	'First and foremost, I believe an individual's heritage language determines where they come from and who they are as an individual. Language is the backbone of a culture. I would like to carry on my Dene heritage therefore I am willing to learn my native language to carry on my ancestor's heritage. I also want to learn because I would like to teach my 13 year old son how to speak it.'
German	'It shows and tells who I (truly) am. I want to able to pass it down to my kids.'
English as a second language	
Chinese national	'I started to learn English from my middle school, as one of the required course. From then on, I had to kept on learning English meet the requirement at high school and to get the university degree in China. When I started to work after leaving university, I had to work with a American colleague in my office. The need in daily-work, which is not even very much, forced me to learn English further by speaking, reading English. In order to get the chance to study in this University, I had to pass several standard examinations, like TOEFL. So, in the last several years before I came here, the main reason to improve my English is to pass those tests and make the life in Canada easier.'

Table 15.1 (*Continued*)	
Student's background	*Response*
German national	'In high school I had to decide weather to take English or French. I choose English because it is most widely used. I went to the US to travel just 2 months before, not enough of the students chose French, so there wouldn't have been a course offered anyhow. The main reason throughout high school was that I had to take English up until grade 11, there was no other choice. In Grade 12 and 13 one still has to have one foreign language. I decided to take English because I was much better in it than in Latin (my other foreign language) and I liked our English teacher. When I decided to study in Canada, I had no other choice than to improve my English. a) to be able to meet the prerequisites (TOEFL 550 points) b) to follow in class c) to communicate with people (Listing a,b,c is not weighted I guess they are all equally important)'

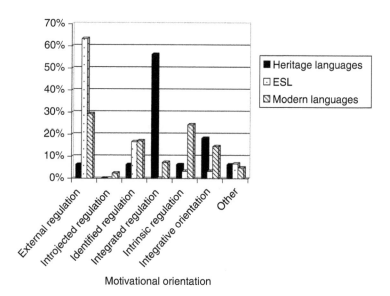

Figure 15.1 Percentage of respondents who endorse each orientation as a function of the language learning context

Autonomy, Competence and Relatedness: Fundamental Human Needs and the Role of Significant Others

The development of an integrated, autonomous self is not an unproblematic journey. This human propensity interacts with aspects of the social and physical worlds that either nurture or thwart its unfolding. To achieve integration and self-determination, SDT posits that certain psychological 'needs' must be met. People within the learner's network play an important role in supporting (or undermining) these needs, in effect providing the 'nutriments' for internalisation and self-actualisation. SDT posits three fundamental needs, including autonomy competence, and relatedness (Ryan & Deci, 2002).

Autonomy in language learning is a topic that has been extensively addressed (see Benson, 2006, 2007 for recent reviews). Indeed the website hosted by Hayo Reinders concerning autonomy and language learning contains over 700 articles (Reinders, 2007). Benson (1997) and Oxford (2003) have forwarded similar models to synthesise the various perspectives on autonomy in language learning. Autonomy as conceptualised in SDT does not focus on the technical skills that students must develop to pursue a learning activity outside the classroom, nor does it address how ideological positions and socially-structured relationships privilege or constrain self-authorship. Rather, it fits into Benson's psychological category and lies between Oxford's psychological and sociocultural I (Vygotskian) categories. Autonomy refers to the experience of initiation and regulation of behaviour by the self:

> Autonomy ... concerns the difference between behavioral engagement that is congruent and fitting with one's values, interests and needs (i.e., with one's self) versus alienated, passively compliant, or reactively defiant. (Ryan & Deci, 2004: 450)

Autonomy does not imply that one acts independently of environmental influences, and/or acts counter to the influence of generalised norms or the demands of specific individuals. If, upon reflection, we concur that such mandates are consistent with our values and interests, we would be acting autonomously. People in the social world can support this phenomenology of autonomy in a variety of ways, such as providing appropriate choices, encouraging self-initiation, minimising the use of controls, and so on.

Within SDT, competence refers to the feeling that one has the capacity to effectively carry out an action. Because of the need for competence, people seek out opportunities to challenge themselves and thereby develop their skills and capacities. Feelings of competence are promoted by communicating expectations that are challenging without being overwhelming, providing a rationale for how behaviours are related to consequences, and giving guidelines and feedback that explain how behaviours can be changed to become more skilful and effective.

Relatedness refers to a sense of belongingness with other people in one's community. It involves both a sense of caring about and being cared for by others – in other words, a sense of affection and a feeling of security. Grolnick *et al.* (1997; Ryan & Solky, 1997) maintain that an atmosphere of warmth, security, and acceptance is necessary to act in a 'spontaneous and authentic way' (Horney, 1950: 455). The exploratory spirit in all humans is most robust when persons are operating from a 'secure base' (Grolnick *et al.*, 1997: 138). The feeling that one matters to others is enhanced when others demonstrate sensitivity and responsiveness to one's concerns, devote time and resources to that person, and perform other kinds of personally validating actions.

A growing body of research supports the claim that an internalised orientation for language learning is associated with these three experiences. For instance, Noels (2001b) found that those students of Spanish who perceived their teacher as less controlling and as providing informative feedback felt a stronger sense of autonomy and competence in language learning, which in turn was associated with stronger endorsement of internalised and intrinsic reasons for learning the language. Several other correlational studies of students of French, English and German have likewise demonstrated the positive link between strong perceptions of autonomy, competence, and relatedness and more internalised reasons for language learning (Noels, 2005; Noels *et al.*, 1999, 2000, 2001).

To look more closely at how people in the learners' social world are implicated in their motivation, we asked students, including heritage and nonheritage learners, registered in undergraduate-level German courses across Canada to complete a survey concerning their motivational orientations and feelings of autonomy, competence and relatedness (Noels & Saumure, submitted). We also asked them to tell us about how controlling their teachers, family members and members of the German community were of their efforts to learn German, how informative their feedback was for developing a sense of competence, and how concerned and responsive they were towards the student.

We found that, for nonheritage learners, competence, relatedness, and most strongly autonomy, predicted a more internalised orientation for learning German. The teacher played the most significant role in supporting these fundamental needs, although informative feedback and interpersonal involvement from members of the students' families and the German community also fostered a sense of relatedness. A different picture emerged for the heritage language learners. In their case, feelings of competence were relatively unimportant, and interestingly, relatedness was at least as strong a predictor of an internalised orientation as autonomy. Regarding the role of significant others in supporting these feelings, the teacher played only a small part. Instead, the family members and members of the German community played the leading roles in promoting heritage learners' autonomy, competence, and relatedness.

There are two main points to take away from these findings. First of all, this comparative analysis again emphasises that the social context dramatically affects motivational dynamics, even for students registered in the same course. Different people played more or less significant roles in students' internalisation of language learning. Indeed, in some circumstances the teacher's impact may be inconsequential relative to the weight that family and community members bring to bear. The second point pertains to the importance of autonomy in supporting self-determined regulation. These results emphasise that although autonomy is important, it is not the sole basis for internalisation. Rather competence and particularly relatedness are also foundational for self-determined motivation.

What are the Implications of Internalisation for Social Identity?

Research carried out in our lab and by researchers elsewhere has demonstrated that more self-determined extrinsic motivation and intrinsic motivation have several implications, including more positive affective responses to learning the language (e.g. less anxiety, more positive attitudes), increased motivational intensity and engagement in the language, better linguistic skills (e.g. grades and self-assessments), and increased use of the target language (see Noels, 2001a, for review). An issue that we have been exploring in several recent studies is whether more internalised reasons for learning a language are linked to increased identification with the target language group. It would seem reasonable to suggest, at least in contexts where a target language community is readily identifiable, that as language learning and use become increasingly integrated within a person's sense of self, one might increasingly feel a sense of belonging to that ethnolinguistic community.

Some studies support this contention. For instance, several correlational studies indicate a link between self-determined extrinsic and intrinsic orientations and ethnic identity or integrative orientation (Noels, 2001b, 2005; Noels *et al.*, 2001). To look more closely at this issue, Erin Goldberg and I studied graduates of French immersion and other intensive language programs in which students receive a substantial portion of their academic curriculum in French (Goldberg & Noels, 2006). The university students who participated were registered either at the English-speaking campus of a western Canadian university or at the university's French-language campus. None of them had a Francophone ancestral background. We were interested to know if the students' choice of campus was related to their motivational orientations for learning French. More specifically, we reasoned that those people who opted to pursue their university studies primarily in French would have internalised the language to a greater extent than those people who decided to study in English. We also thought that if students felt that they were learning the language because it corresponded with their values, interests, and sense of self, they might engage in a more Francophone lifestyle and adopt a Francophone identity.

The results provided some support for this hypothesis. Although quantitative measures did not show a difference between groups, qualitative responses to the question 'Are you continuing your French language training? If so, why and if not, why not?' were coded into categories reflecting the motivational orientations posited by SDT. Students at the French-language campus described their orientations in a more self-determined style than those at the English-language campus. Moreover, several people at the English-language campus indicated that they had no reason to study French or had postponed their studies until a later time, although none at the French-language campus did.

This difference between groups in how internalised their reasons for language learning were corresponded with differences in patterns of identity. For both groups, Anglophone identity was stronger than Francophone identity across all situational domains examined (i.e. with family, with friends, at school, in the community). This pattern indicated that learning French did not interfere with the students' feelings of identity with their culture of origin, suggesting these people experienced an additive form of bilingualism. However, the differentiation between identities was attenuated for the French-campus students in the school domain. For these students, their Francophone identity was stronger and their Anglophone identity was weaker in the school domain than in other situations. Moreover, their Francophone identity was greater and Anglophone identity weaker than that reported by the English-campus students, but only in the school domain. Hence, being immersed in a French environment at school, which includes opportunities to interact in French with classmates and professors, had an enhancing effect on these students' Francophone identities. By no means do I want to suggest that simply because a person feels that learning French is an important part of who she is, she will be able to successfully claim an identity as Francophone. Certainly more is involved in such identity claims, including meaningful use of the language and receptivity and validation from members of that community. But an important piece of the puzzle is the student's own sense of ownership of the new language, which would help to legitimate such identity claims in her own eyes as well as the eyes of others.

The students examined in this study might well be considered advanced language learners who have had considerable exposure to the language and possibly the French community. To test the generalisability of this link between internalised motivation and ethnolinguistic identity, we looked at this issue in students registered in a first-year French course at a western Canadian university (Noels, 2007). The participants, who were all native speakers of languages other than French (primarily English), completed a questionnaire that assessed their motivational orientations; sense of autonomy, relatedness and competence in the language learning context; their effort and engagement in language learning; and their feelings of ethnic identity in the educational domain. We analysed the relations between these variables using structural equation modelling, and the results showed a good fit of the proposed model to the data (see Figure 15.2). The more that students felt that their needs for autonomy, competence and relatedness were satisfied, the more they indicated intrinsic and self-determined extrinsic reasons for learning the language, and the less they felt amotivated. More intrinsic and self-determined reasons for language learning corresponded with more motivated engagement in language learning, which in turn was linked to increased identification with French speakers. Thus, consistent with Goldberg and Noels's (2006) findings, the results indicated that if learners feel that they are learning the language because it is expresses their values and interests, they will likely identify with the target language community.

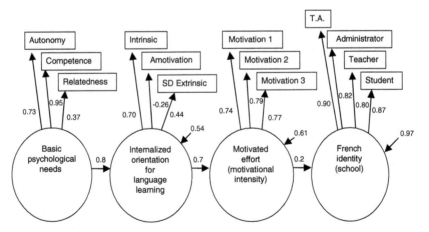

Figure 15.2 Final structural equation model for first-semester French students, with standardised coefficients. Note: $\chi^2 = 88.92$, $p < 0.01$, CFI = 0.93, RMSEA = 0.08

Issues to Consider

I hope so far to have demonstrated the utility of SDT for understanding language learning motivation. The theory organises many, seemingly disparate, ideas regarding motivational orientations in a manner that can be applied across a large range of contexts. It is a useful guide for posing research questions and effectively predicts patterns of relations between many of the variables that have interested scholars who study the sociopsychological processes involved in language learning. It underscores the central role of the self in language learning, particularly the importance of internalisation of the learning activity, which is a topic of considerable interest in recent discussions of motivation. For instance, it is closely aligned with Dörnyei's (2005, this volume; see also Csizér & Dörnyei 2005a, 2005b) discussion of a motivational self-system that regulates behaviour, cognition and affect. Drawing from the work of Markus and Nurius (1986) and Higgins (1987), Dörnyei argues that the capacity to visualise oneself as a member of a language community of some kind is the key mechanism by which motivation is sustained (cf. Norton's (2000) 'imagined community'). In line with SDT's differentiation between more or less internalised forms of extrinsic motivation, Dörnyei maintains that more idealised guides for language learning are associated with a self-promotion focus (e.g. studying to realise an important aspect or potential of the self). In contrast, guides associated with an 'ought' self are prevention focused (e.g. studying because of a sense of duty or obligation).

The SDT framework is not inconsistent with recent calls by sociocultural theorists to reconceptualise the monolingual language learner as a multilingual language user. It fits in very nicely with approaches to learning that emphasise the role of social interaction, the importance of zones of proximal development and optimal challenges, and the idea that human beings are self-regulating organisms (cf. Ryan & Powelson, 1991; Ushioda, 2006). SDT has been quite mute on the themes that critical theorists have raised regarding power and ideology in specific social interactions and the struggle of learners to recraft their sociostructural position to bring about personal and social change. Recently, however, Landry *et al.* (2005) have argued that language socialisation involves not only the experience of self-regulation as outlined by SDT but also the experience of conscientization (cf. Freire, 1983), and have attempted to integrate these experiences and others in a comprehensive model.

But there remain several issues that I feel need to be more extensively addressed with regards to this theory. Over the years various critiques have been levelled at SDT. Space precludes an extensive discussion of these but I will suggest three areas that I feel are particularly important, not only because of what they might tell us about language learning and use, but also because of what they might have to say about motivation and the self more generally. First, the claim of a true, authentic self runs counter to the assumptions of many constructivist theorists. Many scholars have forwarded the idea that we have dynamic, multiple, relational selves, which are constructed and negotiated within specific interpersonal interactions in particular social contexts. These multiple selves are a normal, adaptive part of human life, and are not necessarily indicative of identity fragmentation or distress. This perspective contrasts with the arguably positivistic overtones of the SDT notion of an 'authentic' or real self that is fostered or undermined by the social context. From this perspective, when identities are relatively isolated, compartmentalised, and 'disintegrated', one is likely to experience poorer well-being; when identities are integrated and unified within the psyche, they represent the full endorsement of the self, and this contributes to better well-being (Ryan & Deci, 2003). A rapprochement between these contrasting points of view is sorely needed, perhaps one that speaks to a dialectical balance between constancy and change in self-processes.

The second pertains to the differentiation of intrinsic motivation from internalised forms of extrinsic motivation. Koestner and Losier (2002) describe many similarities between intrinsic and identified regulatory styles, including high levels of involvement, positive affect, and internal sense of control. They differ from each other, however, in terms of their motivating force and regulatory guides. Personal importance is the motivating force in identified regulation, such that one regulates one's behaviour in terms of personal values and identity. In contrast, attraction or interest in the activity is the motivating force for intrinsic motivation, and the emotions that emerge as a result of engaging in the activity serve as the regulatory guide. I puzzle, however, over the notion of 'interest' – surely an activity cannot be itself inherently interesting, but rather interest must originate from the person. Moreover, to be interested in something suggests that one makes, or at least would be inclined to make, meaning of that activity. If this is true, then intrinsic motivation is defined quite similarly to internalised extrinsic motivation, in that one's motivation derives from that which one finds personally meaningful. Perhaps Koestner and Losier (2002) have resolved this definitional indeterminacy by positing that regulatory guides are learned in the case of identified/integrated regulation and genetically inherited in the case of intrinsic motivation. It is plausible that some people may be genetically predisposed to enjoy verbality generally, which eventually becomes channelled into enjoying learning new languages. In contrast others may only come to enjoy language learning as a result of socialisation and internalisation. It remains to be seen how this premise could be tested.

Evidence for the distinctiveness of internalised extrinsic motivation and intrinsic motivation might come from their different associations with fundamental needs and behavioural consequences. Koestner and Losier (2002; see also Ryan & Deci, 2002) claim that, although autonomy is an important antecedent for both motivational types, it combines with competence to support intrinsic motivation, but combines with relatedness to foster internalisation. With regard to behavioural consequences, internalised extrinsic motivation and intrinsic motivation have been shown to differ in how well they predict behaviour relevant to achieving long-term goals: somewhat counter-intuitively, identified regulation is often the stronger predictor, a pattern that we have also seen in our own research, whereby identified regulation more strongly correlates with the intention to continue language studies than does intrinsic motivation. Koestner and Losier (2002) suggest that seeing an activity as interesting may not be sufficient to engage fully and effectively in that activity, but rather one must see the activity as personally important. Hence they suggest that it may be often worthwhile to encourage the development of an identified style of regulation in addition to intrinsic motivation. In sum, there is arguably a conceptual overlap between intrinsic and internalised extrinsic motivation, and differentiation between these constructs merits more theoretical consideration, empirical inquiry, and reflection on their implications for application.

In my view, the greatest challenge for SDT, and for the concepts of autonomy and agency more broadly, arises from the premise that autonomy is universally the cornerstone of motivation. The primacy of autonomy seems appropriate in Western societies where individualism is a deeply vested cultural value. Its centrality, however, must be examined in other, so-called 'collectivistic' societies where autonomy may not be as emphatically cherished. Although investigation of SDT in non-Western societies has only just begun (see Ryan & Deci, 2006, for a brief review), the cross-cultural relevance of autonomy for language learning has been well discussed and debated, particularly with regard to language education in Asian countries. Some claim that traditional pedagogical approaches that include authoritarian teaching styles and exacting assessment criteria are detrimental to students' sense of competence and autonomy (e.g. Yang, 1998). Others maintain that stressing autonomy in language education may be inappropriate in contexts where social interconnectedness and respect for authority are emphasised (cf. Farmer, 1994; Ho & Crookall, 1995; Jones, 1995; Riley, 1988). Still others argue that autonomy in Asian countries may assume a form different from autonomy in Western nations, where collaboration and interdependent learning rather than solitary and independent learning are encouraged (Aoki, 1999; Aoki & Smith, 1999; Littlewood, 1996, 1999). To date, however, there has been little empirical work to examine learner autonomy and language learning motivation from a cross-cultural perspective. Such a comparative approach, along with a consideration of other dynamics such as relatedness and competence, I believe will help us to better understand the place of autonomy in motivation and self-regulation.

Conclusion

I began this chapter by highlighting two questions that seem to run through much of the recent work on the social psychology of language learning. The first concerned how we might better support students' motivation to learn a new language. The second pertained to the implications of motivated involvement in the learning process for feelings of social identification. I hope that I have convincingly demonstrated that SDT, which highlights the importance of internalisation and self-determination for motivated effort, can serve as a useful guide for answering these questions. At the same time it is important that one not be 'in thrall' to this or any other theory (cf. Thomas, 1997). Although I find SDT to be an insightful standpoint from which to consider language learning motivation, I believe that our understanding of this domain will grow as we test the limits of our theories, and stretch beyond their boundaries.

References

Aoki, N. (1999) Affect and the role of teachers in the development of learner autonomy. In J. Arnold (ed.) *Affect in Language Learning* (pp. 142–154). Cambridge: Cambridge University Press.

Aoki, N. and Smith, R.C. (1999) Autonomy in cultural context: The case of Japan. In S. Cotterall and D. Crabbe (eds) *Learner Autonomy in Language Learning: Defining the Field and Effecting Change* (pp. 19–28). Frankfurt am Main: Lang.

Benson, P. (1997) The philosophy and politics of learner autonomy. In P. Benson and P. Voller (eds) *Autonomy and Independence in Language Learning* (pp. 18–34). London: Longman.

Benson, P. (2006) Autonomy and its role in learning. In J. Cummins and C. Davison (eds) *The International Handbook of English Language Teaching* (pp. 733–745). Norwell, MA: Springer.

Benson, P. (2007) Autonomy in language teaching and learning. *Language Teaching* 40 (1), 21–40.

Clément, R. and Kruidenier, B.G. (1983) Orientation in second language acquisition: I. The effects of ethnicity, milieu, and target language on their emergence. *Language Learning* 33 (2), 273–291.

Clément, R., Noels, K.A. and MacIntyre, P. (2007) Three variations on the social psychology of bilingualism: Context effects in motivation, usage and identity. In A. Weatherall, B. Watson and C. Gallois (eds) *Language, Discourse and Social Psychology* (pp. 51–77). Basingtoke: Palgrave Macmillan.

Csizér, K. and Dörnyei, Z. (2005a) The internal structure of language learning motivation and its relationship with language choice and learning effort. *The Modern Language Journal* 89 (1), 19–36.

Csizér, K. and Dörnyei, Z. (2005b) Language learners' motivational profiles and their motivated learning behavior. *Language Learning* 55 (4), 613–659.

Deci, E.L. and Ryan, R.M. (1985) *Intrinsic Motivation and Self-Determination in Human Behavior*. New York: Plenum.

Deci, E.L. and Ryan, R.M. (2002) *Handbook of Self-Determination Research*. Rochester, NY: University of Rochester Press.

Dörnyei, Z. (2005) *The Psychology of the Language Learner: Individual Differences in Second Language Acquisition*. Mahwah, NJ: Lawrence Erlbaum Associates.

Dworkin, G. (1988) *The Theory and Practice of Autonomy*. Cambridge: Cambridge University Press.

Farmer, R. (1994) The limits of learner independence in Hong Kong. In D. Gardner and L. Miller (eds) *Directions in Self-Access Language Learning* (pp. 13–27). Hong Kong: Hong Kong University Press.

Freire, P. (1983) *Pedagogy of the Oppressed*. New York: Continuum.

Gardner, R.C. (1985) *Social Psychology and Second Language Learning: The Role of Attitudes and Motivation*. London: Edward Arnold.

Goldberg, E. and Noels, K.A. (2006) Motivation, ethnic identity and post-secondary education language choices of graduates of intensive French language programs. *Canadian Modern Language Review* 62 (3), 423–47.

Grolnick, W.S., Deci, E.L. and Ryan, R.M. (1997) Internalization within the family: The self-determination theory perspective. In J.E. Grusec and L. Kuczynski (eds) *Parenting and Children's Internalization of Values: A Handbook of Contemporary Theory* (pp. 135–161). New York: Wiley.

Haberman, S.J. (1978) *Analysis of Qualitative Data: Vol. 1 Introductory Topic*. New York: Academic Press.

Higgins, E.T. (1987) Self-discrepancy: A theory relating self and affect. *Psychological Review* 94, 319–340.

Ho, J. and Crookall, D. (1995) Breaking with Chinese cultural traditions: Learner autonomy in English language teaching. *System* 23 (2), 235–243.

Horney, K. (1950) *Neurosis and Human Growth*. New York: Norton.

Jones, J.F. (1995) Self-access and culture: Retreating from autonomy. *ELT Journal* 49 (3), 228–234.

Koestner, R. and Losier, G.F. (2002) Distinguishing three ways of being highly motivated: A closer look at introjection, identification, and intrinsic motivation. In E.L. Deci and R.M. Ryan (eds) *Handbook of Self-Determination Research* (pp. 101–121). Rochester, NY: University of Rochester Press.

Landry, R., Allard, R., Deveau, K. and Bourgeois, N. (2005) Autodétermination du comportement langagier en milieu minoritaire: Un modèle conceptual. *Francophonies d'Amerique* 20, 62–79.

Littlewood, W. (1996) 'Autonomy': An anatomy and a framework. *System* 24, 427–435.

Littlewood, W. (1999) Defining and developing autonomy in East Asian contexts. *Applied Linguistics* 20, 71–94.

Markus, H. and Nurius, P. (1986) Possible selves. *American Psychologist* 41, 954–969.

Noels, K.A. (2001a) New orientations in language learning motivation: Towards a model of intrinsic, extrinsic and integrative orientations. In Z. Dörnyei and R. Schmidt (eds) *Motivation and Second Language Acquisition* (pp. 43–68). Honolulu, HI: University of Hawaii Press.

Noels, K.A. (2001b) Learning Spanish as a second language: Students' orientations and perceptions of teachers' communicative style. *Language Learning* 51, 107–144.

Noels, K.A. (2005) Orientations to learning German: Heritage background and motivational processes. *Canadian Modern Language Review* 62, 285–312.

Noels, K.A. (2007) Identity and the internalization of language learning into the self-concept. Paper presented in the Invited Colloquium Individual Differences, Language Identity and the L2 Self, AAAL Annual Convention, Costa Mesa, April 20–25.

Noels, K.A., Clément, R. and Pelletier, L. (2001) Intrinsic, extrinsic, and integrative orientations of French Canadian learners of English. *Canadian Modern Language Review* 57, 424–442.

Noels, K.A. and Giles, H. (in press) Social identity and second language acquisition. In T.K. Bhatia and W.C. Ritchie (eds) *New Handbook of Second Language Acquisition*. Leeds: Emerald.

Noels, K.A., Pelletier, L. and Clément, R. (1999) Perceptions of teachers' communicative style and students' intrinsic and extrinsic motivation. *Modern Language Journal* 82, 545–562.

Noels, K.A., Pelletier, L., Clément, R. and Vallerand, R.J. (2000) Why are you learning a second language? Orientations and self-determination theory. *Language Learning* 50, 57–85.

Noels, K.A. and Saumure, K.D. (submitted) Motivation for learning German as a heritage vs. foreign language: A self-determination perspective on the role of the social context in supporting learner motivation.

Noels, K.A., Saumure, K.D., Adrian-Taylor, S., Johns, K. and Chu, J. (in preparation) A content analytic comparison of the importance of the social context for the motivation of heritage, second and ESL learners.

Norton, B. (2000) *Identity and Language Learning: Gender, Ethnicity and Educational Change*. Harlow: Longman/Pearson Education.

Norton, B. (2007) Personal communication, April.

Oxford, R.L. (2003) Toward a more systematic model of L2 learner autonomy. In D. Palfreyman and R.C. Smith (eds) *Learner Autonomy Across Cultures: Language Education Perspectives* (pp. 75–91). Basingstoke: Palgrave Macmillan.

Reinders, H. (2007) http://www.hayo.nl/autonomybibliography.php. Retrieved November 1, 2007.

Riley, P. (1988) The ethnography of autonomy. In A. Brookes and P. Grundy (eds) *Individualization and Autonomy in Language Learning*. London: Modern English Publications in Association with the British Council.

Ryan, R.M. and Deci, E.L. (2002) An overview of self-determination theory. In E.L. Deci and R.M. Ryan (eds) *Handbook of Self-Determination Research* (pp. 3–33). Rochester, NY: University of Rochester Press.

Ryan, R.M. and Deci, E.L. (2003) On assimilating identities to the self: A self-determination theory perspective on internalization and integrity within cultures. In M.R. Leary and J.P. Tangney (eds) *Handbook on Self and Identity* (pp. 253–274). New York: The Guilford Press.

Ryan, R.M. and Deci, E.L. (2004) Autonomy is no illusion: Self-determination theory and the empirical study of authenticity, awareness, and will. In J. Greenberg, S.L. Koole and T. Pyszczynski (eds) *Handbook of Experimental Existential Psychology* (pp. 449–479). New York: Guilford Press.

Ryan, R.M. and Deci, E.L. (2006) Self-regulation and the problem of human autonomy: Does psychology need choice, self-determination, and will? *Journal of Personality* 74, 1557–1586.

Ryan, R.M., Huta, V. and Deci, E.L. (2008) Living well: A self-determination theory perspective on eudaimonia. *Journal of Happiness Studies* 9 (1), 139–170.

Ryan, R.M. and Powelson, C.L. (1991) Autonomy and relatedness as fundamental to motivation and education. *Journal of Experimental Education* 60, 49–66.

Ryan, R.M. and Solky, J.A. (1997) What is supportive about social support? On the psychological needs for autonomy and relatedness. In G.R. Pierce and B.R. Sarason (eds) *Handbook of Social Support and the Family* (pp. 249–267). New York: Plenum.

Thomas, G. (1997) What's the use of theory? *Harvard Educational Review* 67, 75–104.

Ushioda, E. (2003) Motivation as a socially mediated process. In D. Little, J. Ridley and E. Ushioda (eds) *Learner Autonomy in the Foreign Language Classroom: Teacher, Learner, Curriculum and Assessment* (pp. 90–102). Dublin: Authentik.

Ushioda, E. (2006) Motivation, autonomy and sociocultural theory. In P. Benson (ed.) *Learner Autonomy 8: Teacher and Learner Perspectives* (pp. 5–24). Dublin: Authentik.

Yang, N.D. (1998) Exploring a new role for teachers: Promoting learner autonomy. *System* 26, 127–135.

Chapter 16
Possible Selves in Language Teacher Development

MAGDALENA KUBANYIOVA

Introduction

This chapter draws on the qualitative dataset of a larger longitudinal mixed methods study of the development of English as a Foreign Language (EFL) teachers in Slovakia (Kubanyiova, 2007). The L2 Motivational Self System (Dörnyei, 2005; see also this volume) and the broader conceptualisation of future identity goals in possible selves theory was applied to explain the research participants' idiosyncratic developmental patterns in response to a specially designed in-service teacher development course in L2 motivational strategies. The analysis of the qualitative data revealed that teacher conceptual change is a function of the interplay among the multiple identity goals language teachers adopt in their educational and sociocultural contexts and the dissonance between the teachers' actual and desired future selves is a key catalyst for the teacher learning process. This is seemingly in contrast with findings in the teacher motivation domain where dissonance between teachers' ideals and the educational reality they are confronted with is viewed as detrimental to their motivation and commitment. The purpose of this chapter is to throw some light on the nature of this contradiction and argue that insights into the content of the participants' possible selves can enhance our understanding of why some teachers change as a result of reform initiatives, while others, having similar backgrounds and working in comparable contexts, remain completely untouched by the reform input even if they appraise it positively (cf. Kubanyiova, 2006).

Possible Language Teacher Selves: Forging the Link Among Teacher Cognition, Teacher Motivation and Teacher Development

Language teachers' cognitive development, also researched under the labels of belief change, conceptual change, teacher development or teacher learning, has been investigated within the domain of language teacher cognition, a fairly well established sub-discipline of applied linguistics (Borg, 2003, 2006). The results generated in this field of study have highlighted the variable degrees to which teacher education programmes and in-service teacher development initiatives facilitate development. Some of the widely explored factors that have been found detrimental to development include teachers' pre-training cognitions with a proven track record of being resistant to change, and the various constraints of sociocultural contexts in which the teachers' practices are embedded. However, the picture of teacher cognitive development painted thus far by the language teacher cognition domain seems to be far from complete. We know, for example, that affective factors play a significant role in teacher growth (Golombek & Johnson, 2004). Yet, the attention that this dimension of teacher development has received is far from systematic. Even more puzzling is the domain's lack of explicit engagement with dispositional and motivational factors and this omission becomes particularly pronounced in the context of this volume, which puts motivation at the centre of any developmental process.

On the other hand, consulting the domain of teacher motivation does not appear any more satisfactory. Admittedly, the various typologies of micro- and macrocontextual factors impacting on motivation to teach which have resulted from the largely fragmented research in this area (see review in Dörnyei, 2001b) have generated important insights into the aspects that could potentially facilitate or hinder teacher learning. However, these do not contribute to our understanding of how motivation is transformed into action and how cognitive, motivational and contextual factors interact in the highly dynamic and complex individual as well as socially constructed process of language teachers' development.

I believe that the theoretical framework of possible selves can provide the all important bridge and shed light on the relationship among these factors. As postulated by possible selves theory, not all cognitions that affect peoples' behaviour are anchored in the social reality. Some, on the contrary, constitute an important imagined future dimension that transcends direct experience and functions as an incentive for development and change. This future dimension of language teachers' cognition is conceptualised here as *Possible Language Teacher Self*, which, in accordance with possible selves theory, embraces personalised as well as socially constructed (Markus & Nurius, 1986) language teachers' cognitive representations of their ideal, ought-to and feared selves in relation to their work as language teachers.

In keeping with the L2 Motivational Self System (Dörnyei, 2005) and self-discrepancy theory in particular (Higgins, 1987, 1998), Possible Language Teacher Self is in this chapter operationalised as (1) *Ideal Language Teacher Self*, which constitutes identity goals and aspirations of the language teachers, that is, involves the self which they would ideally like to attain; it is assumed that, irrespective of what the content of this ideal self is, teachers will be motivated to expend effort to reduce a discrepancy between their actual and ideal teaching selves; and (2) *Ought-to Language Teacher Self*, which refers to the language teachers' cognitive representations of their responsibilities and obligations with regard to their work; this may involve latent expectations of colleagues, parents and students as well as the normative pressures of the school rules and norms. As opposed to the previous type of possible self, the teachers' activity geared towards reducing the actual versus ought-to self discrepancy is motivated by extrinsic incentives and the primary source of this motivation is believed to be the teacher's vision of negative consequences.

Although not explicitly conceptualised in either the L2 Motivational Self System or self-discrepancy theory, the teachers' vision of negative consequences is taken here to represent a distinct third type of possible self: *Feared Language Teacher Self*. It refers to someone that the teacher could become if either the ideals or perceived obligations and responsibilities are not lived up to. Self-regulatory efforts towards reducing the actual-versus-possible selves discrepancy are likely to increase when teachers have 'balanced' possible selves, that is, when their desired future states (ideal and/or ought-to) are accompanied by well defined feared counterparts (Dörnyei, 2005, this volume; Kubanyiova, 2007; Oyserman *et al.*, 2006).

The aim of the following sections is to document the multiple identity goals that the current research participants adopted in their respective teaching contexts and illustrate an uneasy relationship between teachers' possible and present states as these interact with the teacher development input and determine its ultimate impact. This chapter also throws light on the contradicting role dissonance plays in the context of language teacher conceptual change. Before I explore these themes, let me provide a brief background to the research study, findings of which have informed theoretical deliberations in this chapter.

The Study: Promoting Conceptual Change Among In-service EFL Teachers in Slovakia

The purpose of this longitudinal classroom-based mixed methods study was to explore the impact of a specially-designed 20-hour experiential in-service teacher development (TD) course on conceptual change among eight non-native speaking EFL teachers in Slovakia. Seven out of the eight research participants worked in the state sector, with four of these teaching in secondary schools, one in a primary school and two working in the tertiary context. One of the research participants was employed in the private sector.

The TD course content focused on strategies for creating a conducive psychological climate in the L2 classroom, particularly motivation-sensitive and autonomy-supporting teaching approaches and group-building strategies (Dörnyei, 2001a; Little *et al.*, 2003), and encouraged a reflective approach to teaching. While prospective language teachers in Slovakia receive robust training in linguistics and language teaching methodology, issues such as learner motivation and group climate that later become of primary concern to practising teachers (cf. Hadfield, 1992), remain unaddressed on the majority of teacher education programmes. Thus, in this context, the TD course input concerned approaches to language teaching that were novel for its participants and is therefore referred to throughout this chapter as reform input.

The qualitative fieldwork involved five phases of data collection spread over the course of the Slovak school year starting in September 2004 and ending in June 2005. Each phase lasted approximately two weeks and involved delivering a five-hour session of the TD course (apart from the fourth phase, during which the session could not be delivered) followed by field visits. These entailed classroom observations, informal conversations and more formal in-depth qualitative interviews with the research participants. Classroom observations (55 in total) were of ethnographic nature, generating extensive descriptive data of the teachers' instructional behaviours, classroom discourse and student engagement patterns. The interviews (31 in total, producing just over 29 hours of audiorecorded data) explored three main thematic strands: the research participants' profiles (i.e. their language learning and language teaching history, motivation to enter the teaching profession, personal history and beliefs about language education), observed lessons and TD course-related issues. Data from several non-participating informants, such as students, head teachers, university teacher trainers and research participants' colleagues, were also added to the dataset. Further details of the study, the description of the quantitative component and the theoretical foundations of the TD course can be found in Kubanyiova (2006, 2007).

The qualitative data analysis can be characterised as following a theory-building path. That is, the data were examined for emerging themes and recurring patterns and this process has led to the development of the novel theoretical model of language teacher conceptual change (LTCC, see Kubanyiova, 2007). The following discussion focuses on a specific aspect of the LTCC model, the construct of Possible Language Teacher Self, and illuminates how its relationship with the reform input determines a degree of language teachers' cognitive development.

Ideal Language Teacher Self: A Central Cognition

One of the key findings of this research project concerns the centrality of the Ideal Language Teacher Self in the teachers' cognitions and the pivotal role reform-induced dissonance between actual and ideal selves plays in teacher conceptual change. This section shows how probing motivational orientations of the research participants uncovered a link between teacher motivation and the construct of ideal self and thus led to the above conclusions.

The first part of this section provides a brief account of the research participants' reasons behind pursuing the teaching career. A more in-depth discussion in the second part will demonstrate that these individual motivational orientations in fact penetrated multiple facets of the teachers' work, thus suggesting salience of a more encompassing motivational construct. These findings have led me to the proposition that the concept of ideal self may offer a powerful theoretical framework for understanding not only why teachers choose their career but also why they engage in specific classroom practices and, being particularly relevant here, why some of them develop as a result of a reform input while the cognitions and practices of others remain unaltered.

Key motivational patterns in the current research sample

An in-depth exploration of the teachers' motivation to pursue their career revealed two major incentives. The first concerned the participants' positive attitude towards the subject matter, which, according to Csikszentmihalyi (1997), constitutes one component of intrinsic motivation to teach. This is in agreement with findings in other Eastern European contexts, such as Poland (Johnston, 1997) or Slovenia (Kyriacou & Kobori, 1998), where positive attitudes towards the English language and the desire to improve English proficiency have been found to be primary motives for people who pursue or consider an EFL teaching career.

The second set of distinct and by far the most pervasive motives discerned from the data of the current research sample related to the teachers' more general psychological needs. That is, for some of the research participants, the teaching job was an important means of fulfilling their striving for recognition, appreciation, respect and authority, a set of motives which does not typically feature in teacher motivation frameworks. Because the focus of these goals centres primarily on the self rather than the subject matter, the educational process or the students, I term these motives 'ego-related' and will further illustrate their nature in the second part of this section.

A particularly noteworthy and surprising finding was the absence in most participants' data of the most frequently cited source of teachers' motivation to teach – the educational process itself (Csikszentmihalyi, 1997). That is, a desire to facilitate students' learning did not seem to be central in the research participants' motivational composites. This is also in sharp contrast with the conclusions reached in a number of empirical studies involving EFL teachers (Hayes, 2005; Michlizoglou, 2007; Tardy & Snyder, 2004; Watzke, 2007), where students' 'moments of learning' (Tardy & Snyder, 2004: 122) were quoted by the teachers as the most important factor in fuelling their motivation to teach. It is not the purpose of this chapter to speculate whether such a contradiction is due to particular characteristics of the sociocultural contexts investigated or research methodologies employed. Rather, the aim of the next section is to demonstrate that the research participants' motivation to teach, whatever the actual motives, bore a strong identification loading, and that the notable absence of identity goals linked to the educational process can also explain the absence of change in this research study.

Links between teacher motivation and ideal self

The link between motivation and some kind of identification element emerged as the data analysis progressed. It became obvious that the research participants' motives to pursue their career as well as to engage in the current teacher development initiative permeated all facets of their data and were in various ways reflected in their classroom behaviours, discourse and thinking. What is more, there seemed to be a striking overlap between these motives and the frequent occurrence of diverse self-related constructs identified in the initial phases of the coding process (e.g. self-esteem, self-perceptions, self-image, perceived superiority, ego-related goals), which pointed towards the relevance of an overarching self-concept theme. Let me illustrate this by examining in more detail Iveta's ideal self.

Ego-related concerns were a hallmark of Iveta's data and her identity aspirations of being valued and appreciated were obvious from the way she reflected on her teaching as well as on her participation in the research project, talked about her personal and professional history and behaved during the TD course. In the extract below (Iveta's feedback on TD Session 1), she identifies the following benefits of her joining the project, all converging into a single theme of her desire for recognition:

> the fact that I have joined the project gives me more confidence. Perhaps this seems to have no connection, but I feel that I am doing something for myself, that I am not just a 'dumb colleague' as we are sometimes addressed by XY (her colleague)....And lastly, the kids love me more, because they say it is so nice of me that I allowed them to write their own opinion about me and that I want to change

because of them...they told me that no one had ever done that for them before.

Pursuing her ego-related goals is also clearly traceable in the observational data of her instructional practice. The following is a lesson excerpt (26 April 2005) in which she is explaining a usage of future tenses (note: the underlined text represents Iveta's use of L1, whereas the 'xxx' symbol marks inaudible content):

So. We are dealing with going to? But so as not to confuse it with another structure, let's look at page 43? *(they all open the books, the T waits)* we have exercise number 5 there. Tenses. So we are going to look at will and going to. So will is *(reads what the coursebook says)*, so for example, if you want to say, xxx *(very fast speech in L1 follows, explaining when they would use it by giving examples of what they might want to say in what situations, etc.)*, so when it's certain, you'll use will.

While prior to this episode, the students generally interacted with the teacher either verbally or non-verbally (frequently nodded and 'uhmed'), the teacher's mini-lecture documented here was accompanied by complete silence, suggesting that the students may not have grasped the explanation (and, I have to admit, I could not quite follow it either). However, Iveta did not seem to pick up this clue and, despite the students' lack of interaction, spoke markedly faster than usual and made very definite statements. It seems that her ideal self as a respected and appreciated teacher (in this case an expert linguist able to readily provide an explanation for a particular grammatical structure) was central to her self-concept and thus obscured her ability and/or willingness to examine whether or not the students understood. Findings from other data sources indicate that this kind of behaviour by Iveta was usually linked with her lack of self-confidence in grammatical knowledge. The current conceptualisation enables us to understand how preventing students from questioning the explanation she herself might not have been sure about was a crucial strategy for Iveta to avert the imminent threat to her identity goal of being appreciated for her expertise. Focusing on reducing the discrepancy between her actual (i.e. uncertain) and ideal selves was, understandably, Iveta's priority and her observational data contain numerous instances where she did so at the expense of the goal of facilitating student learning.

How then does self-discrepancy theory explain the lack of develop-ment in Iveta as well as the other research participants? As has been mentioned earlier in this chapter and elsewhere in this volume, the main premise of self-discrepancy theory is that people are motivated to reach a condition in which their actual selves match those future desired selves that are personally relevant to them. The awareness of the discrepancy between who someone is and who he/she desires to be, which is accompanied by emotional dissonance, is critical in triggering people's self-regulatory activity towards achieving such a condition. The key focus of the TD course (creating motivating conditions for students' learning) in no way tapped into the future identity goals of most research participants. Thus, because facilitating students' learning was not a central part of the teachers' future vision of themselves, there was no ground in which dissonance could be induced by this specific reform input and therefore the possibility of development was significantly reduced.

An Arsenal of Ought-to Language Teacher Selves

Teaching would undoubtedly be a more attractive job if it was only ideal selves that the teachers pursued in their work. This is, unfortunately, rarely (if ever) the case and the everyday reality of a teaching job brings with it numerous external pressures, demands and requirements (cf. Shoaib, 2004). It seems, therefore, that apart from personally relevant internalised visions, language teachers' work is also driven by a different type of incentive, such as the effort to comply with outside expectations or a desire to avoid dreaded disaster. As has been mentioned earlier, these externally-defined images are operationalised here as *Ought-to Language Teacher Selves,* because they represent language teachers' non-internalised perceptions of what is expected of them as teachers in specific contexts, and the failure to comply with these obligations typically has significant identity implications.

For classroom-based researchers, the most well-known case of teachers' ought-to selves in action is probably the so called 'observer paradox', whereby teachers' classroom behaviour is not so much a representation of their normal routines, but rather their attempt to display what they believe are desirable and sought-after practices. Let us have a closer look at this type of, what I term, reform-related ought-to self that the current research participants adopted, before examining a set of context-related ought-to teaching selves.

Reform-related ought-to selves

The early stages of data analysis revealed certain discrepancies in some of the research participants' data. This indicated the possibility that they were, in a way, working with their assumptions of what was expected of them and tried to live up to these expectations even though they may not have personally identified with them. In the initial phases of data analysis, I developed a whole coding tree of such instances with a working name 'Living up to expectations' (see Kubanyiova, 2007: 229), which seemed to feature particularly strongly in at least three research participants' data.

For instance, even though half of the participants did not incorporate the reform input into their teaching in any way, the other half made, or reported to have made, several attempts to either replicate the course activities in their classrooms or adapt the reform input for their own teaching situation. However, in order to understand the true nature of the TD course impact, we need to establish whether these implementation instances were a result of the teachers' ideal (i.e. internally defined) or ought-to (i.e. externally imposed) selves. This distinction is believed important in determining whether the implemented practices could potentially represent true conceptual change or were likely to be abandoned once the teachers' perceived pressure of the project's requirements was over (cf. Gutierrez Almarza, 1996). Let me now present Monika's account, which provides evidence of the existence of some temporary, externally defined identity goals guiding her classroom behaviour during the research project.

Monika seems to have adopted a vision of a committed research participant, eagerly taking on all the tasks associated with the project, including her active attempts to implement the course input into her classes. However, as she herself admits in Interview 4 (10 May 2005), her frequent reform implementation was usually restricted to classes immediately following the most recent input session (which often happened to be classes scheduled for observation), and did not reflect some long-term implementation plan:

> You know it could be that I didn't do many activities recently? (3) Very recently yes, after the [TD course] session. And I'm very much like, you know, during the course, I always feel like, OK, on Monday I will be like the best teacher! (laughs) and on Friday I will always forget.

It seems, therefore, that the self Monika was projecting was a temporary response to the project's requirements and was associated with the feelings of frustration and even anger when it was difficult to reconcile with other competing responsibilities:

> while I'm enjoying something, it's great, but when all my energy's gone, that's it. (laughs). Humanist or no humanist. Yeah, like what does she want from us! (meaning the researcher) (laughs). Yeah, I was, within me, angry, like what does she, all the time, what does she want?! I've got other things to think about. (*Interview 2, November 2004*)

Yet, it was clear that she continued to 'deliver' despite her frustrations. For example, when I asked her, six months after the project ended, whether she thought experimenting with new things was possible in the state school system, she was quite sceptical. To my question whether she, despite the system, ever attempted to do that type of activity, she replied:

> I think I did. In the year when we attended the seminar, certainly yes at that time…

Monika's students, too, were quite aware that when I was there as an observer, their lessons were markedly different from their regular ones. When I asked them during the focus group interview whether they noted some differences, they seemed to be unanimous (note S1–S4 refer to individual students):

S1: Absolutely.
S2: Definitely.
S3: No doubt.
S4: Like we always know that when you're gonna be there, we would have some kind of games and fun.

This, of course, is not to say that the research participants' desire to live up to the project's expectations was a negative phenomenon and should be dismissed, as it often is in classroom research, as the 'observer paradox'. On the contrary, in research projects with transformational agendas such as this one, teachers' efforts to integrate innovation into their teaching should be welcomed, because what may initially represent an externally motivated possible self (i.e. ought-to self), can transform along the way to an internalised ideal self. Such a proposition is, after all, considered plausible in both the L2 motivational self-system discussed in this volume and in self-determination theory, and the teacher's experience of success with the implementation undoubtedly plays a key role in this process (Kubanyiova, 2007). As Monika, reflecting on her experience, confirms:

> Even though I tended to moan, like this will not work and this is easy to say to someone who hasn't tried it, but really it did pay off. (*Interview 5, 31 December 2005*)

In fact, what the previous brief account has demonstrated is that the two prerequisites for teacher conceptual change outlined in the previous section on the ideal self were fulfilled: (1) the content match between the reform input and the possible self, and (2) dissonance between actual and reform-related possible selves. Indeed, Monika and some of the other research participants experienced dissonance between the kind of teacher they perceived themselves to be (actual self) and the kind of teacher implied by the reform input (reform-related ought-to self) and, as a result, felt the pressure to implement the reform input in their classes, even though they may not have personally identified with it at the outset. Thus, even in the absence of relevant ideal selves, complying with these reform-related ought-to selves could potentially be an important starting point in the teachers' internalisation of the relevant reform-induced self and thus an alternative stepping stone towards conceptual change.

Unfortunately, for most of these research participants the reform-related ought-to selves were short-lived and of limited impact on their development. Instead, a number of competing context-related ought-to selves played a considerably more significant role in guiding their ultimate response to the TD course, and what follows is an explanation of why this may have been the case.

Contextual demands as competing ought-to selves

The negative effect of unfavourable contexts is nothing new. After all, research on teacher cognition, teacher motivation (Dörnyei, 2001b; Shoaib, 2004) or school change (Sarason, 1996) have all concluded that pressures of the system coupled with heavy workload, limited resources, prescribed curriculum, lack of autonomy or unsupportive colleagues have a negative impact on teacher commitment and development. However, as the following discussion indicates, there are a number of unanswered questions about the exact role of context in teacher development. I believe that adopting the construct of the ought-to self goes some way towards helping us address those questions, and can thus contribute significantly to our understanding of the role contextual constraints play in language teacher development.

The excerpt below documents a struggle that often results from the interaction of the teachers' reform-related possible selves and their efforts to conform to various external expectations and normative pressures of the school culture, operationalised here as context-related Ought-to Language Teacher Selves:

> I hear [colleagues] say, look how perfect her class is, what order she has in her class! But what's her relationship with the students, how do the students perceive her? You know she would say I'm the boss, I'm the captain here and everybody will obey me. And I say, well, maybe from the outside it may look to her that they are listening to her, but...are they really? I don't know whether this is the right relationship (*intonation as if seeking approval*). Like, what's the aim? To have authority and have everybody listen to me? And [let them] say nothing? Or will I value if [the students] tell me that this is something they don't like, that I do give them space to speak up. Hmmm. This is what I'm struggling with. It's easier when you're a captain from the outset. It's easier. Simply, this is how things will be done around here and you don't give them any space. And they often do need a firm hand. But what I'm trying to prove is that it can be done without it, too. Although with more effort, but it can be done. (*Monika's Interview 1, 22 September 2004*)

Unfortunately, the determination that we see at the end of this excerpt was infrequent in the dataset and even those rare instances were often quickly stifled by a variety of competing ought-to selves primed by the educational and sociocultural contexts of the research participants. These selves typically contained well elaborated socially constructed images of how teachers should or should not behave in the classroom, what relationship with the students they should have, and what content they should teach and for what purposes, the majority of these contradicting the reform input and therefore inhibiting teacher development.

There are several reasons why contextual constraints are operationalised here through the construct of ought-to selves. To start with, it is clear that although the research participants' concerns about contextual demands, including the system, resources, time or students' and colleagues' expectations appeared frequently in the current dataset, there seemed to be differences in the way different teachers appraised similar constraints, and the detrimental type of dissonance was not always the outcome of these appraisals. For instance, Tamara was adamant that her circumstances simply did not allow her to engage in a more reflective approach to teaching which the current TD course advocated as essential for change to occur. Her account in the following excerpt eloquently expresses this:

> this sort of self-reflection as we do here...for me, I told you, the first class when it was finished, perhaps just on the way to the staff room I would just say it worked or it didn't work, that was good, that wasn't good, that's it. Sometimes it happens to me that the bell rings, the class has ended and at that moment I start thinking about the following class. That I have no personal time to sit down and jot down a couple of notes. (*Interview 3, 13 January 2005*)

It appears that this teacher's dissonance appraisal of her teaching context (i.e. her conclusion that her resources were insufficient and there was therefore nothing she could do to even consider a reflective approach) was indeed detrimental to her development. On the other hand, Denisa, whose workload was equally demanding, could see possibilities of engaging in such an approach despite the contextual constraints, which she was well aware of, but, in contrast with Tamara, was prepared to fight:

> I started to write my feedback on almost every class I teach – something you asked me in the interview, e.g. how and why I met my objectives, but also everything I want to do differently next time. I know that we were recommended to do something like this in our methodology seminars, but...there was no time for that....I know that during that interview I realised things about that class that didn't even cross my mind during the class itself. And it helped

quite a lot. So I now try to reflect on each class for about 15 minutes (even if it means it has to be done before I go to sleep) and I write it down so that I don't forget it. It is just great. I have known for some time that I want to teach, but only during the interview it came to me how much it means to me. That's why this reflection writing does not seem to me a wasted time. (*Feedback on Session 1*)

Thus, while the issue of an unsupportive system and 'institutional resistance' (Vieira, 2003) was a recurrent theme in the data of most of my research participants, it affected their readiness to experiment with the new teaching approach quite differently and did not become a factor negatively affecting the possibility of sustained conceptual change for all of them. Two of the eight teachers, in fact, responded quite radically to the system constraints and, rather than complying with the pressures, decided to set up their own English language schools during the course of the project in which they could 'teach the way they wanted'.

The possibility of not satisfying students' expectations emerged as a particularly influential contextual factor preventing the research participants from implementing the reform in their classrooms. In the following excerpt Iveta assesses the possibility of integrating more interactive tasks into her regular classes (as opposed to conversation classes) through the lens of students' expectations:

No. I personally can't do that. I can't integrate it in [my normal lessons]. I can't. And [the students] also... Even if I tried something of that sort, they don't cooperate .... For them, it somehow doesn't fit into a normal class. (*Iveta, Interview3, 3 January 2005*)

In a similar vein, Monika expresses worries with regard to an autonomy-supporting teaching practice:

I am a bit skeptical about [learner autonomy] unless we all [teachers of all subjects] start doing something about it. I do believe it is very important and something that is my priority, but my own experience is that I have not reached much understanding from students, on the contrary, the effect often was that I am not serious (or maybe competent) enough about teaching. (*Feedback on Session 4 of the TD course*)

These are just some examples of what was a strong theme in several teachers' data: their fear that by adopting a new approach to teaching they would fail to meet the students' expectations. This type of dissonance appraisal of the teaching context clearly hinders development.

Interestingly, however, its closer scrutiny also reveals that the students' expectations were in most cases interpreted by the teachers through their own identity goals rather than based on some kind of objective evidence of what the students really expected. Let me just provide one illustrative example from Tamara's post-observation interview excerpt (describing a warm-up activity that involved having blindfolded students guess whose voice among their classmates they were listening to) that attests to a more general pattern in her as well as other teachers' appraisals of students' expectations (The numbers in brackets indicate silence in seconds):

> **Interviewer:** And you said [to the students]: 'You might have found this a stupid activity'.... Do you think there was a possibility that they thought it a stupid activity? Or did you have the feeling they did?
>
> **Tamara:** (3) You know (uncertain), I have to admit that I didn't notice this in particular. I have to admit I didn't notice that, I did not inspect their faces, yeah? That is one thing that should be there, ... one doesn't concentrate on that ..., you see that's a good point, (1) but I had the feeling that it seemed to them as non-sense because they responded immediately, see? They didn't think who it was, but they knew instantly...
>
> **I:** Aha, so during the activity you noticed that it was easy-
>
> **T:** -easy and that's why I thought what's easy must be nonsense. (*laughs*)

Thus, although the research participants were generally concerned with students' expectations, they were often unable to provide data-based evidence for what these actually were. Instead, they tended to interpret these through the filter of their own theories ('what's easy must be nonsense'), beliefs about a good language class (each lesson should contain 'a new grammar exercise'), or their various ego-related concerns ('they didn't appreciate it much'). These cognitions seemed to be a reflection of the Ideal or Ought-to Language Teacher Selves the research participants had adopted and, as the excerpts presented here show, the fear of not meeting students' or any other type of external expectations indeed proved to be associated with the fear of identity implications (i.e. being perceived as a teacher who is 'not serious enough', 'incompetent', and therefore 'not appreciated' by the students), and were accompanied by negative emotions such as anger, embarrassment and disappointment when such implications were directly experienced.

The data of this research project indicate that the fear of not meeting students' expectations becomes a factor inhibiting change when it is associated with an imminent threat to the teachers' identity goals, irrespective of whether or not the students' real expectations are at play. Similarly, the extent to which a variety of contextual demands, such as heavy workload or the unsupportive school culture, produce detrimental dissonance depends on the teachers' internal appraisal of these conditions. These are, in turn, determined by those possible selves that are most central in their working self-concept. Therefore, in order to understand the detrimental impact of sociocultural contexts on teacher development, we need to examine the degree to which the teachers had adopted contextually primed ought-to selves as their self-guides.

The Role of Dissonance: Unravelling the Contradiction

One final point that deserves clarification concerns dissonance and the seemingly contradictory role it plays in the process of conceptual change. Adopting the framework of possible selves in self-discrepancy theory enables us to see that the two types of dissonance result from fundamentally distinct mechanisms.

On the one hand, dissonance appraisal is triggered by the reform input and results from course participants' realisation of a discrepancy between their ideal/ought-to selves represented by the reform input and their actual self represented by their current practice. Dissonance in this sense appears to be an essential (although not sufficient) condition for conceptual change to occur and this ties in closely with the findings across disciplines (Dörnyei, 2005; Farrell, 2006; Freeman, 1993; Golombek, 1998; Golombek & Johnson, 2004; Gregoire, 2003; Higgins, 1987; Johnson, 1996; Posner *et al.*, 1982; Visser & Cooper, 2003). In keeping with self-discrepancy theory, then, without individuals' awareness of a discrepancy between their actual and possible selves, which is accompanied by dissonance emotions, there is no gap to be reduced and therefore no motivation to further engage with the reform input.

In contrast, dissonance triggered by unfavourable contextual factors has been shown to undermine motivation and inhibit development. As has been demonstrated above, this happens when the contextual pressures and expectations have been elaborated into the teachers' specific ought-to selves, and when the vision of the negative consequences of not satisfying those expectations (i.e. counterpart feared selves) is equally well-defined and central in the teachers' working self concept. It is clear that in this case a reform input which contradicts such ought-to selves represents a threat to the teachers' identities. Dissonance that results from this realisation will therefore compel the teachers to employ strategies for minimising the threat by actively avoiding engagement with the reform input.

Based on some tendencies in the current dataset, we could speculate that the language teachers who experience dissonance between their actual selves and the reform input (i.e. not only is the reform input consistent with the teachers' intrinsic aspirations, but they also recognise a discrepancy between their current and desired end-states) are less likely to be negatively influenced by the various context-related ought-to selves and therefore less likely to centre their effort on prevention. This is because in their pursuit to reduce the discrepancy, the teachers are likely to employ self-regulatory strategies with the aim to minimise the impact of contextual constraints on their development. Although more empirical evidence is needed to support this claim, its plausibility is also confirmed in the data of Lena, a research participant in White and Ding's (this volume) study. Despite the constraints she encountered on the way, Lena pursued her vision of herself as a teacher who creates authentic learning experiences for her students in an online environment. Because this vision seems to have been central in her working self-concept, other competing ought-to selves were rendered insignificant in guiding her behaviour and therefore did not distract her from her developmental path.

Conclusion

Prior cognitions have been identified in language teacher cognition research as a filter through which language teachers process the content of a reform input. The main argument of this chapter was that central to these cognitions are the teachers' future-oriented cognitive representations of their Possible Language Teacher Selves, encompassing Ideal, Ought-to and Feared Selves, though not all of them necessarily available and/or readily accessible to every teacher.

The findings presented in this chapter suggest that in order to understand why teachers develop (or do not) as a result of a reform input, the relationship between the reform content and the specific orientations of teachers' multiple possible selves needs to be interrogated. It appears that the reform input will be effective in motivating behaviour and promoting change only to the extent to which its basic premise (which, in this case, entailed the importance of teachers' proactive intervention to create conditions conducive to students' L2 learning) had been incorporated into the teachers' relevant possible teaching selves. Without such specific cognitive representations of future identity goals, 'there should be little instrumental behavior in the direction of mastery' (Markus & Nurius, 1986: 961), and thus little prospect of language teacher conceptual change. Even if it appears counter-intuitive and directly contradicts both theoretical conceptualisations and some empirical evidence regarding EFL teacher motivation, the data presented here have shown that facilitating the learning process may not necessarily be a central aspiration of all language teachers.

Two immediate implications arise from these conclusions. First, it seems important for language teacher education programmes to make sure not only that prior cognitions are made explicit (Freeman, 1991), but that, first and foremost, reform-related ideal teaching selves are proactively primed rather than assumed. Empirical evidence generated in research domains outside the field of applied linguistics demonstrates the effectiveness of specific educational interventions designed to this end (Oyserman *et al.*, 2002, 2006) and thus gives us optimism as well as invitation to engage in similar endeavours in our field. Secondly, it is clear that if language teachers do not experience reform-induced dissonance between who they are and who they want to become, their ideal self, even if congruent with the reform content, is unlikely to impel them to self-regulatory action. Teacher education programmes therefore need to find ways of destabilising teachers' established cognitions, while at the same time facilitating the development of strategies for coping with the potentially detrimental impact of their teaching contexts.

To conclude, this chapter has introduced the construct of possible selves as a theoretical framework for a better understanding of language teacher cognition and development. Its particular appeal is in the way it addresses the current gap in the language teacher cognition domain and bridges the various cognitive, motivational, affective and contextual factors which play a role in language teacher conceptual change. Judging from the fast advancing research in L2 motivation documented in this volume, possible selves have the potential to open up promising new avenues for conceptual and empirical inquiry in the domain of language teacher cognition.

References

Borg, S. (2003) Teacher cognition in language teaching: A review of research on what language teachers think, know, believe, and do. *Language Teaching* 36, 81–109.

Borg, S. (2006) *Teacher Cognition and Language Education: Research and Practice.* London: Continuum.

Csikszentmihalyi, M. (1997) Intrinsic motivation and effective teaching: A flow analysis. In J.L. Bess (ed.) *Teaching Well and Liking It: Motivating Faculty to Teach Effectively* (pp. 72–89). Baltimore, MD: The Johns Hopkins University Press.

Dörnyei, Z. (2001a) *Motivational Strategies in the Language Classroom.* Cambridge: Cambridge University Press.

Dörnyei, Z. (2001b) *Teaching and Researching Motivation.* Harlow: Longman.

Dörnyei, Z. (2005) *The Psychology of the Language Learner: Individual Differences in Second Language Acquisition.* Mahwah, NJ: Lawrence Erlbaum.

Farrell, T.S.C. (2006) The first year of language teaching: Imposing order. *System* 34, 211–221.

Freeman, D. (1991) 'To make the tacit explicit': Teacher education emerging discourse, and conceptions of teaching. *Teaching and Teacher Education* 7 (5/6), 439–454.

Freeman, D. (1993) Renaming experience/reconstructing practice: Developing new understanding of teaching. *Teaching and Teacher Education* 9 (5/6), 485–497.

Golombek, P.R. (1998) A study of language teachers' personal practical knowledge. *TESOL Quarterly* 32 (3), 447–464.

Golombek, P.R. and Johnson, K.E. (2004) Narrative inquiry as a mediational space: Examining emotional and cognitive dissonance in second-language teachers' development. *Teachers and Teaching: Theory and Practice* 10 (3), 307–327.

Gregoire, M. (2003) Is it a challenge or a threat? A dual-process model of teachers' cognition and appraisal processes during conceptual change. *Educational Psychology Review* 15 (2), 147–179.

Gutierrez Almarza, G. (1996) Student foreign language teacher's growth. In D. Freeman and J.C. Richards (eds) *Teacher Learning in Language Teaching* (pp. 50–78). Cambridge: Cambridge University Press.

Hadfield, J. (1992) *Classroom Dynamics*. Oxford: Oxford University Press.

Hayes, D. (2005) Exploring the lives of non-native speaking English educators in Sri Lanka. *Teachers and Teaching: Theory and Practice* 11 (2), 169–194.

Higgins, E.T. (1987) Self-discrepancy: A theory relating self and affect. *Psychological Review* 94 (3), 319–340.

Higgins, E.T. (1998) Promotion and prevention: Regulatory focus as a motivational principle. *Advances in Experimental Social Psychology* 30, 1–46.

Johnson, K.E. (1996) The vision versus the reality: The tensions of the TESOL practicum. In D. Freeman and J.C. Richards (eds) *Teacher Learning in Language Teaching* (pp. 30–49). Cambridge: Cambridge University Press.

Johnston, B. (1997) Do EFL teachers have careers? *TESOL Quarterly* 31(4), 681–712.

Kubanyiova, M. (2006) Developing a motivational teaching practice in EFL teachers in Slovakia: Challenges of promoting teacher change in EFL contexts. *TESL-EJ* 10 (2), 1–17. Retrieved October 13, 2006 from http://tesl-ej.org/ej38/a5.pdf.

Kubanyiova, M. (2007) Teacher development in action: An empirically-based model of promoting conceptual change in in-service language teachers in Slovakia. PhD thesis, University of Nottingham.

Kyriacou, C. and Kobori, M. (1998) Motivation to learn and teach English in Slovenia. *Educational Studies* 24 (3), 345–351.

Little, D., Ridley, J. and Ushioda, E. (2003) *Learner Autonomy in the Foreign Language Classroom: Teacher, Learner, Curriculum and Assessment*. Dublin: Authentik.

Markus, H. and Nurius, P. (1986) Possible selves. *American Psychologist* 41 (9), 954–969.

Michlizoglou, C. (2007) Teacher motivation: A systems approach. A study of EFL teachers in secondary education in remote places. MA dissertation, Hellenic Open University, Patra, Greece.

Oyserman, D., Bybee, D. and Terry, K. (2006) Possible selves and academic outcomes: How and when possible selves impel action. *Journal of Personality and Social Psychology* 91 (1), 188–204.

Oyserman, D., Terry, K. and Bybee, D. (2002) A possible selves intervention to enhance school involvement. *Journal of Adolescence* 25, 313–326.

Posner, G.J., Strike, K.A., Hewson, P.W. and Gertzog, W.A. (1982) Accommodation of a scientific conception: Toward a theory of conceptual change. *Science Education* 66 (2), 211–227.

Sarason, S.B. (1996) *Revising 'The Culture of the School and the Problem of Change'*. New York: Teachers College Press.

Shoaib, A. (2004) What motivates and demotivates English teachers in Saudi Arabia: A qualitative perspective. PhD thesis, University of Nottingham.

Tardy, C.M. and Snyder, B. (2004) 'That's why I do it': Flow and EFL. *ELT Journal* 58 (2), 118–128.

Vieira, F. (2003) Addressing constraints on autonomy in school contexts: Lessons from working with teachers. In D. Palfreyman and R.C. Smith (eds) *Learner Autonomy Across Cultures: Language Education Perspectives* (pp. 220–239). Basingstoke: Palgrave Macmillan.

Visser, P.S. and Cooper, J. (2003) Attitude change. In M.A. Hogg and J. Cooper (eds) *The Sage Handbook of Social Psychology* (pp. 211–231). London: Sage.

Watzke, J.L. (2007) Foreign language pedagogical knowledge: Toward a developmental theory of beginning teacher practices. *The Modern Language Journal* 91 (1), 63–82.

Chapter 17
Identity and Self in E-language Teaching

CYNTHIA WHITE and ALEX DING

Introduction

Language teachers are often called upon to adjust or restructure their pedagogical and professional practices in response to changes in curricula, materials, classes and learners, and in response to shifts in broader understandings of language learning and teaching. In the past decade for example, significant developments in language teaching have occurred as new technologies are used to provide novel ways of configuring and accessing language learning opportunities. In this field an enduring focus for both research and practice has been the development of virtual learning environments and descriptions of their potential for language teaching; only more recently has attention been given to teachers and learners, and the ways they respond to and work within the new learning spaces. Moreover, studies of teachers new to technology-mediated language teaching focus primarily on the professional challenges and issues they face, together with changes in their roles and skills. Questions about the internal world of the teacher, about teacher identity and teacher self associated with a re-envisioning of what it means to be a language teacher, have remained largely unasked.

The aim of this chapter is to address that gap, drawing on a longitudinal qualitative study of experienced language teachers new to e-language teaching participating in a collaborative teacher learning initiative. Here we examine the subjective and intersubjective experiences of teachers over a period of nine months, noting how they negotiate their identities as part of those experiences; we also explore how the individual, dynamic nature of the self-system (Dörnyei, 2005) shapes and is shaped through the actions teachers take both individually and collectively, impacting dramatically on the course and nature of teacher learning. We argue that the teacher self is an important catalyst for teacher learning impacting on the nature and degree of involvement in teacher learning opportunities, with teachers evidently motivated by ideal and/or ought-to self orientations. To begin with we critically examine prevailing understandings of teacher learning followed by our perspectives on teacher identity and teacher self which together provide the rationale for this chapter.

Teacher Learning

Language teachers – who they are, what they do – have been looked at through their learning processes, their cognition and practices, and more recently through narratives of their experiences and daily lives (see for example, Borg, 2006; Richards & Farrell, 2005; Senior, 2006). Interest in 'the language teacher's development' (Mann, 2005) has generally been expressed in terms of teacher education frameworks and professional development models, accompanied by critiques and acknowledgement of their limitations. Here we examine paradigms which have teacher learning at their core, touching on three interrelated areas central to this study – experienced teacher learning, workplace learning and teacher learning about new technologies.

Teacher learning in relation to technology presents a number of unique challenges, including not only major shifts in technical and pedagogical knowledge and skill areas across a combination of roles (Hubbard & Levy, 2006), but also the ability to orient students to new ways of accessing target language learning opportunities. Further complexities stem from the fact that learning in this domain is not a matter of coming to know what is already known or being oriented to existing practices: there is no codified body of knowledge to access, and technological and pedagogical goal posts continue to shift. Moreover, there is uncertainty about how to optimise the development of teacher expertise. Workshops for language teacher development in new technologies, for example, have been critiqued as disaggregated and decontextualised, divorced from contexts of use, with the result that there is often little sustained transfer to the situated practices of teachers (see for example Reynard, 2003). Attempts to address these limitations in learning to use new technologies include the use of experiential learning opportunities (Hampel & Hauck, 2004), collaborative action research (Murray & McPherson, 2006) and the use of reflective journaling combined with observation by a 'critical friend' (Lewis, 2006). The advantages of these approaches is that they represent a move away from casting teachers 'as "technicians" whose job it is to implement defined "algorithms" for teaching' (Butler *et al.*, 2004: 436), opening the door for teachers to develop personalised approaches to using technology which cannot be predefined (Hampel & Stickler, 2005). However, arguably the most crucial challenge for teachers taking up e-language teaching comes not from changes in knowledge, roles, skills and practices per se, but from challenges to teacher identity and teacher self in each of these domains (White, 2007). Thus in this study we adopt an approach to teacher learning based on the notion of intersubjective collaborative autonomy (Ding, 2005) which frames learning as a situated process, emphasising the social and dialogic nature of knowledge and thought.

Relatively little attention has been given in applied linguistics to either experienced teacher learning or workplace teacher learning. In the general education literature studies at the intersection of these two broad areas suggest that teacher learning is often spontaneous and non-linear, with learning through interacting with others as a common thread. For example, in a study of experienced teacher learning in higher education carried out by van Eekelen *et al.* (2005), the unplanned and unstructured character of most learning experiences of teachers was an important finding. Teacher workplace learning has also been found to be largely unconscious in character (Eraut *et al.*, 1998; Kwakman, 2001, 2003), often arising from and seeking to resolve a specific problem situation, dependent on individual motives and interests, and shaped by interaction with other people. Kwakman (2003), for example, concludes on the basis of two robust studies that participation in professional learning activities depends to a large extent on the personal character-istics of teachers: that is, while task and work environment do affect participation, this effect is mediated by such personal characteristics as appraisals of meaningfulness and professional attitudes. Kwakman (2003) also notes that teachers perceive the task and work environment very subjectively and attributes these differences in perception to differences between individual teachers. What is important in this research from our point of view is that engagement with workplace learning opportunities is seen as interacting with the perceptions and goals of teachers. In identifying and taking account of personal factors affecting teacher participation in professional learning activities, Kwak-man's research breaks new ground, though she does not extend this to a consideration of teacher personhood, teacher self or teacher identity. This is the subject of the next section.

Teacher Identity and Teacher Self

Riley (2006: 295) observes that much has been written about teachers' aims, beliefs, skills, concepts, and practices but 'surprisingly little attention has been paid to the person who is the locus of such notions'. A focus on teacher identity and teacher self addresses this omission, with the potential to extend our understanding of both 'who language teachers are' and 'what language teaching is' (Cross, 2006). Teacher identity has a far greater reach than the notion of teacher role, which is an assigned term concerned primarily with function (White, 2007), whereas identity 'voices investments and commitments' (Britzman, 1992: 29). Identity is multiple, dynamic and conflictual, closely related to sociocultural contexts, and is constructed, enacted and negotiated largely through discourse and interaction.

Research into teacher identity in the wider educational literature has tended to concentrate either on the development of personal beliefs and the effects of these beliefs on the way an individual understands him/herself (Connelly & Clandinin, 1999; McCarthey, 2001), or on the institutional role expectations and how these influence professional identity (Geijsel & Meijers, 2005). The formation of teacher identity is seldom conceptualised as a learning process. An exception is the work of ten Dam and Blom (2006); they argue that a fundamental problem of teacher education is the development of a professional identity, since it involves making sense of and giving meaning to learning, and seeing oneself as a central participant in activities and processes. In this chapter we argue that identity development occurs in an intersubjective field and can be best characterised as an ongoing process of interpreting oneself as a kind of person and being recognised as such in a given context.

Turning now to the notion of the self, Martin (2007) notes that both expressive and managerial selves underlie the research practices of educational psychology in the areas of self-esteem/self-concept and self-regulation/self-efficacy. Both share a common emphasis on the interior functions and processes of individuals. However, our concept of self, that is the organised representation we have of our theories, attitudes and beliefs about ourselves (McCormick & Pressley, 1997), is socially constituted since we encounter and understand ourselves in relation to others, shaped by particular sociocultural contexts and practices. In this chapter we maintain that any notion of self is enriched by taking account of the socially constituted nature of self. Drawing on personality psychology, Dörnyei (2005: 99) identifies the notion of 'possible selves' as a compelling construct for understanding motivation – 'representing the individuals' ideas of what they *might* become, what they *would like* to become, and what they are *afraid of* becoming'. Life goals develop and are influenced by the individual's idea of what they are like, and what they may turn out to be, as well as by their hopes, dreams and aspirations about how they would like to be, and what they would want to avoid. While there have been few theoretical models or empirical studies of teacher motivation in applied linguistics, the notion of possible selves is a useful lens to bring to examining how experienced language teachers envision and re-envision themselves in the new domain of e-language teaching.

The relationship between the notions of identity and self in applied linguistics, as in related fields, is blurred and indeterminate. Conceptually the main difference seems to be that identity is understood to be external – negotiated during social intercourse, while self is understood as internal – a set of beliefs about who we are. This distinction, however, is rather contrived and over-simplistic since the self is determined by social relationships, while the social personae we create in interaction are based on our notions of self. Van Lier (2007) differentiates the constructs as follows: identities are ways of relating the self to the world, through cycles of perception, action and interpretation. He continues:

> ideally the self is in harmony with the environment (including the physical, the social and the symbolic environment) through well-fitting and satisfactory identities that are shaped by both self-perceptions and other-perceptions...when our lives change significantly...new identities (ways of linking the self to new worlds and words) need to be forged that bridge the gaps between the known and the new. (van Lier, 2007: 58)

In this chapter then we extend van Lier's definition of learner identity and self to the teacher whom we see as 'a person with a social, embodied mind, with dreams, worries and beliefs, and in need of forging productive identities that link the personal self to the new worldly demands' (van Lier, 2007: 62); in this case the new worldly demands are presented not by a new language, but by the new contexts and practices of e-language teaching.

The Study: Teacher Learning in E-language Teaching

This research project took place against a complex and dynamic backdrop: the key role technology plays in universities' internationalisation policies of recruiting and educating a growing body of diverse non-native students; a growing awareness of the importance of e-literacy for both language teachers and students in academic contexts; and the need for language teachers to employ technology in sustained, embedded and pedagogically appropriate ways. The aim of the nine-month E-learning Autonomy Project (ELAP), involving 23 tutors based at three universities in China, UK and New Zealand, was to follow how language teachers collectively and individually explored using technology in their teaching. Key to this project was to identify how innovations in technology impacted on their collective and individual identities and professional autonomy. During the course of the project, it became increasingly evident in interviews and online discussions that teacher engagement with learning opportunities interacted profoundly with aspects of teacher personhood, teacher self and teacher identity; examining these aspects then became an important focus of our enquiry.

The study was bounded by a broad framework allowing teachers to choose a technology (for example, PowerPoint, VLEs, podcasts, multimedia) and to configure it in ways they could explore further in their teaching. In order to facilitate collaboration and capture dialogue a

Google group, the E-learning Autonomy Group, (ELAG) was set up. At various stages of the project the authors carried out individual and group interviews with participants; some participants kept a reflective journal or blog recording their experiences, and the authors exchanged observations, reflections and ideas using a blog. Prompts used in the reflective journal and the online discussion group were open, inviting participants to report and reflect on their experiences, and did not focus directly on questions of identity and self; similarly the questions used in the interviews were wide-ranging and non-specific in terms of identity and self:

(1) What prompted you to take part in ELAP (E-learning Autonomy Project)?
(2) What do you expect to gain from taking part in the project?
(3) What challenges have you experienced in ELAP so far, in working with new technologies?
(4) Can you think of any critical incidents or episodes – a turning point, a breakthrough? What happened? What did you do? What did it change?
(5) In ELAP you are in a context where other people are learning about new technologies too – does that have an influence on you? What does that afford you? How might this be different if you were completely on your own?
(6) What does the online discussion give you?
(7) How does your experience in this project orient you to students' experience trying out new technologies in the classroom?
(8) What has been the impact of the project on you so far? On you as a teacher? What has changed?

Recordings of the interviews and discussions were listened to intensively and repeatedly to develop an understanding of the contents. They were then transcribed noting interruptions, pauses, silences and paralinguistic features such as laughter and hesitation markers. Where the conversation moved to more tangential issues, these remained in the transcribed material, in case their significance emerged at a later date. Transcripts of the ELAG discussion, of the reflective journals and of the participants' blogs were compiled to complete the data set for the study. Initially this data set was examined and responses were identified and coded according to two broad categories of identity and self. The processes of coding the data for key themes, re-examining the key themes after further background reading, looking for patterns and making interpretations linked to theory all took place as concurrent cycles of activity, until we were satisfied that no new themes or interpretations were available. For the individual case study we asked the teacher herself (Lena) to read and comment on our analysis to make sure it represented a valid interpretation of herself. Ethical procedures were followed in conducting the research including informed consent, with care taken to ensure anonymity and confidentiality of participants. We were also conscious of our roles at different points of the project and of potential difficulties in fulfilling these roles with integrity throughout the process. We managed this by sharing our decisions and reflections on a joint researchers' private blog, by remaining open to the wishes and perspectives of participants, and by making our roles explicit at different stages of the project.

Brief Illustration of Findings

In the remainder of the chapter we examine aspects of teacher identity and teacher self that emerged in the project, through the study of an individual teacher, Lena, and then through the study of an intact group of four EAP teachers. But first as background to the two studies, we will briefly present excerpts from interviews and discussions with five participants, illustrating something of the range of aspects of identity and self which emerged in this context of teacher learning.

A common perspective by participants was that they were motivated to take part in the project – often somewhat reluctantly – to avoid being seen as a teacher with a limited range of skills, who had not kept up-to-date:

> I know I need to do this – things have changed – but it isn't as easy as for some others who have more time. – *Leslie (individual interview)*

One participant clearly motivated by such an ought-to self orientation, took a utilitarian approach to the project:

> I have had to develop...I think...what do I need from what is available...this is what I do. – *Michel (individual interview)*

Another participant viewed team work and colleagues from a similar perspective, as the means to endorse actions taken and products produced:

> I work well in a team.... You need people to look at what you have done objectively...to evaluate what you have done...they are a good resource. – *Catherine (individual interview)*

In this case any sense of group identity did not extend beyond this perspective. Working with colleagues was based around personal development and affirming an identity as a materials producer working largely individually:

> My strengths lie in producing materials.... I enjoy those projects most where I am producing something. Sometimes they are used by others. – *Catherine (individual interview)*

A sense of frustration arose when the possibility of realising this identity was curtailed:

> I find it difficult.... I have ideas for projects I want to work on but I am not allowed to because it is not seen as a priority...or I am told you have other things to do. – *Catherine (individual interview)*

Another participant saw e-language teaching as a way of realising his ideal self – as a teacher who projects himself as a real person to the students and who can produce a rich learning environment:

> I became interested in online teaching because I wanted the students to have access to experiences in the language that are real and vivid – through music, sounds and images. I wanted them to be able to know me as a person, and for me to gain a full sense of them as learners – I saw that online environments offered the means to that end. It has been a lot of work but I am inspired by that possibility – and I have made that a reality. – *Peter (group discussion)*

Alternation between the combination of ideal and ought-to self orientations was also common in the reports of some participants, as in:

> I saw technology as a way to solve a problem associated with certain classes I was teaching...I found it very frustrating because I couldn't work out how to configure WebCT but actually deciding that I was going to have to do it, that made the difference, and really wanting to do it that I really wanted to do it, that was more motivating...and I could see how I wanted things to be for my classes. – *Malcolm (individual interview)*

From this brief sample of teacher selves as expressed in a new language teaching domain we turn to the in-depth individual case study of Lena.

Identity and Self: Teacher Case Study

The choice of Lena as an individual case study for this chapter was based on the clear personal vision of her ideal teacher self she articulated at different stages of her experience of e-language teaching. Lena's vision was evident in what she hoped to realise and express in both her personal and professional identities. Aspects of her vision are also evident as they emerge, develop and are made over in her interactions with others. Here, after some background, we focus on Lena's initial motivations linked to her identity and ideal teacher self and then explore how the collaborative context which developed through the project impacted on her. We close with a view of Lena's ideal teacher self as expressed towards the end of the project, noting how it incorporates her learners, her use of technology and the identity she is in the process of constructing as a distance language teacher.

Lena agreed to participate in the project in the first year of her appointment as a university lecturer in German. As an experienced tertiary lecturer in English for Academic Purposes and a researcher of language maintenance among German immigrants to New Zealand, in an early interview she saw her new position as an opportunity to 'rediscover' her roots in teaching German, albeit through a very new medium, online distance language teaching. In the project she chose to explore the possibilities of e-tandems linking tertiary learners in New Zealand and Germany in a series of bilingual activities exploring contemporary issues such as race relations in both contexts. Lena reported and reflected on her experiences over a period of eight months in the ELAG discussion group, in interviews, in small group discussions and in a reflective journal.

Lena's ideal self as a distance language teacher was articulated at the start of the project as being someone who could provide students with authentic online learning opportunities that are 'engaging and inter-active'. Lena saw technology as offering possibilities to realise this ideal self, but the experiences required to reach her goals were seen as very challenging:

> at the beginning it was very daunting because I was still learning so much about other things because I was new to the institution, it was all coming at once like a big tidal wave – *Interview*

In her reflective journal she describes the possibilities as 'exciting and frustrating at once, seeing the great potential but also the huge learning curve in front of me'. She continues:

> But what a responsibility too, to my students, to whoever might be the 'other' in the tandem.... I had never done this before, what if it didn't work out? How would I find a suitable group of students in the target language context? Sites facilitating tandems existed, but many of these aimed at pre-University level students. – *Reflective journal*

Finding a German partner institution took time and she was very aware that much would depend on the relationship with her German counterpart, Karen. 'An intense dialogue on possibilities' took place with Karen using the same text and voice tools the students would use (WebCT and Wimba), asking:

> Who were our learners? What could possibly bring them together – the target languages, topics of interest, other? What were the practical and pedagogical considerations? Who were we, what

were our own personal and professional expectations? How could we pursue a relevant research goal at the same time? – *Reflective journal*

Here questions about self point to the ways in which notions of self, identity and possibilities were questioned, negotiated and jointly constructed at the outset and throughout the project. All the 'imponderables' in the project were explored through 'the joint approach with my German counterpart', requiring a good deal of collaboration and personal investment from both participants:

> At times the project design and planning became quite time consuming and seemed out of proportion with the actual size of the project. But at the same time, with every communication between Karen and myself, we would chip away at something, be it the wording of the project description, the setting of tasks, the adoption of a research instrument or the choice of platform. – *Reflective Journal*

A number of key values – respect, openness, flexibility – were identified as features of interactions with Karen contributing directly to Lena's identity which aligned with her ideal teacher self:

> We were feeling our way not only in terms of developing a tandem project but also in relation to who we are and how we do things at either end. A real strength in this has been the high level of mutual respect, openness and flexibility which I believe has enabled us to do a good job, affording our students a new learning experience. – *Reflective Journal*

Lena also emphasised the contribution of colleagues in her Department in affirming the trajectory she was on. One who was more experienced with Wimba Voice tools was helpful in showing her what was possible in the context of his course while 'most of my other colleagues were new to Wimba too so that I didn't quite feel so inadequate' (Reflective Journal).

For both Lena and Karen a key point in the project was when the students began to engage with the learning environment, the activities and most importantly, to gain a sense of the other participants:

> Another breakthrough was when we saw the students talking to each other when things actually started to take shape. They were beginning to get a sense of each other because they were clearly quite different people...we took some pictures and put them online...then students from the other side responded and they began to emerge as people... – *Interview*

And most importantly for Lena this corresponded with her goal of providing authentic, interactive experiences for her students:

> it changed everything basically. I am already working in a different way doing distance teaching, but doing the tandem, bringing in the overseas dimension brought more authenticity into it. They were not just partners in a classroom, they were people in different countries talking to each other, in a way emulating everyday life where people talk to each other, join a chatroom....the e-tandem gave us a chance to do things that emulate life, being interactive and collaborative, and that's possible despite the lack of face-to-face contact. – *Interview*

An unexpected aspect of the project for Lena was becoming an academic mentor for Karen, an emerging academic in the German context:

> Karen is younger than me and has less experience – in hindsight I think she looked for guidance from me – when I was there I felt she was enabled in that she did something that worked well, that gave her professional connections, with someone else who gave her respect – she could really establish herself as someone who could work well professionally and educationally...in a new area, internationally. I met her Professor, he was positive, that gave her some standing – *Interview*

This new-found sense of herself as a valued collaborator and academic mentor was made all the more meaningful as it coincided with a return visit to Germany after many years of absence:

> she [Karen] felt enabled through this as much as I know I was... and being in that context, in Germany, put me into my own home ground again...the personal and the private were combined. It was quite different to come into this context as a professional – meeting the students, seeing them interested was a very reassuring experience seeing the learners, in their context – *Interview*

Towards the end of the data-gathering cycle, Lena articulated a shift in her sense of how she enacts her identity as a teacher. Through her online experiences she moved from seeing technology as something abstract to seeing technology as the means to construct and project herself as a teacher for her students:

> ...[the technology tools] constitute part of me, they are no longer abstract things. It impacts on how I see myself as a teacher, not as someone who uses technology in some sort of abstract way but I am someone now for whom technology has a constructing function, it constructs me as a teacher – I can make myself now appear in front

of my students, even just my voice, in a way I could not have anticipated in the past. I feel I have been able to add to what I do – *Interview*

Lena's closing reflective comment reveals the way her collaborative experiences in the project extended her vision of her ideal self as an academic with acknowledged expertise:

One other very personal aspect of working on the project has been a new emphasis on the German dimension of my role as an academic and pedagogue. German had not been part of my professional domain for a number of years, which only changed after taking up my current position in 2006. The project has meant increasing opportunity to engage in professional and academic dialogue in German and to build networks in Germany, both at a distance and even face to face during my visit to Germany. This is an experience I have found greatly validating in terms of what I do and who I am. In this sense the project has become a bridge for negotiating my own crossings between cultural contexts, similar to those my students will hopefully repeat. – *Reflective Journal*

Interestingly Lena ends her commentary, referring not to herself but to her students, confirming again that they are central to her ideal teacher self.

Lena's journey in the project involved negotiating many aspects of her identity in the context she constructed through her activities with other professionals and learners. The stakes for her were great, as a teacher, a colleague, an academic taking part in an international collaborative project, and for herself in the German aspects of herself. Lena's motivation to engage with workplace teacher learning can be best understood through the lens of her ideal teacher self and how that relates to the virtual landscapes she traversed coupled with the relationships she developed and the identities she managed to negotiate and forge for herself. Through Lena we have insight into how her ideal teacher self was a powerful motivator in the early stages of the project, how it was enhanced by her interactions with her German counterpart, leading ultimately to seeing herself as a teacher for whom technology is essential in enabling her to relate her self to the world of distance language teaching.

Identity and Group: A Case Study

The EAP group is made up of four tutors – Will, Terry, Tim and Paul – whose experience of EAP includes teaching in the UK as well as in Europe, the Middle-East and the Far-East. The group agreed to participate in this project during a period of intense innovation and development of their teaching activities. The articulation and enactment of group identity explored here was forged through collective reflections and actions based on innovations in teaching using technologies. The group shared a number of common concerns and divergent perspectives which surfaced in group and individual interviews, postings on ELAG, and discussions with the authors. The focus here is less on an analysis of the group's collective identity and more on an exploration of the dynamic process of group identity formation. This approach draws on Martin's critical appraisal of conceptions of self, arguing that very little of the work on selfhood attempts to theorise the self as constituted through social interactivity with others (Martin, 2004, 2007). Martin suggests further that just because social and cultural contexts are considered 'does not mean that selfhood is considered as a communal rather than a predominately individual achievement' (Martin, 2007: 86). In this group case study we provide some insights into how group identity, including ideal group identity, emerges through engagement with and orientation to others and the tools, language, concepts and understandings that are communally shared, even if contested.

Within the context of this study, engagement within and beyond the EAP group was fundamental in shaping the group. In interviews and online discussions a recurrent theme involved exploring and analysing the impact of technological innovations on students.

> We tend to do things we see as responding to a [student] need and we use the parts [of technology] that actually do respond and ditch the rest – *Will (individual interview)*

> But if we can give [students] a little bit of extra somehow.... provided through WebCT – they might be encouraged to do it if they think they're going to get a little bit extra to what they get in class. – *Will (group interview)*

The (ideal) identity of the group and the aims of the group are closely linked to their students and meeting their students' needs; this points to the group's growing awareness of the extent to which their emerging identity and motivation are strongly tied to how students respond to their innovations. It is primarily the students and interactions with students that frame and direct the further activities and reflections of the group.

> I think we probably...overestimated students' use of WebCT. From speaking to students I don't think that they use WebCT very much in their departments. I kind of thought they used it a lot more. – *Tim (group interview)*

Whilst collectively meeting students' needs combined with a growing awareness of the role of others in helping them to achieve this aim are key to understanding the identity formation of this group, the ongoing dialogue within the group was of equal importance.

> As a group we all did the basic training and that was good but, more than that, the fact of all being together, experimenting together and being able to tell each other and help each other that was what really pushed it along – *Will* (*individual interview*)

A sustained, supportive and open-ended dialogue of competing explanations and solutions runs throughout the interviews (and observations of the group) motivating and engaging the group to explore areas of intrinsic group interest and to find solutions to problems, both on an affective level (to avoid 'demotivation' and getting 'too upset') and on a pedagogical level, without leading to conflict and division within the group.

> [T]here are all sorts of issues but at least now we know what we have or haven't achieved so far. And what would be feasible. – *Terry* (*group interview*)

From uncertain beginnings ('being in the dark', 'going ahead willy-nilly', 'inventing as we went along') the group gained sufficiently in experience and expertise in technology to reach the point where group innovation

> has got an autonomous life of its own now…purely from interest. That seems to be more the way that we work. – *Will* (*individual interview*)

Both the group itself and its members widened their horizons not by turning in on themselves but by actively engaging with and attempting to understand their intersubjective world of group members, students, and university colleagues. Perhaps more significantly, the transformation of group identity can be read against a shift from ought-to selves struggling with the imperative to engage with new technologies and failing to fully meet perceived students' needs, towards ideal selves, collectively and successfully shaping (as well as being shaped by) innovations through intra and inter group interaction sustained not only by intrinsic interest, experimentation and motivation but also by a greater awareness of and engagement with others.

Conclusion

The ideal teacher self perspective offers a paradigm for understanding how experienced language teachers engage with a new learning and teaching domain, and the ways in which they create, contribute to or resist opportunities for workplace learning. From the close following of teachers' experiences over a period of nine months we can see that 'possible selves' are powerful motivators, shaped and realised within experiences, activities and practices mediated by others. We also have a view of the open, contingent nature of workplace learning experiences comprised of a wide array of encounters, relationships, events and exchanges during which identities were shaped, maintained, challenged and negotiated. At the heart of the study lies the teacher self seen as socially constituted, dynamic, evolving representations of not just the individual self but of others, and of what it may be possible to be or become. In this chapter we have argued that it was the teacher self which acted as a catalyst for the nature and degree of teacher involvement in the project, for the cycles of action, dialogue and reflection – with and through others – which in turn formed the course and nature of teacher learning. Here we focused on those parts of the project which had an evident ideal self dimension, concerned with growth, development and the hope of satisfying professional relationships. In our study there were also instances of participants motivated by an 'ought-to' self: in some cases this was evident in a reluctant concern to avoid being seen as behind-the-times, as a way of protecting a career; in some cases it led to minimal involvement with the project, shielding a sense of self from change; in other cases it led to a sheltering from others; in still other cases it led to a utilitarian view of peers, with project participants positioned as helpers or as experts who could endorse the actions taken or the products produced. And there were also participants motivated by an ideal self based on personal, individual achievement with a minor role assigned to the impact of their actions on learners or on their relationships with others. We mention this because our study should not be seen as a blueprint for experienced teacher learning. Instead our study highlights teacher self and teacher identity as the core of teacher learning, shaping and shaped by the actions teachers take, their dialogue and reflections. Teacher learning emerged clearly as being contingent, fraught with unknowns and both disruptive and challenging of teacher identities and self concept. And perhaps most importantly our study reveals something of what we may uncover when we manage to access how language teachers envision and re-envision themselves in a new domain, their hopes, dreams and aspirations of what they would like to be, what they would like to become and what they would like to be part of.

References

Borg, S. (2006) *Teacher Cognition and Language Education*. London: Continuum.

Britzman, D. (1992) The terrible problem of knowing thyself: Toward a post-structural account of teacher identity. *Journal of Curriculum Theorizing* 9 (3), 23–46.

Butler, D., Lauscher, H.N., Jarvis-Selinger, S. and Beckingham, B. (2004) Collaboration and self-regulation in teachers' professional development. *Teaching and Teacher Education* 20, 435–455.

Connelly, F. and Clandinin, D. (1999) *Shaping a Professional Identity: Stories of Experience*. New York: Teachers College Press.

Cross, R. (2006) Identity and language teacher education: The potential for sociocultural perspectives in researching language teacher identity. Paper presented within the symposium Languages, Teaching, and Education at the Australian Association for Research in Education Annual Conference, Engaging Pedagogies, 27–30 November, 2006, University of South Australia, Adelaide.

Ding, A. (2005) Theoretical and practical issues in the promotion of collaborative learner autonomy in a virtual self-access centre. In B. Holmberg, M. Shelley and C. White (eds) *Distance Education and Languages: Evolution and Change* (pp. 40–54). Clevedon: Multilingual Matters.

Dörnyei, Z. (2005) *The Psychology of the Language Learner: Individual Differences in Second Language Acquisition*. Mahwah, NJ: Lawrence Erlbaum Associates.

Eraut, M., Alderton, J., Cole, G. and Senker, P. (1998) *Development of Knowledge and Skills in Employment*. Brighton: University of Sussex.

Geijsel, F. and Meijers, F. (2005) Identity learning: The core process of educational change. *Educational Studies* 4, 419–430.

Hampel, R. and Hauck, M. (2004) Towards an effective use of audio conferencing in distance language courses. *Language Learning and Technology* 8 (1), 66–82.

Hampel, R. and Stickler, U. (2005) New skills for new classrooms: Training tutors to teach languages online. *Computer Assisted Language Learning* 18 (4), 311–326.

Hubbard, P. and Levy, M. (eds) (2006) *Teacher Education in CALL*. Amsterdam: John Benjamins.

Kwakman, K. (2001) Work stress and work-based learning in secondary education: Testing the karasek model. *Human Resource Development International* 4, 487–501.

Kwakman, K. (2003) Factors affecting teachers' participation in professional learning activities. *Teaching and Teacher Education* 19 (2), 149–170.

Lewis, T. (2006) When teaching is learning: A personal account of learning to teach online. *CALICO Journal* 23 (3), 581–600.

Mann, S. (2005) The language teacher's development. *Language Teaching* 38 (3), 103–118.

Martin, J. (2004) The educational inadequacy of conceptions of self in educational psychology. *Interchange* 35 (2), 185–208.

Martin, J. (2007) The selves of educational psychology: Conceptions, contexts and critical considerations. *Educational Psychologist* 42 (2), 79–89.

McCarthey, S. (2001) Identity construction in elementary readers and writers. *Reading Research Quarterly* 36 (2), 122–151.

McCormick, C. and Pressley, M. (1997) *Educational Psychology: Learning, Instruction, and Assessment*. New York: Longman.

Murray, D. and McPherson, P. (2006) Scaffolding instruction for reading the Web. *Language Teaching Research* 10 (2), 131–156.

Reynard, R. (2003) Internet-based ESL for distance adult students – A framework for dynamic language learning. *Canadian Modern Language Review* 60 (2), 123–142.

Richards, J. and Farrell, T. (2005) *Professional Development for Language Teachers*. New York: Cambridge University Press.

Riley, P. (2006) Self-expression and the negotiation of identity in a foreign language. *International Journal of Applied Linguistics* 16 (3), 295–318.

Senior, R. (2006) *The Experience of Language Teaching*. Cambridge: Cambridge University Press.

ten Dam, G. and Blom, S. (2006) Learning through participation. The potential of school-based teacher education for developing a professional identity. *Teaching and Teacher Education* 22, 647–660.

van Eekelen, I., Boshuizen, H. and Vermunt, J. (2005) Self-regulation in higher education teacher learning. *Higher Education* 50, 447–471.

van Lier, L. (2007) Action-based teaching, autonomy and identity. *Innovation in Language Teaching and Learning* 1 (1), 46–65.

White, C. (2007) Innovation and identity in distance language teaching and learning. *Innovation in Language Teaching and Learning* 1 (1), 97–110.

Chapter 18

Motivation, Language Identities and the L2 Self: Future Research Directions

ZOLTÁN DÖRNYEI and EMA USHIODA

Introduction

The two editors of this volume have known and respected each other for many years, yet this anthology constitutes our very first direct cooperation. This is no accident: although we have always found common points in our overall thinking of L2 motivation, our specific research approaches could not have been further apart. Drawing on the traditions of quantitative social psychology, the majority of Dörnyei's work has focused on presumed motivational universals aggregated from large sample groups, whereas Ushioda was attracted right from the beginning to a situated, qualitative, interpretive approach, viewing motivation as part of the individual learner's thought processes. This book owes its existence to the fact that in it we found a common denominator: *identity* and the *self*. In Chapters 1, 2 and 11 we described in some detail the rather different avenues that had led us to this shared platform, and we are pleased to see that our views have also resonated with several other scholars in the field, as attested to by their contributions to this volume. It seems that motivation conceived as part of the learner's identity/self is a workable concept from several perspectives – we were indeed heartened by the wide range of theoretical paradigms represented in this volume that successfully accommodated motivational self issues.

In this concluding chapter we would like to concentrate on two topics that lie at the heart of much of the research reported in this book as well as our own thinking: (a) motivation conceived in terms of future self guides, as in Dörnyei's L2 Motivational Self System, and (b) a situated, dynamic view of motivation as expressed in Ushioda's 'person-in-context relational view' of emergent motivation.

Future Self-Guides and the L2 Motivational Self System

The language facets of the learners' ideal and ought-to selves have been seen in this volume as a primary motivational force because of the learners' desire to bridge the gap between the actual self and their projected goal states. This motivational capacity has been acknowledged by most contributors to this volume and all the studies that attempted to operationalize the self system in some empirical way produced results that supported the claim that future self-guides are potent motivators. The quantitative studies by Al-Shehri (this volume), Csizér and Kormos (this volume), MacIntyre *et al.* (this volume, Chapter 10), Ryan (this volume) and Taguchi *et al.* (this volume) generated statistical evidence that add up to a powerful cumulative validity argument, and the investigations by Kim (this volume), Kubanyiova (this volume), Lamb (this volume) and White and Ding (this volume) have successfully used the possible selves lens to interpret the diverse situations they examined in their qualitative studies. These positive takes on the topic and the fact that aspects of the L2 Motivational Self System have been applied to such a wide variety of contexts indicate that this line of research has a great deal of future mileage in it; as MacIntyre *et al.* (this volume, Chapter 3: 50) put it, 'The potential strength of the L2 self formulation lies in its ability to map out new conceptual linkages by taking the self as the starting point'.

Although possible selves theory is undoubtedly a powerful paradigm, it also raises a number of questions that will need to be addressed by future research. MacIntyre *et al.* (this volume, Chapter 3: 53–58) list several areas where cautions are warranted, although they kindly add that these 'arise primarily from the complexity of studying the self, rather than specifically from Dörnyei's (2005) L2 self system'. We agree that the points they raise are important, and we would like to contribute to their critical analysis by discussing six issues below that are specifically related to the L2 Motivational Self System:

(1) The first broad issue concerns the *uniqueness* of the self-guides. The key question in this respect is whether learners have several different desired possible self images of themselves (as Markus and Nurius, 1986, assume) or only one broad ideal self with various facets (as Higgins, 1987, proposes). In either case, only future research can tell the extent to which alternative selves/self facets compete with each other and the consequences of any potential conflict of this type. With regard to the ought-to self, it is likely that the projected views of different authority figures in one's life show some diversity, so the question as to whether a certain degree of 'self harmony' is necessary or desirable to motivate effective learning behaviour is even more acute in this area.

(2) A second uncharted area concerns the temporal *evolution/change/ development* of the future self-guides: how stable are the ideal and ought-to selves? They appear to be, by definition, fairly robust since

they concern self-images that are built up over a period of time, but until we have a clearer understanding of how they come into being and then evolve, we cannot make any strong claims in this respect. We will also need to find out more about the sources of change that can cause any substantial self developments, an issue that has obvious practical implications for motivational teaching. Finally, a related question is how we can conceive the concept of 'demotiva- tion' (i.e. negative change) in self terms?

(3) A third broad area that awaits future investigation both in SLA and mainstream psychology is the relationship between *emotions* and future self-guides. As MacIntyre *et al.* (this volume, Chapter 3: 47) point out, 'The emotions experienced are critical to understanding the motivational properties of possible selves....Emotions are fundamentally important motivators. Without a strong tie to the learner's emotional system, possible selves exist as cold cognition, and therefore lack motivational potency'. We fully agree with this claim and would also add that the imagery component of possible selves offers an obvious link with emotions, as one of the key roles of the sensation generated by experiential images is exactly to evoke emotional responses.

(4) A fourth issue concerns the *relationship* between the ideal and the ought-to L2 selves, a question addressed at least partially by several contributors in this volume (e.g. Kim; Kubanyiova; White & Ding). As Dörnyei (this volume) argues, at the heart of the issue lies the question of the internalisation of external influences, which is a key concern in Deci and Ryan's (1985) self-determination theory, as discussed in Chapter 15 by Noels. Because humans are inherently social beings, all their self-perceptions are originally socially grounded (i.e. they emerge in a continuous interaction with the social environment). Given this significant social influence, at what point in the internalisation process can we claim with confidence that a desired possible self is 'ideal', that is, fully owned by the learner, rather than 'ought-to', that is, imposed on the learner by others? We suspect that one way of addressing this question will involve concentrating on the imagery element that needs to accompany a fully-fledged ideal L2 self.

(5) A fifth issue is related to any *cross-cultural variation* in the impact and/or composition of the L2 Motivational Self System. As MacIntyre *et al.* (this volume, Chapter 3) point out, past research has shown that the self in general is subject to a great deal of cross- cultural variation, and talking more specifically about the L2 Motivational Self System, Segalowitz *et al.* (this volume: 190) state that there is a need to understand whether the different facets of 'ethnolinguistic language identity and of the L2 Motivation Self

System are specific to a language-learning context or whether at least some of these facets may be "universal", common to a variety of language teaching and learning situations'. An indication of the complexity of this issue is offered by Taguchi *et al.* (this volume), who compared three Asian foreign language learning contexts and found that although the broad structure of the L2 Motivational Self System construct applied to all three examined environments, there were some salient differences in the weights of the components. In addition, Csizér and Dörnyei (2005) demonstrated that in the cases of learners who are simultaneously engaged in the study of more than one L2, the multiple L2-specific ideal self images show some interference.

(6) The sixth and final issue we would like to address is one that was also highlighted by MacIntyre *et al.* (this volume, Chapter 10): the question of operationalising the self system in *measurement* terms. This is clearly a key concern, because we can only use constructs in mainstream SLA research if we have reliable empirical measures of them. The particular significance of developing possible self indices has been stated by Markus and Ruvolo (1989) as follows:

> To the extent that we can develop methods for measuring the degree of elaboration of a possible self, we should be able to predict performance more precisely than measures of level of aspiration or achievement motivation, which assess only one aspect of the individual's orientation to the goal. (Markus & Ruvolo, 1989: 236)

As several studies in this volume (along with the attached instruments they used) prove, the various components of the L2 Motivational Self System lend themselves to self-report assessment. Scales of the ideal and ought-to L2 selves as well as the L2 learning experience have been administered to thousands of language learners of various ages, academic status and proficiency levels, and the results displayed good internal consistency reliability (as measured by Cronbach alphas). Thus, it is fair to conclude that the way the components of the L2 Motivational Self System have been operationalised and assessed meets the standards of scientific measurement in motivation research in general.

Having said that, we must also realise that there exist alternative ways of assessing future self-guides and at this point we cannot be certain as to which type of measure captures the essence of one's future goal-oriented vision best. Talking about possible selves in psychology, Hoyle and Sherrill (2006: 1691) emphasised that 'Unfortunately, operational definitions of the possible selves construct have not kept stride with the conceptual definition. There is neither a standard measure of possible selves, nor a standard index that is extracted from possible-selves measures'. Indeed, in the studies reported in the literature we find a variety of indices of future self-guides; for example, some participants have been asked to simply list the possible selves relevant to them, while others rated or rank-ordered lists of possible selves they were given. Interestingly, closed-ended items of possible selves like the quantitative measures presented in this book have hardly ever been reported in the psychology literature, possibly because such items can only work with very specific target domains such as the language self. Furthermore, we cannot recall a single study which measured the imagery aspect of possible selves, and therefore Al-Shehri's (this volume) investigation is pioneering in this respect.

Motivation as a Situated, Dynamic and 'Person-in-Context Relational' Concept

As mentioned earlier, placing the self at the centre of our motivational thinking opens up a wide range of novel research directions. However, proposing a tripartite construct such as the L2 Motivational Self System runs the risk of ending up with a rather static category system that does not take into account sufficiently the process-oriented nature of motivation or the dynamic interaction between motivation and the social environment. This is in contrast with the central tendency in recent individual difference (ID) research in SLA, described by Dörnyei as follows:

> The most striking aspect of nearly all the recent ID literature is the emerging theme of *context*: It appears that cutting-edge research in all these diverse areas has been addressing the same issue, that is, the situated nature of the ID factors in question. Scholars have come to reject the notion that the various traits are context-independent and absolute, and are now increasingly proposing new dynamic conceptualizations in which ID factors enter into some interaction with the situational parameters rather than cutting across tasks and environments. (2005: 218)

This is the point where the second main strand in this volume, the situated and dynamic conception of motivation at the level of the individual learner comes into its own. Ushioda (this volume) labelled this approach the 'person-in-context relational view' of motivation to outline a perspective that focuses on the intentional agency of real people embedded in an intricate and fluid web of social relations and multiple micro- and macro-contexts. She highlighted the complexity of the system and the non-linear relationships of the multiple contextual elements from which motivation emerges organically. Within this approach there are no clear-cut and predictable cause-effect relations because the emphasis is on the complexity and idiosyncrasy of a person's motivational response to particular events and experiences in their life.

This individual-centred social approach offers a viable alternative to the group-based methodology that has traditionally dominated L2 motivation research and it is also in harmony with the broader 'social turn' in SLA research, which has been discussed extensively in a recent Focus Issue of *The Modern Language Journal* (Lafford, 2007). The intriguing question from our point of view, however, is whether there is a way of going beyond the somewhat 'schizophrenic' situation prevailing both in SLA and L2 motivation research, characterised by a range of contrasting dichotomies such as positivist-interpretive, quantitative-qualitative or cognitive-sociocultural. In other words, can we form bridges between the existing 'two parallel SLA worlds' (Zuengler & Miller, 2006) at least at the level of motivation research?

A real possibility for achieving such a convergence has been recently offered by the interrelated theoretical paradigms of dynamic systems theory, complexity theory and emergentism. These approaches concern the behaviour of complex systems that contain multiple interconnected components, and due to the manifold interacting influences, any development in such systems is characterised by a non-linear growth curve, displaying a contextually sensitive, moment-to-moment trajectory of change (for recent discussions within SLA, see for example, de Bot, 2008; de Bot *et al.*, 2007; Ellis & Larsen-Freeman, 2006; Hawkins, 2007; Larsen-Freeman & Cameron, 2008; for a recent overview, see Dörnyei, in press). It does not require much justification that this description is in accordance with Ushioda's 'person-in-context relational view', and in a recent reconceptualisation of individual differences in dynamic system terms, Dörnyei (in press) has proposed that future self-guides can be seen as broad attractors with attractor basins that overlap cognitive, emotional and motivational domains. Thus, reframing language learning within a dynamic systems framework might potentially integrate the two strands of motivational thinking that underlie the material in this book. Moreover, such integration would further consolidate the growing synergy between our field of inquiry and mainstream SLA (see Chapter 1) by ensuring that L2 motivation research continues to keep pace with and contribute to new theoretical developments in SLA.

References

Csizér, K. and Dörnyei, Z. (2005) Language learners' motivational profiles and their motivated learning behaviour. *Language Learning* 55 (4), 613–659.
de Bot, K. (2008) Second language development as a dynamic process. *Modern Language Journal* 92 (2), 166–178.

de Bot, K., Lowie, W. and Verspoor, M. (2007) A Dynamic Systems Theory approach to second language acquisition. *Bilingualism: Language and Cognition* 10 (1), 7–21.

Deci, E.L. and Ryan, R.M. (1985) *Intrinsic Motivation and Self-Determination in Human Behaviour.* New York: Plenum.

Dörnyei, Z. (2005) *The Psychology of the Language Learner: Individual Differences in Second Language Acquisition.* Mahwah, NJ: Lawrence Erlbaum.

Dörnyei, Z. (in press) *The Psychology of Second Language Acquisition.* Oxford: Oxford University Press.

Ellis, N.C. and Larsen-Freeman, D. (2006) Language emergence: Implications for applied linguistics – Introduction to the special issue. *Applied Linguistics* 27 (4), 558–589.

Hawkins, R. (ed.) (2007) *Current Emergentist and Nativist Perspectives on Second Language Acquisition.* (Special Issue): *Lingua* 118 (4).

Higgins, E.T. (1987) Self-discrepancy: A theory relating self and affect. *Psychological Review* 94, 319–340.

Hoyle, R.H. and Sherrill, M.R. (2006) Future orientation in the self-system: Possible selves, self-regulation, and behavior. *Journal of Personality* 74 (6), 1673–1696.

Lafford, B.A. (ed.) (2007) *Second Language Acquisition Reconceptualized? The Impact of Firth and Wagner (1997).* (Focus Issue). *Modern Language Journal* 91.

Larsen-Freeman, D. and Cameron, L. (2008) *Complex Systems and Applied Linguistics.* Oxford: Oxford University Press.

Markus, H. and Nurius, P. (1986) Possible selves. *American Psychologist* 41, 954–969.

Markus, H. and Ruvolo, A. (1989) Possible selves: Personalized representations of goals. In L.A. Pervin (ed.) *Goal Concepts in Personality and Social Psychology* (pp. 211–241). Hillsdale, NJ: Lawrence Erlbaum.

Zuengler, J. and Miller, E.R. (2006) Cognitive and sociocultural perspectives: Two parallel SLA worlds? *TESOL Quarterly* 40 (1), 35–58.

Author Index

Subject Index

Lightning Source UK Ltd.
Milton Keynes UK
UKHW021446090519
342385UK00003B/233/P